THE ART OF INTERACTIVE DESIGN
A Euphonious and
Illuminating Guide to
Building Successful Software

THE ART OF INTERACTIVE DESIGN

A EUPHONIOUS AND ILLUMINATING GUIDE TO BUILDING SUCCESSFUL SOFTWARE

Chris Crawford

NO STARCH
PRESS

San Francisco

Publisher: William Pollock
Editorial Director: Karol Jurado
Cover and Interior Design: Octopod Studios
Composition: 1106 Design, LLC
Copyeditor: Judy Ziajka
Proofreader: City Desktop Productions
Indexer: Broccoli Information Management

Distributed to the book trade in the United States by Publishers Group West, 1700 Fourth Street, Berkeley, CA 94710; phone: 800-788-3123; fax: 510-658-1834.

Distributed to the book trade in Canada by Jacqueline Gross & Associates, Inc., One Atlantic Avenue, Suite 105, Toronto, Ontario M6K 3E7 Canada; phone: 416-531-6737; fax 416-531-4259.

For information on translations or book distributors outside the United States and Canada, please contact No Starch Press, Inc. directly:

No Starch Press, Inc.
555 De Haro Street, Suite 250, San Francisco, CA 94107
phone: 415-863-9900; fax: 415-863-9950; info@nostarch.com; http://www.nostarch.com

Library of Congress Cataloguing-in-Publication Data

Crawford, Chris, 1950-.
        The art of interactive design : a euphonious and illuminating guide to building successful
software / Chris Crawford.
                p. cm.
        ISBN 1-886411-84-0 (pbk.)
            1. Interactive multimedia. 2. User interfaces (Computer systems)   I. Title.
QA76.76.I59 C73 2002
006.7--dc21

                                                                                    2002001562

DEDICATION

To three friends who stood firmly behind me in my hour of need:
Laura Mixon, Veronique Raingeval, and Dave Walker.

BRIEF CONTENTS

CONTENTS IN DETAIL

PART ONE: FUNDAMENTALS

1

WHAT EXACTLY IS INTERACTIVITY?

2

WHY BOTHER WITH INTERACTIVITY?

3

SPEAKING

4

THINKING

5

LISTENING

6

THE INTERACTIVE LOOP

7

ARCHITECTURES

PART TWO: DESIGN ADVICE

8

GUIDELINES

9

ANTHROPOMORPHIZATION

10

BLOOPERS

11

CLOCK SETTING

12

THE DESIGN PROCESS

13

ADVICE FOR SPECIFIC FIELDS

14

DEDICATED DEVICES

15

WHY LEARN PROGRAMMING?

16

SOFT MATH

PART THREE: THEORY

17

PROCESS INTENSITY

18

LINKMESHES

19

PLAY

20

ABSTRACTION

21

INDIRECTION

22
LINGUISTICS

23
METAPHOR

24
ANTICIPATION

PART FOUR: SOCIAL AND ARTISTIC ISSUES

25
A HISTORY OF INTERACTIVITY

26
CONTROL VERSUS INTERACTIVITY

27
THE TWO-CULTURES PROBLEM

28
INTERACTIVE STORYTELLING

29

SUBJUNCTIVITY

30

FUTURES

Index

READ ME

This book is written for designers of interactive products. If this description fits you, then you should read this book.

If you have no direct professional interest in interactivity design, but want to understand something more about the significance of computers, you should concentrate on Parts III and IV.

If you consider interactivity design to be a variation on traditional human factors design, then you should hurl this book away from you with vehement force; its carefree disregard for the eternal verities of your field will only upset you.

This book was NOT written for programmers. If you want to learn the latest, greatest, fastest techniques for 3D animation, this is NOT the book for you.

This book boasts (or suffers from) a discursive style, especially in the later chapters. It's not formal enough to be a textbook, nor is it a cookbook for those who want to learn great design techniques in one reading.

This book is about understanding interactivity, not simply using it.

The breakneck pace of technology induces many designers to grab for quick solutions. But it is precisely the torrid pace of development that requires us to concentrate on understanding the fundamentals rather than snatching quickie patches. Today's solutions will be obsolete in a few years, but the fundamentals (and this book) will still be useful decades from now.

This book will educate you, not train you.

PART ONE
FUNDAMENTALS

1

WHAT EXACTLY IS INTERACTIVITY?

The term *interactivity* is overused and underunderstood. I choose to define it in terms of a conversation: a cyclic process in which two actors alternately listen, think, and speak. The quality of the interaction depends on the quality of each of the subtasks (listening, thinking, and speaking). And many things commonly held to be interactive are not.

Interactivity is one of the buzzterms of the times and as such is much abused. It's not that interactivity was heretofore unknown; on the contrary, I remember lengthy discussions on interactivity in the early 1980s. But the computing community didn't catch on to the importance of interactivity until recently. In the early 1990s, I garnered plenty of derision by insisting that interactivity was the core idea of computing.

So at least we're buzzing in the right general direction. But popularity has its costs, one of which is the way popular terms are given a different spin by every user. The result is that the poor term ends up spinning one way and then the other, becoming hopelessly dizzy with all the abuse. I'm reminded of the wonderful story from The Martian Chronicles about a Martian who visits a town of earthlings and is unable to prevent himself from transforming, chameleon-like, to meet the expectations of everyone he encounters. Thus, overwhelmed by these expectations, he dies from the frenetic effort.

So it is with the term *interactivity*, yanked around so much as to be half-dead, a pallid, bloodless nothingburger of a word. I'll bet that one day you'll walk into the grocery store and find a box of laundry detergent with a big banner slashing diagonally across its top, saying, "NEW! IMPROVED! INTERACTIVE!"

For example, take a gander at these photos:

Or consider this definition of interactivity offered in a popular book: "By definition, the things people do on computers have always been interactive." Not very illuminating, is it? Or here's another definition offered on a website: "Interactivity . . . concerns itself with the various means by which human beings implement actions." Rather mushy, eh?

So let's start with a humbling realization: We really don't have a clear idea of what interactivity is. Plenty of people have slapped it onto their work and tried to sell "The Same Old Same Old Stuff" as "New Interactive Technology!" and, with all the hype, we've lost track of the word's true meaning. But let's not be too hard on ourselves; after all, any word that can launch a book this heavy surely has plenty of tricks up its sleeve. So let's roll up our own and get to work.

Defining Interactivity

I used to think that definitions were important, sort of like linguistic rules of the road, erected to keep people's utterances from crashing into each other in a demolition derby of language. But nowadays, I take a more easygoing view of definitions. Any idea worthy of my attention is probably too big and too complicated to be reduced to some schoolmarmish formula. The joy of thinking comes from all of those fascinating nooks and crannies that lurk in nuance. My task as a lexicographer is just as important as a cartographer's, but I don't see the scenery by perusing a map; I get out there and walk the ground. Nevertheless, a definition is a good way to get started, so I'll draw the map first, and we can start walking the ground later.

interaction: a cyclic process in which two actors alternately listen, think, and speak.

I'm using the terms actors, listen, think, and speak metaphorically, although the terms are literal to the most commonly experienced form of interactivity: conversation. Conversations, in their simplest form, begin with two people, say, Gomer and Fredegund. First, Gomer says something to Fredegund, at which point the proverbial ball is in Fredegund's corner. Fredegund then performs three steps in order to hold up her end of the conversation:

Step One: Fredegund listens to Gomer, paying close attention to Gomer's words (we hope). She gathers in all of Gomer's words and then actively assembles them into a coherent whole, requiring effort on her part.
Step Two: Fredegund considers Gomer's words. She contemplates and cogitates. The wheels turn in her mind as she develops her response to Gomer's statement.
Step Three: Fredegund responds to Gomer. She turns her thoughts into words and speaks them.

Now the tables are turned, and the ball is in Gomer's court. Gomer must listen to Fredegund, think about what she is saying, and react. Then he must express his reaction to Fredegund.

This process of conversation cycles back and forth, as an iterative process in which each participant in turn listens, thinks, and speaks.

We can generalize this notion of the conversation as an interactive process to any human interaction, although when we do, we must use the terms listen, think, and speak metaphorically. If we want to get academic, I suppose we could replace listen, think, and speak with input, process, and output, but that's so gauchely techie.

Here's a key point about the interactive process: There are two actors, not one. If I'm out in the woods and I hear to the sound of a tree branch breaking, and I meditate on the implications of such a sound emanating from my zenith, jumping out of the way just as the branch crashes to earth, I am *not* interacting with the branch; I am reacting. This is a crucial factor that many, many people don't understand, and it leads to lots of silly designs. You can't converse with a brick wall. It takes two people to have a conversation, and it takes two actors to have an interaction. If you, dear reader, were of an argumentative temperament, you might suggest that the branch is an actor. I will concede your point in the most technical of senses: The branch does something, so it must be an actor. But I am using the term actor in the more common sense of a purposeful creature.

Extending the branch argument, some claim that when you open a refrigerator and the little light inside turns on, and then you close the door and the light turns off, you are interacting with the refrigerator because it responds to your actions.

Now I suppose that a person graced with sufficient open-mindedness (several cubic light-years' worth!) could accept such an argument, but the box inside which I think is a lot smaller than that. I have difficulty imagining Nintendo refrigerators with millions of people all over the country opening and closing their refrigerators for the sheer fun of it. Of course, if you want to get academic about this argument, then yes, the fridge listens (to the opening door), thinks (with all the processing power of a single switch), and speaks (by turning on the light). But this kind of interaction is silly and beneath the intellectual dignity of almost everybody. I'm concerned with interactivity that has some blood in its veins.

The Nintendo refrigerator offers us some intellectual utility, however, even if it can't entertain us, because some people will, in fact, be entertained by playing the refrigerator door game. As any exasperated mother will testify, small children can find a refrigerator light more entertaining than a television. So here is our puzzle: Is the refrigerator door game interactive or is it not? Surely it is interactive for the small child, and just as surely is it not interactive for adults. Does interactivity exist in the eye of the interactor? If my friend calls a rock interactive, do I have any basis for challenging her? Is interactivity utterly subjective?

Plenty of people claim that everything is subjective, so I won't try to convince you if you belong to that tribe. But if you're willing to grant the existence of occasional objective truths, here's an explanation that offers some practical value for a designer.

Degrees of Interactivity

We tend to think of interactivity as a Boolean property (either you have it or you don't) like virginity. But why not think of interactivity as a continuous variable with relative measures, more like our weight? In other words, we might speak of interactivity as high, moderate, low, or even zero, thus solving our problem with the subjective nature of interactivity. By using such measures, rather than the simple either/or proposition, we make it possible to accept that anything can be interactive and simply discuss the degree of interactivity subjectively. This, in turn, gives us a happier solution to the refrigerator challenge: The refrigerator does indeed interact with the user, but it does so at a low level.

But we still have a problem: How do we tell the difference between "high" and "low" interactivity?

Let's attack this problem by returning to our founding concept, the conversation. After all, most of us have amassed a wealth of experience with conversation and should be able to agree on which factors contribute to a good, intense, or rewarding conversation, and which factors ruin one. I'll formulate those factors in terms of the three standard steps of the conversation we looked at earlier, between Fredegund and Gomer.

Listening

If you want to have a good conversation, you have to listen well, and so does your partner. How many times have you been caught in Pointless Conversation Number 38, with someone who refuses to listen to what you're saying? He nods his head and smiles idiotically while you're talking and then resumes his single-minded lecture or reiterates the point you just demolished. Moving to the other end of the scale, have you ever had the magical experience of conversing with somebody who understands exactly what you are saying? The conversation soars, and you want it to last forever.

Thinking

The next requirement for a successful conversation is that both actors think well. This is fairly obvious; surely you can recall at least one conversation with a slow thinker. He gives it his best: He knits his brows in determined attention, he takes some time to let your words rattle around inside his head, but when his mouth opens, the words that come out just don't mean anything interesting. While this poor dolt doesn't anger us like the unlistening jerk, our conversation with him is just as useless.

The opposite extreme is also illuminating. I can recall several conversations with Alan Kay, a red-blooded genius of a computer scientist if ever there was one. I'd knit my brows and listen really hard as the ideas tumbled out of him and washed all over me. Most of the time, I'd respond with a deeply-considered "Yup," because I just couldn't keep up. But I'll never forget The Day I Kept Up With Alan Kay. He was talking about a subject in which I was thoroughly versed, although from a different background. I kept hitting him with arguments from my particular angle, and his ripostes were dazzling and fascinating. My mind was reeling from the implications of his ideas, and he seemed to be enjoying our conversation, too, which may be why he scowled when the phone interrupted us. I can still feel the glow from that conversation. Good thinking can make a conversation sparkle.

Speaking

Here's another obvious requirement for good conversation: You gotta spik good if you wanna converse fust-class. Ever tried to communicate with your local computer genius? Sure he's bright and pays attention when you talk, but the hodge-podge of acronyms and verbified nouns that he calls English might as well be Hungarian (assuming you don't speak Hungarian). This conversation with him is dead on arrival; you thank him for his brilliant solution and resume banging on your computer with your coffee cup.

No Trading Off

To interact well, both actors in a conversation must perform all three steps (listening, thinking, and speaking) well. Doing a good job with one of the three steps does not compensate for a bad job with the other two. In each of the preceding examples, the failed conversationalist performed two of the three jobs well but failed with the third, and that one failure was enough to botch the entire conversation.

The same principle applies to all forms of interaction. The most common design error in interactive products arises from a failure to appreciate this principle. The designer does a slam-bang job with two of the three steps but blows the third step, believing that the strengths of the first two will outweigh the weakness of the third. But one weak area in an interactive product (or a conversation) is like a weak link in a chain. The chain breaks regardless of the strength of the rest of the links.

Things That Aren't Interactive

Let's augment our definition of interactivity by discussing some things that aren't interactive. Printed books are my first target because you can't interact with them. A book can't listen or think. It can only speak; it speaks its words as we read them. It is therefore a combination of the worst traits of the jerk and the idiot mentioned earlier.

Do you disagree? Just say the word! Don't be shy, tell me what you really think. It's not that I don't care, but I'm not listening to you and I can't hear you; I'm sitting in my office in Oregon, which may be hundreds or thousands of miles away from you. Obviously, I also won't be thinking about whatever it was that you just said.

Of course, if you're frustrated, you are welcome to throw this across the room, but even then, there still won't be anybody listening to your frustrations or thinking about them. [Editor: This is *not* a good place to put my email address. Ha-ha-ha!] {Reader: ccrawford@Inet.com—Heh-heh-heh.}

Many writers (as well as my publisher) will object to my assertions, because, they argue, reading is indeed an interactive process. They point to the emotional engagement one experiences when reading a book, and to the active state of the reader's mind while reading between the lines and interpreting meaning.

Their assertions are true, but they do not support a claim that reading is interactive. Instead, they describe intense reaction, and interaction is not reaction on a higher plane of existence. There exists no continuum with reaction at one point on the continuum and interaction somewhere else. Interaction and reaction are apples and oranges, horses of different colors, tigers of different stripes. A stronger and stronger reaction does not transcend its nature and become an interaction. You can turn up the reaction volume as high as you want, but playing Beethoven's Ninth Symphony at 20,000 watts does not make it a painting.

The Greeks and Romans understood well the vast difference between the non-interactive written word and the interactive spoken word, perhaps because they were closer to the invention of writing and thus more sensitive to its weaknesses. For example, in Plato's dialogue "Phaedrus," Socrates says:

> "I cannot help but feel, Phaedrus, that writing is unfortunately like painting; for the creations of the painter have the image of life, but if you ask them a question, they remain silent. The same may be said of words. You would think them to be intelligent, but if you want to inquire further, and put a question to the words, you always get the same words for an answer. Once

words have been written down, they are scattered everywhere, among people who may not understand them, and may not know whom to ask about them. If these words are misused or misinterpreted, their creator cannot protect or explain them, and they cannot protect or explain themselves."

Cicero, in the Tusculan Disputations, Book 2, wrote "Certainly many examples for imitation can be obtained from reading, but fuller nourishment comes from the living voice, as they say, especially the voice of the teacher." Seneca wrote, "The living voice and the intimacy of a common life will help you more than the written word."

Other Non-interactive Activities

While dancing with another does provide an avenue of interaction, the interaction is between the dancers, not between the dancers and the music. Dancing alone to the music is not interaction; it is participation. The dancer doesn't set the beat or in any fashion provide feedback to the music makers (who could just as well be a compact disc). Participation is not the same thing as interaction, and really, really good participation isn't "upgraded" to interaction. They're different beasts.

Movies, too, garner a nix from me in the interactivity sweepstakes. (Remember, I'm not arguing that interactivity is the sole gauge of merit; it's simply a different dimension of measurement, and in that dimension, movies rate a zero.) It's not that I have anything against movies; some of my best friends are movies. But as of this writing, you still can't interact with a movie. How many times has your heart protested as you watched the protagonist in a movie do something disastrous? The car breaks down on a stormy night, and the only house nearby is a dark, looming mass with pairs of red eyes peering out. Nevertheless, our sprightly and fragile heroine gaily chirps, "I'll just ask for help at that nice house there!" Every bone in your body shrivels in terror at the prospect, yet she obliviously marches straight to the house.

If the movie were interactive, you might see our heroine pause and say, "Gee, I think I heard somebody in the audience urging me not to enter the dark house. I think I'll take that advice." But this *never* happens! The protagonist always does that stupid thing that you or I would never do in a million years. More important, the protagonist doesn't listen to anything you say. You can beg, you can plead, you can get down on your knees before the TV screen, but she's still going to knock on that creepy door with the gargoyle doorknocker. And surely she's not going to think about your protestations — when was the last time you saw a videocassette engaged in deep contemplation?

So there you have it: Movies don't listen to their audience, nor do they think about what the audience may be saying. Like books, movies can only speak to their audiences, and they do that very, very well. Let's appreciate them for what they are good at instead of press-ganging them into something they're terrible at.

The situation changes slightly when we get into performance art. While it's obvious that a pile of paper, a strip of videotape, or a lump of rock can't listen or think, performance artists can. Capability is not the same thing as action; performance artists seldom interact with their audiences at any deep level.

I've often heard the claim that plays are interactive because the actors are aware of the audience and allow its moods to affect their performance. This is true, I suppose, but let's be honest: Just how much time does an actor have to listen to the audience, consider its mood, and modify his performance to better satisfy the audience? I suppose that if you're one of the guys holding a spear in the background, you'd have the time, but if you're playing Falstaff and you have a few hundred lines of Elizabethan English to make intelligible to non-Elizabethan Americans, I don't think you'll spend your time on stage gauging the facial expression of each member of the audience and thinking how you can improvise something better than Shakespeare.

While actors are certainly capable of interacting with an audience, most devote the vast majority of their considerable talents to the speaking part of their jobs, not the listening part. Yes, plays can be said to be interactive, but I'd give them about a 0.01 on the 10-point Crawford Scale of Interactivity.

NOTE *An exception must be made for the modern experiments in interactivity, in which the audience plays a more active role than usual. In one project, audience members are guests at a wedding party populated with actors. These experiments certainly boast much higher interactivity than traditional plays, and I expect that we shall learn interesting lessons from them.*

Other performers can sometimes obtain higher levels of interactivity. Audience size is the most important factor in permitting interactivity in performance art. Brute statistics make it impossible for one performer to meaningfully interact with thousands of fans, but as audience size shrinks, the statistical factors become less adamant. We try to limit class sizes because smaller classes afford more interactivity between student and teacher. The student-to-teacher ratio is one of the best simple indicators of the quality of a school.

User Interface

Let's be careful to differentiate the study of interactivity from some older fields, such as human factors engineering, which arose from the time-and-motion studies of the early twentieth century. The goal of human factors is to increase the productivity of industrial workers, and so, it places considerable emphasis on formal experiments designed to measure the time it takes a person to perform a task under controlled conditions. We're talking about hard science here; aesthetic factors play no role because efficiency is this field's sole concern.

The study of user interface is a modern offshoot of human factors. Its focus is narrower, with the goal of optimizing the communications between people and electronic devices. Consequently, some people prefer to refer to this as the study of human-computer interface. Its focus is more on communication than interactivity.

Interactivity design, on the other hand, addresses the entire interaction between user and computer. While it shares much with the study of user interface, interactivity design differs because it considers thinking in the process of optimization. The user interface designer optimizes the design towards the computer's strengths in speaking and listening, and away from its weaknesses in these same areas. The user interface designer never presumes to address the thinking content of software (the algorithms that determine its core behaviors).

The interactivity designer optimizes the design for all three dimensions of interactivity; this entails additional balancing considerations and could conceivably produce results that the user interface designer, using his narrower considerations, would reject as incorrect. We can grasp the task of the interactivity designer by regarding the thinking content of software as its function, and the user interface as its form. In this frame of thinking, the user interface designer considers form only and does not intrude into function, but the interactivity designer considers both form and function in creating a unified design.

Another, more subtle factor that distinguishes the interactivity designer from the user interface or human factors designer is the combination of generational factors and two cultural factors (see Chapter 27 for a discussion on the wars between the science/engineering culture and the arts/humanities culture). The human factors people have been in the business a long time, and have developed a large body of truth for their field, most of it arising from experience with "big metal": mainframe computers, weapons systems, power plants, and the like. Their field is heavily "academized": You must have a Ph.D. to be taken seriously, and you spend a lot of time carrying out experiments to measure the efficiency of a design.

The user interface people tend to be less starchy. As a group, they're younger, less concerned with degrees, and sometimes less certain of themselves. Their expertise arises from the two decades of experience the world has had working with personal computers. Because the field is so rapidly changing, there's less confidence in eternal verities. And, like the human factors people, the user interface people are stronger on the math/science side of the problem than on the arts/humanities side of the problem. Indeed, most of them would say, "*What* arts/humanities side?"

By contrast, interactivity design people tend to come more from the "Webby" generation than the "Personal Computer" generation. They're younger, less technical, and stronger in the arts/humanities. They tend to be less technically adept than the human factors or user interface people.

Interactivity design faces an obstacle in the territoriality of the older and established human factors and user interface people, whose work is valuable and relevant. The problem is that user interface design is a more narrowly focussed field than interactivity design, and yet the user interface people seem to resent the intrusion of interactivity design into "their" field. They're perfectly willing to tolerate studies of interactivity — so long as those studies closely adhere to and build on the established traditions of the user interface field.

The pernicious effect of this attitude lies in its refusal to recognize the paradigm shift implicit in interactivity design. Much human intellectual advance arises from the steady refinement of an established set of ideas; occasionally, however, progress is more readily achieved by rearranging established truths under a new paradigm. Interactivity is such a new paradigm. Interactivity designers do not deny the hard-won lessons of the past; they seek to incorporate them in a wider perspective, which, in turn, requires some rearrangement. We must incorporate the wisdom of older fields into the larger design framework of interactivity.

Graphic Design and Multimedia

The web has enticed a great many graphic designers and multimedia people into the computer biz. These people have, in turn, provided a life-saving dose of vitamin C to a deathly scurvied industry. Their expertise in applying aesthetic considerations that improve the effectiveness of websites has opened the eyes of a great many technical people.

Unfortunately, these creative people have yet to shake off some of the inappropriate predilections of their earlier careers. In particular, some seem to confuse graphic design with interactivity design. While designing a visually effective page certainly demands great skill and creativity, page design alone is only part of the overall task of interactivity design.

Another common misconception is that the design process can be broken into two steps: the graphic design step and the "interactivizing" step. As you will see in later chapters, this is a serious error because good interactivity design integrates form with function. Those who cling tightly to the firm foundation of their expertise in graphic design, refusing to let go and strike out into the briny deep of interactivity design, will forever be graphic designers — not interactivity designers.

Summary and Conclusion

I have offered a definition of interactivity. I don't claim this to be the only good definition, or even the best; I really don't care to establish lexicographical dominance over anybody. I do insist that this definition is useful: That is, it generates guidelines for good design that make sense. Once interactivity becomes established in our culture, the academics will get a hold of it, and then you'll have more "high-quality" definitions than you ever thought you needed.

Review Questions

1. Are rugs interactive? Explain in your own words why or why not.

2. Come up with your own damn definition of interactivity.

3. Throw this book across the room. Measure the distance it traveled and the angle of impact. Draw appropriate conclusions in crayon.

2

WHY BOTHER WITH INTERACTIVITY?

Interactivity is important for designers because it is a new and revolutionary communication medium, yet a tried and true way to learn. Interactive communication is superior to conventional, one-way communication. Interactivity is also the computer's intrinsic competitive advantage. For artists, interactivity represents an exciting and unexplored field of effort.

The computer is so good at so many things that we have difficulty discerning the one factor that truly makes it unique. Remember desktop publishing? Mobile computing? Multimedia? Connectivity? Workgroups? Full-motion, full-frame video? 3D graphics? With all these fads and buzzwords inundating us, it's easy to lose sight of the enduring fundamental truth: Each new generation of designers makes the same mistakes as the previous ones, and little forward progress is made. Therefore, let's look at the reasons why interactivity is of primary importance in the design of all things that are computer related.

It's New! It's Revolutionary!

Let's start with the obvious argument. Yes, interactivity is new and revolutionary, yet few realize the degree of novelty and the significance of the interactivity revolution.

Strictly speaking, interactivity as a deliberate behavior in animals is several million years old; most mammalian infants learn basic skills through interactive play (more on this in Chapter 25). What's new is automated interactivity—interactivity effected by means of computing machinery. Mechanization has invaded almost every aspect of human life, mostly to our great benefit, but human interactivity has resisted mechanization.

Take the art of conversation, our most familiar form of interaction. Despite the automated nature of today's electronic world, the dynamics of a conversation between two people today are no different from those of a conversation between Gilgamesh and Enkidu. While the carrier of that conversation has changed, and conversations are carried on from one end of the world to the other, the conversation's interactive dynamics have not changed. Conversation itself is still our fundamental means of communication. Email, interestingly enough, has exploded into our lives precisely because it is an extension of conversation, yet it's greatest weakness is the absence of conversational cues, leading to embarrassing misunderstandings.

Automated interactivity, made possible by the computer, has made possible a profoundly different kind of conversation. Human-to-human conversations are driven by the differences in knowledge or opinion of the conversers. While such differences may seem huge, they pale in comparison to the difference between human and computer, because the computer's thought processes are stupendously different from a human's. We can grasp emotional situations that a computer could never comprehend; the computer can multiply two numbers faster than we can read them. Which leap is greater: that from walking to jet planes, or the leap from conversing with people to conversing with such an utterly alien entity?

It's Tried and True!

Yes, friends, not only is interactivity new and revolutionary, but it's also tried and true! As I'll show in Chapter 25, it carries the seal of approval of millions of years of natural selection; billions of satisfied customers from a broad range of species will attest that it yields whiter whites than Brand X (schools) and fresher breath than Brand Y (expository media). Herewith some actual testimonials:

"I flunked Stalking 101; my teachers said I'd be eating kibbles for the rest of my life. But after just two months of playing with my friends, I was stalking my teachers!"

"My friends all laughed when I crouched down to challenge Spike; they didn't know that 12 weeks of intensive play had given me lightning-fast reflexes!"

It's Better

Interactivity is superior to all other forms of human expression in one way: it engages the human mind more powerfully than any other form of expression. When we truly interact with someone or something, we are truly engaged.

In contrast, non-interactive forms of expression do not hold our attention so tenaciously. The greatest movie in the world can lose our attention to the sound of munching popcorn; our involvement with a great book will surrender itself to a buzzing fly. But interactivity wraps its tentacles around our minds and doesn't let go. Active, direct involvement always demands greater attention than passive observation. As the Chinese proverb says, "I hear and I forget; I see and I remember; I do and I understand."

Well-executed expressions in other media will always outperform interactive expressions in their superior texture, polish, and detail, but the interactive expression has its own unbeatable advantage: people identify more closely with it because they are emotionally right in the middle of it.

It's the Computer's Basis of Competitive Advantage

The first rule in business is that you must identify your basis of competitive advantage and then exploit it to the fullest. Let's take me as an example. I'd be a fool to go into business as a cabinet maker because I handle a file like a chainsaw; I'm much better off speaking, writing, or pontificating on interactivity design. And I don't want to go into any business that mixes pontificating with cabinet making, because that dilutes my basis of competitive advantage.

The same rule applies to designing with the computer. Sure, the computer can offer beautiful graphics, but any kid with a few bucks can pick up a calendar with much better graphics. Sure, it's got wonderful sound capabilities, but how much does a music CD cost these days? Yes, the computer offers lovely video, but for one measly dollar I can rent a videotape with much better video. Software designers who try to compete with movies, music, or printed graphics are guaranteed to lose. The one and only place where we can beat those other industries is in our interactivity, so we should exploit interactivity to its fullest and not dilute it with secondary business.

I'm not saying that we should eschew graphics, sound, or video; I'm saying that we shouldn't make these factors the selling points of our work. Winemakers put their wine in bottles, and they make every effort to make those bottles attractive, but I certainly wouldn't buy from a winery whose advertisements emphasize its lovely wine bottles.

People claim that the computer's true essence lies in its ability to crunch numbers, or handle mountains of information. While these are desirable features, they don't lie at the core of what makes the computer so important to our civilization. Remember, we had plenty of number-crunching and data-cubbyholing computers in the 1960s and 1970s, but we don't talk about "the computer revolution" until the 1980s. The revolutionary new element was interactivity.

Before personal computers, a computer was a frighteningly expensive machine ensconced in special air-conditioned quarters, accessible to the user only at a distance, and in batches. You submitted your "job" to the computer operators, who took your punched cards into the sacred vault and fed them into the computer, which "processed your job" and printed it all out on striped green-and-white paper. You collected your printout hours after submitting your job and went off to analyze your results. If something was wrong, you modified your punched cards and tried again. If you were fortunate, you had access to a data terminal that permitted you to communicate directly with the computer through a 300-baud modem. This reduced the response time of computers from hours to minutes—but even that was slow enough to destroy any sense of interactivity.

The personal computer revolution put a computer on every desk, thereby reducing the response time to fractions of a second. You could organize your data (numbers, formulas, or text) one way, examine the consequences, and try something else, without ever drumming your fingers in frustrated waiting. Interactivity had been strangled by slow computing; personal computers unleashed viable interactivity and changed the world.

It's Unknown Territory

Let's suppose, though, that you are not some crass businessman concerned only with base issues of profit and loss; let's suppose that you are an artiste, complete with beret, concerned only with the creative process. What great artist could resist the opportunity to explore a completely new field of artistic endeavor? This is the biggest artistic opportunity in history: a major new field is suddenly opening up, and you're one of the lucky generation to be in the right place and at the right time to change the world. The doorway to each of the other Muses was slowly pried open by the combined efforts of many artists; but the doorway to interactivity was blown open overnight. Our interactive Bachs, Michelangelos, and Shakespeares are probably out there right now, flunking school. We are living in Florence during the Renaissance. Hey look! Wasn't that da Vinci going into that restaurant?

Interactivity is important, and deserves our attention, because it is new and revolutionary, yet tried and true; it has communicative advantages no other medium shares; it's the essence of the computer revolution; and it's exciting, unexplored territory.

Personal computers changed all this, but not by merely putting a computer on everyone's desk. The revolution was driven by software, and if any program can be singled out as contributing the most to getting the computer revolution going, it has to be VisiCalc, the first microcomputer spreadsheet program. Created by Dan Bricklin and Bob Frankston, VisiCalc was released in 1980, and quickly became the biggest software hit of the computer industry. People bought computers just to be able to use VisiCalc.

There were spreadsheet programs on big computers long before VisiCalc came along, but they didn't change the world, because they offered poor interactivity. You punched up your budget figures, submitted your job, and waited for the printout of your spreadsheet to come back. If you wanted to change a number, you ran the program a second time, and it printed the new version of your job. The whole process was slow and clumsy. In the best of circumstances, you could run the spreadsheet program from a remote terminal and enjoy response times of perhaps a minute—still too slow to be usefully interactive.

But VisiCalc permitted you to make changes and see the results instantly. The unforeseen consequence of this was that businesspeople starting playing around with their budget numbers, changing them willy-nilly to explore a variety of what-if scenarios. Suddenly, the spreadsheet became a powerful tool, something every business needed. It wasn't the number-crunching or data storage that made these programs suddenly useful—those features were just as good on the old mainframe spreadsheets. It was the interactivity that made this new generation of spreadsheets so exciting.

The same thing goes with word processing. There were plenty of "text processing" programs on mainframes back in the 70s. They were almost useless; you entered your text, ran the program, and then went to the computer center to collect your printed output. The whole process was so slow as to make it useless. But with personal computers—especially the Macintosh, which first introduced true WYSIWYG (What You See Is What You Get) word processing—you could edit your document, see what it looked like on the screen, make a change, and instantly see the result on the screen. The now-standard writing cycle of read-edit-reread was unheard of in the 1970s.

The essence of the change is that the interactivity of the writing process has been catapulted from ghastly slow to breathtakingly fast.

3

SPEAKING

We begin our close-up examination of the three steps of interactivity with the most familiar: speaking.

Speaking, in the special sense that I use it in the definition of interactivity, is the process by which the computer communicates to the human. It has two channels: visual and auditory. The fineness of output is still not up to human sensory capabilities.

A Note on Terminology

I use the term *speaking* loosely to apply to any effort to move information from one person to another. I could, of course, use the more precise term *output*, but that would distance us from the definition of interactivity. Perhaps the definition should have been expressed not in terms of *listening, thinking,* and *speaking,* but rather in terms of *inputting, processing,* and *outputting.* Such a change would, I think, have led us in entirely the wrong direction, however. The problem we face in getting computers to work better is not that humans need to become more computer-like, but that computers need to behave in a more human-like manner. We must impose human ways of thinking on the design process if we are to make our designs more understandable to humans.

A Vast Accumulation of Expertise

Humans have developed speaking into myriad special forms: literature, theater, music, cinema, the visual arts, rhetoric, dance, and more. Humankind has accumulated vast experience in expressing itself. If you add up all the people in the world engaged in creating such works (writers, teachers, graphic artists, poets, musicians, moviemakers, actors, dancers, journalists, and poets), then surely you would obtain a sizeable fraction of the earth's population. We sure do spend a lot of time speaking. This is understandable; speaking is the primary means of transmitting culture, and we 6 billion have developed a lot of culture to transmit.

When we first began to build software, we rushed to apply this vast expertise in speaking. It was difficult in the early days; computers had lousy visual and auditory outputs. But computers have come a long way, and we are no longer so tongue-tied. There are now four measures of the expressive power of a computer: pixel count, color depth, frame rate, and sound output.

Pixel Count

Pixel is a miscontraction of the technical term *picture element*, which in turn is a single dot on the screen. I suppose that the alteration of the contraction is a happy one; imagine how you'd feel if I asked you how many *pickels* you have on your screen.

The image on a computer display is composed of thousands of tiny square pixels. Some are white, some black, some red, some blue, and so on. The pixels form a complete image. On a typical computer screen, each pixel is about a third of a millimeter wide—just small enough for your eye to combine groups of pixels smoothly. Back in the early days of computing, pixels were about a millimeter wide, and you could really see the graininess:

```
This is an example of standard video
resolution from the early 1980s. Each
line is only 40 characters wide.
```

More pixels permit more image. For example, the text above uses only 9,282 pixels. This is how the same text appears on my display screen, drawn to the same scale:

> This is an example of standard video
> resolution from the early 1980s. Each
> line is only 40 characters wide.

This image, however, requires 32,308 pixels. As you can see, more pixels permit a better-looking image. Or they can be used to provide more low-resolution text. Either way, more pixels means more image.

Screen Size versus Pixel Count

Some people prefer to think in terms of physical screen size rather than pixel count. To their way of thinking, a 21-inch screen is 50 percent bigger than a 14-inch screen and has 225 percent of the surface area, so it is more than twice as good as the 14-inch screen. And in fact this is correct, so long as we are comparing pixels of the same size. The confusion arises from the fact that most display systems offer the user a variety of screen resolutions. The user can have a great many tiny pixels or fewer large pixels. I think that pixel count is a more useful measure of what we interactivity designers must work with. It is true that some monitors permit tiny pixels and thereby cram a great many into a small screen, but I regard this as a secondary exception; most people don't bother to use those resolutions. The proper measure is how many pixels the user can see at his preferred size. And of course, a bigger screen always permits more pixels. But remember, we're working with pixels, not inches.

Back in the early 1980s, most computer displays used television screens and so offered screen sizes of 480 horizontal pixels and 320 vertical pixels, although at these high resolutions, the pixels were smeared horizontally. This amounted to 153,600 pixels. The first Macintosh in 1984 offered 512 horizontal pixels by 340 vertical pixels, or 174,080 pixels. By the early 1990s, screen displays were up to 640 horizontal pixels by 480 vertical pixels, for a total of 307,200 pixels (307 kilopixels). Currently, the market has settled on 17-inch screens with resolutions of 800 by 600 (480 Kpx) or 1024 by 768 (800 Kpx). I expect that we shall creep up to a megapixel over the next few years. The limiting factor is not in the silicon chips; the memory needed to display a megapixel is 4 megabytes, currently priced at under $40 retail. The limiting factor is now the monitor: as I write this, a 17-inch monitor costs about $300, and a 21-inch monitor costs $800. Prices of monitors have been coming down over the past decade, but with nowhere near the precipitous plunge that is typical of silicon chips. Therefore, my hunch is that interactivity designers should be able to count on and design for a full megapixel of screen capacity by 2003.

Why is this important? Because computer displays speak to the human eye, and therefore, for optimal results, it is important that output capacity of the display match the input capacity of the eye. Our visual systems suck in information, and the straw through which they suck in that information should be neither too small nor too large.

Unfortunately, it is impossible to precisely calculate the input capacity of the human eye, because the human visual system is marvelously optimized for a dynamic, three-dimensional world. We can get a handle on the problem, however, by considering the lessons we have learned from the two-dimensional world of reading. Newspapers are printed at 600 dots per inch (dpi) and books at about 1200 dpi; the highest-quality printing uses about 2400 dpi. For our purposes, we can safely use 1200 dpi as our working figure for the resolution of the human eye. Compare this with the 80 dpi that is common on most computer screens today, and you can see that we have a long way to go.

But there's another critical factor to consider: the effective visual field of the eye. This is especially difficult to estimate because the eye is in constant motion, darting all over the image, gathering information as needed. Our guide-line here shall be the standard sheet of paper at 8.5 inches by 11 inches. Since we must read all the way across the page for each line, let us guess a standard visual field of 7 inches in width. However, our field of view is not symmetric; we tend to see horizontally better than vertically. This is why televisions and movie theater screens are wider than they are tall. The ratio of width to height is called the *aspect ratio*, and it varies from 1.77 for a television screen to 2.38 for a movie screen. Let's take an intermediate value of 2.00 for our assumed aspect ratio. Combining this with our other figures leads us to calculate 35 megapixels for the working area of the human eye. Compare this figure with the half-megapixel we get with the typical computer monitor, and you can see why most people pre-fer to print a long chunk of text rather than read it directly on the screen.

Consider the difference between the number of pixels the eye would like to see (35 Mpx) and the number we can feed it (< 1 Mpx), and you can see why these considerations are important. Our users are starving for pixels! It is vital that we software designers make best use of every single pixel we have.

Unfortunately, we can't wait for technology to bail us out of this problem. With current technology, a 35-megapixel monitor would measure about 100 inches (8 feet) diagonally with an extrapolated cost (if it were technically possi-ble, which it isn't) of about a quadrillion dollars. Even if Moore's Law applied to monitors (which it doesn't), it would take 50 years to get the price of such a monitor down to $1,000.

I will not offer advice on screen layout; this is a well-understood variation of conventional graphic design. You can find many books about graphic design; this book is about the rarer topic of interactivity design. However, there is an immense difference between traditional graphic design and computer screen lay-out: the computer screen can change in the blink of an eye, while paper images are forever. Thus, traditional graphic design presents us with a good starting point for screen layout, but it does not take us far enough. The role of anima-tion in screen function is crucial to good interactivity design. You will find more on this issue in the discussion of frame rate.

Color Depth

The next major factor in computer output is color depth. This is the fineness of shades of color that our screen can present. If you have two screens with the same number of pixels, but the first screen has more color depth than the sec-ond, then you can display more information on the first screen. For example, you can show text at a smaller font size, and it looks better:

four bits of color resolution
one bit of color resolution

This is what the preceding text looks like magnified:

four bits of color resolution
one bit of color resolution

Color depth is measured in bits of color resolution. The absolute lowest level of color depth is 1 bit: black and white. The lower sample text was written with 1 bit of color resolution. An 8-bit display can present 256 colors; a 16-bit display offers 65 thousand colors; 24 bits yields 16 million colors. We can congratulate ourselves and thank the monitor designers for having attained adequacy; the 24-bit display (now common) offers more color depth than the human eye can perceive. Thus, unlike pixel count, the color depth of our display screens is good enough as far as the human eye is concerned.

With 16 million available colors, we can display natural-looking photographs and other artwork, but the most common benefit of all those colors lies in *anti-aliasing*: the fine shading of pixels at the edge of a line to suggest angles not displayed properly on a tessellated display. Here's another example showing more closely how anti-aliasing works:

This example shows the letter *"l"* in italic; the left character is in 1-bit mode, and the right is in 4-bit mode. The angled line of the letter on the left doesn't line up neatly with the gridwork of the pixels, so we see a blocky image; this problem is called *staircasing*. The letter on the right uses intermediate-value grays to suggest parts of the line, and when you look at it in its proper size, it looks much better:

l l

Thus, displays with more color depth can present more information to the user.

Anti-aliasing is now standard on screen displays, especially word processors; only the older, slower machines are incapable of handling anti-aliasing. Be aware, however, that many older books on screen layout did not take anti-aliasing into account.

Frame Rate

The next major factor in computer output is frame rate, the speed with which animations can be run on the computer. Much of the excitement over multimedia arose when computers crossed the speed threshold for a reasonable frame rate, about 16 frames per second. This was the standard for the old black-and-white movies; it is obviously jerky, but the eye can tolerate it. The current standard for movies, 24 frames per second, works fine for most people. Televisions use a weird scheme that makes their frame rate hard to define; a programmer would call it 30 frames per second, and a marketing person would call it 60 frames per second, and they'd both be right.

The frame rate a computer can achieve depends on the size of the animated frame. Because a computer can move only so many pixels per second, a big frame with a lot of pixels takes longer to assemble than a small frame with few pixels.

NOTE *The not-Impossible Dream here is for full-screen, full-motion (FSFM) video, which also assumes full color depth as well. This would mean that your entire screen could be animated at 30 frames per second; in other words, someday your expensive computer might become powerful enough to do what your television does. As yet, this ideal remains a dream, but we're getting close; I reckon we'll be popping champagne corks in a few years.*

From the point of view of an interactivity designer, animation might be thought of as a means for squeezing more utility out of each screen pixel. After all, it is possible to change each pixel 60 times per second; thus, in a single second, you could theoretically display 60 screens worth of information. Even a small 800 by 600 monitor could put out 28.8 Mpx per second! Now that's expressive power! Unfortunately, there is a catch: the human eye doesn't work that way; animating the screen that way wouldn't work. Fortunately, we don't need to push matters to this extreme; a great deal can be accomplished with much less ambitious designs. The key point of this paragraph is that animation is not some magical element existing in isolation from all other components of the design; it is instead just one more way to communicate information—to speak—to the user.

To use animation effectively, we must again consider the capabilities of the human visual system. Our eye sees randomly flickering pixels as "television snow"—you might be presenting the encoded complete text of, say, the user manual for Microsoft Word, or some other humongous document, but to the eye, it's just a snowy mess. Our eyes are optimized to recognize certain types of motion, and those are the types that you must use in your designs. Here are some of the animations that the human eye is keyed to recognize:

Translation: Objects moving across the field of view.

Expansion/Contraction: Objects expanding or contracting; this is perceived as approach or recession.

Brightening/Dimming: Objects growing brighter or dimmer; this is perceived as approach or recession.

Vibration: Objects moving small distances in a fast and regular pattern.

Rotation: Three-dimensional objects appearing to rotate.

Facial animation: The visual system has special facilities for recognizing facial expressions.

These are the fundamental animation components you have to work with. However, two constraints must be kept in mind. First, temporal discontinuity is not good. An animation shouldn't simply pop from one image to a completely different one. The visual system has all sorts of algorithms built into it that assume a continuous universe; if something pops up instantly, the visual processing system is momentarily befuddled. Windows 98 incorporates this design concept in its menus, which quickly expand out of their source rather than simply popping up.

The second constraint upon your use of animation is its power as an attracting annunciator. Whenever something flashes or blinks, our eyes are attracted to it. That's very useful when we want to insist upon getting our user's attention. It's very bad when some minor animation distracts the user from the task at hand. An overly animated display looks—literally—busy. For example, in one commonly used program, if you happen to leave the cursor over an icon, then that icon's little explanation phrase (known as a *tooltip*) will pop up and remain there. If you then start typing, each keypress turns off the little explanation phrase, which then pops back up after every pause of a few seconds. Thus, at the instant you pause to consider a phrase, that damn pop-up distracts your attention—a perfect example of animation-distraction.

Pop-up Animation

The most commonly used animation technique seldom strikes us as animation: the use of pop-up displays. Pop-up displays take many forms: pop-up menus, tooltips, help bubbles, even dialog boxes and alternate windows are part of this family. The underlying concept is simple: the screen display is not two-dimensional, but two-and-one-half dimensional. We imagine the display to be a stack of partially overlapping planar images, which we can bring to the fore with various commands. This change of display is the simplest form of animation, but it multiplies the number of pixels available. A single text option embedded in a pop-up menu occupies perhaps 2,000 pixels; if that pop-up menu contains just ten items, it offers an additional 20,000 pixels of almost free screen space.

The *tooltip* is a single word or short phrase meant to explain the meaning of an icon. It is most often activated by leaving the mouse motionless over an active icon for longer than about a second; this causes the tooltip to pop up underneath the icon. What puzzles me is that designers have stopped short in utilizing this idea. If you can pop up a short phrase, why not pop up a full sentence, or a whole paragraph? In fact, this idea has been implemented and is called a *help bubble*. Whereas a tooltip gives us a few hundred free pixels, a help bubble grants us several thousand free pixels. The capability to provide help bubbles is built into both the Mac and the Windows operating systems, yet most software designers seem content with tooltips.

One would expect that well-designed applications rely heavily on these pop-up techniques to increase their effective screen space many times over, but such is not the case. My examination of a variety of software applications reveals a ratio of this virtual screen space to real screen space ranging from 75 percent to 250 percent. I am pleased to report, though, that the more modern programs tend to have the larger ratios. However, the great majority of this virtual screen space takes the form of plain drop-down menus and their secondary menus. As yet, pop-up menus, tooltips, and help balloons are little used to multiply effective screen space.

The design problem we face in implementing pop-up systems lies in defining a clean command system for the user to bring up these secondary image planes—but I'll address such issues in Chapter 5, "Listening."

Full-Motion Animation

There is one application of animation for which discussions of user control are less important: the playing of video. The central issue is that the user can't interact with canned video, other than using the standard controls such as start, stop, single-step, rewind, and so forth. True interactive pre-recorded video is a contradiction in terms. As soon as you start thinking about interrupting that carefully controlled video stream pouring from the DVD player, design hell breaks loose. How often will you permit the user to interrupt the video? What if the user interrupts it at an inconvenient time? If the user interrupts the video stream because s/he desires to interact with it, how can you respond if the only video you have is the canned stuff? What can you do with a video stream other than play it non-interactively? If you want to design software that turns a computer into an overpriced DVD player, by all means do so, but you might want to ask yourself, what's the point of your efforts?

I have seen a great many attempts to deal with this problem, and none of them impress me. The best relegate the video stream to a minor role in the overall interaction. The primary imagery is calculated by the CPU itself; because it is algorithmic, it can be interactive. In other words, the user interacts with the little stick figure running around in the foreground, while magnificent video plays irrelevantly in the background. Occasionally the video does change, perhaps in response to the user's change of environments. In these uses, video works well because it's not getting in the way of the interaction.

The only general-purpose way to tackle full-motion animation is to calculate the images on the fly. The first decent example of this was the computer game Doom—which is one reason why it was such a sensational success. By cleverly constraining the types of images handled, the designers were able to achieve FSFM video that was calculated in interactive response to the user's actions. Unfortunately, without those clever constraints, the calculation of most imagery in real time remains at the fringes of research. Some impressive results have been achieved with certain kinds of imagery, but the ability to calculate in real time the entire image set for, say, *Jurassic Park* remains out of reach.

Sound Output

The most important use of sound is to demand attention. A user's eyes may wander wheresoever they please, but sounds reach out and grab even the least attentive user. Unfortunately, little progress has been made in this elementary application of sound; we continue to use the age-old standard system beep (permitting users to replace it with quacks, toots, sneezes, or other custom variations). Computer sound channels these days can carry more information. For example, designers could apply a graduated scale of warnings, from a low-volume, mid-frequency grunt for progress reports ("Now printing document"; "Waiting for connection") to a deep, loud growl for pre-emptive warnings ("Are you sure you want to format the hard disk?") and a high-pitched scream for post-disaster announcements ("Your program just crashed"). A particularly effective application of sound output would be for anticipated decision announcements (see Chapter 24).

Music is another way to bring sound to bear on an interaction, but music is difficult to apply interactively. Music's power arises from its holistic nature; the emotional value of a composition does not spring from a simple addition of all the notes; it is instead the internal relationships reaching over the entire composition that render music so effective. Break the music into individual phrases, play them independently of each other, and you get auditory mishmash. Thus, musical compositions must be presented in their entirety to work their magic—and how can you interact with something that refuses to alter itself in response to your actions?

Still, there have been some impressive efforts in this direction, which indicate that much potential for music remains. As early as 1983, a computer game called Preppies sported sprightly tunes during game play, and the tunes acceptably segued at transition points in the game. Similarly, many first-person shooter games are embellished with musical sequences that can change with the environment.

However, in all such cases, the degree of interaction is low; the music changes only occasionally. We do not enjoy the kind of rapidly changing music that we hear in movies. Why? Because when composing for a movie, the musician knows what's coming next, and can build that knowledge into the flow of the music. This is much more difficult to do in interactive products, because the designer cannot know in advance what the user will do, and therefore cannot program the algorithms for rapid shifts in tone. Fortunately, there has been much progress of late in algorithmic music generation, and over the next decade we will hear music with increasingly faster response times.

Speech Synthesis

We have had basic speech synthesis for several decades now. While the early results sounded mechanically Swedish, they were recognizable as human speech. We have made much progress since then: we ditched the accent and have added rudimentary voice tonality. You can have the computer speak with, say, the voice of a man, a woman, a boy, or a girl. There are even programs that can figure out the tonal traits of your own voice and mimic them adequately. But the general solution to tonality—the ability to specify almost any voice—eludes us yet.

Even worse is the problem of inflection. The goal here is to have the computer say "Not with *my* daughter, you don't!" with the proper inflection on *my* to communicate indignation. Much preliminary work has been done on this problem; no solution has emerged that is good enough to command wide adoption.

A more fundamental weakness of speech synthesis is its transitory nature. If I set my computer to print a document, and then go grab a cup of coffee, the spoken advisory, "The printer is out of paper," will go unheard, leaving me ignorant and irritated upon my return. For this reason, speech can seldom be used as a primary mode for speaking to the user. Its use will most likely be confined to declarations of assumptions and intermediate processes, similar to the manner in which members of a work crew coordinate their actions by announcing them as they proceed.

NOTE *Some pessimists warn that the use of any sound can be disruptive in an office environment. I think this is true only in the case of ill-mannered sound. Every office buzzes with quiet conversations between co-workers, and a quiet conversation between user and computer is no different. The designer should apply sound with the same sense of civility that guides office conversations. Keep it short, confine attention-getting noises to serious situations, and don't raise your voice.*

Assembling the Pieces

Putting it all together, we see that we have a machine that can efficiently present moderately detailed images with lots of color, some animation, small snippets of prerecorded sound and—soon—synthesized voice output. Interactivity designers would therefore best utilize this device by using color liberally, resolution next, animation third, and sound last. (This is not to say that sound deserves little attention; in annunciation situations (for example, "You've got mail!"), use of sound is the best way to speak to the user, and it's also the best way to declare anticipated decisions.)

As technology improves, you'll have more of everything, and the ratios may shift. Certainly as screen sizes increase, you'll be able to spread out your screen layouts and indulge yourself in some much-needed whitespace. Larger hard disks will permit greater use of animation.

A Final Warning

Last, I warn you to be especially wary of a dangerous pitslope in interactive design: the tendency to speak too much. Several forces push you in this direction. First, speaking media are well understood, and you probably already possess expertise in one of these media.

We always prefer to solve problems with techniques we have already mastered. For example, my wife once started a new job by discovering that her subordinates were carrying out a manufacturing step by cracking nuts with big rocks. She inquired as to the reason for the rocks: safety? efficiency? The workers were surprised by the question and allowed as how they'd never done it any other way. She asked, had they used hammers; they had, but hammers did too much damage. Well, she said, have you tried plastic deadblow hammers? Silence. The new deadblow hammers tripled productivity. Moral: don't use rocks to crack interactivity design.

Second, the computer is intrinsically better at speaking than at listening. We spend more money, memory, and machine cycles on visual display than on any of our input systems; think about how cheap and simple a mouse is compared to your 19-inch color monitor. The stores are full of special display cards that will give you even more graphics power than already comes with your machine, but have you ever seen a special card to enhance the computer's listening?

Lastly, our own egos egg us to hog the conversation. In regular conversation, the disapproving stares of our interlocutors serve to rein in our rampaging egotistical loquacity; no such helpful feedback constrains us in interactivity design. So we blather away at our users, hosing them down with impressive imagery, astounding animation, and sensational sounds. An ego trip, yes; good interactivity design, no.

As an interactivity designer, you must maintain constant resistance against these forces. At every step in the design, you must ask yourself, am I talking at my user or talking with him?

The dimensions of speaking available to the interactivity designer are measured by resolution, color depth, frame rate, and sound. Of these, only color depth exceeds the natural limits of the human eye. Resolution falls far short, while frame rate falls between these extremes. Sound is an underutilized medium of communication to the user.

4

THINKING

Thinking is the delivered content of all interactivity designs. It uses algorithms: mathematical procedures for determining results, built up from many tiny building blocks. Algorithms can be created from many sources.

Human Thinking Versus Machine Thinking

While *thinking* is a handy term for the purposes of this book, it surely misleads the reader about the realities of designing this second step in interactivity. Computers don't think, and they never will; what goes on inside their CPUs is alien to human thought. I use the anthropomorphic term only because it's the closest word available. But remember: the notion of computers thinking is about as strained as the notion of Mr. Sperm in love with Ms. Egg.

The difference between biological thinking and machine thinking is profound. Nervous systems process through pattern recognition. All considerations are expressed as patterns; all decisions are manifested as patterns of muscle activity. These patterns can be temporally sequenced: when we decide to speak the sentence "The cat threw up a hairball," the decision is a pattern, but the actual utterance is delivered serially. Pattern-recognition thinking is ideally suited to the needs of an organism: it is easily scalable from the simplest wormy thoughts to the overwrought contemplations of homo sapiens. It yields fast results—always good for an organism coping with a real-time environment—and its default configuration permits the widest latitude in processing sensory inputs (for example, "Grunt, that berry is red and round, so it fits the pattern for edible berries. Barf! Gee, maybe I need to refine my pattern for edible berries.").

Machine thinking, by contrast, is about as far away from pattern recognition as a thinking system can be. It reduces all thinking to the most elementary logical atoms, using bits as data and the three fundamental logical operators (AND, OR, NOT). All machine thinking is nothing more than combinations and sequences of these operations. Because these operations are so logically microscopic, huge numbers of them must be assembled to accomplish anything we humans consider useful. The building blocks of computer logic are assembled into towering pyramids of logic to create useful functions.

Many non-technical designers are appalled and intimidated by the size of the intellectual pyramid they must build. Harkening back to their childhood building-block play, they fear that any pyramid they build will necessarily collapse of its own weight. So they never make the attempt.

You must indulge yourself in some hubris to design interactive applications. Unlike the wooden blocks of your childhood, the building blocks of computers snap together neatly like Lego pieces. With enough Lego parts, you could have created edifices reaching up to the stars, but your brother had lost the crucial pieces. When designing with the computer, your supply of Lego pieces is infinite.

I'll demonstrate the process by showing you how I would go about designing a word processor. I'll use both *top-down* and *bottom-up* approaches. Top-down design starts with the broadest statement of the design objective and then steadily breaks it apart into smaller and smaller chunks until all the chunks are small enough that their implementation is obvious. Bottom-up design starts with the capabilities of the computer and works upward in the general direction of the objective. The two strategies meet somewhere in the twilight zone of software design.

I start at the top by deciding that my goal is a program that will allow the user to type some text, edit it, save it for later use, and print it. I flit back to the bottom and note that my fundamental data structure will be the text itself: a long table of characters, one slot for each letter or punctuation mark that the user types. Bouncing back to the top, I observe that my program must organize that text into a page. The table itself is a long line of characters; if I were to print it directly, I'd get something like a ticker tape of text. So now I must figure out how to organize all that text into a page.

A Digression about Verisimilitude

Consider this document:

Why shouldn't our word processor be able to reproduce this document? The task in interactivity design is the same as in any art: to create, not an exact duplicate of reality in all its confusion and messiness, but an image or representation of reality that focuses the user's mind on some singular truth. The designer deliberately distorts reality in a manner reflecting the designer's own point of view. Whenever you design an interactive application, you are not delivering reality to your user, you are imposing a worldview upon your user. That worldview has purpose or human desire woven into its fabric. The distortion that your worldview imposes is a falsehood, a failure of verisimilitude—a lie. But it is a useful lie, a clarifying lie, and therefore valuable to your user.

Consider the Declaration of Independence as printed by a computer:

When in the Course of human Events it becomes necessary for one People to dissolve the Political Bands which have connected them with another, and to assume among the Powers of the Earth the separate and equal Station to which the Laws of Nature and Nature's God, a decent Respect for the Opinions of Mankind requires that they should declare the causes which impel them to the Separation.

We hold these Truths to be self-evident, that all Men are created equal, that they are endowed by their Creator with certain inalienable Rights, that among these are Life, Liberty, and the Pursuit of Happiness—That to secure these Rights, Governments are instituted among Men, deriving their just Powers from the Consent of the Governed, that whenever any form of Government becomes destructive to these Ends, it is the Right of the People to alter or abolish it....

See how dry and lifeless the computer version is! It lacks the tiny skips where the quill left the paper; in the real document, you can almost hear the scraping, scribbling sound of quill on paper. Look how stately that title is, with its beautiful calligraphy and exquisite flourishes, and how utterly the computer version fails to capture its magnificence. And what about the signatures? What computer output could ever match the boldness with which John Hancock put his life on the line?

All these observations are true, but irrelevant. The word processor used in this example is built on the worldview that a document is composed of its text, pure and simple. It captures the words and the language perfectly, deliberately neglecting the sensuousness of the original work. If you want to build a sensuous word processor, by all means do, but if so, you must place sensuousness at the center of your design, subordinating all other considerations to your design objective.

End of digression.

Meanwhile, Back at the Ranch . . .

My task here is to reduce the messy complexity of a real document to some simple construct that I can compute with. I need some simplifying concept that stands intermediate between a single character and a page. An obvious solution pops into my head: a line of text. Looking bottom-up, a line is a short string of characters; looking top-down, a page is a stack of lines.

Now I must translate that insight into computable terms. What data will I need to completely specify the nature of the line? What numbers must be computed?

Line length is an obvious beginning. Clearly, the line must fit inside the margins of the page. This can get tricky, though, because the line length depends on how many characters are in the line, and I can't know that until I actually have the text at hand. Ergo, the computer itself will have to make the decisions about how to fill lines. I'll have it build each line the same way a sixteenth-century typesetter would: start at the beginning of the line and place the first letter, then the second letter, and so forth, until we get to the end of the line. If I can't get the last word to fit into the line, then I have to break up and hyphenate the word, or move the entire word to the next line, leaving a long space on the current line. The human typesetter measures the length of the line simply by fitting it into the typeframe; the computer uses a different method. I store a table of the widths of every single character in my typefont; then whenever the computer adds a letter to the line abuilding, it adds the width of that character to the summed length abuilding. When the summed length exceeds the allowed line length, the computer goes back to trim the end of the line. We can express these plans in the elemental terms of the computer:

```
1.    START A NEW LINE
2.    SET THE LINE LENGTH SUM TO ZERO
3.    GET THE NEXT LETTER FROM THE TABLE OF TEXT
4.    PUT THAT LETTER IT INTO THE LINE ABUILDING
5.    LOOK UP THE WIDTH OF THAT LETTER IN THE WIDTH TABLE
6.    ADD THAT WIDTH TO THE LINE LENGTH SUM
7.    QUESTION: IS THE LINE LENGTH SUM LESS THAN THE PERMITTED LINE LENGTH?
```

```
8.      IF THE ANSWER IS YES, THEN DO THIS:
9.      GO BACK TO LINE 3 AND WORK FORWARD FROM THERE
10.     BUT IF THE ANSWER IS NO, THEN DO THIS INSTEAD:
11.     TRIM A WORD OFF OF THE LINE, AND THEN GO TO LINE 7
```

This little bit of imaginary computer program will perform the thinking function of deciding how to lay out the text inside each line. It doesn't do a great job: there's only one font and no variations within that font. Nor does it specify how to "trim the line," but that's a job for another little snippet of computer code.

Now comes a big idea: I can give this little snippet a name, say, BUILD A LINE and then use it as a bigger building block in creating the next layer of the pyramid. At a higher level of the program, there will be line of program code that says USE "BUILD A LINE" NOW. So we go, building ever-bigger blocks. The elementary blocks perform truly stupid operations, but we assemble them into larger blocks that perform merely dumb operations and then assemble those into larger blocks, continuing until we get some interesting or useful thinking.

Algorithms

This little snippet is not a computer program: it's an algorithm. A computer program is an actual working piece of software that you can run on a computer; an algorithm is a generalized plan for a piece of software. An algorithm is a blueprint for a portion of a computer program; it must be translated to a computer language such as Java before it can be run on a computer.

Who designs algorithms? Heretofore, algorithms were always designed by the same programmers who wrote the code. Effective interactivity designers wrest that responsibility from the programmers, or sometimes they become programmers themselves. Algorithms are the fundamental units of computer thinking. To design the thinking, you must design the algorithms. You must therefore learn the principles demonstrated in the word processing example. You must be able to construct algorithms using the elementary components of computer processing. If you don't want to design the algorithms, then go draw artwork, or write a marketing plan, or do something you're good at. Just don't botch interactivity design by relegating the thinking part to somebody else. All three parts (listening, thinking, and speaking) must be an integrated whole.

I can hear you protesting, "But I lack the mathematical expertise to design algorithms. I'm a designer, not an engineer!" This may be true, but engineers lack the design expertise to create algorithms. It might take you a while to recall your high school algebra, but it'll take a lot longer for an engineer to develop your artistic sensitivity. Somebody's got to do the job, and yours is the shortest path to the goal.

Also: shame on you! Was there ever a great artist who was allowed mere technical problems to obstruct the path to greatness? Leonardo studied light and anatomy; Michelangelo learned metallurgy; many modern sculptors are quite handy with a welding torch. Indeed, most of the advances in metallurgy before 1800 were made by artists seeking new forms of expression. Technology serves art—but only for those artists willing to learn the technology.

How to Create Algorithms

Algorithms come from the same depths of the human mind that produce poems, paintings, and symphonies. Like other works of art, they are metaphorical in some deep sense. The basis of the metaphor, however, lies not in how things appear or sound, but in how they operate. The crash of cymbals and blare of trumpets in Siegfried's *Death and Funeral March* are blatant metaphors for the wails at a funeral. More subtlely, the four-part handling of the theme of the fourth movement of Beethoven's *Ninth Symphony* metaphorically evokes an intricate interplay of sadness, nostalgia, and joy. But an algorithm might metaphorically treat the dispersion of people from a crowded subway exit as the paint emerging from a spray nozzle, or a person's losing his temper as the rupture of a water pipe.

In the demonstration algorithm presented earlier, I used an explicit metaphor: the sixteenth-century typesetter. The line of text on the screen is just like a line of type in a typebox; a character on the screen is just like a single piece of type. That metaphor enabled us to see exactly how the algorithm would work. It was the basis of the act of creation.

Most low-level algorithms are as simple as this example, and quite easy to design. At the higher levels of design, however, the task becomes more difficult, and the metaphors more subtle. I have used a great many metaphors in my work, some of them quite exotic. I once used a metaphor involving Mayan arithmetic to solve a screen display problem. The Mayans had a weird way of calculating that was, in this case, ideally suited to my problem. Their system never developed fractions, but they figured out how to get around the problem. Similarly, 8-bit computers could not use fractions, so I used the Mayan's technique on the computer.

On another occasion, I wanted an algorithm to calculate the affinities of a group of imaginary friends inside the computer. If Fredegund likes Mary but hates Gomer, and Mary likes Gomer, how does that affect Fredegund? This is tricky business, because each pairing of people must be considered. My metaphorical solution was to attach imaginary springs to each person, one spring going to every other person, and then setting the length of the spring to be the amount of antipathy that they had for each other. Then I used some simple spring equations from physics to model their behavior and move them around in a 'social space' that was a metaphor for the social universe of the group.

Twenty-five years ago, while I was an undergraduate physics student, I faced an interesting problem that was, in essence, an algorithmic challenge. I needed to randomly select one of eight pairs of lights to be illuminated, and I needed to do this at random times. Nowadays, this problem would be ridiculously simple to solve with a random-number generator in a computer, but back in 1971 we didn't have such technology. I needed to design a random-number generator that would also randomly select one of eight targets.

I cast about for random processes in the real world; there are precious few indeed. One is radioactive decay; however, detecting individual decay products would have required some fairly expensive equipment. I had to do the entire project on a budget of $270.

Another random process is the motion of particles in an ideal gas. We normally think of a gas as a set of molecules in free motion, but there's no law of physics that requires an ideal gas to consist of molecules. The particles could just as well be much larger than molecules and still show the same behavior as an ideal gas. I reasoned that I could just as correctly use ball bearings. Moreover, there is nothing in the physics of an ideal gas that requires it to operate in three dimensions; two dimensions will work just as well. This provided the basis for my physical algorithm.

I started with a piece of plywood and nailed some 3/8-inch wooden strips to it in the form of a rectangle with a funnel at the bottom. At the bottom, I placed a metal propeller attached to a motor. Then I placed some ball bearings in the chamber, tilted the plywood slightly so that the balls would naturally roll down towards the propeller, and turned on the motor.

When the propeller hit a ball, it imparted energy to the ball, which then took off to the upper reaches of the chamber, colliding with other balls. In the lower half of the chamber, motions were dominated by the action of the propeller, and so it didn't act like an ideal gas, but in the upper portion of the chamber, the motions were primarily affected by ball-to-ball collisions, and so the system acted like an ideal gas.

I made a small exit hole at the top of the chamber, and balls occasionally (randomly) escaped through the hole. They then rolled down a ramp to enter a Pascal cascade made of nails, bouncing left or right in three sequences to enter one of eight channels. In rolling down one of these channels, a ball would pass over two microswitches of my own design (two strips of copper foil held apart by a bit of electrical tape at one end), closing the microswitches and activating the lights. After exiting the switch channels, the balls rolled down another ramp to return to the lower portion of the ideal gas chamber.

By adjusting the tilt angle of the plywood and the number of balls in the chamber, I could get any desired rate of activity. My advisor had a good laugh over my Rube Goldberg setup, but the system worked perfectly during the 12-hour experimental run.

Algorithms come from your experience and your knowledge; ultimately, algorithms are wherever you find them. I believe that a broad education is an important factor in algorithm creativity. If you're good at spatial thinking, geometric algorithms are always handy. Perhaps you can draw a schematic representation of the problem, thereby converting difficult concepts into points, lines, or angles. If you're designing an entertainment product based on a love triangle, why not use an actual triangle in your algorithms?

Some Useful Metaphors for Algorithm Creation

There are as many metaphors to use as there are ideas in your head. Here are some particularly productive veins of thought to mine for metaphors.

Spatial and Geometric Metaphor

Spatial and geometric relationships are the most heavily used base for metaphors, largely because programmers excel at spatial reasoning. The trick here is to identify the most important relationship among the components of the problem, and treat that relationship as a distance. For example, I once designed an algorithm for emotional interaction in a group of people by thinking in terms of the "emotional distance" between any pair of people. If two people liked each other, they were physically close in my imaginary diagram, and if they hated each other, they were physically distant. In a political simulation, one might define half a dozen major political issues, and measure each voter by where she stands along a spectrum of opinions about the issue; combining those six dimensions geometrically allows you to determine a political "center" against which candidates can be judged.

Physical Metaphor

Physical metaphors apply processes from physics or chemistry to a problem. In the emotional distance model I just described, I imagined springs stretched or compressed along the lines connecting every pair of characters; these represented the social pressures that pulled people apart or pushed them together. To see how people's relationships changed, I simply allowed the whole system of springs to relax to its most stable positions. The ideal gas law could be applied in a number of ways to analyze the behavior of users at large websites, the better to serve their needs.

Musical Metaphor

Although I am impressively ignorant of musical theory, the richness and high degree of conceptual polish in music tantalizes my hunger for new sources of algorithmic protein. Specifically, music offers a variety of ways for thinking about sequences of events. The rules of melodic composition, and the basic plan of establishing a pattern and then violating it in a pleasing way, offer a great many opportunities for entertainment software design. Concepts of harmonics and chord progressions could be applied to algorithms in educational software to alleviate the tedium of certain kinds of material.

Business or Economic Metaphor

A variety of concepts from the fields of business and economics offer useful sources of metaphor. Competition between similar entities can be applied in a great many conflict simulations, and the relationships among price, supply, and demand can be applied in almost any resource management simulation, even when it includes no explicit price mechanism. A great many algorithmic problems involving prioritizing tasks can also be addressed with metaphorical price mechanisms. Website traffic analysis can be enhanced with models that compare the "price" of a page (its time to download) with the "demand" for that page (how often it is accessed). In a more technical application, certain types of operating system problems involving the management of machine resources can be addressed with schemes analogous to the "put" and "call" systems of the stock market.

Emotional Metaphor

There's an interesting irony here. Designing emotional algorithms can be a difficult task, requiring recourse to other metaphors. However, algorithms based on metaphors for human emotion can be especially useful in handling certain types of user interface problems. (More on this in Chapter 9.)

Bureaucratic Metaphor

Bureaucracies exist because certain social tasks are so complicated that they require a formal division of labor. Software has grown increasingly complex, too, and managing software complexity is the central thrust of all modern software development philosophies. However, we have yet to tackle the concomitant problem of presenting all that complexity to the user in a coherent and usable form; much software is better organized internally than externally. We all love to deride the inefficiencies of bureaucracies, but the brutal truth is that, since Roman times, bureaucracies have proven themselves to be the best way to handle messy problems. So why not organize your design along bureaucratic lines? More on this in Chapter 9.

Data Structures

Creation of algorithms goes hand in hand with creation of data structures; when I hit a brick wall trying to come up with an algorithm, I back up and try the different approach of trying to come up with a data structure that covers the problem. A data structure is simply a reduction of the key elements of the problem to numerical form. For example, suppose that you are designing an educational program about history. Reducing historical processes to algorithmic form is a daunting task, so it might be easier to define the data structures first. A simple data structure for this job might take the form of a sentence, with a date, subject, verb, and direct object:

Year	Subject	Verb	Direct Object
800	Pope	crowns	Charlemagne
1225	Genghis Khan	conquers	Persia
1347	Black Death	enters	Venice
1939	Adolph Hitler	starts	World War II

The components of this data structure, such as subject, verb, and direct object, are called *fields*. Each of these can be represented by numbers representing entries in a table. A program using this data structure would then have a long table of historical actors, such as Genghis Khan, Adolf Hitler, Attila the Hun, and Florence Nightingale. Each table would contain all the necessary additional data on the actor, such as name, birth and death dates, competencies, and so forth. Another table would list the verbs and their characteristics.

Here's another example. A data structure for a human face might contain the following fields:

Nose length

Mouth width

Lip thickness

Interocular distance

Height of face

Pointiness of chin

Eye color

Eyebrow thickness

A simple number for a distance in millimeters can be used for most of the fields in this data structure. Pointiness of chin might require a number for the angle of the chin. Eye color would require three numbers, one for the red component, one for the green component, and one for the blue component.

This set of numbers can then be used as a basis for writing a program to draw a human face. The program would use these numbers to do its job. You could feed the program any set of numbers, and it would draw that face.

Thus, creating a data structure is often a good starting point for creating an algorithm. Note, however, that data structures seldom encompass the fullness of the reality. There's a lot more that goes into making a human face than the eight numbers offered here. But those eight numbers give us a good start, and we can always add more numbers to our data structure if we want to beef up the quality of the overall algorithm.

Ask yourself: What data structures will I need to tackle my problem? How can I reduce the messy reality with which I must deal to something that can be expressed numerically? How complete must my data structure be to solve the design problem adequately? How would various additions to the data structure enhance my ability to improve the interactivity?

Perhaps you object that reducing people to mathematical ciphers is an outrage against your artistic sensitivities. If so, consider that most art in some way reduces the human soul to some physical object: a painting is just oil on canvas, a sculpture just metal or rock. The printed page can present Proust or pornography. A medium does not affect the human values of art; what matters is the expression that the medium carries. If you can express some deep truth of the human soul in algorithmic form, who cares that your truth is communicated via silicon and plastic?

The Significance of Thinking

Although I have argued that each of the three steps of interactivity (listening, thinking, and speaking) must be designed well, there is one asymmetric factor to consider: thinking constitutes the content of your work. Listening and speaking are crucial enabling steps, but thinking is the goods.

A spreadsheet, for example, must have a clean display layout and a practical input system, but ultimately the value of the spreadsheet lies in the calculations that it performs for the user. If the calculations offered are inadequate to the user's needs, then the best-designed listening and speaking are useless. A word processor must have good user interface, but when the rubber hits the road, it is the way that the software organizes and reorganizes the words on the paper that matters most. Game designers have learned that snazzy graphics and sounds are vital, but without good gameplay, their designs are DOA.

The web might seem to offer a counterexample; after all, most of the "thinking" on the web consists of little more than links. These constitute a weak form of thinking. We must remember, however, that the web is still in its infancy; we are nowhere near to mastering this medium. Indeed, the salient trend in the evolution of the web in the last few years has been the augmentation of its simple hyperlink-based thinking with enhancements using CGI and Jjava. Moreover, our designs are currently distorted by the ghastly slow speed of the connections. These slow connections lead us to think in terms of static pages. We need to shift gears.

Here's one way to think about it: what if somebody put a word processor on the web? If you don't have a word processor of your own, you just go to that website and type your document. You can edit it, rearrange the margins and the paragraph settings, and when you like the result, you can print it. This may strike you as silly—after all, the web is so slow that you'd spend most of your life waiting for the latest edited version of your document to come down the wire. But those long delay times are a temporary artifact of telephone lines designed only for voice transmission. There's no question that the lines will improve, and speeds will go way up. What happens when the Internet is so fast that it can bounce back a page faster than you can type a single character?

Right now, we use the web in hunt-and-peck fashion; our interaction with a website is thin, distant, muted. Recall my initial observation that conversation is our clearest metaphor for interactivity. Suppose that all conversations between humans had always been carried out at web speeds—delays of 3 to 20 seconds between each sentence. Conversation wouldn't be much fun or much use, would it? Suppose one day some savior delivers us from this evil predicament, and suddenly we can speak to each other at our current speeds. Consider how profoundly the nature of conversation would change. That change is precisely the same change that will steal over the web as connections speed up.

Stop thinking about the web as a collection of pages. What you've been calling a page is really a window into a niche of thought. Assume that your user will interact with your website as intimately as he might interact with a word processor. This implies, of course, that your website will boast software as rich and intricate in its algorithms as a word processor. That's a lot of work. But it's the future.

Link-based thinking was appropriate when the web was tiny and pages were few; it's not difficult to link up a few dozen pages by hand. But as technologies grow, methods that worked fine in their youth fall into obsolescence. The web has enjoyed explosive growth in size, but much slower conceptual growth. Hand linking thousands of pages doesn't work, and browsing is inadequate when dealing with thousands of pages. Search engines bring a bit more thinking to the process, and already we find that they can't keep up. We need ever-smarter techniques to get what we want from the web. We don't need better graphics or more buttons—we need better thinking. That's why Java has generated so much excitement: it brings vastly greater computational (thinking) power to the web. Over the course of time, cosmetic designers will be shouldered out of the way by those designers who can express their thinking processes (not merely their thoughts).

Algorithm creation is the deepest challenge of interactivity design. It requires profound integration of breadth of knowledge with soaring creativity. The great designers of the next generation will distinguish themselves with their brilliant algorithms.

Closure

At the deepest level, successful interactivity design demands that you offer ideas to your customers. Furthermore, it is not enough, as it is with other media, to offer merely a hodgepodge of interesting, useful, or edifying ideas; the designer must create a closed, complete, and consistent working model of whatever the product addresses. (More on this in Chapter 7.)

Traditional media are organized differently. In this book, for example, I include a good many ideas and facts, the range of which covers a great deal of territory. There's some linguistics, a touch of anthropology, a little mathematics, some physics, and a bit of history, among other things. By wandering into other territories, I add depth to the primary content. But suppose I was saddled with the Editor From Hell who demands that any topic I touch upon must be completely covered. After all, it's a disservice to the reader to supply a partial truth, and besides, we all know that a partial truth is also, because of its incompleteness, a partial lie. Therefore, any subject I broach must be fully addressed. I think that you can agree that such a demand would be impossible to satisfy; nobody can live up to that ideal. So in books (and other media), we accept the principle that any given expression will be incomplete. Thus, noninteractive media tend to be scattershot affairs, containing lots of interesting bits and pieces that spread out over a great range but don't actually enclose the entire intellectual territory. Shakespeare's *Macbeth* says a lot about karma, but it certainly doesn't say everything there is to say on the subject.

But the interactive expression must be complete and closed in its coverage; every failure of closure will inevitably result in problems for the user. A word processor that can't handle the letter Z would obviously be a disaster, but even a lesser shortcoming, such as an inability to handle the ¢ key, will cause serious problems for some users.

Here's an example of why a lack of closure can be disastrous. In the Bad Old Days, when CPUs were slow and RAM was tight, some word processors used embedded characters to control document formatting. For example, the text <##PB##> would cause the program to generate a page break, and the text <##SK3##> would tell it to skip three lines. These strings of text would be sneakily inserted into the text you typed, but never shown on the screen or in the printout. The only problem was, if a user just happened to type one of those magic text formulas into her document, say, <##SK999##>, all hell would break loose. The designers told themselves that this would never happen, and perhaps it never did happen, but if some hapless user just happened to type the wrong text, can you imagine the disaster that would unfold? The fundamental source of this disaster is the failure to close the set of text strings that can be used by the word processor.

Have you ever noticed that some web pages crash your browser? It's often traceable to a closure problem. The browser receives the various commands it needs to build the page, and it receives a command in a context that wasn't anticipated. The command is misinterpreted, and the browser bites the dust. Every single byte that comes down the wire into the browser must be recognizable by that browser. Getting it 99.99 percent right isn't good enough when a user can suck in 9,999 bytes in less than a second.

The only solution to the problem of closure is to accept a smaller, more compact handling of the material. The user must be able to wander freely without falling off the edges or bashing into walls. In attempting to interactivize *Macbeth*, you will be forced to say everything there is to say on your subject, and you'd better keep the subject small enough to permit you to do so.

This also places sterner demands on your creativity. It must be bolstered with a heightened sense of artistic integrity. A non-interactive expression can play fast and loose with dramatic reality, asking the audience to suspend disbelief and go along with the dramatic bandwagon; the artist's primary task is to build enough momentum into the storyline that the audience is swept right past the unavoidable inconsistencies. How many movies have you picked apart for their absurdities? I refer not only to the silly action movies that perpetrate drama molestation; even the more serious cinematic dramas demand leaps of faith from their audiences. In *Apocalypse Now*, why does Marlon Brando's character acquiesce to his own murder? Why did he grant Charlie Sheen's character freedom to roam the encampment? Why didn't he simply kill his prisoner—he certainly had no compunction about brutally killing hundreds of other people. His actions heighten the mythical feeling of the movie, but would you have done that? Have you never wondered what would have happened had Brando's character acted differently?

Francis Ford Coppola undoubtedly created a masterpiece, but he couldn't have done it without distorting reality. An interactive artist must also distort reality, but with less freedom to do so blatantly. The interactive expression must address all reasonably conceivable variations, and that, in turn, requires the artist to consider the issues at hand with more thoroughness and more integrity. Of course, since the world is so big, the only way to achieve that degree of integrity is to narrow the scope of the expression.

Thus, interactive expressions must be deep rather than broad. Completeness implies depth, while closure implies narrowness. Think of it in terms of planes and spheres. A noninteractive expression is like a splash of paint on a plane, spreading out over a particular area, with bits and pieces nearby. The user is always aware of the edges of those painted areas. An interactive expression, though, is like a sphere covered with paint. The user can wander all over the sphere, never encountering an edge. Your job as an interactive designer is to take that flat splash of paint and wrap it neatly around a sphere.

> *Algorithms are the creative substance of computing. While their expression inside a computer is necessarily mathematical, their raw material comes from all walks of life. Designing the data structure is often the first step in designing the algorithm. In designing an interactive product, the designer must create a closed and complete set of algorithms.*

5

LISTENING

 Listening is the most difficult step in interactivity design. Computer hardware is not well-suited for listening. The designer must invent the language the user listens with.

Ah, the impossible art of listening! The pride of individualism that makes us Westerners so enterprising, so curious, and so indefatigable in pursuit of our personal goals also makes us lousy listeners. We love to talk and have developed a vast treasury of wisdom in the art of speaking well, but as listeners we are failures. "Man can neither make him to whom he speaks, hear what he says, or believe what he hears" (Thomas Fuller, 1647).

Nor can we write this off as due to the ephemeral quality of the spoken word. Get on the Internet and lurk in one of the discussion groups. It need not be an inflammatory topic—almost any topic with lively discussion will demonstrate clearly that the correspondents don't pay attention to what is written. What fraction of the messages are devoted to clarifying simple misunderstandings? "I didn't mean it that way" and "I thought you meant something else" are surely the two most common noncommercial messages traversing the Internet.

Our culturally congenital inability to listen is our greatest hindrance in learning interactivity design. As I have already pointed out, effective interactivity requires effective speaking, effective thinking, *and* effective listening, and a failure in one area destroys the interactivity regardless of how magnificently executed the others might be. Listening to the user, therefore, is just as important to the final result as thinking and speaking.

Natural Languages

Human languages provide a misleading example for the interactivity designer, because they are imposed from above. I can communicate to you in this English language only because English is standardized (mostly). We agree on the meanings of most of the words and the interpretation of most of the grammar. This agreement was enforced by our teachers, who crammed "correct English" down our throats. The words that I speak with are the same words that you speak with—our communication is symmetric.

Whatever we speak falls short of our meaning. Someday I hope to speak or write the perfect sentence: an utterance of such clarity, precision, and power that it communicates my meaning with absolute perfection. I doubt that I shall ever succeed, but it's a fine goal. Sometimes my words fall so far short of my meaning that my interlocutor requests me to run that by him one more time. Thus, everything I say is more or less misleading or false. I will never utter a perfect truth.

Second, my channel of communication is inevitably noisy. In vocal communication, the delicate nuance of voice intonation is drowned out by the sounds of blaring televisions, screeching brakes, or the jackdaw prattle of my neighbors. My hearer can never enjoy the full benefit of those delicate intonations. If I appear on television, my face cannot be seen with the clarity that it would be in a face-to-face encounter; hence, micro-expressions and subtle lifts of the eyebrow are lost. If I write a book, I abandon all hope of incorporating nuance into my words and must rely on dead letters on a printed page.

Third, my interlocutor never understands my meaning in the same way I meant it. Even if I eschew obscure terminology, you will still interpret my words in a slightly different manner than I mean with them. My *arrogant* is probably less vainglorious than yours—I always connect it semantically with *arrogate*. Even my facial expressions and voice intonations won't communicate exactly the meaning that I have in mind. My expression and intonation for "sardonic cleverness" strikes some people as "conspiratorial."

A Visual Metaphor

Here's an illuminating way to think about word meanings and the process of communication: Let's imagine words as if they were like fragments of the keys we use in our locks. The particular shape of the teeth constitutes the meaning of the word. Thus, my word *cat* might look like this:

Now when you hear me say the word *cat*, you conjure up a meaning for it in your mind, which presumably is a perfect fit for my word *cat*:

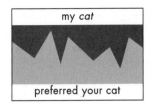

Sad to say, it never works out this well. The truth is, your interpretation of the word *cat* is slightly different than mine; after all, your knowledge and experience of cats is unique. Thus, the fit between my word *cat* and your word *cat* is imperfect:

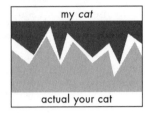

Thus far, all we have is a graphical means of imagining the previously mentioned fact that we never understand each other perfectly. But now let's examine some variations on this theme. Consider, for example, how this scheme applies to bland words such as *thing*:

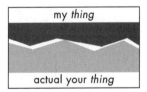

The teeth in this word are fewer and flatter than those of a more specific word such as *cat*, so my version of *thing* makes a better fit with your version, even though the two meanings are still different. Taken to the other extreme, when I use the word *dactylodeiktous*, whose meaning you don't know, we get a fit like this:

This demonstrates why, when I use words with big nasty teeth, they simply break against your lack of definition. Of course, if you happen to share my penchant for ridulously obscure words, and therefore know exactly what dactylodeiktous means, then the picture looks like this:

Oh, what a rapturous fit! What ecstasies of semantic intimacy!
Now, let's extend the concept from individual words to entire sentences:

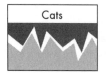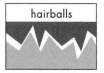

This is how the words look when they are lined up individually, but when we assemble them into a sentence, they are required to fit each other laterally as well:

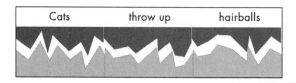

This additional requirement drives the meanings further apart, because there are now more teeth to fit together in a more complicated pattern. Your individual word *hairballs* matches mine best when you shift the meaning slightly to the right, which is no problem when we consider the word in isolation. But when coupled with the verb *throw up*, the meanings clash in opposite directions. Moving your *throw up* to the right to keep in step with your *hairballs* causes your *throw up* to clash against the teeth of my *throw up*, forcing your sentence away from my sentence.

The longer the expression, the more teeth there are to mismatch. Imagine what happens when we try to fit together a bookful of words—it's a wonder if you understand even half of all the ideas I write!

Herein lies the fundamental failure of all noninteractive communication: adding more precision of expression (more, longer, and sharper teeth) makes matters worse if your audience's context differs from your own. Greater precision helps only to the extent that the audience's context matches yours.

Interactivity's advantage is that it invites resolution of the subtle contextual differences that can ruin a noninteractive communication. A great many successful conversations concentrate on resolving such contextual differences. The speaker's original point is not challenged; rather, the context in which it is correct is exposed by a series of probing questions.

In the visual metaphor we've been discussing, interactivity encourages jiggling the teeth around to get a better fit. If my *cat* is a fluffy, cute, lovable friend, and your *cat* is a hissing, scratching sneak, my statement that "I found a lost cat today" means to you something entirely different than I meant. But if the statement is made as part of an interactive conversation rather than a noninteractive book, you will note the apparent contradiction between my statement and the smile on my face and converse with me about cats, thereby discovering the difference between us and resolving the contradiction. Interactive communication helps us resolve subsurface clashing contexts.

Conversations with Computers

For good or ill, the relationship between user and computer is neither standardized nor imposed by a third party, nor is it symmetric. People and computers do not use a common language in speaking with each other. The computer speaks with video and audio, but the human speaks with keyboard and mouse. The precise meaning of the keystrokes and mouse clicks is the creation of the designer. We designers listen to the user speak in a language that we ourselves create. Who then controls the utterance: the user who speaks the words or the designer who creates and defines them?

If you would listen well, then you must give your user the language to speak well.

Imagine yourself in a nightmare in which the people around you are doing something terrible, yet when you open your mouth to object, nothing comes out but muffled croaks. You gesticulate frantically, grunting, and they merely shake their heads and smile at your inarticulateness. This nightmare lurks only in our sleep and our software. How many times have you felt the same frustration with the computer? You shout at it, point to the screen, stab the keyboard with your fingers, and you know perfectly well that the computer sees you as a grunting, inarticulate deaf-mute. You know what you want, but can't find the words to say it to the computer. Are we therefore to conclude that you are a blithering idiot who couldn't talk your way through an open door? Of course not! The failure arises not from your lack of communications skills, but rather from the deficiencies of the language offered by the designer.

Don't think that this problem is confined to beginners. Just the other day I wanted to retrieve some email with my browser rather than my usual email program. When I asked the browser to get my email, it curtly informed me that I had not yet provided my identification information. So I went to the appropriate spot in the browser and found that my identification information was already there. But when I tried again, the browser insisted that it lacked the information it needed. I have yet to figure out how to tell that damn browser who I am.

Anatomy of a Computer's Ear

In designing a language for our user, we must first assess the parts at our disposal. Just as the human vocal tract determines the content of human languages, so too do the input devices on the computer determine the content of the language you create for your users.

Before we begin, however, I'd like to present a simple table of the critical technologies in each of the three steps of interaction:

Step	1980 Technology	2000 Technology	Improvement Factor
Speaking	24v x 80h B&W character display	800h x 600v x 24-bit display 44 KHz stereo sound	1000x
Thinking	1 MHz, 8-bit CPU 16K RAM	300 MHz 32-bit CPU 64 MB RAM	4,000,000x
Listening	Keyboard	Keyboard + Mouse	2x

As you can see, all the glorious advances in technology over the past 20 years have bypassed the listening side of our task. This suggests that some minor improvements in listening hardware will work major advances in overall interactivity.

Keep this in mind as we consider various listening technologies.

Single Button (Yes or No)

Many years ago, I had a dinner conversation with one of the early exponents of interactive television. This fellow regaled me with his clever schemes for studio design, camera mobility, and all manner of other snazzy ideas. My ignorance of television production left me no choice but to nod, smile, and keep my mouth full of food. After he'd run out of steam and finally started working on his now-cold meal, I asked one of the few intelligent questions available to me: "And how does the audience communicate its input to the show?"

Perhaps the salmon had captured his attention; with an airy wave of his fork, he told me that the home audience would be provided with a button to push at appropriate times. "A button?" I asked, gauchely failing to conceal my incredulity. "With a button you can only say two things: yes or no." He was unruffled. "Sure! It'll keep 'em happy!"

Now, let me take you back for a moment to the 1960s and the premier broadcast of a bold television show: *Star Trek*. In that first broadcast episode, Captain Christopher Pike has been horribly injured by some space-type accident; he is confined to a high-tech futuristic wheelchair that looks like a cardboard box from which his head protrudes. His body is so completely destroyed that he cannot speak, and his face is unanimated with any flicker of emotion; he just sits there like a bust on a box. What an artistic challenge for the actor! Fortunately, he is not completely without means of self-expression; the ever-ready prosthetic engineers of the twenty-fourth century have equipped him with a little light that he can blink, perhaps by twitching his kidneys. One blink signifies yes, and two blinks mean no.

Shed a tear for the tragic condition to which this once-mighty starship captain has been reduced. Unable to speak, to smile, or to laugh, this poor wretch stares helplessly across a huge chasm at the rest of humanity. His family and friends will never know his thoughts, hear his needs, or share his feelings. He can never initiate any conversation or volunteer any thought; he can only react to other people with his pathetic two-word vocabulary. Consider the horror of this man's position! Imagine the loneliness of such a life, the emptiness of such an existence! I would surely call this a living hell. And this was the role that my interactive TV friend intended for his audience.

Lose the pushbuttons.

Joysticks

Let us now move up the scale to an input device no longer in common use (except in video games): the joystick. The standard switched joystick allowed but five syllables: up, down, left, right, and button. These syllables could be combined into exactly 18 words, such as *up-left-button*, *down-left*, or *button*. (The eighteenth word is *silence*).

Consider how little you could say if you were confined to an 18-word vocabulary. While it beats all heck out of *yes* or *no*, this vocabulary is not the fodder for profound self-expression. It's adequate for moving around a two-dimensional space and performing a single action, such as firing a weapon, but not much else. Isn't it a remarkable coincidence that this was precisely what all the early videogames offered?

A simple principle emerges from these examples: the input device determines the size of the vocabulary available to the user. Clearly, we want to use input devices that give our user maximal vocabulary.

Keyboards

Let us move on to the keyboard. Now here's an input device you can say something with! Its 101 keys standard, plus a variety of prefix keys (Shift, Control, Option, and so on), give this baby a vocabulary of upwards of 400 words.

But there's a catch. The keyboard is the perfect input device for entering text; it's a disaster for anything else. The keys are labeled with the various text characters, which is good if you're typing text, but if you're trying to do anything else, those labels are misleading or confusing. The keyboard can even be difficult to use with text characters, if they aren't mapped clearly; try finding the key for the £ character, if you have one.

There have been attempts to use a keyboard for input functions other than text entry. The most striking of these are some of the flight simulators, which use the keys to handle the myriad complex functions of an airplane. Thus, the *g* key might activate the landing gear, the *f* key might operate the flaps, and the *q* key might increase the resolution of the ILS system. Note that we can't always obtain good mnemonics when we use a keyboard. I take a dim view of such input systems. Memorizing all those keys is just too difficult for most people, especially because there are no cues to aid memory other than the occasional fortuitous use of the first character—which is violated just often enough to generate intense confusion at times.

Reliance on the keyboard for nontextual input lies behind one of the stupidest and most avoidable blunders in classic user interface design: *darkness paralysis*. Imagine it's four in the morning and the dog is whining in the garage. You stumble out of bed and creep through the house, groping your way toward the door. You're too sleepy to remember to turn on the light. The path you must take is direct and unobstructed, yet you move slowly and carefully, imagining at every moment a toe-stubbing chair or nose-crunching wall to be just in front of you. The absence of light dramatically changes a simple and obvious task into one that is difficult, confusing, and intimidating. Always keep this feeling in your mind, for although users operate the same program that designers create, the designers see the program in the light of complete knowledge, and the users navigate in total darkness. The designer cannot understand the user's confusion; having laid out the room, examined it from a thousand different angles, gone over every square inch with a magnifying glass, the designer can walk across it with his eyes closed. He simply cannot understand the user's confusion.

I hold in special contempt those designers who dismiss users' fears with RTFM (Read The Manual); I'd love to lock them in a dark room at four in the morning with a 400-page manual explaining how to turn on the lights.

Those 101 keys that give us so much expressive power as designers constitute terrifying responsibility in the eyes of the user. At every juncture of uncertainty, the user attempts to second-guess your intentions. It's reasonable for the user to assume that you as designer have competently addressed every problem. This suggests that every single key should perform some function. The thought that you would leave some keys unused never occurs to the user; after all, you are the omniscient designer, addressing every contingency, anticipating every need, using every resource—and assigning a meaning to every key. Yet upon first encountering a program, the user cannot possibly memorize all those program functions; therefore, she balks at doing anything, certain that there's something out there just waiting to stub a toe.

Many computer keyboards in the 70s and 80s were meant for use on computer terminals; one of the most important functions in those days was interrupting the computer to order it to terminate some mistaken instruction gone wild. Back then, this key was placed in the upper-left corner of the keyboard and was labeled ABT, meaning "Abort current job," but when that verb became politically charged, keyboard manufacturers with nightmares of newspaper headlines about "computerized abortions" changed the label to BRK, meaning "Break off executing current job." These same keyboards were used in manufacturing the early personal computers. Many were the first-time users whose faces blanched upon discovering this key. Clearly, it said "break," but what, precisely, would be broken by pressing it? The computer? The disk drive? The world?

Nowadays that key is labeled ESC, for "escape," a much happier term. Unfortunately, *esc* in Latin is the verb root for *eat*; fortunately, ancient Romans don't use computers.

We therefore come to a clean conclusion: the keyboard should be used for all textual input, and nothing but textual input. There is a single exception to this rule: the provision of shortcut keys for power users. Those users who have mastered an application resent the often-slower input systems that sustained them when they were beginners. For such users, it is appropriate to provide keyboard shortcuts for common verbs, and you have no responsibility to organize those keyboard shortcuts in any logical system. Power users seem to revel in arcana; indulge them. Just make sure that the beginning users are unaware of the existence of this mess.

The Mouse

At long last we come to the most common and most important input device in personal computing: the mouse. Many are the variations on the basic theme of mousousity. There are one-button mice, two-button mice, three-button mice, and on upwards; I don't know what the world record is, but I have suggested that the ultimate in mouse design could be achieved by attaching rollers to the bottom of a keyboard, thereby unleashing the limitless power of the 101-button mouse.

A related device, the trackball, is really just a dead mouse. The latest versions, called trackpads, are dead, roadkilled mice. Then there are the optical mice, which have been emasculated.

These devices all function in the same way: user prestidigitation moves a cursor on the screen to a hotspot where further prestidigitation performs some action.

The Mouse Is Itself an Interaction

My theoretician's hormones gush when I contemplate the significance of the mouse. It is a second-generation input device; previously, input devices were boxes at the end of a wire that transmitted some defined signal to the computer when activated. The mouse, by itself, has no defined meaning; its input depends completely on the context of the screen. The concept of the mouse includes more than just the plastic doodad we roll around our desks; it necessarily includes the cursor on the screen. We demonstrate our appreciation of this concept whenever we refer to the cursor as the mouse.

Yet "mouse" comprises even more than roller plus image: there's also the software inside the computer that moves the image in response to the motions of the roller. We have to include the CPU in the definition, too, because it's what actually executes the mouse software.

Here's where we get weird: the mouse is an input device for interaction, but it is itself a complete interactive process. You speak by moving the mouse; the computer listens to your motion, thinks about it, and speaks back by moving the cursor. You listen by watching the cursor move on the screen, think by comparing its position with your objective, and speak again by moving the mouse some more. Thus, the mouse as an input device is an interaction within an interaction.

The deep power of this interaction can easily be demonstrated by resorting to a practical joke masquerading as an experiment. We could write software to discombobulate the normal relationship between mouse motion and cursor motion. We could then load this software into our friend's PC and hide so we can watch the fun. He moves the mouse up, and the cursor moves left. Confused, he moves the mouse down, and the cursor moves up. Befuddled, he stops altogether, and cursor slowly creeps downward.

The interactive factor endows the mouse with a gigantic advantage over all other input devices: the ability to match vocabulary size to function count on the fly. With a mouse, you can offer your user a single button to push, thereby focusing his attention narrowly (for example, "System crash; press here to restart"). If the situation calls for two buttons, you can offer exactly two buttons, no more, no less (for example, "Format disk" and "Cancel"). You can provide exactly the number of buttons required by the context; you thereby banish darkness paralysis completely, as there need never be any nonfunctional buttons. The upper limit on the number of buttons is the number of pixels on the screen, usually several hundred thousand. Don't dismiss this as an absurdity; paint programs and photo-retouching programs treat every pixel in the image as a mouse-addressable button.

Variable Vocabulary Size

These are just the static capabilities of the mouse; dynamically, it's even more expressive. These are the words you can say with a mouse:

Move over an object

Pause over an object

Click an object

Click and hold on an object

Double-click an object

Triple-click an object

Click and drag an object

Prefix key click

This is merely what is possible with a single-button mouse. With a two-button mouse, we can separately invoke each of these gestures save the first two.

More buttons would let us perform even more tasks, but we must acknowledge human motor limitations. It's theoretically possible to have a five-button mouse, with one button for each finger, and make use of sequenced gestures (two or more buttons held down at the same time), in which case we could have 265 different words to say—but we'd have to remember that pinkie-ring-thumb-middle-index means "perform a Gaussian transformation" while "pinkie-ring-thumb-index-middle means "copy this formula down through the spreadsheet." Anybody up for learning the pental numbering system?

How Many Buttons?

Macintosh mice have one button, and Windows mice have two or three and sometimes a little scrollwheel between the two. What's the ideal number of mouse buttons? This has been the subject of fierce opinion wars. I believe that the original single-button mouse of the Macintosh was ideal for the first ten years of GUIs, but the increasing vocabulary requirements of software demands more of our input devices, and the use of more buttons on the mouse is undeniably superior to the use of double-prefix key commands (for example, Shift-Control-K) now starting to creep into software.

I suspect that the practical upper limit is the two-button mouse with a scrollwheel, the Windows standard as I write this. More buttons will be too complicated to be practical. My own mouse has five buttons, each with separately assignable meanings for different applications, but I have found all that expressive power to be, well, overpowering. Ninety percent of my clicks go to the main button, 9.9% to the second button, and about 0.1% go to the third button. The two-button-plus-scrollwheel device will likely become the standard.

Unfortunately, Microsoft's laissez-faire definition of the functions of the two mouse buttons has led to more confusion than freedom. The two mouse buttons should perform completely different classes of tasks. I suggest that the left button should be used for actions and the right button for inquiries. This would guarantee that there is no overlap between the two buttons. The Microsoft mouse in its current incarnation roughly follows this guideline but includes enough exceptions to make matters completely confusing. In earlier days, software was simple enough that there wasn't a great need for inquiries, but nowadays our software is so complicated that there is always a question to ask as we use it. Apple's excellent balloon help system would function better if it were actuated by a right-button click rather than a modality.

Hotspots

First comes the problem of indicating the presence of active portions of the screen. We have quite a hodgepodge here. There are some clearly defined standards: we all know what pushbuttons, radio buttons, check boxes, and scrollbars look like, even though we can't agree on their nomenclature—what Mac people call a scrollbar, Windows people call an elevator. Other active elements are moderately well standardized, such as butcons (icons that operate as buttons) and hyperlinks. But there is also a cackling flock of odd-bird screen objects, demonstrating the triumph of graphic design over interactivity design. The typical application screen jabbers at the user with cute little icons and graphic indicators. For example, can you tell what each of the following mini-icons does:

Each one of these chirpers actually does something. They're easier to pick out in their spatial context—but then, context is recognizable only to someone with experience. Our first task, then, is to make those active objects *recognizable* as active objects; our second task is to communicate their function. Few designers appreciate the importance of the first task. A good example here is the third mini-icon from the left, which is used to split a window into two panes, so that the user might compare two distant parts of the document. While it is widely used, only the most computercentric person would believe that the majority of users are aware of this tiny image. I am not arguing against the use of this mini-icon; I am arguing only that relying on its natural visual recognizability just doesn't work. Designers need a more effective way to tell the user that it does something.

My personal horror story about this problem involves the fourth mini-icon from the left. It nestles along the bottom edge of the program window, next to another mini-icon in which the black triangles are larger. Could you guess that those black triangles represent mountains? Clicking the larger mountains zooms in on the main image, making it appear larger. Clicking the smaller mountains zooms out from the main image. Of course, I had no way of knowing this without reading the (...) manual, so I searched in vain in the menu structure for a way to zoom in or out, to no avail. One day it occurred to me that those two mini-icons might be active. I clicked one and instantly realized their function. If only the designers had made it obvious that those mini-icons were functional!

I opine that the best way to flag an image's ability to provide a function is to include a standard color, the *hotcolor,* somewhere in the image. If every active element on the screen contains the hotcolor, either on its border or in its text or its imagery, and no inactive element contains the hotcolor, then the user has a simple and reliable visual indicator of active elements.

An oft-used alternative is the *auto-highlighting object.* This is an image that becomes highlighted when the cursor passes over it. I think that this is a lousy way to solve the problem: it reduces the desperate user to randomly sweeping the cursor over every possible image on the screen, hoping to find something that will light up.

Another bright idea, the *tooltip,* not only reveals functionality, but also explains that functionality. If the cursor pauses over an active item for longer than, say, one second, a tiny text box of an indicative color pops up, providing the user with a short phrase explaining the function of the active element. The tooltip is basically an auto-highlighting object with an added benefit and its concomitant cost. The benefit is that the function is explained; the cost is that a delay is imposed on the user.

All too frequently, the tip, a single word or short phrase, is only somewhat less cryptic than the graphic icon. For example, the little beasty in a word processing program (you'll never guess which) doesn't mean much to the inexperienced eye. Holding the cursor over it yields the unilluminating phrase "document map." If you already know what a document map is, then you don't need the tooltip. If you don't know what a document map is, the tooltip phrase doesn't help. Only after I actually clicked the mini-icon did I discover that it produces a list of the first significant words of each paragraph.

The killer objection to tooltips, however, is that they rely on a delay imposed on the user. Delays are inimical to interactivity, as I explain in Chapter 8. Any design element that deliberately imposes a delay on the user is bad for interactivity and bad for the user.

Moreover, tooltips are unnecessary; the balloon help system devised by Apple some years ago is superior. First, it is readily available on request and stays out of the way if not wanted. Second, it provides complete explanations. It still requires, however, the minesweeping methods required by auto-highlighting and tooltips. Apple's balloon help, augmented with my hotcolor system, and accessible directly through a second mouse button, would be a better solution.

A third approach to the problem of identifying active screen elements, sporadically used, changes the cursor when it passes over the object. For example, the default north-northwest (NNW) arrow cursor changes into an I-beam cursor when it enters an editable text field; this clearly indicates that pressing the mouse button will place the blinking text cursor directly underneath the mouse cursor. Presently, cursor manipulation is a hodge-podge. Some of this is unavoidable. For example, many image editing programs use special cursors to indicate the nature of the tool being applied to the image. Aside from these, however, the great majority of programs use only 10 to 20 cursors, of which only a few standards are recognized, most of which were defined by Apple as early as 1983:

 Standard north-northwest cursor

 Rectangle-selection or pixel-targeting cursor

 Text insertion cursor

 Watch cursor for indicating delays

 Animated spinner cursor for indicating delays

 Single-click activator cursor

Grabber cursor for moving objects

Unfortunately, cursor alteration can suffer from two problems. First, there can be so many different cursors that the user cannot fathom their multitudinous meanings. Consider this collection of cursors used by a single

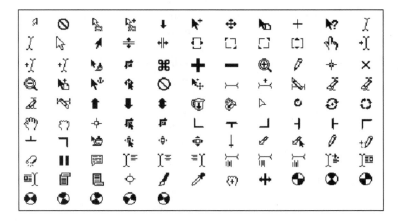

program:

Can you guess what they all mean?

The second problem with multiple-identity cursors is that some programs are a bit slow to change them. You can therefore end up staring at some non-sensical and confusing combination of cursor and background. This problem is readily solved with more careful programming. Right now, too many sloppily written programs are on the market.

I believe that a clean system for organizing the user's expressive possibilities can be built with cursors. There are only eight classes of active elements on the screen:

1. Something that executes an action when single-clicked, such as buttons, scrollbars, check boxes, and hyperlinks

2. Something that executes an action when double-clicked, such as controls for files and applications

3. Something that can be selected for a subsequent operation by a single-click

4. An object that can be moved to another location

5. An object that can be moved vertically only

6. An object that can be moved horizontally only

7. Menu

8. Editable text field, such as a word processor document, file name field, or spreadsheet cell

(A ninth class applies to pixels whose value can be changed, as in a painting document, in which case the cursor must indicate the tool employed.)

I assign cursors to the eight classes as follows:

Class	Passing over Image	Holding or Dragging
Single-clicker		
Double-clicker		
Selectable		
Draggable		
Horizontally draggable		
Vertically draggable		
Menu		
Editable text field		
Incactive area		

These cursors can be graphically combined to denote objects with multiple capabilities:

File (moveable, selectable, and openable)

Selectable and openable

Selectable and moveable

In all these cases, the right button could be used to bring up balloon help, thus eliminating the need to set a help mode by recourse to the Help menu.

One rather silly reason why such a system has yet to be implemented is that cursors have traditionally been restricted to 16 pixels in height and width. This made sense in the bad old days of tiny black-and-white displays, but the vastly greater screen real estate available these days makes 32-by-32-pixel cursors more than feasible. This limitation will require some fundamental changes to operating system software to overcome, but the technical problems are headaches, not many-fanged monsters.

Voice Input

Another much-discussed input device is the microphone feeding into voice recognition software. This technology is just now coming into its own; the worst obstacles have finally been overcome, and we are now able to explore (with some restrictions) the possibilities of this technology. I have high hopes for voice recognition; it is far and away the most natural form of input.

We must be careful, however, to differentiate between two entirely separate issues: voice recognition and language recognition. The former refers to recognizing individual words or short phrases; the latter brings syntax into the picture because we combine those words into a larger communication. Our ability to process language falls short of our ability to process voice. The computer can recognize individual words well enough, but the goal of understanding a sentence is still far beyond its reach.

Current language recognition software is good enough to handle simple sentence structures with no use of metaphor, but not much more. For this reason, many observers reject all forms of voice input for the computer. This, I think, is throwing out the baby with the bathwater. Voice recognition software can be put to immediate use as a second channel of user input, thereby speeding up the interaction. Commands can be single words used in conjunction with the keyboard and mouse. Thus, a graphic artist drawing a picture would not have to bounce the cursor between the image and the tool palette; the mouse could remain in position, and the various tools could be called up with voice input. Similarly, a writer on a word processor might not need to remove her hands from the keyboard to handle the various nontextual commands; voice commands could parallel many of the mouse commands.

It is true, as some people object, that voice input suffers from problems of background noise, but I think people will adjust just as they have learned to keep their voices down when somebody in the next cubicle is on the telephone. Voice input will elevate the office loudmouth to a higher plane of obnoxiousness.

The problems of language understanding, and some possible solutions, are presented in Chapter 22.

Other Input Devices

The lack of viable alternatives to the standard keyboard-plus-mouse is certainly not due to any lack of imagination on the part of hardware engineers; a great variety of alternatives has been proposed. Sadly, the community and the industry have not greeted these innovations with the same exuberance that they accorded video boards, MIDI boards, and other speaking devices.

One of the more interesting devices I have seen is the force-feedback mouse, a mouse operating on a special pad that, under control of software, can push the mouse in various directions. Thus, the user can feel the frictional resistance of dragging an object across the screen, or feel a slight edge when crossing a window boundary. This kind of tactile feedback enhances the notion of the mouse as a nested interaction and extends the utility of the mouse.

Sad to say, I am dubious that this innovation will catch on; most people won't be willing to pay the extra dollars to gain the extra expressiveness. The irony lies in the amount of money that people are willing to pay for speaking hardware: the audio-video capabilities of most personal computers typically account for about 25 percent of the total cost of the computer. You would think that, after spending hundreds of dollars on audio and video, people would be willing to spend a bit of money on better listening capabilities. Oh well.

A wilder idea was tried at Atari in the early 1980s: a brainwave input device. A band wrapped around the user's head picked up the faint EEG signals emanating from the brain; this would permit the user to control a videogame with his thoughts! Biofeedback meets Atari! The idea sounded great, but there was a hitch: the faint electrical signals from the brain are much weaker than the electrical signals emanating from the muscles of the forehead. Therefore, most users found it quicker and easier to control the device by scrunching the muscles of their head. After a long or intense session with a videogame, the user invariably developed a monstrous headache. So much for that idea.

Light Pens and Other Devices

Light pens and similar devices promised so much 20 years ago and yet languish in obscurity today. The user simply points to a spot on the screen and clicks. There's no need to maneuver a mouse at your side; what you point to is what you get. The killer problem has been the vertical monitor screen; it's tough to control a light pen on a vertical surface. Some people argue that, once we go to flat-panel displays, we can mount our displays horizontally, and light pens will render the mouse extinct. They fail to consider the positioning of screen and keyboard. Since the keyboard must sit over your lap, the screen must go, at best, somewhere beyond the keyboard. I can reach only a few inches farther than the top of my keyboard; using a light pen would require me to bend forward in a spinally incorrect posture. For the foreseeable future, you can afford to ignore light pens.

Another fascinating possibility is the touch-sensitive screen. You poke the button on the screen to talk to the computer. These are already in use in many businesses, especially restaurants. They suffer somewhat from the fatness of our fingers; we can't use tiny buttons. But as computer monitors grow larger, we can afford more pixels for our applications, and the Fat Finger problem sheds some weight. Certainly most websites could be used almost as well with touch-sensitive screens. Touching the screen causes the cursor to jump to the point of contact and simulate a button press. Unfortunately, the touch-sensitive screen does not offer a perfectly smooth upgrade path from a mouse. Double-clicking is slower with touch, and dragging is much more difficult. Moreover, touch-sensitive designs must deal with the spotty nature of cursor movement, arising from the user's lifting his finger to move more quickly to other screen locations.

There is no single best input device; future improvements in computer listening will involve the combination of several input devices. This will surely prove difficult; look how much trouble we have had coordinating the mouse with the keyboard. There are still plenty of people who consider the mouse a childish crutch for those who aren't man enough to handle a keyboard. Such attitudes are ignorant nonsense, for they fail to appreciate a fundamental truth of expression: pointing is a fast form of specifying. We have an entire class of words—pronouns—whose sole job is to semantically point at something. In many, many situations, pointing is the fastest means of specifying something. Spelling it out is always clumsier, but sometimes we have no alternative. Thus, the mouse and the keyboard complement each other neatly. The mouse points, and the keyboard provides detailed specification. Good design uses the mouse for pointing tasks, and the keyboard for textual tasks; the difficulty comes in tasks such as menu selection that can be treated as either pointing or textual; this is why many menus are accessed through the mouse but provide command-key equivalents.

Combining input devices will be politically difficult because it requires coordination across a huge industry. If somebody comes up with a better software input scheme such as the icon bar—it's a simple matter for others to copy the idea. But introducing a third hardware input device raises a great many new problems. Why should a software designer limit her market by taking advantage of a device that falls short of universal adoption? Why should a hardware manufacturer trying to beat the competition on price bundle such a device into the package?

Language Design

These then are the basic tools to work with, the elements out of which you as an interactivity designer can fashion your language of interaction. How do you design such a language?

Verb Specification

The first rule of all interactivity design is to start with the verbs (see Chapter 8). What do you want your user to be able to accomplish with your program? Imagine yourself acting (through your software) as the user's servant. What skills do you have to offer, and how might your user most easily take command of those skills?

Suppose that you are designing some sort of productivity application. Exactly what do you want your user to be able to do better and faster? Do not indulge in vague generalities about improving the lives of your users or empowering them; write down exactly what tasks you will help them perform. Now imagine yourself as the computer-servant eager to perform those tasks. What must your user tell you for you to be able to do your stuff? What's the easiest and quickest way for the user to get her requirements across to you? What actions (verbs) most directly express the user's goals?

Or suppose that you are designing a retail website. You might think that your first and most important verb is *buy*, but that's the most important verb for you, not the user. The user's desired verb set is more complicated. He wants to quickly find exactly what he's looking for, evaluate its appropriateness to his needs, discover all the gotchas such as shipping charges and delivery times, and determine how competitive the price is. Your user will likely want to compare your offering with others on the web. You want to facilitate this process in a way that most flatters your product. These questions characterize the verbs that you must offer your customer.

If you are developing an educational program, what is the likely mindset of your user? What does she already know, and what do you desire to teach? Do not look at it from your point of view as the teacher; look at it from the student's point of view. Specifically, don't just organize lots of information into tidy little structures that make perfect sense to somebody who already understands everything. Try to imagine yourself ignorant; what questions would you ask? By what circuitous routes might your curiousity lead you to the information? Remember that you can't teach anybody anything; you can only facilitate a person's own learning process. What actions, then, would a curious student need to take to learn the material?

Concise verb design is especially important in games, which require fast learning curves. The user of a word processor need not master style sheets to begin using the software, but the user of a game needs to know immediately how to fire the gun in order to stay alive. This mandates a small verb set; the game designer's task is then to come up with the most powerful small set of verbs possible. The best game designers adjust the design to permit that ideal set of verbs; this most often requires a higher level of abstraction in the verbs. For example, "pull the trigger" can be abstracted to "fire the weapon" to obtain greater expressive breadth—that is, to give the player access to more weapons. It can be further abstracted to "use the device," thereby granting the user access to a large array of tools and devices. The trick that makes this work is the creation of tools that have only one possible use. A tool with two distinct uses could not be used in such a design. "Do it" is an even more abstract form of the command; it requires that the verb in question be set up previously by grabbing the device or otherwise unambiguously specifying the "it" to be done.

Once you have prepared your list of ideal verbs, you face the hardest task of all: expressing those verbs in a form achievable with computer input devices. If the user's verbs are textual, then your decision is a no-brainer: you use the keyboard. Otherwise, you'll want to start with the mouse as your prime candidate.

Menus

Three primary constructs dominate all mouse-based interactivity design: menus, maps, and gizmos. The former are obvious but take a number of forms. Drop-down menus are the most common form; their worst deficiency is their requirement to present the verb in a word or short phrase that fits into a menu; sometimes a simple concept refuses to yield any short descriptive verbal expression.

Menus are nevertheless a powerful component of the designer's toolbox, because they neatly solve a difficult dilemma. On the one hand, we want to present our user with a complete list of the available commands to ward off darkness paralysis. On the other hand, screen space is a precious resource in our designs; we dare not waste kilopixels listing rarely used options. The menu uses lots of pixels to present options, but only when the user asks to see the options. From a designer's point of view, the menu provides more pixels, at the cost of some indirection imposed on the user, who must access the menu to see those extra pixels.

Three extensions to the basic menu design make drop-down menus especially versatile. First is the now-standard *ellipsis* to denote the existence of a follow-up dialog box. This is used when the menu item triggers a multi-argument verb. Those multiple values are presented in the dialog box and made available for editing.

```
                                                              8.5.1
   Printer:  LaserWriter 4/600 PS  ▼        Destination:  Printer  ▼

   General                       ▼
                    Copies: 1        ☐ Collated

                    Pages: ● All
                           ○ From:        To:

           Paper Source: ● All pages from:    Cassette            ▼
                         ○ First page from:   Cassette            ▼
                           Remaining from:    Cassette            ▼


   Save Settings                              Cancel    Print
```

For example, this dialog box allows the user to specify seven values: the destination, the printer, the format of the output, the number of copies to print, whether they should be collated, which pages to print, and which paper source to use while printing.

A second extension to menus is the *nested* or *hierarchical* menu: a menu inside the parent menu. The most common example of the nested menu is the Style menu on the menu bar of many textual applications; inside this Style menu will be a Font menu item; selecting the Font menu item raises a pop-up menu listing all available fonts. Menus can be nested many layers deep, but deeply nested menus are unstable; slight mouse-handling errors can cause the entire menu structure to collapse. This problem was particularly severe before pull-down menus were replaced by drop-down menus. (Pull-down menus require the user to hold the button down while accessing the menu; drop-down menus require a single click to open and a second click to dismiss.) Nested menus are most practical for input structures shaped like broadly and deeply branched trees; the user navigates down the tree to the final choice.

The last extension to the basic menu concept is *disabling* a menu item by dimming it. Users now recognize this as a standard indication that contextual requirements for the use of the verb must be satisfied before it is enabled. Ofttimes those unsatisfied contextual requirements are obvious, but there are plenty of situations in which the user might not be able to guess the reason for the dimming of the item. The user wants to send the mail, and right there in front of him is a menu item reading "Send my mail," but it's dimmed, and the user can't figure out what he has to do to get it undimmed. This is a user interface disaster, and it arises in almost every program I have used. My disgust for this problem is heightened by the ease with which it can be eliminated. There are two good solutions to this problem.

Instead of dimming an item to disable it, reword the item by prepending the word "Can't" and enclosing the resulting phrase in parentheses. Present the item text in italic style to further differentiate it from available items. Then attach a few lines of code to the beginning of the menu-handling code, asking if the selected item is written in italic; if so, display an "I can't handle that" (see Chapter 8) dialog box explaining what the user must do to enable the menu item.

The other solution is even better: Apple's balloon help system, which can automatically explain why a menu item is dimmed.

Pop-up menus (appearing when the user clicks an item in the main window area) are another useful form of the basic menu idea. They are used to present a default value that can readily be changed by the user. They are especially handy in designs that are tight on screen space.

Another variation on the basic menu concept is the icon menu, often called a *palette*. I seldom use these devices; their weaknesses outweigh their utility. In the first place, icons are not, pixel for pixel, superior to text in their expressiveness. A small number of icons in an application can serve you well, but the scores of icons swarming over palettes in some applications are confusing. The one undeniably effective use of a palette is in presenting a selection of background patterns or colors for a paint program or any other directly visual (as opposed to indirectly iconic) use. Icon bars are a more refined version of the icon palette and can work well if they are confined to a small number of icons.

A second deficiency of menus arises when the height of the menu exceeds the available screen height. The common fix, a scrolling menu, contradicts the whole point of the menu, which is to present the user with all available options; it is an abomination. Let us consider the two most common appearances of overly long scrolling menus: font menus and country menus.

Font menus show all the fonts available in, say, a word processor. If the user stuffs her machine full of fonts, how can the designer avoid a long list? The basic answer is to use hierarchical menus, and I can offer you not one but two organizing principles. You might organize the fonts by their type: sans-serif, serif, ornamental, all caps, and so forth. This would require you to obtain this information about the font, which might not be technically possible, but you could simply maintain an internal table of all known fonts and refer to that table; any font not appearing on your table goes into the Miscellaneous submenu. Another organizing principle is frequency of use. The main menu has four menu items: Frequently Used, Occasionally Used, Rarely Used, and Never Used. An even nicer approach, if screen space allows, is to present the frequently used fonts on the main menu and relegate all other fonts to submenus.

The same organizing principle could be used to shorten those ghastly long menus on websites that want your address. It is silly that millions of people must scroll past countries they've never heard of to get all the way down to "United States." It would be much better to put a few heavily used country names at the top of the list and then the remaining countries under a divider.

Maps

Another broad construct for mouse input is the map, which makes each pixel in an area of the screen a hotspot. The simplest example of this is a painting program with a single-pixel pencil tool. If you click a pixel, it changes color. Each pixel on the screen stands for one pixel in the paint image. You can also act on groups of pixels with some of the tools, such as a paintbrush, a paint bucket, or the various geometric shape tools.

Mapping techniques are most useful in situations that assume some sort of two-dimensional spatial structure: painting programs, drawing programs, CAD programs, photo-retouching programs, and map-reading programs.

Mapping constructs also offer great utility in some situations requiring complex or finely shaded input structures. With a map, every pixel in the active area is a button; in extreme cases, this can amount to several hundred thousand buttons. Add to that the natural spatial logic built into mapping constructs, and you have a powerful way to reach into your user's mind. The trick lies in recasting your input problem in spatial terms; this requires great cleverness.

The most familiar application of mapping is the placement of file icons in a file manager (Finder on the Macintosh, Explorer in Windows). Such systems map onto screen space all the components of the user's computer system: primarily the files on the hard disk, but also ancillary devices such as CD-ROMs, printers, trash bins, and so forth. A window here is nothing more than a scheme for mapping the contents of a directory onto a chunk of screen space. All the associated behaviors of windows (opening and closing, collapsing, resizing and repositioning, overlapping in "two-and-a-half dimensions") serve only to make the task of accessing files easier.

By the way, the value of GUIs demonstrates a principle that underlies much of the development of interactivity design: as computer systems grow bigger and more complex, completely new methods of interacting with them are necessary. The simple command-line operating systems of yesterday (and Linux today) are not universally inferior to GUIs—in fact, they are better at handling small systems. After all, if you're working with only a dozen files on a floppy disk, a simple list of the filenames is all you need. When the typical number of files increased to a few score, however, we moved from flat systems, in which all the files on a diskette are listed at once, to hierarchical systems, in which files are grouped into directories that the user can open and close at will. But a typical general-purpose computer system these days has thousands of files; even a hierarchical list of directories is cumbersome. Windowing systems are better because they allow us to organize the file hierarchy more easily. Of course, the evolution of file systems was actually more of a co-evolution; the software became more powerful only as the hardware became more powerful. Trying to run Mac OS 9 on an Apple II with 64K of RAM and a 1 MHz 8-bit CPU simply would not work. The simpler microcomputers couldn't handle the more complex filing systems of today. The old command-line systems were about all that would work in such a constrained environment.

The recent surge in popularity of Linux is often misinterpreted as support for all manner of reactionary conclusions. Unix-based systems have two advantages over GUIs: they're great for programmers to mess with, and they handle single-task functions, such as file servers, with great reliability. For most of the tasks that we expect of computers, Linux doesn't offer a complete or integrated feature set.

The mapping system of the desktop generated intense excitement during the 1980s, and there were many attempts to extend the spatial mapping system in other directions. There were quite a few schemes for expanding the "virtual desktop" to a "virtual office" complete with virtual filing cabinets, virtual telephones, and so forth. But the metaphor had already been stretched to its limits; these products never caught on. I suspect that the vast amounts of energy expended in all these efforts has sufficed to expose all viable extensions within our reach. For the next few years, mapping systems will probably yield few new results in interactivity design. Of course, when our machines are a hundred times bigger and a hundred times faster, and have a hundred times as many files, it'll be a whole new ball game.

Gizmos

The term *gizmo* covers all those odd screen doodads that you use to make things happen. They are higher-level schemes for enhancing the expressiveness of the mouse. You already know them, although you may not use the same terms I use. There are buttons: click them and they do something. Check boxes require a click to toggle (reverse from off to on, or vice versa). Radio buttons allow you to select one and only one option from among a group of options. Scrollbars allow you to set some continuously variable setting, such as the portion of the document that your word processor presents on the screen. These four classes of gizmos allow the user to say almost anything that can be said with mouse and monitor; each tackles a distinct and clearly defined expressive problem. I consider the application of these gizmos to be obvious, but if you have any questions about their proper use, by all means consult Alan Cooper's excellent book *About Face*, which devotes entire chapters to each of these gizmos.

Complex Mouse Expressions

There remains an odd class of expressions available to the designer: the complex expressions that combine a number of motions. One such approach much toyed with is *gestural input,* in which the mouse's motion as well as its position are taken into consideration. A good example of gestural input is in a game, Eric's Ultimate Solitaire. The user can click a card to pick it up and then flick the mouse a short distance in the direction of the intended destination of the card; the software will take over and float the card to its destination. This trick works because there are many constraints on where cards can go, and it's normally easy for the software to figure out the intended destination even though the user's gestural movement might be vague. Gestural input has poor resolution; you'll be lucky to get 45 degrees of angular resolution. Moreover, it seldom offers truly unique input expressiveness; any gesture toward some on-screen object must always be replaceable by explicit traversal to that on-screen object. Gestural input with the mouse, then, provides some reduction of effort for the user, but little more.

However, some other input devices can benefit from gestural input. The mouse is handicapped by weak directional calibration; what with the bends in the shoulder, elbow, and wrist, the user can never be quite sure of the direction of motion until she sees the cursor motion on the screen—too late with gestural input. Trackpads, on the other hand, are directionally calibrated; the user's body geometry facing the screen and finger positions give plenty of cues as to the true direction of an anticipated gesture. Touch screens are even better with gestural input. Accordingly, designs for mouse use should probably avoid gestural schemes, but designs that can be confined to trackpads or touch screens might take advantage of this capability.

Even more complex is the extended gesture, or path tracing system. An excellent case study is provided by the Apple Newton and the Palm Pilot. The Newton used path tracing to allow normal handwritten input on its touch screen; this required considerable intelligence on the part of the Newton to recognize hand-drawn characters. Sad to say, handwriting recognition (more properly, hand printing recognition) lay within the reach of the Apple engineers but not within their grasp; the Newton never did attain sufficient recognition accuracy for most people.

The designers of the Pilot, by contrast, made a bold compromise: they imposed an artificial alphabet called Graffiti on the user. This simplified version of the conventional alphabet was optimized for ease of entry but posed some minor problems of recognition on the user. The result was fast, clean, and inexpensive. The Apple designers had their hearts in the right place, but they attempted more than they could deliver. The Newton boasts better technology, but the Pilot has better design.

Extending Sequentiality

When you have a limited number of basic atoms of expression, such as we have with the computer, the best way to extend their expressiveness is to combine those atoms into sequences. We combine 26 letters into several hundred thousand words and then combine those words into an uncountable number of sentences. These linguistic models of input are addressed in Chapter 22.

> *The computer's ears are small and weak, so you must exert special effort to listen well. You must design a complete language with which the user can speak to your design. For the computer to listen well, you must give the user a language that permits him to speak well.*

6

THE INTERACTIVE LOOP

Interactivity moves information in a loop between the two actors. Better information flow through the loop usually indicates better interaction.

My definition of interactivity calls it a "cyclic process in which each actor alternately listens, thinks, and speaks." Now that we have closely examined listening, thinking, and speaking, we can step back and look at the "cyclic process."

What exactly is the stuff that's cycling through the interactive loop? My answer is perhaps overly academic: information. It may strike you as cold-blooded to describe a conversation as a loop through which information flows, but I do not ask you to accept this description as comprising the totality of conversation; I ask only that you play this academic game along with me so that we might arrive at some useful understanding of the process of interactivity.

I therefore ask you to think of a conversation as a loop through which information flows, changing its content and character with each pass through the loop. Imagine the intense brainstorming conversations you have had with a close colleague, a comrade in thought, who can finish your sentences for you. An idea floats murkily between the two of you; your first attempt to describe it fails badly. Your comrade stands on the shoulders of your attempt and takes her own stab at it; again, she fails to capture its essence, but her contribution shows you the idea from a different angle, suggesting a new approach. Together, the two of you build on each other's thinking, passing the idea back and forth between you as you each chisel away some portion of the matrix of confusion in which it is embedded. The information content of your interactive loop increases with each cycle, until after much effort you have exposed the idea with complete clarity. This is the most compelling example of what I mean by information flowing through a loop.

Of course, this isn't a typical conversation; most conversations are more mundane:

"How was work, honey?"

"Lousy. The boss yelled at me again for being too slow."

"That's a shame, honey. What would you like for dinner?"

"How about spaghetti?"

"Did you stop by the store and pick up some milk like I asked?"

"Oh damn! Sorry, I had so many other things on my mind...."

While this conversation may not match the intensity of the intellectual bolero described above, it's still an information loop, albeit an asymmetric one. The husband cyclically requests information that the wife provides. That such loops can be lopsided does not deny their underlying architecture; they're still information loops, just lopsided ones.

Indeed, the symmetry of information contribution to the conversation is one of our unstated criteria for successful conversation. My impressively academic phrase "symmetry of information contribution" is expressed just as clearly (albeit reversed) in the phrase "hogging the conversation." A good conversation is a balanced cycle to which each speaker contributes an equal share. I am only rewording a truth you already understand, but this rewording sheds light on the interactive process.

The concept of symmetry of information contribution can be applied by the interactivity designer. We can use this concept to evaluate design concepts. For example, the dark shadow of suspicion immediately falls on those "reference CDs" that put encyclopedic information at your fingertips. These are worthy applications, to be sure, but we all know that they haven't set the world on fire. People buy computers to get on the Internet, or to process words, or to crunch budget numbers; they don't buy computers to accelerate the process of flipping through an encyclopedia. If you've ever wondered why software encyclopedias haven't added much more than a few shingles to Bill Gates' metropohouse, you now have your answer: software reference works offer lopsided interactivity. That's nowhere near as much fun as, say, fiddling around with the latest budget numbers on your spreadsheet, or adding just the right turn of phrase to your letter to your father-in-law, or blasting monsters in a dungeon.

Of course, sucking in information without gurgitating any in return is a common and necessary part of our lives, so interactivity designers should certainly investigate better methods of doing so. The trick is to keep in mind the importance of symmetry of information flow through the interactive loop. Most designers who have a large mass of information to make available start on the wrong foot by focusing on the information itself: how can it be organized, categorized, and hyperlinked? The better way to start is by focusing on the user: what questions will prompt the user to approach this mass of information? How can it be arranged so as to most conveniently answer those questions? Four methods are available to the designer: keyword search, database query, browsing by structure, and convergent iteration. I shall explore these in the context of the most common problem of mass information handling: search engines on the web.

Searching by Keywords

Keyword searches are most often used at the beginning of a search. First you cast your net with a keyword search; then you scan through the results looking for a likely page. Going to that page, you begin browsing from there. The problem here is twofold: search engines have different algorithms for collecting the background data, and you often get far more matches than you can scan. Keyword searching is not good enough for most people, but we hobble along with it as the best we have.

Let's follow an example of a web search problem. Suppose that you're an engineer wishing to find out how to use the latest generation of charge-coupled devices (CCDs). You've just been told that these third-generation devices are exquisitely sensitive, and you'd like to learn about their sensitivities. So you start with the keyword *CCD*. Bad move: you just got 15,238,916 matching pages. You forgot about all those retail sites selling CCD cameras. Okay, so you narrow the search with *CCD* AND *sensitivity*. This is much better: you've eliminated 99.9 percent of the matches. Unfortunately, this leaves you with 15,237 matches. You scan through the match list looking for the pages that are cluttering you up. There are still plenty of retail sites; you jump to one and realize that the sales blurb boasts about the sensitivity of the camera. Damn! So you make it *CCD* AND *sensitivity* AND *third generation*. This drops you down to just eight sites, but you quickly discover that all of them are retail sites trying to sell you expensive scientific equipment using third-generation CCD technology. You give up at this point.

Browsing by Hyperlink

The web brought this approach to the fore, although it was in use much earlier. This method is simple, direct, easily adapted to almost any system, infinitely extensible, and all sorts of other great things—that's why it's so popular. There's one little catch: all those links have to be set up by hand. Sure, there are plenty of mechanized links on the web, but those tend to take all the fun out of browsing. Generally speaking, you browse through hand-crafted links; you search through manufactured links. And with the explosion of web pages, browsing is less practical until you get very close to your destination.

Returning to our example search for CCD specifications, perhaps you could get closer to your goal if you found your way to a site that might be close and then browsed from there. So you search for *CCD* AND *specifications* AND *technical* and get a healthy 350 sites. Sampling a few, you browse, looking for anything that might get you closer. Lo and behold, you've struck it rich: here's a page that lists hundreds of pages of specifications of all sorts of CCDs. Unfortunately, it's not sorted by generation, so you have to plow through the whole list to find the few that you want. There's gotta be a better way.

Database Querying

Sometimes it is possible to search using numerical tests. The keyword search considers only text; a database query system allows you to constrain your search by some numerical trait. For example, bibliofind.com, a purveyor of used books, allows you to specify the maximum price in any search; only the books that cost less than your maximum will be presented. Full-scale database query systems permit all kinds of complicated specifications (for example, "Computer, show me all available women under 35 whose height in centimeters divided by weight in kilograms exceeds 3.2 inches). These systems give you a better handle on the search problem. In the CCD example, you could narrow the search even further by looking for any CCD with sensitivity less than 0.01 lux. That would get you to your goal. Unfortunately, database queries work best in numerically organized problems. If you want to know why the sky is blue, a database query won't help.

Convergent Iteration

There's a fourth method, though, that I think would be faster than any of the preceding ones, although it would take much more work on the part of the designer. The key observation here is that each of the search systems is designed to be a single-shot proposition: you enter your search specification or click a link and off you go to one or more answers. The search specification for such a jump must be onerously precise. Why couldn't the process be designed to be interactive, with an expectation that multiple steps are required to reach the goal? In practice, all searches are multi-step processes, with the user honing the search procedure based on results of previous searches. Why couldn't we build this concept into our search engines?

As it happens, the concept is already in operation at NorthernLight.com. Its search engine is even smarter than the one in my description. When I tried my CCD example on NorthernLight.com, I first used the simple keyword *CCD*. This yielded 417,779 hits organized into a dozen categories, one of which was Telescopes. This led me to 9,174 items with another dozen subcategories. I chose the Questions and Answers subcategory, which led me to 72 items, many of which looked just right for my needs.

This system is superior to conventional search engines because it is more interactive. Rather than ask the user to divine the ideal set of keywords, this scheme permits the user to enter one broad keyword, which the system uses to look up a huge set of possibilities. At this point, the scheme does two things that conventional keyword searches don't do: it thinks, and it speaks back to the user. Specifically, it analyzes the set of web pages that fit the initial keyword and figures out the secondary keywords that most efficiently divide up those web pages into neat subcategories. It then tells these secondary keywords to the user, who can then select the most likely keyword for additional searching.

Technical people might object that this scheme requires too many cycles and too much background storage. But who's supposed to do all the work here: computers or people?

Measuring Information Flow

As with many other areas of interactivity design, games best demonstrate the importance of information flow. Of course, the information flowing through the loop of a videogame is simple: where you are, what's coming at you, and so forth. Nevertheless, videogames derive much of their power from the amount of information racing through their loops. We can actually measure the information flowing in a videogame by asking two questions: how much information on the screen is changing, and how much information is the player transmitting to the computer? In a standard 3D shoot-'em-up game, the screen image is constantly in motion; the amount of visual information transmitted through the screen is at least 10 MB per second. By contrast, my word processor presents me with a fairly static image that changes only by small increments as I type; it's giving me perhaps a few kilobytes per second. Looking at the input side, though, the information flow is lopsided the opposite way. A kid frantically punching at his joypad at, say, two moves a second transmits about one byte every second. I can readily type four to six bytes per second. Even so, note the extreme disparity between how much information the computer transmits and how much information the human transmits. Let's face it: fingers were never designed to move information at high bit rates.

But raw information flow, measured in bits, is not a reasonable assessment of the value of the information flow through the loop. I could write a program that would dump the contents of the New York City telephone directory onto your screen in 4.73 seconds, but that doesn't mean that this program is somehow better than my word processor. We must take into consideration the value of each of those bits of information moving around—an entirely subjective decision. The pearls of wisdom flowing through my fingertips into the keyboard as I sit here writing this book—who is to say that they are more valuable bits than the jerky movement orders coming out of a kid's video-game joypad?

There is another means of assigning relative values to the bits that flow through the loop of any human-to-computer interaction: how much processing does the information trigger inside the human brain? If computer thinking is the delivered value of a piece of software, is not the human thinking that this stimulates a measure of the received value of the software? This point of view remains subjective, of course. A kid playing a video game might evaluate the oncoming monsters and decide to duck around a corner; how does this decision making compare to my mulling over the structure of this sentence as I use this word processor?

While these considerations of information flow are unquantifiable, they do provide the designer with important gauges of utility. Over and over again, you as designer must reflect on the state of the user's mind and what information processing is going on inside that brain that pays your salary. How can you keep that brain going at full speed? What information will stimulate it to its highest levels of desirable activity?

Human-Human Interaction versus Human-Computer Interaction

Some people think that the human-to-human interaction of a conversation is somehow fundamentally different from the human-to-machine interaction in software. There are differences, but they are confined to the particulars of each step. Humans think holistically whereas computers think sequentially. Humans speak in natural language, whereas computers speak with audio and video. Humans listen with their ears, whereas computers listen with the mouse and the keyboard. These are profound differences, to be sure, and much of the hard work of interactivity design lies in surmounting the obstacles imposed by these differences. The process as a whole, however, remains the same in both cases. Human-human interactivity is at root the same thing as human-machine interactivity; the basic cycle of listen-think-speak remains unchanged. The asymmetry of listening and speaking styles makes your job difficult; the asymmetry of thinking processes provides you with the point and purpose of your work in the first place. If the computer thought just like a human being, who'd want to talk to it rather than the real thing?

Interactivity establishes a loop through which information flows. More information flow usually means better interactivity. However, the value of the information flowing is crucial to the quality of the interactivity.

7

ARCHITECTURES

Architectural diagrams of interaction help us better understand the design problems we face. A variety of commonly used strategies are available, but most suffer from some serious defect. A bushy tree is required for good interactivity. One way to judge the interactive quality of a design is to examine the ratio of accessible states to conceivable states.

One of my physics professors used to say, "When in doubt, draw a picture." Any tough problem can be clarified by some sort of diagram laying out the elements of the problem and their relationships. For many people, myself included, drawing a picture serves the same purpose that vocalizing a feeling has for many people when they're upset: it may not by itself solve the problem, but it's a good start.

Interactivity design presents us with many tricky problems, and it can be especially difficult to articulate those problems because of the dynamic nature of interactivity. Accordingly, drawing a picture might have some value, not as an engineering diagram or a blueprint, but rather as a way to visualize the problem. I hijacked a standard diagramming scheme from computer science and modified it slightly to apply to problems of interactivity. It's ridiculously simple, but that simplicity makes it applicable to a wide variety of design problems. In this chapter, I'll present the diagram and show how it illustrates many of the problems and mistakes of interactivity design. Although I'll be using games and interactive storytelling as my primary examples, the principles apply to any kind of interactive application, as I shall later illustrate. Moreover, the design problems show up most clearly in games.

A Simple Interactivity Diagram

I shall begin with a simple diagram that presents the structure of a story:

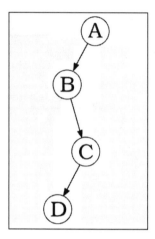

In this diagram, each circle represents an event or action, while the arrows show the connections between the events. A story is thus a simple sequence of events:

A. Once upon a time there was a noble youth named Culhych.

B. His stepmother told him that he must win a beautiful girl named Olwen.

C. But to do this he had to gain the help of a great king.

D. So Culhych set out for Arthur's court. . . .

Note that the sequence of events is linear; that's why we refer to this structure as a *storyline*.

Now, how can we evolve this structure into something that is interactive? Some people don't bother to ask this question; they just take a story and cram it into a computer, add a few meaningless technological tricks, and pronounce it "interactive." I shall dismiss such travesties without further exercise.

For the purposes of this chapter, we need to focus on a single critical component of interaction: the element of choice on the part of the user. The user gets to make decisions, to effect choices. If the user doesn't get to make a choice, we don't have interaction; we have a plain old story. A choice would be expressed in our little diagrammatic scheme with something like this:

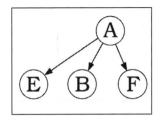

This is called a *branchpoint*, a term taken from programming. The user comes to a point in the story where she gets to make a decision. She has several options: that is, the story can proceed in any of several directions. The user decides which option to take. The important fact is that there is more than one choice—the user has a meaningful choice that will influence the future direction of the interactive story.

Now, how do we put this structure into our storyline? Well, the obvious thing to do is to simply cram it into the storyline structure like so:

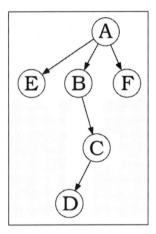

Of course, this creates a new problem: what falls below the empty nodes E and F? The obvious thing to do now is to continue the process of giving the user options by tacking additional branchpoints onto the structure. This yields a *storytree*:

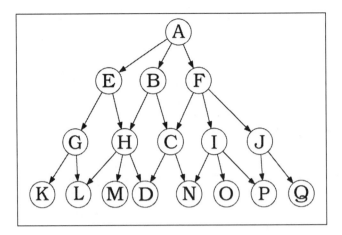

Now I'd like to ask, how many layers should the structure have? That is, how many rows should there be in the pyramidal structure? I have drawn just four layers, but what would a real interactive storyteller have?

A quick way to answer this is to look again at the storytree with one portion highlighted:

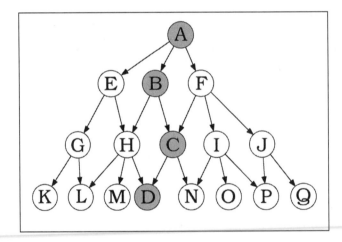

The highlighted portion, you will note, is exactly the same as the storyline at the beginning of this example. In other words, a storytree is a storyline creator; a single path through a storytree yields a storyline. We can therefore apply what we know about stories to estimate the appropriate depth of a storytree. A movie, for example, will have many more than ten events or actions in it, and certainly less than 10,000. In other words, I think that a movie has something like a hundred or a thousand events or actions in it. Novels tend to be longer, perhaps.

Let's be conservative so we get the smallest reasonable number of nodes. Let's assume that our interactive story-thing needs only a hundred events or actions. In other words, there will be 100 layers in our interactive story. Let us further assume that each branchpoint will have only two choices available to it—this is the absolute minimum required. This means (according to a standard calculation) that the storytree will have a total of 2^{100} nodes in it. How many is that? About 10^{30}. And how big is that? If you employed every human being on this planet to create nodes, each person making one node every second, working 24 hours per day, 365 days per year, then it would take 5 trillion years to make the nodes necessary to build that single storytree. You're going to have difficulty making your deadline.

Foldback

A variety of solutions to this problem of the geometric growth of nodes have been developed over the years. One of the earliest solutions, first presented 30 years ago, had a structure like this:

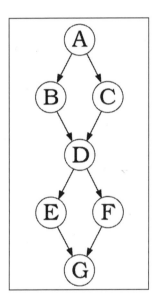

I call this trick *foldback*. The storyline folds back on itself. For example, consider the first four nodes, labeled A, B, C, and D. Suppose that node A represents Eloise saying to Bart, "I'm just not attracted to wimps like you, Bart." Suppose further that node B represents Bart wringing his hands and pleading with Eloise, while node C has him sneering at her, "Ha! I can find better sex in a broom closet!" Now, node D might represent Eloise declaring, "Oh, Bart, don't say that—I'll take you back!"—which response is appropriate to either of Bart's actions. It's clever, but the problem with this method is that it robs the interactivity of any meaning. Whatever Bart does, Eloise is going to take him back. Indeed, if you step back from this diagram a few feet, it doesn't look any different from a regular storyline. This is nothing more than a storyline masquerading as a storytree. This is fraudulent interactivity.

Kill 'Em If They Stray

Here's another approach:

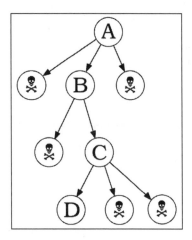

I call this the *kill 'em if they stray* approach to storytree design. The designer allows the user many options, but almost all of the options lead to the death of the user or the termination of the story. This scheme merely spruces up a linear storyline with many opportunities to fail along the way. This is not what I call user-friendly. Moreover, it's still essentially linear. Many adventure games and puzzle stories fit this model.

Obstructionist Stories

Another variation on this is the *obstructionist* scheme wherein the user is presented with a linear sequence of story nodes separated by obstacles:

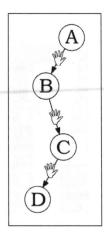

The user runs into a brick wall at each stage in the story and must solve the puzzle to proceed to the next stage of the story. This is interactive after a fashion; the user is permitted to interact with the puzzle. But, of course, there's no interaction with the story itself. This is Skinner Box interactivity, reducing the user to the status of a rat in a maze, required to push the correct levers to get the reward—and punished for failure. Despite its serious flaws, the technique has been used in a number of commercially successful products. I consider it to have the staying power of any other fad.

Hand-Wired Storytree

Next comes the *hand-wired storytree*, too messy to diagram. The designer sits down and draws a big diagram showing how every node connects with every other node. He builds the entire structure by hand, plotting connections and figuring pathways. This sounds better; after all, it's hand tooled and surely must be finely tuned. The problem with such designs is that they are sorely limited by the amount of time that the designer can put into them. Even the largest such designs sport no more than a few hundred nodes. Moreover, these are often crippled in other ways. They support only the most primitive of Boolean connection schemes. In other words, the pathways in the system are opened or closed by the simplest of yes-or-no decision schemes involving such lame-brained factors as whether the user uses the correct item, whether he recites the magic incantation, or some other such simple-minded pap.

Combinations of the Above

Then there are the combinatorial schemes, which combine various elements of the other architectures. A bewildering array of such methods have been tried. One such scheme attempts to solve the problem of the gigantic storytree by linking together a group of smaller, more manageable storytrees. The links between the small storytrees are simple, direct connections.

This is a common approach in graphic adventures. Each small storytree is used to establish a particular subgoal. The first storytree might determine whether you wheedle the orange key from the one-eyed pirate. With the orange key, you can enter the secret room where the purple dragon awaits; now you enter a new storytree whose outcome, if successful, advances you to the next storytree.

This system fails because each subtree produces a simple success-or-failure result. This means that we can replace each of the small storytrees with a single node that asks the question, "Did the user succeed at the assigned task?" It operates in exactly the same way that the obstructionist story operates.

In general, combinatorial schemes fail because there are no exploitable synergies between the various strategies. Simple combination of two dissimilar components seldom accomplishes anything; there must exist some relationship between the two that permits a useful synergy to emerge from the combination. A metal alloy works because the atoms of the two metals are different sizes and will fit together in a tighter, stronger structure. Cramming random bits of metal together doesn't make better metal.

The Desirability of Bushiness

A good storytree is rich and bushy; a storytree that is narrow or scraggly is not particularly interactive. Why? There are two ways to answer this question.

One way is to think in terms of user choice. The user wants to make choices. Choice is the means by which we express our free will; choice is the manifestation of our personalities. Hence, a good design offers the user many choices—many branches emerging from each branchpoint.

Another way to look at this problem is to think of the interaction as an act of individuation. When our user enters our storytree, she desires to find her own personal resolution to the challenge presented in the interaction. This could be her own document or even her own spreadsheet. This is fundamental to human nature. In anything we attempt, we seek not to replicate the results of the masters, but to create our own unique solution. What cook fails to make some small individuating adjustments in the recipe in the cookbook? It is an act of self-expression, of asserting our individuality.

What do we do to the users of our interactive entertainment? We cram them into a slot, demanding that they follow *our* storyline. We narrow their options, declaring some options to be correct and others to be incorrect. We give them only a few choices, because we are too lazy to recognize just how varied our users are.

If we wish to offer our user a truly satisfying interactive experience, it is imperative that we allow each user to express her individuality during the experience. There should be billions of pathways through the storytree, so that each user can find her own path through, coming to her own conclusion—and it's no fair declaring that only a handful of such pathways are correct. The average user should be able to make her own choices and still find a pathway with a satisfying conclusion. The user of a word processor wins or loses according to her own writing standards, not those of the designer. Thus, we want to create a storytree that is thick and bushy, with billions of pathways leading through it. This is the only way to guarantee that each user will be able to find an individuating pathway through the storytree.

Broader Applications

These concepts can be applied to design areas other than games or interactive storytelling. To do so, I must engage you in a long-winded and roundabout reasoning process. It begins with another one of my simple diagrams:

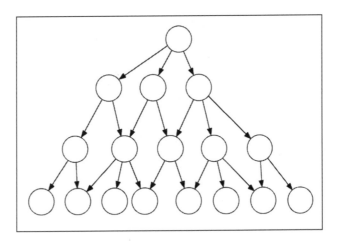

By the way, we need a shorthand label for these diagrams. Computer scientists use the term *graph* for something similar to this, and some people prefer to use *state diagram*, but each of these is used in somewhat different ways than we need. To avoid confusion, we should use a distinct term, and I suppose that this burden falls upon my already fatigued shoulders; I therefore propose the wildly immodest term *Crawford diagram* to refer to them. At least it's better than *dactylodeiktous diagram*.

This tree structure could just as well be applied to a word-processing program, the only difference being that, instead of two or three branches at each node, we would see about a hundred branches: one for each key on the keyboard. The top node is a blank page. If this diagram were applied to a website, then the top node would be the home page.

To use the word processor, the user starts at the top of the tree with a blank page and selects a letter to type, which creates a new state, a document with that single letter. This act also moves him down one layer in the tree. He then selects another letter to type, which takes him to a new state and the next lower layer, and so on until he reaches the bottom of the tree and his document is complete. The bottom of the tree contains zillions of nodes, each representing a document containing characters in some sequence. The great majority of these imaginary documents would be nonsensical collections of characters, but one in a zillion might be a Shakespearean sonnet. Thus, in this way of thinking, the user does not write a document so much as he chooses a document through a long sequence of small choices (keystrokes).

Differences between Word Processors and Games: Two New Concepts

But there is a big difference between word processors and games: the former do their job better than games. My word processor does everything that I want to do, and then some. By contrast, I have yet to play a game that gave me such a sense of satisfaction. Every game I have ever played restricted my freedom of action, refused to permit me to do the things that I wanted to do. How can it be that games and word processors can yield such different results when they are structurally identical? What is it that word processors do that games don't do? The answer to this question will tell us how to make any interactive application—including word processors—better.

To answer that question, I shall introduce two new concepts. The first is the set of *accessible* states in a tree. These are all of the states that the user can get to as he moves down the tree. In a word processor, this is the humongous set of all documents that the user could theoretically create; in a game, it is the set of all realizable paths through the game; in a storytree, it is all the different stories that could be experienced.

The second concept is a little more difficult; it is the set of all *conceivable* states. These are the states that the user might expect to be able to access. In the case of the word processor, these would include all the documents that a user might want to create. In a game, it would include all the game endings that a user might visualize. In a storytree, it is all the ways that the user might imagine that the story could develop.

A Criterion for Excellence

I now direct your attention to the ratio of the number of accessible states to the number of conceivable states. You calculate this ratio by dividing the number of accessible states by the number of conceivable states. I suggest that this ratio provides us with a criterion for evaluating the overall merit of a product.

Consider now that the source of my satisfaction with my word processor lies in the fact that "anything I want to do, I can do." In other words, any state that I expect to access, I can access. Let's make up some plausible numbers for a word processor to see how the ratio works. Let's say that I can expect 100 gazillion states, but my word processor can't quite handle all of them; it can reach only 99.9 gazillion states. So we might calculate the ratio for a word processor as follows:

```
interactive excellence     = accessible states / conceivable states
                           = 99.9 gazillion states / 100 gazillion states
                           = 0.999
```

The ratio of accessible states to conceivable states is very nearly 1. On the other hand, I do not have the same experience with games. Many times in games I feel trapped by the design, unable to do the thing that I want to do. In other words, the state that I expect to access is not there. Thus, with games, the calculation might look like this:

```
interactive excellence     = accessible states / conceivable states
                           = 20 gazillion states / 100 gazillion states
                           = 0.20
```

We have here a way of gauging the interactive excellence of any interactive design. Now, I'm not suggesting that one should literally perform this calculation by counting up all the accessible states and all the conceivable states; I don't have a gazillion fingers. But we can use our imaginations to get a hunch as to whether the ratio is big or small.

More important, this suggests a way to improve our designs: the more closely the ratio approaches 1, the better our design will be. There are only two ways to increase a ratio: increase the numerator or decrease the denominator. I shall take up the latter case first.

Decreasing the Number of Conceivable States

Decreasing the number of conceivable states sounds silly, doesn't it? How can a designer lower the expectations of users, short of including in the package a coupon for a free frontal lobotomy at the nearest hospital? As it happens, we designers have a great deal of power, for we set the expectations of our users with the cues we give them and with the language of interaction that we provide to them. Most programs inflate user expectations and then confound those expectations. We do this by suggesting that the software universe inside our program is larger than it actually is.

What we need here is the closure discussed in Chapter 4. A good interactive design presents a closed and complete universe. Leave out the petty things so that you can implement the important features completely. The emphasis is not on parsimony but on closure, although parsimonious design is often necessary to achieve closure. Just remember that every chink in your system's closure will leak users into the void of unanticipated feature space. Your users, strangling in the vacuum, will perceive a deficiency and blame you for it—quite rightly. The expressive range of your design must be hermetically sealed against such leaks.

There are two means by which you can fail to achieve closure: your choice of feature set and your user interface. Too many designers succumb to overweening pride in creating products that attempt too much. In their eagerness to expand the universe of their design, they toss in features willy-nilly without recognizing the geometrically increasing expectations that such features instill in the users. Whenever you add a new feature to a design, that feature can interact with every other feature in your design. You may never consider what might happen if the gamma correction tool were used in conjunction with the Korean language translator, but some of your users certainly will. It is incumbent upon you to anticipate all those possible combinations and provide for them.

But the problem extends beyond the mere possibility of unanticipated combinations of existing features. A new feature added to a program often suggests related features to the user. If you add a hyperbolic sine function to your productivity application, you'd damn well better put in the hyperbolic cosine function and the hyperbolic tangent function, as well as the inverse of each of these functions; by creating one function, you have also created the expectation of five others. If you permit the user to export a special file format, then you must also permit the user to import that file format. If your game shows a door, the user must be able to open that door. If your word processor offers superscripts, it must also offer subscripts.

A good example of the user interface side of this problem is the *command-line interface*, such as used in DOS. You may not remember this once-ubiquitous operating system, so I'll describe it here. The screen was not graphical but textual; you saw a bunch of obscure text codes on the screen. Then you might type a command like this:

```
>C:\MYDIR\WORDPRO.EXE
```

This is one of the simpler commands. It directs the computer to run a program that can be found on the hard disk (C:) in a directory called MYDIR, and the program itself is called WORDPRO.EXE.

This looks simple enough, but personal computers kept growing, adding ever more capabilities and complexity. To cope with this growth, designers kept adding new commands to the basic set. The commands grew longer and more complicated; there were so many that only the experts could remember how to use them.

There is no question that command-line systems are inferior to the graphical user interfaces (GUIs); except for UNIX, a hoary and hairy command-line operating system for programming wizards, and Linux, its open-source derivative, the industry has abandoned such interfaces in favor of the GUIs. But the shift away from DOS was not arbitrary or accidental; there were fundamental reasons for it. The most important of these is that command-line interfaces increase the number of conceivable states far beyond the number of accessible states. You can type zillions of different expressions on a keyboard, and given the exotic spelling of DOS commands, almost anything you type looks reasonable, but only a few thousand of them will actually do anything useful. In other words, for DOS, the calculation looks like this:

```
interactive excellence    = accessible states / conceivable states
                          = a few thousand states / 100 gazillion states
                          = 0.000000...0001
```

That ratio is the best explanation for why DOS is dead.

The term *command-line interface* is usually applied to operating systems. When we talk about the same thing used inside an application program, we call it a *text parser*—and text parsers are an even worse disaster than command-line interfaces, because these latter use a parsimonious set of contractions. For what it's worth, you can be pretty sure that neither UNIX nor DOS will have a command as long-winded as, say, *dissimulate, DSMLT*, or *DSMT*, perhaps, but never anything so obvious as the actual word. Text parsers, on the other hand, purport to recognize a subset of normal English vocabulary. You can type expressions such as "Pick up the rock," and the parser will understand what you mean; isn't that wonderful? But there's a vicious devil lurking in the details of all parsers. A parser suggests to the user that any valid English expression will be accepted by the parser, but in fact most parsers have working vocabularies of a few thousand words. "Pick up the rock" might work, whereas "Pick up the stone," "Grab the pebble," "Take hold of the geode," or "Seize the stony slab" won't. Thus, text parsers perpetrate a cruel falsehood on a user. They create gazillions of conceivable states, but they provide only a few million accessible states (at best).

The simplest, easiest, and most honest way to decrease conceivable states is seldom used: tell the user candidly what you can't do. The hype-driven world of computers has closed its eyes to the clarifying power of the disclaimer. I'm sure that all the marketing suits out there will reach for the garlic and silver cross when I suggest that a little truth goes a long ways. I realize that marketing considerations require you to put a positive face on your software, but I warn you that a positive face does not compensate for a negative reality.

For example, it would have been much easier on us if all of Windows' capabilities *and* incapabilities were clearly presented somewhere. By including hundreds of obscure functional keypresses in the operating system, Microsoft ensured that reasonable people would suspect every key combination of doing something—and by failing to explicitly deny such expectations, it compounded the problem. Windows should have a little warning box that pops up whenever a user types some oddball combination of keys. The warning box should say something like, "Here is a list of all the oddball key combinations that do something, as well as their functions. And here is a list of all the oddball key combinations that don't do anything at all."

The same thing goes for mouse input. Every time a user clicks an inactive screen object, a pop-up window should explain why that object is inactive and what might make it active, if anything. A good system will go further and refer the user to controls that might accomplish what the user seems to be driving at. As I explain in Chapter 5, dimming menu items declares that they aren't functional, which is good, but it's even better to explain why they are dimmed and what can be done to activate them.

This rule of negativity is especially important with websites. The typical browsing user has a pretty clear need in mind and seeks only to determine if your website can satisfy that need. We all know that a website can be gigantic; that creates the expectation that it just might have what we want. So we browse and meander through the website, examining all manner of useless pages in search of our goal. The bigger and more thorough a website is, the more time we are likely to waste searching for our grail. It would be much better if every website devoted some page space to describing what it does *not* include; that might save the users lots of time. For example, I wasted a good deal of time at the Apple website trying to locate a bug report page, as I had found a couple of bugs in AppleWorks and I considered it my solemn duty as a user-citizen of the AppleWorks world to report bugs. Although my expectation of a bug report page was entirely reasonable, no such page was accessible, and the only way to learn this was by trying and failing repeatedly. Remember, negative information is every bit as useful as positive information.

If you build a big website all about George Washington, but you have no information about his financial affairs, you might as well say it up front. The user who pokes all through your website looking for that information is going to be just as disappointed either way; do you want her to be angry with you as well?

To conclude: we can decrease the number of conceivable states by carefully designing our listening structures to suggest nothing more than we intend. Where ambiguities remain, we should explicitly disclaim reasonably conceivable (but inaccessible) states. Remember that great black-and-white photographers pay just as much attention to shadow as to light.

Increasing the Number of Accessible States

How might we increase the number of accessible states? How can we make our trees thicker and bushier? The obvious answer is to provide more branch-points from each state—more verbs. Here are some techniques that will suggest more verbs.

Add More Variables

The first tactic we might use is to increase the number of variables used in our designs, most often by replacing a constant element of our application with a variable element. This is the most commonly used way to increase the power of applications, although in most cases I suspect it is used unconsciously, as an indirect result of other (less strategic) considerations. The earliest word processors, for example, did not permit multiple fonts; there was just one standard font. It didn't matter back then, as the printers also offered only a single font. The decision to add font capability to word processors could also be described as a decision to transform the printing front from a constant to a variable. Designers then gave control of that variable to the user. In general, adding more variables to your design always increases its flexibility and power. Thus, this one change led to other possibilities: new variables in font size and style.

Sometimes the constants in your program are not immediately recognizable as constants. For example, imagine a web page with a button that takes the user to another page. That link is constant; would it be more useful as a variable? A search function, for example, could be thought of as a variable link whose value depends on the search text entered in the associated text field.

There is a dark side to this power: button-mania on the part of the designer often instills button-phobia on the part of the user. Every variable you add is one more chore for the user to handle, one more page in the user manual to be read. An old concept from game design is useful here: the *color-to-dirt ratio*. Every new feature that a game designer adds increases its colorfulness. If I were to add, say, stock speculation to Monopoly, that would certainly make the game more colorful to play. It would give the users more choice in their financial decisions, more flexibility, and more game-playing power. But it would also entail a whole raft of new rules, more cards for the Chance and Community Chest sets, some special spaces on the board, and so forth. All this bureaucratic detail constitutes *dirt* in the game design. The designer must then ask, "Is the color I'm adding with this feature worth all the dirt it brings in?" Similarly, the designer of any interactive application must always consider the color-to-dirt ratio of any contemplated feature. More variables add more color, but they also add more dirt.

For example, a great many programs now offer "configuration sets." These are different versions of the preferences options available in so many programs. The use of preferences allows the user to set up the program exactly the way she likes it. For example, preference files might contain information about the default font to use, the most commonly accessed server, the size and placement of the window for a new document, and so forth. Preferences are a great idea, and most programs now have some kind of preferences system. But some programs go even further: they make the preference file itself a variable, so that the user can choose among different groups of preferences by selecting one of several preference files. If you're in a mood for something exotic one morning, you can choose the Exotic preference file to get odd-shaped windows with that Asian-looking font. Later in the day, when you are to demonstrate something for your boss, you might change to the "Safe and Staid" preference file to give the program a more conventional look. I'm sorry, folks, but this is carrying the use of variables too far: you don't get much color for a lot of dirt. Sure, there are a few hundred geek users around the world who love the feature, but the great majority of users are too staid to appreciate such a feature.

Replace Boolean Variables with Arithmetic Variables

When you do add a variable, you should usually make it an arithmetic variable as opposed to a single-bit Boolean variable. A Boolean variable can take only two values: 1 or 0, yes or no. There are plenty of variables that require Boolean treatment. For example, in the Print dialog box, the check box for collation presents a Boolean variable. Let's face it; collation is something you either do or don't do; there's no partial form of collation. Thus, the user must answer the simple question, "Do you want it collated?" with either a yes or a no—a Boolean variable. We normally use check boxes to allow users to control Boolean variables.

An arithmetic variable, by contrast, is a number; it specifies how much or how many instead of just yes or no. In general, you should strive to find uses for arithmetic variables rather than the more limited Boolean ones. Don't simply keep track of *whether* the user has entered any keystrokes in the word processing document—record *how many* keystrokes he has entered. That way, instead of merely refusing to save an unchanged document, you can more intelligently advise your user: "You've typed 5,000 keystrokes without saving; why not take a break and let me save them for you?"

On a website, you can keep track of how many times a unique visitor has hit each page in the last 10 minutes; this knowledge permits you to treat that visitor in a more responsive manner. Perhaps he's lost, perhaps he's uncertain, perhaps he could use some guidance. An addendum to the page might just help him out.

For your educational software, if you are testing a student, don't just ask whether the answer was wrong; determine how many times the student answered the same type of question incorrectly. In some cases, you can even measure just how far off the mark the answer was. This information can be profitably put to use devising material to assist the student later.

Even some game genres are still stuck using Boolean variables when they should have graduated to arithmetic variables. Interactive fiction has a particularly egregious attachment to Boolean variables. The field could develop much more richness if it started using variables like "how big a rock does he carry" rather than "is he carrying a rock or is he not?"

Eschew Hard-Wired Branching for Computed Branching

Another wrong-headed practice is the use of explicitly defined branches in a tree. I have never seen this error in productivity applications, but it is depressingly common in games and educational software, and central to the organization of websites.

Whenever a designer creates an explicit link between one node and another, she implicitly rules out the many variations that might pop into a user's head. Explicit links are like Boolean variables: either you follow the link or you don't. A user whose needs are not as starkly defined as the choice you offer will expect a greater range of choices. Simple arrangements like this are acceptable for the basic navigational operation of a website, but for delivering greater value, you'll need to build your pages on the fly to meet the individual requirements of each user. Why must your pages be cast in stone before the user even arrives?

Every time you use a search engine, it builds a custom page presenting the results of your search. Why must customization be confined to something so simple as a list of items from a database? Instead of building 3,000 pages for your users to delve tediously through, why not organize your site more algorithmically, and build custom pages for each user? If you're designing a small website, explicit links are fine, but as sites grow larger, the need for more powerful listening powers increases dramatically—and text is far more expressive than mouse clicks. Let your users type what they want and then calculate how to give it to them.

Use Indirection

As much as possible, push your design thinking away from the concrete and towards abstraction and indirection. This is a complicated issue; I'll come back to it in Chapters 20 and 21.

Crawford diagrams provide another way of thinking about interactivity designs. They illustrate some of the common errors, and suggest some useful desiderata. They are not adequate as design blueprints. The ratio of accessible states to conceivable states is a good measure of the quality of the interaction. Work to decrease conceivable states and increase accessible states.

PART TWO
DESIGN ADVICE

8

GUIDELINES

Always design the verbs first. Don't start with the technology. Be on guard against the egotistical tendency to speak. Response to user actions must be fast. Organize verbs into logical groups. Prioritize verb accessibility according to frequency of use. Tree architectures should be as square as possible. Design the loop as a whole. Don't set up false expectations. Say what you mean. Don't describe the problem—offer the solution. Speak with one voice in four tones.

It has taken seven chapters, but you now have enough of the fundamentals under your belt to actually start applying them. This chapter offers guidelines—not absolute rules! There are always exceptions to these guidelines, and I'll try to characterize some of those exceptions.

Start with the Verbs

This is the first and foremost rule of good interactive design, and the word *rule* is truer than *guideline* in this case. At the outset of the design process, after you have established the goals of the design but before you have begun work on the design itself, you must ask yourself the question, "What are the verbs in this design?" All through the design process, you must ask that question again and again.

As I pointed out in Chapter 4, listening is the hardest step to design. That in itself should make verb design the first task of the interactive designer. In any difficult project, you should always tackle the toughest task first. If you fail, there's less work to throw away. If you start with something other than the verbs, the unavoidable constraints of verb design will twist your design around into a pretzel. Hold off adding the salt and baking it until the twisting is complete.

By verbs, I mean the choices available to your user. These are *not* the keystrokes, button clicks, scrollbar actions, menu choices, and hotlink selections that are part of the standard user interface toolbox. The verbs are the actions you intend to make available to your user. The details of precisely how you will make your verbs accessible to the user can be worked out later. But before you begin laying out radio buttons and check boxes, you need to make more fundamental decisions. If it's a word processor you are designing, what do you want the user to be able to do? Don't think in terms of your internal model—think in terms of the final product. Should the user be able to print pages upside down? Should the user be able to artificially stain the printout with virtual tears? How, exactly, are you empowering (gad, how I hate that word!) your user?

If you're designing a website, ask yourself what you expect the user to be able to accomplish on your site. Should he be able to compare your prices with your competitors'? Should he be able to see your inventory to determine whether the product is in stock? Should he be able to contact you directly, or perhaps through a standard form? Make these decisions first—then and only then can you start designing the user interface.

Sit down with a piece of paper and write—in plain English, not computer terminology—what your software will enable your user to accomplish. You will probably encounter difficulty with the intrinsic vagueness of defining goals. Don't be frustrated; attack the vagueness. Your job as a designer is to figure out the best scheme for organizing all these things in your user's mind. Continue this process of attacking vague wordings, replacing them with longer and more explicit wordings. Of course, as you go, you'll need to think about the details of the design, and you'll slow down as you start grinding through those details. Remember: during this process, you are specifying what the user does, *not* what the screen looks like or what the program will do or how it will work. Stick to the verbs! Every time you expand something, expand it only in the direction of the user's choices.

I'm sorry to tell you that this strategy will not design the entire product for you. You will not end up with a massive document that need only be handed to a programmer for coding and the product will be ready to ship. Somewhere along the way, the details of verb definition will get so picayune that you'll be forced to tackle the associated thinking and speaking parts of the design.

In the listen-think-speak triplet, the verbs are what you listen to, or what the user speaks with. All three steps are equal in final importance but unequal in difficulty of implementation. Speaking is the cheapest, quickest, and easiest part of the design. Thinking is harder, but the listening step is the great demon that lays low most interactive designs. If you are a project manager allocating budget to an interactive project, you should not allocate approximately one-third of your budget to each of the three steps—set aside the biggest chunk of resource for the hardest part, listening.

To understand why you should do this, hearken back to the previous chapter. The Big Idea there is simple: the ratio of accessible states to conceivable states is a good measure of the quality of the interaction. Verbs are what make states accessible to your user. If you put lots of effort into the verbs, you'll be giving more and more state accessibility to your user. By contrast, every time you speak anything to your user, your words, sounds, or images can trigger all sorts of ideas—conceivable states—inside your user's head. Thus, all those turkeys who spend tons of money getting great graphics, sound, and animation (the speaking part) have got it exactly backwards: they're breeding more conceivable states and doing nothing to improve the number of accessible states.

I promised you some exceptions to this rule, so here are a few. If your design is constrained by a specification that refers directly to either the thinking part or the speaking part, then you don't have much maneuvering room. Consider, for example, the poor soul who was assigned to design the *National Geographic* interactive archive. This was a mammoth project, and the project specification was clearly something like "make every back issue, every article, every photograph available to the user." Let's face it; this is a pure speaking-step project. The images and text (speaking stuff) are the entire point and purpose of the project. The only verbs that were conceivable were verbs along the lines of "let me look at the images and text in this fashion."

Another example might be an input device constraint. Your boss comes to you with a new, electronic, squeezable roll of toilet paper. You can squeeze it, and it sends a signal to a computer! Your assignment is to design the world's greatest interactive thingamabob to show off the wonderful, squeezable, electronic roll of toilet paper. In such a case, the only verb you can give your user is "squeeze the toilet paper."

These, however, are extreme cases, and since they're the best I can come up with in the way of exceptions to my rule, you can see just how imperious that rule is. Throughout the design process, an insistent voice in the back of your mind should nag incessantly, "What does the user *do*?" If you don't have a good answer to this question, then your product is not very good in the interactive dimension.

Don't Start with the Technology

This is the converse of the previous admonition. This error commonly arises when programmers usurp design responsibilities. Programmers love technological tricks, and they especially love new and interesting technological tricks. They therefore spend a lot of time building cute little software oddities and then asking, "How can we turn this into a game?"

I will give this behavior its due before trashing it. There is a place for playful experimentation of this type: the research lab. Many of our most dramatic discoveries come when some bright kid in a lab discovers some odd goo and asks, "How can we turn this into a product?" Every industry needs its research labs to advance this kind of thinking, as it is absolutely essential to the long-term future.

However, the jump from interesting technological trick to working product is a long one indeed, and far too many designs are little more than cute techie tricks shoved into a software shell. This is especially true of the games industry, which has institutionalized opportunistic software design.

Although there have been some striking successes from this strategy, it is far more likely to yield failure. It starts off on the wrong foot. Instead of asking, "What can I do for my customers?" it asks, "How can I convince my customers to pay for this technology?" Whenever you get the relationship between customer and yourself mixed up like this, you are setting yourself up for a disaster.

Be on Guard against the Egotistical Tendency to Speak

This rule applies throughout the design process. Most designers are egotists who would rather inundate the user with their brilliant expressions than actually let the user do something. They begrudge the user his control of the program and regard graphics, sound, animation, and other speaking stuff as their chance to strut their stuff. Like the boor at the party, the egotistical designer wants to do all the talking and never, ever listens. Egotism that robs a designer of her sense of balance and even-handedness is ruinous.

You are not creating your design to make yourself dactylodeiktous by virtue of your vast talent, expertise, or vocabulary; you do this to help your user (or reader) get something done. I do not wish to throw cold water on your healthy ego; my concern is that you apply it maturely. I offer my own towering ego as a model for you to emulate. Was Chris Crawford spoiled by fame? The fawning masses, the rivers of adulatory prose, the crowds of hysterically screaming nubile nymphs—have all these things gone to my head to make me the hopeless egomaniac I now am? No, a thousand times no! Chris Crawford is too big a man to be spoiled by such trivial things! I was already spoiled long before any of this happened to me. Mine is a mature egomania refined and developed since the day I emerged from the womb and took a bow.

Designers lacking healthy egos cannot reach the peaks accessible to their better-endowed colleagues. The egomaniac sets higher goals than she can reasonably expect to achieve. In a poorly defined field such as interactivity design, such is the stuff of creativity. A civil engineer doesn't get too experimental with the bridges he designs, because it is easy to reliably calculate what will and what won't work. But we don't know as much about interactivity. We don't know where the limits are. So we need these foolhardy egomaniacs who blindly plunge into the darkness, boldly going where no one in her right mind has gone before.

The egomaniac has another advantage over the more emotionally balanced person. In the darkest hours of a project, when the problems seem overwhelming and there is no rational basis for hope, a reasonable person would start casting about for ways to scale down the goals of the project. But the egomaniac lies face down in the mud of her own failure and draws herself up, proclaiming, "I am beyond ze reach of failure! I weel find ze way!" Egotism, of course, takes a back seat to reality, and sometimes she fails; but when she succeeds, it seems like magic to the rest of the world.

There are, of course, liabilities created by egotism, such as the deadly difference between pre-project egotism and post-project egotism. The former serves to inspire the designer to greater heights of achievement. The latter convinces her that she has already scaled those heights. Post-project egotism blinds the designer to the flaws in her work and robs her of the ability to learn and improve.

Then there are the embarrassing consequences of an ego that is foisted on other people. There's a big difference between nurturing your ego and unleashing it upon the rest of us. Feel free to smile inwardly in secret appreciation of your untouchable superiority, but it is another thing entirely to tell it to other people. The mature, genteel egomaniac keeps to herself the untold story of her towering intelligence and dazzling creativity.

So don't feel embarrassed by that ego of yours. Go ahead—stand on the craggy mountaintop, lightning bolts playing about you, fist thrust upward and head held high as the furious wind hurls rain in your face. Laugh scornfully at the elements that doubt your greatness. Shout lustily into the tempest, "I am ze greatest designer in all ze universe!" Then scuttle back into your cave and return to work, putting the appropriate amount of energy and creativity into the listening and thinking steps, rather than just the speaking part.

There are no exceptions to this rule.

Keep It Fast

I once served as a consultant for a project that had serious problems. The designers had gotten the software working well, and when I toyed with it at their offices, it worked just great. But then they burned a CD for me to take home, and that's where I encountered the killer problem: their software went out to the CD every time the user did anything, and the two-second delay broke the user's stride. Back at the designers' offices, they ran the software on their big, fast machines with monster hard drives that made everything run like lightning. They couldn't see the problem.

Here's an experiment I urge you to try so that you might appreciate the gravity of this problem. Select a very patient friend and engage him in conversation. Every time your friend says something, stare blankly and look like you're thinking while you mentally tick off two seconds; then respond. See how long you can keep the conversation going before your friend grows irritated.

Try
                                               to
                     understand
                                      a
   sentence
                 that
     deliberately
        breaks
                            the
          timing;
      see
           how
       irritating
                          it
is?

Interactivity has a timing, a rhythm, a stride. Break that stride, and you ruin the interaction. Yet the timing of interaction is intangible; you can't simply look at a JPG file or listen to a WAV file or read a text file to evaluate it. It is imperative that you experience the interaction itself, not its disconnected components. It's not that interactivity is more than the sum of its parts; interactivity is *not* its parts, but the entire dynamic of how they operate together—which includes the timing of that dynamic.

The simplest manifestation of this rule is, you should move your software over to a "typical target user's machine" and play with it, asking yourself if it's fast enough.

How fast should the interaction be? You can't control the user's timing, of course, so you must assume that the user can respond at his leisure. Not so the computer. The time between a user action and the computer reaction is the criterion of quality. My rules of thumb on delay time are:

Less than 0.05 second	Necessary only for multiple keystroke processing.
About 0.1 second	Perfectly good for all other input.
About 0.5 second	Adequate, but keep these to less than 50 percent of all response times.
About 2 seconds	Keep these to less than 10 percent of all response times, and change the cursor during the interval to reassure the user that you haven't fallen asleep.
About 5 seconds	Keep these to less than 1 percent of all response times, and change the cursor.
10 seconds or more	Keep these to less than 0.2 percent of all response times. Post a message explaining the delay. Include a progress bar that indicates how much delay time remains. Offer an abort option.

This table might seem overly strict, but in fact it represents the performance of most good software. I shall use my favorite word processor as an example. Here's a table of its performance with various types of inputs in a typical writing session:

User Action	Delay Time	Count of Uses	Percentage of Uses
Print one page	51	1	0.02%
Start program	5	1	0.02%
Open document	2	2	0.04%
Scroll one page	0.4	15	0.3%
Keystroke	<0.05	5,000	99.6%

(The printer took up 48 seconds of the print job.)

As you can see, my word processor easily meets the requirements of my table. Of course, most other programs do more crunching and so fare more poorly. Here are some results for my programming environment, CodeWarrior:

User Action	Delay Time	Count of Uses	Percentage of Uses
Compile	18	1	0.1%
Start program	7	1	0.1%
Open project	3	1	0.1%
Single-step	0.4	100	8.9%
Scroll one page	0.2	20	2%
Keystroke	<0.05	1,000	89%

Now let's look at the performance of a program that doesn't use many keystrokes: a drawing program. Here is what a typical session looks like:

User Action	Delay Time	Count of Uses	Percentage of Uses
Start program	6	1	0.09%
Load document	0.8	1	0.09%
Scroll one page	0.6	100	9%
All other actions	<0.4	1,000	90%

Note that the scrolling operation in this application sits close to the borderline of my table. Indeed, I find scrolling the most distasteful part of using this program and organize my work to minimize it.

Last, let's put my own work to the test. I present results for a typical session with my program, the Erasmatron:

User Action	Delay Time	Count of Uses	Percentage of Uses
Start program	3	1	0.2%
Load document	2	1	0.2%
Face draw	2	2	0.4%
Background draw	1	3	0.7%
Screentest	1	10	2.5%
Rehearsal	1	10	2.5%
Threadtest	1	10	2.5%
Decision script draw	0.5	200	51%
Keys screen draw	0.5	5	1%
Text screen draw	0.15	50	13%
Main screen draw	0.1	100	25%

As you can see, my own work brushes up against the limits of my rule table in several places. And indeed, the place where it breaks the rule, decision script drawing, is the most irritating screen in the program.

Last, I ask you to consider how these timings compare with typical web performance. Those of us who come in on 28-Kb lines experience typical page jumping delays of three seconds on jumps internal to a site, and maybe 15 seconds on jumps to new websites. In other words, the web egregiously violates my timing rules. Ever wonder why people complain so much about the sluggish speeds on the web?

Particularly nasty is the difficulty of setting the target system for a design. Let's face it: if you design your product to run on the latest, greatest hardware (as the designers I mentioned earlier did), it will surely perform unacceptably on average hardware. Your perception of what constitutes "normal" hardware is skewed. You make your living with a computer; of course you have a better-than-average machine! For that matter, most of your friends, associates, and acquaintances are likely in the same boat. From your point of view, nobody uses that lousy two-year-old hardware. But in fact, that is *exactly* what most people are using. You should assume that low-end consumers are using five-year-old hardware, most consumers are using four-year-old hardware, most business users have three-year-old hardware, and software professionals have two-year-old hardware. You have to design your software to meet my timing requirements on the machine most commonly used by your particular audience.

Are there exceptions to this rule? Of course! Many are the times when a designer must sacrifice speed to attain some important feature. Breaking this rule does not make you an international interactivity criminal; it just makes your users less happy. If you think that the happiness they gain from the feature in question exceeds the irritation they'll feel at the delay, go ahead. Just remember that the irritating effects of long delays are cumulative and synergistic; you can bend the rules once or twice, but any more risks the customer's ire.

A common error made in this regard arises from the cover-your-ass attitude so common in business. We always seem to concentrate our energies on preventing the complainable rather than achieving the best. Feature deficiency is explicitly complainable; sluggish interaction is not. In other words, if your design lacks some gold-plated feature, you can be certain that somebody, somewhere, will complain about the deficiency. On the other hand, if your design is merely sluggish (as the direct result of adding so many features), people will be less likely to pin the blame on you; besides, you can always defend yourself with the old "Get a faster machine!" rejoinder. This is one reason why so many interactivity designs are feature rich and speed poor.

How to Speed Things Up

There is no software that can't be made to run faster. All software requires some combination of three fundamental resources: memory, execution time, and the sweat of the programmers. You can always reduce one of these three by increasing the allocation of the other two. Thus, the easiest and quickest speed boosts are obtained by grabbing more RAM. Turn off virtual memory on your machine and replace it with the real stuff; then watch how much faster those big programs run. Unfortunately, if your program eats up all the free RAM in the computer, other programs can't run—a major pain for your users. Tradeoffs, tradeoffs!

You can also give your programmers a few extra months to tighten up the code; they can often wring a substantial speed improvement out of the program with a few months' work. But the biggest gains are always obtained by redesigning the laggard feature itself. Zero in on the place where the program runs too slowly; why is it running so slowly?

For example, I ran into a nasty problem while designing the Erasmatron. The decision script display took too long to draw. There were two levels to tackle the problem: the programming level and the design level. Since I wore both hats, I pursued both avenues simultaneously. With my programmer hat on, I found that the largest delays arose from my need to perform a series of independent calculations for each and every word that appeared on the screen. In other words, I couldn't simply draw a long stream of text onto the screen—the program would draw one word and then go off to perform more computations, then come back and draw another word, and so forth. All those time-consuming computations between the words were necessary to support a variety of nifty-keen features I had built into the Erasmatron: the ability to click each word separately, different colors and fonts for different classes of words, and so forth. With my designer hat on, my choices were unpalatable: kill one or more of those features, or redesign the entire display structure. At this point, the best option was to throw more RAM at the problem.

Note that this decision required me to balance a design judgment against a programming judgment. Because I can both program and design, I made that decision inside my own head, and I am confident in its correctness. A designer who couldn't program would have to sit through several stormy meetings with the programmers to achieve the same results and would never be sure that he made the right decision. Who knows what those damn programmers are thinking?

Organize Verbs into Manageable Groups

You want to maximize the number of verbs in your software. Of course, you can't simply hurl 100 gazillion options at your user—there's not enough screen space. You need to organize all your verbs into usable groupings.

Often the nature of your design imposes its own structural groupings. A word processor has a number of verbs for laying out the basic page: margins, paper sizes, orientation, and so forth. Obviously, these verbs should be grouped together. Other verbs control the appearance of the individual characters: fonts, sizes, styles, and so on. Again, these provide an obvious basis for grouping.

However, there remain many situations where obvious groupings produce unwieldy numbers of entries. In this case, it is important to recognize the limits of human comprehension. People aren't computers; they can't handle too much input.

Please note that I'm talking about the number of choices at each juncture, not the total number of choices for the entire design. Your user wants to make her choices confident that her decision is sound. If you confront your user with 87 choices on a single screen, the user might well be swamped in indecision.

If the choices are already familiar to the user, then you can have more than you otherwise would. A word processor gives its user about a hundred choices in the keyboard input alone; that's a great many, but all users instantly understand the difference between a *k* and a *w*. Similarly, a stock market program might present the user with a long list of stock symbols from which to choose, but anybody using such a program would know what those symbols mean and so would have no problem choosing one symbol from the long list.

The more difficult the decisions facing the user, the fewer choices you must offer. Picking one stock from a long list is easy because the user already knows which one she wants. On the other hand, a house design program must explain some of the trickier decisions to the user, so it should break the process into a series of small, manageable steps. This situation calls for fewer decisions.

Here are some specific guidelines for organizing your verbs.

Prioritize Verbs by Frequency of Use

Not only must you group your verbs in a logical fashion; you must also prioritize them. Prioritization was not so important in the early days of software design, when the verb count was low. As programs have grown larger, however, the number of verbs they use has increased. Some of these verbs are heavily used, and others are rarely invoked. You want the most commonly used verbs to be immediately accessible, and you want to keep the rarely used verbs in the background, where they won't distract the user. Accessibility here is closely related to visual priority, but don't let that relationship dominate your thinking: putting the most important verbs in the main window and the rarer verbs in dialog boxes doesn't adequately address the problem.

A more useful way to think about the problem is to recall the structure of Morse code. The most common letters are assigned short sequences; the rarer letters get longer, more difficult sequences. Thus, *e* is represented by a single dot, and *t* gets a single dash, but *q* gets dot-dot-dash-dot, and *x* gets dot-dash-dot-dot. You want to lay out your verbs in an analogous fashion.

You have a great variety of devices for segregating verbs by priority; here's a rough sequence in order of accessibility:

- Click or keystroke directly on data
- Double-click directly on data
- Click and drag directly on data
- Click a gizmo (button, check box, and so on) in main window
- Click-keydown or keydown-click directly on data
- Select an immediately executed menu item
- Activate a background window and click directly on its data
- Activate a background window and use one of its controls
- Raise and operate a single dialog box
- Raise and operate a tabbed dialog box
- Raise and operate nested dialog boxes

This list is not exhaustive; there are many more such arrangements. My purpose is to illustrate the concept of accessibility, which is a combination of factors: the number of mouse clicks or keystrokes required to execute the verb, the degree of mental indirection required to access it (operating directly on the data versus using an indirect icon or menu item), and the degree of care required to carry out these steps (seeking the correct window on a crowded screen). If your design uses but few verbs, then you can concentrate them in the upper layers of this sequence. But if you offer a rich and complex verb set, then you must evenly distribute your verbs through this sequence. If a disproportionate number of verbs are clustered in a single level of accessibility, then the design will be cumbersome.

There is also the possibility of inviting your user to set the priorities. This is done with button bars with editable contents. One user can dump that silly drawing icon that he never uses anyway, while another user can include that special font button that's so useful.

Be Square

Suppose you were asked to design a website presenting the collected works of a renowned painter. Suppose also that there are about 350 works. How would you set up user navigation to them? You could, of course, offer several indexes: an alphabetical index by title, or perhaps a list sorted by creation date. But surely many of your users won't recall the title of a painting they want to see, or know its date. How do you help them find it?

Let's suppose now that you decide to organize the paintings in a two-layered tree based on their content. For example, you might come up with the following organization:

Upper Layer

Living Things

Nonliving Things

Lower Layer

Living Things	**Nonliving Things**
Cats	Clouds
Flowers	Mountains
Portraits of men	Houses
Portraits of women	Seashore
Groups of people	Furniture
Trees	Fields
Horses	Ships

This might seem like a logical grouping of the paintings, but there's a hitch: you'll need to stock each of those categories with 25 paintings. Sure, you made the first choice easy (Living Things versus Nonliving Things), and the second choice pretty reasonable, but the third choice is hell. To fit all those thumbnails onto one screen, you're going to have to make them tiny.

You could, of course, break down each of the lower categories into two smaller categories, so that each thumbnail menu holds only 12 images, but that would probably be the wrong solution. The better solution is to look at the upper layer: it has only two choices; you're giving your user too few choices, followed by too many. Suppose that instead you organized your tree like so:

Top Layer

Animals (previously Cats and Horses)

Plants (previously Flowers and Trees)

People (previously the two portraits and Groups of people)

Sea (previously Seashore and Ships)

Domestic (previously Houses and Furniture)

Landscapes (previously Clouds and Mountains)

Fields

Second Layer

Animals	Plants	People
Cats sleeping	Mostly yellow flowers	Portraits of bearded men
Cats playing	Mostly red flowers	Portraits of clean-shaven men
Cats eating	Mostly blue flowers	Portraits of young women
Cats fighting	Multicolored arrangements	Portraits of old women
Farm horses	Single oaks	Big crowds
Running horses	Groups of oaks	Small groups inside
Dead horses	All other trees	Small groups outside

And so on with the other four categories. Here's what's important about this structure: It has seven upper layers and seven lower layers, and each of those lower screens contains seven thumbnails. This is a perfectly square structure; it has the same number of choices at each layer. It can be diagrammed thus:

7:7:7

The first structure, on the other hand, would be:

2:7:25

To be perfectly square, all the numbers must be the same.

This, of course, is theory, and anybody who applies it strictly is guilty of numerology. There are many reasons to violate this guideline. First, it is almost impossible to come up with a breakdown that's so neat and tidy. If, for example, you were required to assemble a website with the collected works of four different painters, your upper layer would surely be the four painters. Now suppose that painter number 2 has 4,073 paintings to be cataloged, and painter number

3 has only 116. There's no way you can get that structure square; it's necessarily lopsided because the painters' portfolios are lopsided.

Another time to chuck this guideline is when one or more of the layers present choices so simple that it's desirable to have many more than seven choices in the layer. Suppose, for example, you are designing a website presenting maps of every major city on the planet. You'd probably want to set up the first layer by continent, the second layer by country, and the third layer by city. The first layer will have only six choices, but some of the pages in the second layer will have several dozen choices. That's not square, but it makes more sense.

Temporal Squareness

There's an additional dimension to consider here: the sequence of steps that the user makes to reach his goal. For example, my examples above presented two arrangements of the paintings: 7:7:7 and 2:7:25. But why must we restrict our design to just three steps? We could just as easily have broken it down into something like 3:5:5:5 or even 3:3:3:3:4:2. In these cases, the structure uses more steps (from the user's point of view) or more layers (from your point of view). Are more steps better? That depends on several factors. The first is the delay time between steps. If your program can present each step lightning fast, then perhaps using more steps is better. But if, for example, you're designing a website, then you definitely don't want lots of steps, because each page takes time to download; you want to minimize the number of steps your user must endure. However, if you have gazillions of options to present, then you have no easy options. This is where the rule of squareness is most applicable.

Game designers face much the same dilemma with turn-sequenced (non-realtime) games, but in their case it's a question of how many verbs they want to give their players versus how many turns they want the game to take. Fewer verbs demand more turns to achieve richness; this, in turn, makes playtest balancing more difficult. There are no free lunches.

These three guidelines for organizing your verb set (manageable grouping, prioritization by frequency of use, and squareness) offer completely different desiderata for the same task; thus, they often conflict. It is simply not possible to organize a large verb set that satisfies all three criteria perfectly. I can offer no guidance in resolving conflicts between the criteria; you must exercise your own judgment in this matter.

Design the Loop as a Whole

In a later chapter, I recommend that the development process be broken down into separate listening, thinking, and speaking efforts. While this is a natural cleavage, it must not erect walls between the three efforts. Inevitably, a feature in one of the three sectors proves impossible to implement. Try as they may, the listening designers just can't come up with a clean input system for a certain feature; or the thinking algorithms for another feature require megabytes of RAM; or the display requirements of a third feature requires three CDs. Some designers try to bull their way past these problems. A more constructive alternative is available: alter the other components of the loop to absorb or compensate for correcting the problem. If you can't come up with a clean and simple verb to activate a feature, perhaps you can use a thinking algorithm to anticipate the user's desire for the feature or perhaps infer the command from some simpler user input. Perhaps the program can be made smart enough to obviate the need for the verb. Perhaps a more expressive screen display can get the user past the problem. Likewise, a tough output problem can sometimes be sidestepped with more expressive input structures; after all, the user may not need so much information if she can exercise more direct control.

This may seem to contradict my earlier warning that you cannot compensate for poor design in one factor by executing better design in another. But here I am recommending correction, not compensation. If your listening structure is badly designed, slapping some irrelevant graphics into the product won't do any good. If you're willing to expend considerable amounts of creative sweat, it is sometimes possible to correct a problem in one sector with a corresponding adjustment in another sector.

Here's a pedestrian example: I used icons overmuch in one of my designs. I realized that the icons had become too complicated for a user to comprehend easily. This was a serious problem with my talking language. I solved it by shifting the problem into the listening sector: I added a feature that popped up a short translation of the icon's meaning if the user held down the button over the icon for longer than a second. This was back in 1987, but the idea was so good that it is now standard (and called *tooltips*) in a great many programs, but with a big improvement: the requirement of the mouse click has been eliminated. If the cursor hovers over an icon for more than a few seconds, a quick pop-up microwindow provides a phrase of descriptive information.

Here's a more practical example: Suppose that you're designing a gargantuan website and are deeply concerned about the number of steps users are required to take to navigate through the morass. You might be able to apply some more thinking to reduce the difficulties your listening part faces. For example, perhaps you could ask your user for a keyword or two that might help zero in on the destination. A search facility takes more thinking than a simple linked tree. It might also be possible to analyze the user's previous history in navigating the tree to divine his likely next goal. If he always goes to the price page for a product before the sales pitch page, perhaps you should take him to the price page automatically, or even present lists of prices for any product class he seems interested in. In all of these cases, you are correcting a problem in the listening phase through the expenditure of more thinking resources.

The one phase that cannot be saved by extra work on the others is the thinking phase. The algorithms, after all, are the meat of the product, the delivered content that makes it valuable to the user. If you don't have enough meat to offer, dressing it up in a snazzy bun won't help matters.

Don't Set Up False Expectations

Featuritis is the uncontrollable urge to slap too many features onto a design. All beginning designers suffer from featuritis, and some never shake the disease. The reasoning is usually "if one feature is good, then ten must be better!" Some of the blame for this stupidity must be placed on those marketing people who perceive competitive marketing as trench warfare with features—God favors the side with the bigger bullet lists. Additional features are never unalloyed benefits;

every new feature interacts with all the other features in complicated ways. The feature interaction inside the program is bad enough—programmers will tell you how often a stable program can blow sky high with the addition of just one little improvement.

Here's a simple example of what I mean. I was designing the Erasmatron, a big, complicated program. There was one variable that showed up in many places in the program. I had originally intended the variable to be defined and modified at a single place in the program. But my tester pointed out that she was constantly modifying this variable, and bouncing back and forth from her workplace to the editing place was a pain in the butt, so I dutifully arranged to make the variable editable anywhere in the program. All seemed well until months later, when somebody chose to edit the variable at a particularly obscure and unexpected location in the program. The variable changed, but a control on the displayed window affected by its value didn't change along with it. This in turn led to the program's crashing when the user accessed that un-updated item. Correcting the problem turned out to be a huge headache.

Of course, in this case, I wasn't adding a new feature but correcting a design mistake I had made earlier, so don't shed any tears for me. But remember that little changes can often trigger big problems.

But there's another, even more dangerous place where features interact: inside your user's mind. Every feature you add creates expectations in the user's mind. Those expectations might not seem logical to you, but then, you have the entire design inside your head. Your user has a weaker grasp of the design's intricacies; the crucial truth that would disabuse her of an illogical expectation might not be known to her. Thus, you must always be careful to consider all the possible expectations a new feature might engender in your user's mind. A feature that sets up false expectations will justly earn your user's ire.

There aren't any examples from the world of real software that I can draw your attention to, because these problems are always caught in testing. Here's a hypothetical example: Suppose that you're designing a word processor and are tackling the footer facility. You figure that editing a footer is just like editing any other text, so you set up the footer editor to be a special case of normal text editing, with all the usual gewgaws such as variable font sizes, margins, paragraph styles, and so forth. How clever of you! And then one day one of your users decides to enter a page break inside a footer. What happens? Well, a page break requires a new page, which in turn requires another footer, which inserts a new page, which requires a new footer. . . . Oops!

Remember that all features interact, both inside the program and inside your user's head. As your program grows, the number of interactions increases geometrically.

Say What You Mean

Back in the bad old days, we were stuck with little tiny screen displays that couldn't hold much information. We learned to conserve screen space. One of our most useful tricks was compressing textual messages. This often took the frm of cntrctns, but we also learned cntrct sntcs. Worked. Saved space. More done. Happy.

Nowadays, the pressure for screen space has decreased a bit. Our screens are bigger, and we have learned new tricks for squeezing more function out of available screen space, such as pop-up devices. But old habits stick to our boots like donkey doo, and we stubbornly retain the habits of yesteryear. Whenever we close a document, we are asked if we want to save it. Some programs ask, "Save changes to *filename* before closing?" and give us the choice of Yes, No, or Cancel. This dialog is unnecessarily terse. The subject of the verb *Save* is not specified; this creates a tiny confusion over who is to do the saving. Is the user expected to do additional work to effect the saving process, or is the computer asking whether it should perform that labor? Most of us, long experienced in the ways of computers, already know the answer to that question, but to a neophyte, the question requires some additional effort to understand, effort that would be unnecessary if the designer had bothered to say, "Should I save the changes to *filename* before closing?" Most old pros will dismiss this as nitpicking, but hell, I cld sv a few cnts wrth ppr by elmntng rdndnt lttrs frm my wrtng, & it tks U jst lttl mr wrk 2 fgr out, rgt? How much work are you willing to do to ensure that your user gets your message clearly?

A second problem with the cited wording is that the choices available to the user are not nailed down as solidly as they could be. Letting the user choose Yes or No requires him to go through the additional mental step of relating the answer to the question. The response would be clearer if the buttons read "Save these changes" and "Don't save these changes."

While each individual manifestation of this problem is itself quite petty in impact, the overall effect of ubiquitous excessive succinctness surely slows down a user. The problem may be small, but the solution is smaller still. So just fix it!

Speak with One Voice in Five Tones

Back in the good old days when dialog boxes first came out, we ancients all thought they were the bee's knees. Of course, there might be only a dozen such dialog boxes in a typical design back then. Nowadays, most applications have at least a hundred. Some are big; some are small. Some are colored; some aren't. Some are centered on the screen; others appear in the upper-left corner. Some are big boxes with tabbed interiors; others are cute little things with a single button. Some are modal; some are nonmodal. It's a hodgepodge.

Remember: whenever a technology expands, it changes in ways that often require a qualitative change in approach. Such is the case with all those dialog boxes. This chattering tribe of dialog boxes has become cacophonous; it's time to bring some order to the chaos.

All screen windows can be fit into five simple categories.

Primary Data Windows

These are the main windows of the application, the places in which the user spends most of her time. They hold the information that the user is most interested in. In a browser, it's the page display window; in a word processor, it's the window containing the user's text. This is the primary window around which all the other windows, dialog boxes, and alerts orbit.

Progress Reports

These contain progress bars and other messages informing the user of ongoing events. Some applications provide this information in a little bar at the bottom of the screen (for example, "Contacting www.erasmatazz.com"). Others put it in a special progress box that shows a progress bar with an estimate of how much time remains in the process. Another variation on this basic class is the initializing splash screen, which often shows, in fine print at the bottom, what program modules are being loaded and initialized.

"I Screwed Up"

This is my term for a variety of dialog boxes describing error conditions. Remember that the customer is always right; he cannot make an error. If an error arises, the only person to take the blame is you. Therefore, every error condition is really the result of a programming or design error and should be presented as such. Tell the user exactly how the program failed and what can be done about it. If possible, give the user a choice of recovery strategies, but don't paralyze him with an overly technical choice. If you have a division-by-zero error, don't give the user the option to proceed with the calculation using the highest value supported by the word size; most people won't have any idea of the implications of such a decision. If the decision is too tricky to make, then make the safest decision for the user, advise him of the damage done, and urge him to save the document and examine it closely. And tell him *where* to look for problems! Your software can't recognize an error without also recognizing its location in the user's work, so go to the small extra effort to specify that location.

"I Can't Handle That"

These replace the rude "Too many farburgles" messages that maculate so many programs. There will always be situations where the user attempts something beyond the specifications of your design. Telling her that she has violated the design specs is not the way to win a customer's heart. When the user wants to do more than you can do, tell her so. Explain the limitation. Suggest workarounds. Request that the user notify you of her experience; if she has bumped her head against this ceiling, you want to know about it so that you can raise the ceiling on the next release of the software.

"I Need More Information"

All programs have plenty of these types of message. Some are the standard information-requesting dialog boxes such as "File name to save document under?" or "How many copies to print?" They also replace all those rude error messages that tell the user that he has failed to establish some item of context needed to carry out the command. Instead of impugning the user's competence with a message like, "You haven't selected a printer to print with." it's better to announce, "I need more information to carry out your command: on which printer should I print this document?"

These five fundamental message types can handle just about every situation you encounter with your user. Here is how I implemented the latter four:

I need more information

 Should I save the storyworld before quitting?

[Never mind; don't quit]　[Don't save it]　[Save it]

I can't handle that

 I can't cope with more than 2,047 verbs; we never thought anybody would need that many.

[OK]

Progress Report

 I am running the story engine now.

[Stop running the story engine]

I screwed up

The script for this role includes a garbage token:

Verb:role

The only recourse at this point is to reset the role script, which will lose all your work on the script itself. Sorry about that.

[Shoot the programmer!]

The uniformity of style is an important attribute of this approach. Each message window has a unique color and a standard title. Each has a face on the left side; in the final implementation, that face communicates the emotional tone of the message. This instantly communicates to the user the expectation placed on him:

I need more information: The user must answer a few questions or fill in some text.

I can't handle that: The user must scale down his expectations of the program.

Progress report: The user should wait or should cancel the action in progress.

I screwed up: The user is in trouble, but it's not his fault and there's little he can do.

Don't Describe the Problem—Offer the Solution

One dark day I encountered this error message:

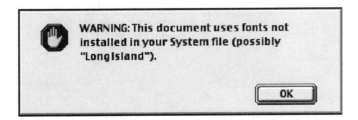

This message is presented upon opening a word processing document. It describes the problem quite clearly, but it doesn't give any inkling as to how I might correct it. It seems to suggest that I could solve the problem by installing the "Long Island" font in my System file—but what if I don't have that font? What I need is to locate the text that uses that font and change it to another font—but the program doesn't give any hint as to how I might accomplish that, eliciting from me a plethora of erudite imprecations.

Here's another example of a truly idiotic error message:

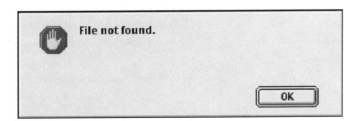

OK, Software Designer; so you couldn't find a file you needed. I'd be glad to try to find it in my archives somewhere, if only you'd tell me what it is. But no! You prefer to bitch and moan without doing anything constructive. And then you ask me to dismiss it by saying OK. It is *not* OK!

It's acceptable to explain to the user the nature of the problem, but that is secondary information. The whole point and purpose of any communication with the user should be to advance her efforts. These should both have been treated as "I screwed up" messages; the designer erred in making the program's function dependent on fonts or files that might not be present and then not providing automatic recovery. The first message should then have looked like this:

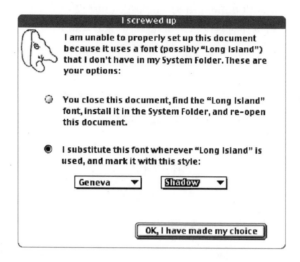

This is how the second message should have looked:

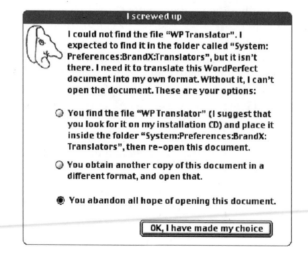

Isn't this a much better approach?

Design the verbs first. Be on guard against the egotistical tendency to speak. Keep it fast. Organize options in manageable groups. Prioritize options by frequency of use. Be square. Design the loop as a whole. Don't set up false expectations. Say what you mean. Speak with one voice in five tones. Don't describe the problem—offer the solution.

9

ANTHROPOMORPHIZATION

The time has come for software designers to accept the necessity of anthropomorphization. While the means to execute anthropomorphization may be marginally adequate, the complexity of software demands it, and the imminent arrival of voice technology adds urgency to the demand.

With Whom Does the User Interact?

Anthropomorphizing computers has always been a sure source of amusement. Remember the old *Star Trek* episodes where Captain Kirk talked his way out of computer-induced jams by confusing the computer with logical conundrums that caused it to spew smoke out its ears and break down? Nowadays, we're not so scared of computers, and many professionals look askance at anthropomorphizing them—it invests them with hidden powers that they don't possess. It's not a person; it's just a machine acting out its algorithms. Talking to it as if it were a person implies that the speaker doesn't understand those simple-minded algorithms and is therefore a worthless, disgusting beginner. The better people don't talk that way.

I'd like to turn the tables on those people who reject anthropormorphization by suggesting that they are doing the reverse: objectifying what is innately a human interaction. The person using your software is interacting with *you*, not the computer. Consider, for example, just whom you converse with on the telephone. Strictly speaking, you're not talking with another human being; you are speaking to a microphone and listening to a speaker, machines both. Those machines are in turn communicating by means of complex digital algorithms with some machines that your interlocutor is speaking and listening to. Yet, while the interaction may technically be carried out with machines, we all recognize the deeper truth that we are, in fact, interacting with another person when we use the telephone.

The same principle is at work when we use a computer. The only substantial difference between the telephone conversation and the computer interaction is the level of abstraction in the communication. The software designer does not provide the specifics of the interaction, but the rules under which those specifics are determined. The fact of abstraction does not alter the underlying reality: the user is interacting with the designer.

If you are confused by this notion that abstraction doesn't alter then substance of the interaction, consider the following analogy. Suppose that you live in a dictatorship that has outlawed, say, the playing of computer games. One day the police burst into your home and catch you playing a computer game. They drag you off to jail. Whom do you blame: the police who actually put you in jail, or the dictator who made the rules under which you were dragged off to jail?

Recognizing your true role as designer makes it easier to visualize the nature of your relationship with your user. You are imprisoned inside the computer, unable to see or hear her. You can hear only her keystrokes and mouse clicks; you can speak to her only by means of video images and sound effects. Much cleverness will be required for you to carry out a successful interaction with your user. Just don't ever forget: the user is interacting with *your* algorithms, *your* ideas—with *you*.

Every Day, In Every Way, Ever More Human

There can be no question that, at some point in the future, we will talk to computers as if they were human, so we might as well get started on the problem now. Indeed, the rapid development of voice technology—both voice recognition and voice synthesis—will soon force our hands. The entire collective experience of the human race does not include a single instance of a person talking successfully with a machine. We talk to people, and only to people, and when we *do* start talking to our machines, it will be impossible to outgrow the feeling that we're talking to another person. Moreover, the brutal truth is that software has already become too complicated for most people to understand. Those "simple algorithms" aren't so simple anymore, and we need to give our users some sort of mental model they can grasp in wrestling with our software. Since our users happen to understand human behavior rather well, we should use what they can understand, not what is convenient to us. The current term we use for this strategy is *agent*. A bit of comic software history communicates the idea:

System crash   Error message   Help system   Agent

Agents are souped-up help systems dressed up to look and act like people. Most designers recognize that this puts a more human face on the computer's interface. But the true benefit of the agent is not the appearance, but the metaphor. Use of an agent implies a human mode of communication. We expect to talk to machines by pushing buttons or turning dials. We expect them to be stupid. The term *agent*, however, suggests that we can talk to this entity by normal human means. This expectation feeds back to the designer, who realizes that the conventions of machine interaction—buttons, dials, and the like—must be jettisoned for human conventions: talking, listening, and thinking. This much is good. The problem is, how far should we go in this process of anthropomorphizing our interface?

The design problems of anthropomorphization should give any competent designer the willies. The truth is, we are nowhere near smart enough to create any decent semblance of a person in software. Any human face we put on our software will surely be a fake, a mask that could all too easily slip off, revealing the true nature of the software in all its ugliness. We won't get away with saying, "Pay no attention to the machine behind the curtain!" The customers will see through our pretension, and that can only hurt our relationship with them.

My solution may seem insanely contradictory: pseudo-anthropomorphization. We present our users with "characters" possessing some small degree of humanity, but the characters are represented by imagery that clearly communicates the limited nature of that personality. The worst possible approach was taken by Apple some years ago when it presented a vision of the future showing an agent popping up in the corner of the screen, offering help to the user. The agent was represented by video clips of a real human being speaking in normal, full-featured English. This probably is close to what we'll have in the future—the far future. For the present, we have to live with agents that are dumber than a doornail.

This approach backfires badly when the speaking part of the agent is much better developed than the listening and thinking parts. Hearken back to Chapter 8, with its warnings about not concentrating on the speaking part. Most agents these days do little more than talk at the user. A little head pops up and announces, "Hi! I'm Agnes, your agent! I'm here to make things so much easier for you! Just listen carefully, and I'll tell you what to do." At which point, we get a talking version of the user manual. Whoop-de-doo.

If you're going to create an agent, then by God, create an agent—not a multimedia user manual. Endow it with ears and a brain! If you can give it only tricycle ears and a tricycle brain, then don't give it a Formula One face and turbocharged talking. A user who sees and hears a normal human being on the screen has every right to expect that it can listen and think like a normal human being, an expectation that turns out to be false. In other words, all that snazzy facial animation and voice synthesis only serves to set up false expectations if it isn't backed up with equally snazzy listening and thinking.

If your agent's listening and thinking are lousy, then use a stick man squeaking in a cartoonish voice. Better yet, emphasize his stupidity by using text instead of voice synthesis, and write the text in third-grade English. Microsoft was on the right track using a paper clip as an agent; the highly cartoonish nature of the image suggests the low level of intelligence in the agent. Unfortunately, the level of intelligence that they gave Mr. Clippie is even lower than what we would expect of a talking paperclip, so the end result is still displeasing to many users.

Use First and Second Person and Active Voice

I don't know why technical people insist on using third person and passive voice in their writing; it's so dehumanizing. Perhaps it's because some of them are self-dehumanized. In any case, 9 out of 10 experts agree: passive voice sucks, and third person is weak. Although these admonitions are given for writing, they apply just as forcefully to software. When you need to tell your user something, you should use first person for the program and second person for the user. Don't say, "File not found"; say "I can't find that file." Don't say, "Number out of range"; say "The number you typed in is too big to use here." (Actually, it would be better to use a scrollbar in this case and prevent the problem from arising in the first place.)

Be Just as Courteous as You Would Be in Public

Actually, this admonition to be courteous applies only if you're a normal human being. If you're one of those troglodytes who sleeps on a cot in your office, then perhaps you should be as courteous as someone *else* would be. In any case, software these days is just plain rude. Imagine an interchange with a waiter operating under software rules of courtesy:

You:	Good evening, garcon!
Waiter:	[Silence]
You:	So, um, is the salmon fresh tonight?
Waiter:	Salmon Capture Time = 16:33 8/11/00.
You:	Okay, I suppose that I'll go with the salmon; but could I have a half-serving?
Waiter:	Invalid number.
You:	Very well; then I'll have the sirloin steak.
Waiter:	Select one: mashed potatoes, rice.
You:	Could I get some french fries instead?
Waiter:	Select one: mashed potatoes, rice.
You	All right then; I'll have neither!
Waiter:	Select one: mashed potatoes, rice.
You	Okay, okay; I'll take the mashed potatoes! Could I get some rosé wine with that?
Waiter:	[Walks away]
You:	Waiter? Waiter?
Waiter:	[Returns] Wine not found.

I ask you, how large a tip would you leave for this waiter? Aren't you glad that software designers don't depend on tips for a living?

And it certainly wouldn't hurt to say "Please" and "Thank you." If a four-year-old can learn to do so, why can't a $500 program?

Use Normal English, Not Your Own Terminology

How many times has a program given you a message referring to something you never heard of? This can sometimes be unavoidable, as when a word processor takes pains to tell you about a problem with a *section* instead of a *paragraph* (and you don't know the difference). But dialog boxes these days are plagued with far too much techie talk and not enough plain English. And, as I warned in Chapter 8, try to avoid overly terse messages.

Don't Feign Infallibility

Have you ever encountered a software error message that apologized for—or even admitted—a mistake? Software is always quick to tell you what you did wrong, but it never seems to admit the possibility that it did anything wrong. In the real world, a person who always blames everybody else and never accepts responsibility for his own mistakes is quickly ostracized. But I have *never* seen a program big enough to admit that it made a mistake. And that certainly isn't because software is infallible. At any given moment, the publisher of any popular program will have a list of error reports containing hundreds, if not thousands, of errors. If software isn't fallible, how come you almost never see a version 5.0.0 of anything? It's always 5.0.3 or 5.1.7. Everybody who uses computers knows full well just how fallible they are. So how come nobody ever admits it?

Some programmers will claim that, as soon as they know the problem, they fix it. If they can recognize the problem, why waste time putting in apologies—it's better to just fix it. I suppose that there are some young programmers who actually believe this nonsense, but no old salt will stand behind such claims. Any reasonably interesting piece of software is chock full of bugs and problems; by the time a program has been cleaned up to the point of being truly bug free, it is most certainly obsolete. Indeed, programmers themselves recognize the fallibility of their work whenever they place an assert statement into their code. This statement declares something that the programmer expects to be true, and if it turns out not to be the case, the program can tell the programmer about the problem instead of crashing. Any place in the code that has an assert statement should also have an apologetic message to the user. The "I Screwed Up" and "I Can't Handle That" standard messages presented in Chapter 8 are ideal for this task.

Conclusion

It may be true that the "better" people don't anthropomorphize their computers, but normal people do. My wife uses AOL (a product for people who are normal, not better), and whenever she signs off, it says, "Goodbye," and like any normal person, she reciprocates with a "Goodbye" of her own. My neighbor with a Ph.D. in electrical engineering talks to his computer in the second person, especially when it doesn't do what he wants it to do. Incorrect it may be, even stupid—but it's what your users are doing, so you might as well use this behavior to your advantage rather than resist it. And if you refuse to be swayed by the ignorant superstitions of the rabble, here's the clinching argument: they do it on *Star Trek*.

Anthropomorphization raises many new and difficult issues, but the first steps in that direction are simple and obvious: use first and second person and active voice, be just as courteous as you would be in public, use normal English, and don't feign infallibility.

10

BLOOPERS

There are as many ways to screw up interactivity design as there are designers. Herewith some howlers.

I'm going to have some good mudslinging fun in this chapter. I'll unleash my inner asshole and vent spleen on design blunders. In the process, I'm sure you'll cheer as I demolish the bane of your digital existence, and gnash your teeth as I gore your favorite sacred ox.

Overloaded Web Pages

Let's start with an obvious clunker: web pages that take too long to download. This is a direct violation of the admonition in the previous chapter to "Keep it fast." Most website designers have long since learned that overloaded pages chase away users, but many of their clients have not. All too often the client demands snazzy graphics, and the designer, after advising against it, acquiesces.

One good compromise arises from the fact that most websites are designed as tree structures. You can make every effort to push the images further down the structure, as far away from the trunk as you can. Thus, the pages that are merely middlemen between the index page and the various information delivery pages can be reduced to simple, fast layouts. The client still gets the satisfaction of knowing that those glorious images showing the product in 16 million colors will still be included—and the user spends less time sitting around waiting.

Video

We have now established beyond all doubt that we can play back video on a computer screen. Whoop-de-doo! Now the question is, so what? Video is anti-interactive; while it's playing, the user is necessarily sitting on his butt, doing nothing. True, video is always stimulating, and it sometimes perks up a dull topic—but we're designing interaction, not video. If your goal is to smear lots of information all over your user's face, you can accomplish this task much better with plain old noncomputer video. Make a videotape! Why should a user drum his fingers while umpty-zillion bytes amounting to a snippet of video dribble down the wire into his computer? In the time it takes to download some of the video on the web, a user can walk to the nearest fast food joint, flip burgers for long enough to earn a few bucks, walk to the video store, use the money earned to rent a videotape with two hours of full-screen, full-motion video, and walk home. That videotape will present him with a video experience superior to anything he can download from the Web. So why do designers waste so much time and money doing video badly when they could be doing interactivity well?

Perhaps you object that the current generation is a TV generation; it was raised on video, it lives, breathes, and thinks video. This is all true, but interactivity is a new medium, just as video was once a new medium. The old fuddy-duddies exerted a braking influence on the maturation of video, but the kids embraced the new form and propelled it forward. Now it's video's turn; the video fuddy-duddies are trying to hold back interactivity by treating it as just a computerized form of video. To the barricades, citizens!

Stupid Thinking

I was using ScanDisk this morning to check my hard drive. It found a tiny problem with a file: its name was too long to be used in DOS. Since I have no interest whatever in raising DOS from the grave to terrorize the world again, I don't care about this problem and told the computer to ignore it. So ScanDisk went off to look at other files and—lo!—it found another file with the same problem. I again told it to ignore the problem. Then came another, and another, and another, until I was reduced to hitting the Enter key frantically, hoping to Gates that there weren't three thousand such files on my hard drive. I was lucky; it took only about a hundred keystrokes. Unfortunately, the last keystroke dismissed the final dialog box telling me the results of the test, so I don't know if ScanDisk approved of my hard drive. I'm sure not going to try that program again!

This is an example of stupid thinking. The designer of the program decided that, if a problem arises, the user should be notified and given a choice as to how to handle it. However, the designer failed to think deeply enough about the problem: what if there are more than a score of instances of a minor problem, all of them to be dealt with in the same way? Clearly, if a human being had asked me ten times about whether I wanted the same minor correction made, I would interrupt him on the tenth query with an angry order to ignore *all* of the damn things. And it's not as if the computer doesn't have enough native intelligence to count. That designer could easily have added some common-sense algorithms that allow a user to short-circuit this kind of nonsense, but he never bothered.

Here's an older example from the Macintosh world: the designers of the Macintosh operating system equipped it with a highly intelligent system for managing big programs. This Memory Manager was even smart enough to know that some resources were not in memory, but stored on a hard disk or a floppy disk. And it was even smart enough to recognize the absence of the required floppy disk, eject the currently inserted floppy, and request the required floppy. That's impressive! Unfortunately, the design had a fatal flaw. In many cases, a program would require resources from both the system file and the application file. The system file resided on the system floppy, and the application file resided on the application floppy. Thus, when you started a program, you might be confronted with a long sequence of disk-insertion requests. "Now I want the system disk," "Now I want the application disk," "Now I want the system disk." I once counted the number of swaps I carried out in this notorious floppy shuffle; it came to 65 disk insertions. That was stupid. Some additional thought on the part of the designer would have created some algorithms to either group all the resource acquisition together or warn me of what I was getting myself into.

Secret Icons

Some designers go nuts with icons, scattering them about like dandelions. I have here a collection of icons lifted from a variety of programs. I don't know what any of these icons mean, so I have provided my own interpretations:

 I can't figure this out. Is that a clothespin holding a scrap of paper?

 A video snippet?

 This is obviously important. Something is going somewhere. What and where, I cannot guess.

 Keep your eye on this folder?

 Duck? Should I migrate? Are you telling me I'm a quack?

 Learn your ABCs? Swirl letters around? Superimpose letters?

 Aha! I recognize this! It's an Apple II!

 Uh-oh. There's no such thing as an Apple I . . . .

This shows just how arbitrary icons can be. All three of these icons mean the same thing: they refer to program plug-ins.

 This is bad! Use of a visually nonsensical image suggests that the function is nonsensical. Who wants to use something that's nonsensical?

Last, we have an exercise in absurdity: the text icons. For some reason, the designer could not bear to simply use a label; that would have been too obvious. No; to be high-tech, the function had to have an icon. So the designer simply wrote the text inside the icon:

UU
(ICK)

BLAH
BLAH
BLAH

Some people defend icons by pointing out that they make more sense in color, and in fact most icons are easier to understand when rendered in color. I chose these icons because they're just as ridiculous in color as they are in black and white. Other people argue that icons should be considered only in the context in which they are used, and that many do, in fact, make more sense in context. But this is a circular argument: once you know what everything means, then you know what the icon means. So how do you learn what things mean in the first place? Does this line of argument boil down to RTFM? Moreover, invoking context as a defense doesn't change the fact that the icon is intrinsically confusing. Read, for example, this sentence:

"Fredegund's sensational test score made her daktylodeiktous all over campus, but not beyond its walls."

The context of this sentence helps you understand the word "daktylodeiktous," but does that make my use of the word appropriate or useful?

Alan Cooper, in his daktylodeiktous-worthy book *About Face*, argues that icons used inside programs really need not make much sense; they are meaningless markers whose only function is to spatially locate a particular function. He therefore recommends that designers use icons frequently, so long as they are for experienced users only, as shorthand for commands that the users have already learned from the menus.

I have reservations about his argument. The first writing systems worked in the same fashion: there was a custom icon for each word, and the scribe had to know all the icons in the system in order to read and write. Inasmuch as the writing systems used several thousand icons, the entire system took several years to learn, and only a very few people learned to read and write. I checked six widely used applications and found that, all together, they sported 424 icons. Do you think that the average user can memorize the meanings of 424 icons?

Icons work well when they are either (a) visually suggestive or (b) few in number. None of the six applications I checked meet these criteria. So enough with the icons, already!

Delayed Response

Desperately seeking new ways to listen to their users using existing hardware, designers have often resorted to using delays as part of the input scheme. The length of time that a button is pushed down—or not pushed down—becomes a new word in its own right. For example, pushing the button for a fraction of a second means one command, but pushing and holding it down for several seconds means another command.

This is a very bad idea, for two reasons. First, there is absolutely no way that a user can guess this behavior. Nothing can be done to suggest it to the user. It can only be explained through the manual, and even then, it is almost impossible to remember. If the user has four buttons to push, how can she possibly recall which button performs which function when held down for an extended time? The clock radio on my (American-designed) car requires that one of its 13 buttons be held down for three seconds to set the clock; consequently, we never set the clock, even in response to the coming and going of Daylight Savings Time. It's easier to remember that the clock never reflects Daylight Savings Time.

The second flaw in this concept is that it defers response until after the button is released. When you first press down the button, the software doesn't know whether this will be a quick-click or a long-click, so it cannot take any action at all. It must wait until you release the button before it can decide what action to take. Therefore, when you first press the button, nothing happens—suggesting to you that perhaps the system is broken, or you didn't press hard enough, or that something else is wrong. You will likely respond to the apparent failure in a manner that sabotages the entire interaction.

Another form of delayed response is less objectionable: delayed response to inaction. This is the method used for tooltips. You simply leave the mouse motionless over an icon, and the tooltip pops up. This still suffers from both of the preceding flaws, but not so obnoxiously. Tooltips have now become so common that most people understand how they work. Still, the whole point of a tooltip is to help the beginner; how can we assume that the beginner already knows such a hidden feature?

Although the time delay used in presenting tooltips is unobjectionable, they do raise a more fundamental problem: in many cases, tooltips appear despite the user's never having asked for them. For example, AppleWorks has a standard toolbar on the left side of the screen; clicking an icon in the toolbar activates the indicated graphic tool. Unfortunately, leaving the mouse stationary over an icon triggers, after a one-second delay, the appearance of a help bubble. (You will recall that a help bubble is a larger, more verbose version of a tooltip.) Worse, the appearance of this help bubble is accompanied by a distracting cute sound effect rather like a smoochy kiss. I will not claim that it is impossible to disable this feature, but I certainly have been unable to discover how to do so.

This raises an interesting design problem. The tooltip is less objectionable when it appears uninvited, because it is tiny and quiet. Of course, its small size ensures that its overly terse explanation achieves little by way of explanation. The help bubble, on the other hand, provides space for a much more satisfying explanation, but its uninvited appearance is more obtrusive. How can we find a reasonable compromise between these competing problems? My answer is that the true problem lies in the fact that both features are uninvited in the first place. The user should get help only when she asks for it. The means for doing so should be the right mouse button, which is as yet underutilized. As I suggest elsewhere, the left button should handle user commands, and the right button should express user requests for information.

Habituation Violation

In Chapter 4, I wrote rapturously of the mouse as an input device with its own interactive loop nested inside the larger interactive loop of the application. I did not address the many demands arising from the tightness of this loop. This is not a primary concern for most interactivity designers, who will piggyback on whatever mouse arrangement is resident in the computer they design for. However, we must all be aware of the delicate ecology of the mouse–user interaction. To be successful, this interaction must insinuate itself into the lower regions of the user's brain. If the user must consciously move the mouse, calculating the motions in advance, then the interface loses its speed and fluidity. Mouse control at its best is an unconscious process for the user. Consequential to this is a certain user inflexibility with respect to mouse control. Our conscious processing can easily change in response to different circumstances, but unconscious processing is not so plastic. For example, all shoelace knots have a direction; some people make clockwise knots and some people make counterclockwise knots. I double-dog dare you to try to lace your shoes in the direction opposite to your normal pattern. I guarantee that you will be reduced to sputtering incompetence, unable to earn that monument of educational achievement, the I-can-tie-my-own-shoes silver star.

My own experience with this is in the use of the mouse in Windows 98. I am a long-time Macintosh user, and try as I may, I simply can't get that mouse to work right. I have fiddled with the adjustments for speed and acceleration, and no matter what combination I try, it just doesn't feel right. Consequently, my every interaction with my Windows machine is soured by the low-level irritation of a balky mouse. After an hour's work, I find an excuse to desist, and I'm cranky for the next few hours. I have developed a gut-level aversion to all things Microsoft, and it's all due to that damn mouse interface being "different."

The serious point for interactivity designers is that we must never underestimate the intensity of commitment that our users hold for the more established habits of their computing lives. Don't ever—*ever!*—mess with the dynamics of the user–mouse interaction. It doesn't matter if your method is superior; you're up against instinct, not reason. Don't push your luck.

This rule applies to all the other conventional elements of user interface. Don't mess with radio buttons, pushbuttons, scrollbars, scroll boxes, or any of the other standardized components of GUI user interfaces.

It's acceptable to experiment with augmentations of the standard components. For example, in one of my designs, I spiffed up a standard scroll box. It presented a long list of items in alphabetical order. Therefore, along the right edge of the scroll box, I placed a set of letters indicating where the scrollbar thumb should be placed to jump directly to that portion of the list. It looks like this:

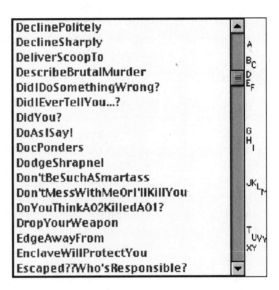

Now, I won't claim this to be a leap forward in user interface design; I'm not even sure that it's a good idea. But my innovation doesn't interfere with the conventional use of the scroll box, so it's a worthy experiment. If other designers like it, they'll copy it, and eventually it might become a standard. More likely, it will disappear into the fog of history.

Changing Things behind My Back

I once got into a battle with a photo-retouching program. In preparing a photo for printing, I clipped out a section of photo, scaled it up to full-page size, and then printed it—but it came out of the printer smaller than a postage stamp. Confused, I checked the size of the document; it had been changed behind my back! As it happens, the program keeps track of three factors that affect the image size: the image size in pixels, the scaling factor, and the resolution. The printed image size is the product of all three of these factors. Thus, there's an intrinsic ambiguity that arises when the user changes a single value. Suppose, for example, that I tell the program to double the image size. Does that mean that it should double the size of the image in pixels (turn a 640h-by-480v image into 1280h-by-960v)? Or should the program print the same number of pixels at a lower resolution (300 pixels per inch instead of 600 pixels per inch)? Both answers yield a final image that is twice as large physically, but they are quite different internally. If you read the documentation carefully, the distinction is made clear—but how many people read the documentation that closely? The better solution would have been to clearly show precisely what is meant in each of the various image size manipulations. Instead, the designers assume that the user understands their intentions and then adjust the image accordingly.

Another example: how many times have you gone to a menu and discovered that it wasn't what it used to be? There are three flavors of this treachery: deleted menu items, reworded menu items, and inexplicably dimmed items. The deleted items are the worst; you blink and ask yourself if your memory is defective. You browse through the other menus, certain that it is in there somewhere. After triple-checking every menu, you consult the manual, where you eventually find a reference to it, but the manual seems to think that the menu item is in menu X, and when you look there, it isn't! You glance over your shoulders, half expecting to see some prankster or poltergeist watching you. After much confusion, you throw up your hands and give up, deciding you'll just have to work around the problem. Half an hour later, while working on something completely different, you bring up the mysterious menu, and to your astonishment, there's the ghostly menu item! What gives?!!?

The villain in this scenario is the well-meaning but ignorant designer who desires to protect you from an overlong menu. The program is constantly shuffling menus around to provide you with only those menu items that are appropriate to the circumstances of the moment. This requires the poor user to keep track of not only *where* menu items are, but *when* they are. This is paternalism warped into fascism.

A kindler, gentler version of this is the reworded menu item. In many cases, the rewording is helpful; for example, a program I wrote alters menu text to refer to precisely what has been selected: the standard Cut command becomes Cut Role when a role is selected and Cut Verb when a verb is selected. Such clarifying additions are always helpful. However, if the rewording changes the nature of the command (for example, if Cut Verb became Paste Role), then the result is just as confusing as the disappearing menu item.

Last, there's the inexplicably dimmed menu item. This goof is universal in software design; I have already presented its solution in Chapter 5. Don't ever dim a menu item without explaining to the user why you have done so.

These problems arise when the designer fails to establish clear responsibility for some value or setting. It's a basic rule in management that making two people partially responsible for the same task is asking for trouble. They'll step on each other's toes; one will incorrectly assume that the other is taking care of the task; they'll point fingers at each other when problems emerge. The same thing happens in a program with poorly defined task responsibilities. In the photo-retouching program referred to earlier, the responsibility for setting the various parameters for the image size was split between the user and the program. Sometimes I get to control it, and sometimes the program gets to control it. This is stupid design. The default condition should always be a clear division of responsibility.

You can certainly take over responsibility for tedious, repetitive tasks—but get the user's (boss's) authorization first! Employees who assume responsibilities too minor for the boss's attention are showing initiative, but if they arrogate something that isn't minor, they get called on the carpet. And the determination of "minor" is not made by the employee (program); it is always made by the boss (user). You need not require authorization for every single instance (see the earlier discussion of ScanDisk); for a suitably concise set of instances, a single authorization at the outset is sufficient.

That's Not My Department

Then there are the designers who go to the opposite extreme: they break up the design into independent fiefdoms unaware of each other. A drawing program once baffled me by printing blank pages instead of my document. I figured there was something wrong with the relationship between program and printer, so I fiddled around with the Page Setup and Print settings, but to no avail. Out of options, I gave up. But a few days later, I came across something in a completely different area of the program. It was in the Format Document menu item, which raised a dialog box for specifying the height and width of the document. I had specified the document to be two pages high by two pages wide, but I had attempted to print the document at a size that required *four* pages high by four pages wide to operate properly. The program became confused and printed empty pages.

The designer's mistake here was an egregiously strict segregation of functions that are, in practice, closely related. Like the pig-headed bureaucrat who smugly refuses to help you because "that's not my department," the designer requires you to trudge from department to department, filling out all the forms in the proper sequence. All I want to do is print a lousy document; does it take an act of Congress?

The proper solution is to create user interface links between tasks that are operationally linked. Every specification related to printing should appear in (or be directly accessible from) a single location. Thus, the standard Print dialog box should include a button that pops up the Page Setup box, and another button that pops up the Document Format box. In programming terms, such changes are ridiculously simple to implement. The problem is not with the programmers; it's with the designers.

Coelacanthous Messages

Oftentimes a programmer will insert various diagnostic messages into her program to alert her to technical problems in the early stages. This is good programming practice, a kind of early warning system for bugs before they actually hit. Most of the time, the message will take the form of a small dialog box with a short message presenting the problem in terms of its location in the code and its precise nature: "RingObj:StepRing ziRing == miRing"; "Interp:PushValue miStack < 0"; and so forth. So far, so good; the goof doesn't arise until later in the development cycle. Now the company is getting ready to ship the product, and the programmer figures that she might as well leave the diagnostic message in place. After all, it can't hurt, and it might help the Customer Service people diagnose the problem if a user actually encounters the problem. However, the project leader insists that it must be made "user friendly," so the programmer rewords the message: "Ring overlap" or "Local stack underflow." That at least explains the problem in human-readable terms. She figures that the user can simply report the magic phrase to Customer Service, and a technician will take it from there. Besides, the problem will never arise anyway—right?

This is idiocy! If the problem occurred often enough and unpredictably enough to require a diagnostic message, then clearly the programmer does not understand it well enough to be confident that it will never reappear. She figures that no fisherman will ever hook this coelacanth—it's lost in the deep blue sea. And of course, somebody always does.

This blooper cannot be shrugged off as one of the inevitabilities of software. Bugs are inevitable: obfuscatory error messages aren't. All programmer diagnostics should be converted into the "I blew it" message form, with the request, "Please call our bug report line at (800) ###-#### and tell the technician: 'I have encountered the Ring Overlap Bug with a ring index of 27 and a stack depth of 5.' The technician will refer it to the programming staff for their diagnostic efforts."

Somewhere along the line, some suit will object that this constitutes an admission of error, exposing the company to legal liabilities, etc., etc. Whoever that person is, just ask him to put his objection in an email so that it can go into the archives for use when somebody does sue the company for covering up the problem.

An Extended Blooper

Most bloopers aren't as obvious as those cited; they arise from a more generalized failure to communicate. While you can't put your finger on any single design failure, there's no question that the overall interaction fails. To demonstrate this, I carried out an experiment: I installed and attempted to use Adobe Acrobat 4.0 on my Windows machine *without* reading any documentation. Of course, this is not a proper test of the design of the product; it's more like a race across Baja California to test the durability of a car design. In one short, brutal session, I busted rear-view mirrors, dented fenders, and overheated the engine. Here is my record of the interaction, exactly as it occurred:

Chris	Acrobat
<Insert CD into computer>	Startup screen with some options.
I'll read "Before you install."	Long, boring license agreement.
OK, I accept your terms.	System requirements, installation hints.
Fine. Now install yourself.	You must quit all other programs!
Sure, sure. Done.	Which country are you in?
USA	License agreement.

Chris	Acrobat
Sheesh, twice? OK, OK.	How complete an installation do you want?
Normal size	Enter your name, rank, and serial number.
Here they are, sir.	Are you sure?
Yes, I'm sure.	Here's what I intend to install. Understood?
Jawohl, mein Kapitan.	Installing.... Here's name, rank, and serial number again. Are they correct?
Yep, just like last time you asked.	Are you in USA, Europe, or somewhere else?
I'm still here in the USA.	Now enter lots of personal information about yourself. If you don't want junk mail, click here. Remember, we will use your email address for spam.
No thanks. Cancel.	You *must* enter your name and address, or the registration process will not be complete and the installation will be aborted!
Ack! OK! OK! Do you want my bank account numbers and passwords, too?	No, but I want other personal information, and you acknowledge that I can use this information for whatever purpose I choose.
But, but, I don't want ...	Select means of registration: fax, email, or US mail.
No! I won't do it! Cancel!	But you won't get all our wonderful services!
I don't care!	Are you sure?
Yes, I'm sure! Cancel, cancel, cancel!	Very well. Installation complete. Shall I restart the computer now?
I thought you were going to abort... OK, go ahead.	<Diddle, diddle, diddle>
Acrobat, Engage! Warp 9!	<Diddle> Empty window with tool icons.
OK, Acrobat, let's play! I want an empty document I can play with. How do I do that? Uh, gee, Acrobat, there's no New Document command in the menu. Perhaps I'm just stuck in my old-fashioned ways. You've probably got some spiffy new scheme that doesn't require New Document commands. OK, so let's see if we can find it.... I know you're in there somewhere, you sneaky little command. Are you hiding in this menu?	No.

(continued on next page)

Perhaps you're hidden in a secondary menu....	No.
Come out, come out, wherever you are! Perhaps if I try a few commands that look remotely like....	No.
OK, OK, I won't be pigheaded about this. Let's just open up an existing PDF file and modify it playfully. We'll open up the first document we see.	ReadMe.pdf.
How apropos! Open it!	File displayed.
Uh, so how do I actually edit this thing? Does this do anything?	No.
Does *this* do anything?	*No.*
Does this?	No.
How about this?	No.
Perhaps this file has been locked—I better find something else to play with. <Rummage, rummage> Ah, here's just the thing: a minor PDF file. They wouldn't bother locking this file. Open it!	File displayed.
So, how do I edit? <Click text>	<Dead, cold silence>
Maybe I need to Shift-click or something....	<Dead, cold silence>
Perhaps if I look under the Edit menu....	Nothing there.
Ah wait: those little icons running down the side of the screen: they look kinda like editing icons I've seen elsewhere. This one here has a big capital *T*—that must mean "text." <Click it>	<Cursor changes to text insertion cursor>
Now let's click some text.	<Selects entire word under cursor>
That's odd; I would have expected you to simply insert a text cursor there. But it's a start. <Type some text>	<Cursor changes to targeting cursor>
What's that mean? Am I supposed to select some target point in the document? And why did you unpress the icon button with the capital *T*? Now you've pressed the icon button with the hand holding a pen. Who's running this show, anyway? Still, this might be a good sign—a hand holding a pen surely indicates some kind of writing. Let's do it your way. <Press some keys>	<Cursor changes to hand cursor>

This is really weird! OK, let's go back to Square One. \<Click capital *T* icon\> \<Click word\>	\<Selects word\>
Good, at least you're consistent. \<Press one key\>	\<Cursor changes to targeting cursor\>
More consistency! Huzzah! This time, however, I'll accept your invitation to select target. \<Click empty spot on page\>	New window: Select signature handler.
What the hay-uh!?!?!? What's a signature handler? I just want to type some text! OK, let's retrench here. Close the signature window. Do you at least have any tooltips? \<Hover over an icon\>	Tooltip: Text selection tool.
Good for you! Such a smart little program! I bet you got a gold star in school for tying your shoes properly. \<Click and drag over text\>	\<Selects several lines of text\>
Now you're talking sense! Now can I actually do anything with this selected text? What's the Edit menu let me do?	Nothing except copy.
That's not very helpful. Let's just try carefully typing letters. \<abcdefghij\>	\<Cursor changes several times\>
Aha! Now I get it! The keyboard isn't for typing—it's for selecting cursors. I suppose you expect me to enter text by prestidigitating the mouse? OK, let's run with that idea. Perhaps you're just too highfalutin a program to dirty your hands with mere text entry. You've got all sorts of powerful features, but entering text isn't one of them. OK, so let's try an experiment: I'll just copy some text onto the clipboard and paste it somewhere else….	\<Dead, cold silence\>
Back to the drawing board. Let's try this here "text annotation tool." \<Click icon\>	\<Cursor changes to text insertion cursor\>
Good. \<Click page\>	\<Text entry box with blinking text cursor\>
Hallelujah! Quick, type something before it changes! Yes, yes, it's working! I'm seeing text appear! It's…it's….	\<Blue text\>
This is not the same as the regular text. Ah, I see! It's an annotation; it's not real text. So how about this other text tool; it says it's a "text touch-up tool." \<Click it\>	\<Cursor changes\>
Good. \<Click some text\>	\<Rectangle appears surrounding line of text. Text insertion cursor appears between two characters of the text.\>

I'm in business at last! <Type some text>	You cannot edit text in this font.
What?!?!? Why not? I'm the boss here, and I want to edit this text! So what do I have to do to edit this text, Your Highness? Do I have to change the font?	<Dead, cold silence>
OK, let's see what we can do. Do the cursor keys do anything? <Press cursor keys>	<Text cursor moves through the text.>
Great galloping gargoyles, I can feel the power flowing through my fingers! Let's really try out some horsepower! <Press Backspace key>	<Letters are deleted.>
So here's what we've got: you'll let me destroy characters, but I can't enter them. This isn't a text editor, it's a Text Terminator. What a concept! Wait a minute, I think I recall something from earlier. <Rummage, rummage> Yes, here it is: a menu item called Touch-up. It has a secondary menu with an item called Text Attributes. I wonder if that will permit me to change the font. <Select menu item>	Text attributes: Font is Palatino-Roman.
Yes, indeed! And sure enough, here's a pop-up menu showing the font in use. All I have to do now is pick some other font from the pop-up menu, and I'm in business! What choices do I have? <Click and hold on pop-up menu>	Long list of fonts
Hmm, this looks fun: Baskerville Old Face. I'll take it. <Release mouse button>	Font is Palatino-Roman.
What?!!?! You didn't change the font? Maybe I screwed up. I'll do it again.	Font is Palatino-Roman.
You dirty, low-down program! Why did you offer me a pop-up font menu if you won't let me change the font? Wait a minute! There's a little check box here that says Embed. Mayhaps it's blocking me. <Uncheck box> Let's change that font now!	Font is Palatino-Roman.
Curses! Foiled again! Perhaps I'm being too adventurous with my choice of fonts. Perhaps I should try one of the most common fonts, such as Times-Roman; perhaps that will work.	Font is Palatino-Roman.

Maybe I'm going about this all wrong. Maybe this document is locked, and I'm not allowed to change the text. Of course, if that were true, why was I able to delete characters? Let's just poke around and see if there isn't some sort of "Unlock this document" command. <Rummage, rummage> Sure enough, here's a Document Info menu item right in the File menu! <Select menu item>	Changing the document: Allowed.
Another dead end! <Rummage, rummage> Gee, this is interesting: under the Tools menu, there's a menu item called Paper Capture. I didn't know that it was getting away. Looky, it's got a secondary menu: Show Capture Suspects. Hoo-boy, this looks like powerful software! And look: just under that, there's a menu item for Find Next Suspect. All it takes is a Ctrl+H. Does the FBI know about this program? Of course, you'd think that a program that can find suspects would be smart enough to let you type some text, but apparently they didn't have any room left for text entry after they'd put in all those powerful features.	<Rectangle moves horizontally.>
I'm running out of ideas here. However, there are two little diamonds on the corners of the rectangle that surrounds the text. Maybe they do something. <Click diamond and drag> That sure is cute; I wonder what it's for? Let's have some fun here: can I move the rectangle all the way off the page? <Click and drag>	<Rectangle moves off page and into empty window space.>
Har, har! I wonder how far I can move it? Can I get it all the way off the.... <Click and drag>	<Rectangle disappears off edge of window.>
Hey, where'd it go? The line is completely gone! I can't even see the little diamonds to get it back! I give up—this program is beyond all hope.	

Discussion

Adobe could quite rightly protest that this is a grossly unfair test of its design, and I would agree that any piece of software, including my own, can be made to look bad by ignoring the documentation. Nevertheless, this brutal experiment condenses and emphasizes genuine bloopers in the software, bloopers that normally become apparent only through extended use; think of it as a caricature rather than a faithful portrait.

The first blooper is the failure to keep track of previous inputs. I had to agree to the license agreement twice, I had to confirm my personal information twice, I had to declare the continent on which I live twice. No conceivable technical argument can justify these intrusions; the designers were just being lazy.

Next, the program demanded a great deal of personal information that I found overly intrusive. Yet when I balked, the program threatened me. I don't object to the need for copy protection mechanisms; entering my name and the serial number on the package is a necessary evil. But the other information has nothing to do with copy protection; it's for Adobe's market research. I now realize that the installation program did not require all the information to proceed; yet the wording of the threat to abort and the presentation of the information boxes gave me the impression that *all* of the information was required. Sure, they wuz just funnin' me; but I didn't laugh. The installation program should have clearly differentiated among the installation process, the registration process, and the market research process.

I can already hear the suits dismissing my arguments as impractical. After all, they'll say, if we tell the users that it's just market research and politely request their cooperation, 95 percent of them won't cooperate. That's true—but are we in the business of serving our customers or cheating them? Obtaining their cooperation under false or misleading pretext is nothing less than cheating.

Let's move on to my attempts to use the program. My first problem was my expectation that I could create a document from within the program. The documentation makes it clear that this feature is not supported by the program. I question the wisdom of the decision to reject a New Document menu item. Every document handling program that I have ever encountered permits the user to create a new document; an aberration of this magnitude demands a damn good justification. I cannot imagine any such justification.

My other problem lay in my attempts to edit the text. Again, Acrobat's documentation makes it clear that text editing is not a supported feature; again, I question the wisdom of this design decision. Acrobat makes available a smidgen of text editing in the form of its Text Touch-up feature. But Acrobat's manual also warns that this feature becomes tedious and laborious for editing more than a single line of text. Why would any software company build a product that they admit is tedious and laborious to use in a commonly expected task?

The only justification for the preceding feature exclusions would be the consequent creation of user expectations that could not be fulfilled. Yet I cannot imagine how these features could create such expectations; they are so common in other programs that users have a clear notion of exactly what can and cannot be done with a text editor.

The problem that disturbs me most, though, is the program's poor response to playful experimentation. I tried to play with this program, and everywhere I went, doors were slammed in my face. My experiments were met with a combination of dead, cold silence, outright refusal to comply, and contradictory behavior. It is certainly reasonable, in this primitive day and age, to expect the user to read the documentation in order to access the entire feature set of the software. But every program should permit its users to get off the ground without reading the documentation, to carry out some simple and slightly productive interaction. There must be *some* support for play.

I eventually discovered that the design problems in Acrobat stem from marketing considerations. Adobe already has an excellent product that meets all my expectations in regard to Acrobat; that product is PageMaker, and it truly is a magnificent product. The problem here is that Adobe wanted something that provides some of PageMaker's capabilities without cannibalizing PageMaker sales. The result was Acrobat. I don't know anything about marketing, but I can say with confidence that the design that resulted is seriously flawed.

A Special Potshot

I have saved the best for last: the most idiotic example of bad interactivity design I have ever come across. It's in Windows 95. Granted, Windows 95 is ancient history, but this blunder is so egregious that I will dredge it out of the dim past for your entertainment. The problem has been fixed in subsequent versions of Windows. Several cleverly orchestrated blunders make the simplest of actions a nightmare. It all starts with old bumpkin Crawford transferring a file from his Macintosh to his PC.

Some Background

The Mac has something called a *resource fork* in each file, a kind of secondary ghost file attached to the main file. This resource fork contains useful information about the nature of the file, including its *file type* and *creator*. The file type determines which icon should be used for the file in the Finder; the creator determines which program is launched when you double-click the file. Windows 95 could do something similar, but it didn't use resource forks; instead, it used a *file extension*: a three-letter suffix attached to the filename, separated from it by a period. For example, MyFile.txt is a text document to be opened with a text editor, YourFile.exe is an *executable file* (that is, a program; Microsoft can't say anything in plain English), and HisFile.zip is a file compressed with the Zip program. This system was basically sound, but it did have a flaw: it could confuse a beginner who accidentally left out the extension in renaming a file. Realizing this, the Microsoft designers came up with a *kluge* (a clumsy corrective action that patches over the problem without truly solving it): they established a special option in Windows 95 that prevents the user from changing the extension, or even seeing it. To protect beginners, this option was turned on when you first installed Windows 95; presumably, the experienced users who need to mess around with filename extensions would know to turn it off. Presumably.

Meanwhile, Back at the Ranch . . . The Tragedy Begins

It all started with old bumpkin Crawford transferring a file from his Macintosh to his PC. . . . Bumpkin Crawford was humming "Old Macdonald had a farm" to himself as he transferred his Mac file to his PC over his LAN. The old fool thought he was pretty smart, using his own little LAN, but he was about to be put in his place by the superior obscurantism of Windows 95. When the Mac file arrived at the PC, it was separated into two files: the main file and a separate file representing the resource fork of the original file. Both files were represented on the Windows desktop as generic, untyped Windows files. The resource fork is like the disembodied tail of a lizard; it's quite useless in its detached condition, so Crawford heaved it into the Trash Bin. Next, the old man decided to rename the file to add its extension so that Windows 95 would know what kind of file it is. He whipped up the Rename command and typed the new filename with its identifying extension. He hit Enter, and Windows 95 obligingly changed the icon to reflect the file's new status as a known and recognized file type. So far so good.

But now Crawford crossed the line where Man Was Not Meant to Go. He realized that he screwed up and entered the wrong file extension. Oh, well; he'll just rename the file again. So he whipped up the Rename command again and typed the name with the new extension. But this time, the icon did not change!

Being your typical computer-illiterate dunce, Crawford repeated the same operation two or three times just to make sure; he succeeded only in proving that human pig-headed repetitiveness can never match computer pig-headed repetitiveness.

Fortunately, Crawford's good friend and Windows expert Dave Walker was but a phone call away; he would have the answer in no time.

Thirty minutes later, Crawford and Walker were still scratching their heads. In a moment of inspiration, Crawford brought up the Properties window for the file. Sure enough, there was the filename, and when Crawford clicked it, a caret cursor appeared in the filename text (a caret cursor is the standard vertical cursor used to indicate the location where text entry will occur). Huzzah! Caret cursors are always associated with text editing, and so he could edit the filename right here in the Properties window.

It is true that caret cursors are always associated with text editing, but there was a special exception in the case of Properties windows; there, the caret cursor served to create expectations that were gleefully smashed. In this case, the Microsoft designers had achieved the dubious distinction of producing a ratio of accessible states to conceivable states that is exactly zero: you couldn't do anything in that text edit box! You couldn't type anything, move the cursor, or delete anything. The only challenge remaining to them now is to get that ratio to less than zero. I'm sure they're working on it.

The two old geezers fumbled and blundered about for a bit longer before Old Geezer Walker remembered something. He instructed Crawford to select the Options menu item from the View menu for the folder; when Crawford did so, a window with a variety of elements appeared. Down near the bottom of the window, you'll find was a check box labeled "Hide MS-DOS file extensions for the file types that are registered." That option was checked on Crawford's system. Under Walker's directions, Crawford unchecked the option and returned to the regular Windows display. Lo and behold, now he could see and even type the filename extensions—and they worked the way they were supposed to! Having once again proven the superiority of Man over Machine, they congratulated themselves, and Crawford tried to remember what he was doing before he began this odyssey.

11

CLOCK SETTING

The task of designing an interface to set the time on a clock would seem to be simple, yet myriad schemes have been designed to handle this interface. Herewith a case study of various efforts.

There are 23 working clocks in my household. My wife and I are not horophiliacs; indeed, our collection of clocks is pretty much the same as you'd find in any typical American home. All of these clocks give us a sizable sampling of the various schemes for setting their time. I shall present these schemes in terms of the interaction required to set them properly.

Scheme A

The simplest scheme appears on the analog clocks: the user rotates a knob that turns the minute hand of the clock. As the minute hand turns, the hour hand advances with it. Turning the knob in one direction advances the time; turning the hand in the other direction reverses the time. Thus, the interaction between user and clock looks like this in conversational terms:

[User] "Clock, advance the minute hand."
[Clock] "Now I read 3:32."
[User] "Advance some more."
[Clock] "Now I read 4:36."
[User] "Advance some more."
[Clock] "Now I read 5:37."
[User] That's too far. Clock, reverse the minute hand a short distance."
[Clock] "Now I read 5:23."
[User] "I overshot. Clock, advance the minute hand just a tiny bit."
[Clock]: "Now I read 5:25."
[User] "Done!"

Scheme B

Scheme A is used on five of the clocks in our house. The only flaw with this scheme is that it can get rather tedious if you have a long way to go. One—and only one—of the digital clocks uses a comparable system: one of the car clocks. The user turns the knob to the right, and the clock advances; the user turns the knob to the left, and the clock reverses. An additional feature is the use of acceleration; if you hold the knob for longer than a few seconds, the rate at which the clock changes increases. This shortens the overall interaction:

[User] "Clock, advance."
[Clock] "Now I read 3:32, now 3:33, now 3:34, now (blur of digits)."
[User] "Stop!"
[Clock] "Now I read 5:28."
[User] "Reverse."
[Clock] "Now I read 5:27, now 5:26, now 5:25."
[User] "Done!"

Scheme C

With the third scheme, used on my bedside clock, we enter the realm of idiotic design. This scheme is similar to Scheme B, with several insane changes. The simple two-switch knob of Scheme B has now been replaced with three pushbuttons. The three buttons as a group are labeled Set; the buttons themselves are labeled Time, Fast, and Slow. This scheme does have the advantage that the buttons are clearly labeled, a minor failure of Scheme B. Unfortunately, the scheme itself is so obscure that it throws away any benefit obtained by labeling the buttons. The user who reads the labels will assume that the Time button must be pressed; doing so accomplishes nothing. Instead, the user must know to press *both* the Time button *and* the Fast button or the Slow button simultaneously.

Nothing on the clock itself indicates this requirement. To make matters worse, the clock advances in only one direction: forward. Should the user overstep by a single minute, then the only recourse is to advance the clock a full 23 hour and 59 minutes. To make this process easier, the designers set the clock to advance at a fast rate of 1 hour per second and a slow rate of 2 minutes per second. Thus, if the user overshoots (a common error), then he must hold both the Time and Fast buttons down for 23 seconds. This gets him only to the current hour; he must then hold down the Slow button for an average of 15 seconds to get to the desired setting. Thus, a typical interaction looks like this:

[User] "Clock, advance fast."

[Clock] "Now I read a blur, with the hours recognizable."

[User] "I'm holding the buttons down for 2 seconds."

[Clock] "Now I read 5:36."

[User] "Damn! I overshot. I am holding the two buttons down for 22 seconds."

[Clock] "Now I read 4:02."

[User] "I'm playing it safe, so I am holding the slow button down for 45 seconds."

[Clock] "Now I read 5:25."

[User] "Done!"

Not content with screwing up the design of the interaction, the perpetrators of this clock also chose to make it mechanically difficult. The three buttons are spaced only $\frac{3}{8}$ inch apart, even though there's plenty of room on the clock for wider separation. This is absurdly close together; the optimum separation for human finger separation can be seen on any keyboard: $\frac{3}{4}$ inch. Moreover, the buttons themselves are small and pointed, with high pressure requirements to actuate. Thus, the user must press them deep into his fingers for dozens of seconds at a time. What a pain!

Scheme D

Wristwatches provide us with the next variation on this scheme. Here, at least, the designers can plead innocence by reason of minusculity. Moreover, watch manufacturers seem to have standardized on a basic system, although each version asserts its uniqueness with some variation just small enough to drive you crazy. On my watch, the scheme works like so:

[User] "Watch, enter Time Set mode" (presses upper-left button).

[Clock] "I'm blinking the seconds to indicate that these will be changed."

[User] "I don't care about the seconds; go to the hours" (presses lower-right button).

[Clock] "Now I am blinking the hours to indicate that these will be changed."

[User] "Advance the hours" (holds down upper-right button).

[Clock] "Now I read 5:37."

[User] "Good. Now go to the minutes" (presses lower-right button).

[Clock] "Now I am blinking the minutes."

[User] "Advance the minutes (holds down upper-right button).

[Clock] "Now I read 5:37, 5:38, 5:39...(40 seconds go by). Now I read 5:25."

[User] "Done! Exit Time Set mode!" (presses upper-left button).

All in all, this looks like a fairly clean interaction, but there are several mistakes in this design. First, the process begins with the seconds, which few people bother with. Worse, the seconds are not advanced or retarded; they are reset to zero when you press the upper-left button. The watch also rounds off the minute when you reset the seconds; if the seconds are greater than 30 when you reset, the watch increments the minute reading, which you might have just set. What idiot thought of that idea?

The other problem is that there are too many modes. You'll notice that I didn't mention the lower-left button; this is the Mode Selector button. My watch has six modes: Time, World Time, Temperature, Alarm, Timer, and Stopwatch. As you might imagine, each mode has its own idiosyncrasies. And all six modes are controlled with just four buttons!

Scheme E

There was one big improvement in Scheme D, buried underneath an otherwise lousy design: the separation of hour setting from minute setting. The previous schemes treat the clock setting as one continuous value that you must change with a single control. But the new, improved approach separates the minutes from the hours. This has a profound effect; the old continuous approach has 1,440 different settings from which to choose, one for each minute of the day. The improvement breaks this down into one choice of 24 (hours) and one choice of 60 (minutes). Moreover, this is a more square arrangement arrangement as recommended in Chapter 8 (24:60 versusvs 1,440).

With fewer choices at each level, the task is simplified. However, a new complication is introduced: the user must distinguish between the two types of settings. In Scheme D, this differentiation is accomplished through the nonobvious approach of pressing a button repeatedly to change the setting value. The big idea in Scheme E is to differentiate these with buttons. My car does this with an admirably simple system. There are just two buttons; an Hours button and a Minutes button. Pressing and holding the Hours button advances the hours; pressing and holding the Minutes button advances the minutes. You can't go backward, but overshooting isn't such a big problem, as there isn't so far to go if you do overshoot. Here, then, is our standard interaction:
[User] "Advance the hours" (holds down Hours button).
[Clock] "Now I read 5:37."
[User] "Advance the minutes" (holds down Minutes button).
[Clock] "Now I read 5:37, 5:38, 5:39...(40 seconds go by). Now I read 5:25."
[User] "Done!"

Let's pause for a moment to reflect on the observation that this scheme is not only simple to understand and execute, but also requires only two buttons. No designer can defend any of the previous schemes on the grounds of manufacturing costs. The only defense of the other schemes is their ability to handle multimodal functions.

Scheme F

Our Macintoshes have a scheme that is slightly better, but not without flaws. Of course, a computer has the advantage over physical clocks in that buttons cost nothing; it's just a matter of screen space. Here is the window used to set the clock:

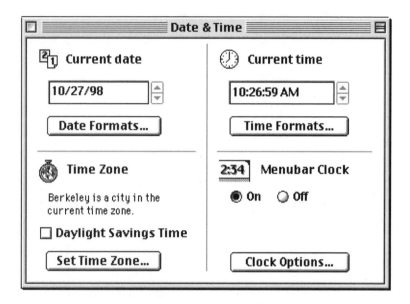

Here we encounter the only flaw in this scheme: where does the user begin? The time is clearly presented and labeled, but there is no indication of how to change it, and the two tiny arrow buttons that might do so are dimmed. How does the user activate them? The answer isn't overly obscure: click anywhere in the time box. The display now looks like this:

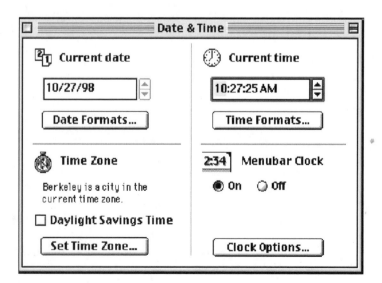

At this point, setting the clock is obvious: the user need merely click and hold the up arrow or the down arrow to change the hour setting. To change any of the other values, click the value and use the up and down arrow buttons. Moreover, the user who wants to use the keyboard can type numbers and switch between the settings with the Tab and Shift+Tab keys. All in all, this is a good system whose only flaw is a minor initial obstacle. Here's the script for our standard interaction:

[User] "I want to change the hours" (clicks hours digits).

[Clock] "Hours digits are now highlighted. I'm ready."

[User] "Advance the hours" (clicks upper arrow).

[Clock] "Now I read 5:37."

[User] "I want to change the minutes" (clicks minutes digits).

[Clock] "Minutes digits are now highlighted. I'm ready."

[User] "Decrease the minutes" (clicks lower arrow).

[Clock] "Now I read 5:36, 5:35, 5:34...(9 seconds go by). Now I read 5:25."

[User] "Done!"

This scheme does have more steps than our best scheme so far, Scheme E, but those steps themselves are quick, so I rate this scheme as a close second to Scheme E.

The clock-setting system used in Windows 95 was similar, but made a classic mistake:

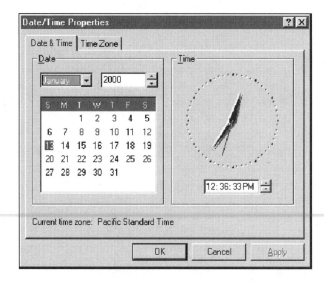

The designers added that lovely analog clock. How sweet; surely that must have made the nondigerati feel less ignorant. Unfortunately, the designers fell afoul of the last guideline presented in Chapter 9: don't set up false expectations. An on-screen clock in a control area begs to be manipulated. Users would click the hands of the clock and attempt to drag them to the correct settings; when this fails, they will feel a twinge that does not make them better inclined toward Microsoft. Oops!

Scheme G

Now we come to the fun one: the VCR. Mine uses a truly idiotic and inconsistent scheme; I suspect that VCR manufacturers have some secret compact to ensure that no VCR will ever have its clock set properly. Here's a device that has plenty of input and output capability; it can listen to its remote controller, which has scores of buttons, and it can talk out of the television display, which doubles as a decent, if small, monitor. Yet with all these resources at hand, the designers still manage to screw up the design.

The user begins the ordeal by pressing the MENU button on the remote control; this pops up an on-screen menu, the top item of which is specially marked with a little triangular cursor on its left edge:

```
MENU


    TIMER SET/CHECK
    TUNER PRESET
    SET VCR+ CHANNELS
    CLOCK SET
    LANGUAGE
    ADVANCED OPTIONS
```

Clearly, pressing the EXECUTE button on the remote will trigger this menu item. But the clock setting item is the fourth menu item, so the user must step down to that menu item by pressing the down arrow button. Once there, pressing the EXECUTE button takes us to the next screen, and here's where things fall apart. The screen looks something like this:

```
CLOCK SET


      • AUTO    MANUAL



    SELECT:  < / >
    THEN PUSH EXECUTE
    QUIT  :   MENU
```

It's amazing how many errors the designers managed to pack into this one little screen. First off, they violated their previously established vertical menu structure; now, for no apparent reason, the menu is horizontal. Of course, this assumes that the user figures out that "•AUTO   MANUAL" is a menu.

Next, the designers cleverly changed the cursor. In the previous display, it was a little triangle; in this screen, they've disguised it as a dot. They've further camouflaged the situation by taking the triangular cursor from the previous screen, coupling it with another triangle pointing in the opposite direction, and placing these both after the SELECT button, separated by a mysterious slash whose significance is discernable only to users of hallucinogenic drugs. To throw the user off guard, they provide one simple, clear sentence: "THEN PUSH EXECUTE." Any fool can see what this means, but by this time, the cogent user is suspicious and wonders what it *really* means. Last, there's the inscrutable line "QUIT   :   MENU." Why is the colon separated from the word *QUIT*? Are QUIT and MENU two additional but independent options, or is QUIT some kind of precursor to MENU? Perhaps the careful positioning of the colon exactly between the two words indicates that they are cosmically balanced in some sort of yin-yang relationship. Does the menu quit, or does quitting raise the menu? I have no QUIT button on my remote control, but I do have a MENU button; unfortunately, pressing it does nothing.

Then of course there's the problem of divining the difference between AUTO and MANUAL. A reasonable person could guess that AUTO means "automatic," but a reasonable person would also wonder, if it's possible to set the clock automatically, why does it need me to do anything at all?

Let us suppose, merely for entertainment purposes, that some person somewhere is cogent enough to figure out the solution to the puzzle, while still preferring to use the manual clock setting. That special person will press the cursor key to the right, thereby moving the little dot from just in front of AUTO to just in front of MANUAL. Pressing EXECUTE, she escapes from the trap and enters the next room of the dungeon:

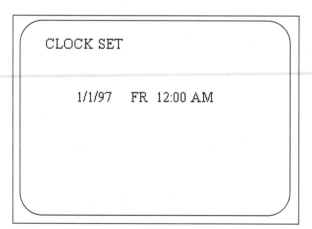

This is the entirety of the display. I doff my hat in salute to the fiendish cleverness of the designers. By setting up the user with a clear command in the previous screen (THEN PRESS EXECUTE), they have ensured that the lack of the concomitant command in this screen will convince their hapless victim that there is no means of escape from this screen.

In an unusual lapse, they have retained the same horizontal menu structure used in the previous screen. However, their creativity was certainly not taxed by the problem of coming up with yet another cursor: this time they blink the first 1 in the date. The trick here, which any experienced text adventurer could immediately see, is to use the vertical cursor keys to edit the values and the horizontal cursor keys to switch from the currently selected field to the adjacent one. And yes, the EXECUTE button will permit the user to escape from the screen.

This scheme sets the record for bad interactivity design.

There are an amazing number of ways to set a clock. Most are magnificent demonstrations of towering incompetence. I challenge the reader to design a clock-setting system for a watch.

12

THE DESIGN PROCESS

Translating a good design into a good product requires real people to do the work. Organizing people is trickier than organizing ideas.

Knowing where you want to go with your design and what mistakes to avoid isn't enough; many's the slip twixt cup and lip. I have seen plenty of good projects ruined by the human realities of the development process. Herewith some advice on setting up the project effort so as to realize the intentions of the design.

Who's the Designer?

The simplest, most easily avoidable source of failure is sloppy assignment of design responsibility. Every project must have one person with sole responsibility for the overall design. The clear assignment of responsibility is one of the fundamental rules of good management, yet interactivity project teams frequently violate this rule. The problem arises, I think, from the necessity of jamming old talents into new slots. We have not yet bred a population of native workers trained in the particulars of interactivity design; most of our workers are immigrants from other fields. Thus, a "graphic designer" becomes an "interactive graphic designer." There is nothing in the definition of interactivity that requires graphic design per se, so the imposition of an alien professional orientation distorts the design process. Since everybody working on the project brings an alien professional orientation, the design lacks any center of gravity.

This dreadful expedient is understandable, I suppose, given the dearth of collective experience in interactivity design. However, the situation is changing rapidly, and the time has come for the industry to commit itself to a rational professionalism. Every project should have a lead designer.

The lead designer is not the same person as the project manager or producer. The latter task is more managerial in style, concentrating on the logistical, financial, and political tasks required to keep the project moving. The lead designer reports to the project manager, and all members of the design team report to the lead designer. The project manager's crucial function is to serve as buffer and bridge between a profit-seeking business and a creatively sensitive design team.

Another symptom of poorly developed professional standards is the intrusion of executives into the design process. This has been especially serious in the games industry, but the problem appears in most interactivity design projects. Because there is no widely acknowledged professional skill called interactivity designer, executives assume that anybody (including themselves) can do it. So they intrude into the design process, always with destructive results. Executives should run the company, not the project!

The lack of recognition of interactivity design as a profession has also led to a minimization of the importance of design on the part of some executives. One marketing executive once boasted to me, "I could sell dog shit in the right box!" To which I replied, "Indeed, you do."

The Project Team

Many variations on the project team structure have been experimented with; most such experiments have yielded disappointing results. Team structures that have worked brilliantly in one situation have failed miserably in other situations. It is therefore impossible to declare any particular team structure as ideal. The highly variable nature of personnel and project requirements makes it necessary to cobble together each team structure with more opportunism than determinism. Nevertheless, I can offer some opinions on the weak points of various organizational charts. Here's a typical org chart for a generic interactivity project:

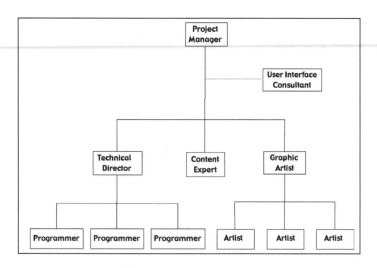

Projects organized this way often fail, because the tasks are broken up by available talents, not by functional requirements. The user interface consultant sits off to the side, fecklessly making recommendations that may or may not be adopted by the programmers. The technical people are segregated from the graphic people in the classic two-cultures style (see Chapter 27)—but programming and art are not the fundamental tasks of the project. Here's an analogously stupid org chart for a baseball team:

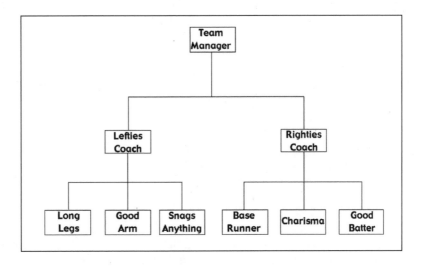

You don't want to organize your effort by the talents of your people; you want to organize it by the tasks you need done; then in filling each box with an actual person, you make the best fit you can. Therefore, a more utilitarian org chart for an interactivity project would look something like this:

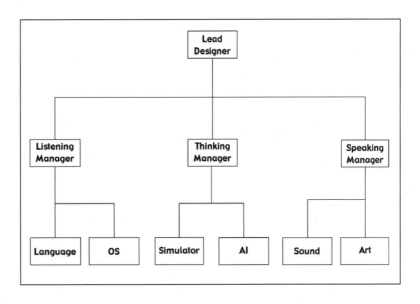

The underlying concept here is to organize the team in a manner that reflects the natural cleavage lines of interactivity design. This will minimize interdependency of people and groups.

Qualifications for the Interactivity Designer

To make this team work, the lead designer must boast a variety of talents. I shall neglect the obvious managerial and fiscal skill requirements of such a position. What does it take to do this job?

The first qualification is the ability to program. This is a painful reality that many will refuse to accept, and there are certainly a number of successful designers lacking this skill. Yet I believe that programming ability is so fundamental to interactivity design that, within ten years, this requirement will have asserted itself in Darwinian fashion.

There are at least 23.7 scads of reasons why the lead designer must be able to program. Some arise from human foibles; for example, programmers often use trumped-up technical excuses to influence the design process. The lead designer must understand the technical strengths and weaknesses of the target platform to best fit the design to the platform. There are also scheduling factors to consider; if you can't program, you'll find it surpassingly difficult to estimate the time required for implementing various features.

The prime reason for learning to program, though, is simple: interactivity design is an ambassadorship between user and computer; anyone who does not speak both languages will fail. It is not necessary that the designer write the code himself; it is not even necessary that the designer be *able* to write all the code himself. It is necessary that the designer have a solid grip on the programming language used in the project. If the project uses C++, then it needs a designer who has written programs in C++.

The best designers are not programmers at heart: they are often people with little or no technical background, who have taught themselves enough programming because they realize how important an understanding of programming is to their work. Don't dismiss these as impossibly difficult requirements to meet. I admit that persons with these qualifications are rare, but this means only that we're talking about an odd combination of talents, not an impossible combination of talents. The primary reason such persons have not emerged is that we haven't yet offered economic incentives for anybody to develop such a combination of talents. Once interactivity-based firms realize the importance of good design, that problem will be eliminated, and we'll have a good crop of designers within a decade or two. Until then, we have to make do.

Empiricism

Back in the bad old days, computer programming projects were monstrous affairs requiring huge teams of programmers slaving away at bits of code that were combined into one massive program. Over and over, the act of combining different code from different programmers inevitably led to mismatches and conflicts that caused the program to malfunction. Millions of dollars were wasted on screwed-up programming efforts that never worked.

The Big Lesson that emerged from those painful experiences was that programmers needed some scheme for managing huge software projects. A great many brilliant ideas were developed in pursuit of this goal: structured programming, strong typing, object-oriented programming, and more. But one idea from those days, still in favor with many programmers, is wrong for interactivity design: the technical specifications document.

This arose as a means of coordinating all involved. In many corporations, there were two documents: the Performance Specifications document, written by the clients (whoever wanted to use the program); and the Technical Specifications document, written by the programming manager and presumably providing a translation of the Performance Specifications document into programming terms. These documents ensured that everybody knew exactly what they were getting and giving; it was in many ways like a contract. As people learned how to use the idea, there arose the belief that a well-written specification would obviate all programming problems. The wisdom was, "If your specification is clear and precise, the task of programming will be so straightforward as to ensure that there will be no problems."

The system worked; a great many big projects were built in this manner, and it definitely lowered the chaos level of software projects. Nowadays, no serious software engineering project is undertaken without a complete and thorough tech specs document. If your programmers are experienced, they will surely insist on such a document.

What I'm about to say will get this book burned on many college campuses: tech specs documents are not a good idea for many interactivity projects. All of your programmers, technical experts, consultants, *and* their dogs will howl with indignation at the heresy of my claim. So you're going to need a lot of good arguments to hold your ground on this important point.

I am not rejecting the use of any kind of coordinating documentation for the project; the more people there are on a project, the greater the necessity for documentation to make certain that everybody is on the same channel. What I am dismissing is a document with *specifications*: formal statements created before programming begins that together constitute a contract between programmers and management. Such a document declares an intrinsically adversarial relationship between you and the programmers, a relationship that must have a contract to ensure that both sides are treated fairly.

Careful planning is indubitably crucial to the success of any project, but we all intuitively recognize the need for a certain amount of flexibility in executing a project. Airline pilots rank among the most by-the-book experts in the world, but every single one of them will deviate from his filed flight plan if a thunderstorm develops along the flight path or to avoid excessive turbulence.

The applicability of formal planning procedures hinges upon the predictability of the circumstances surrounding the project. If the earth's atmosphere lacked weather, all airplane paths could be precisely specified in advance. If you're designing a data entry system for a mail-order company, you can specify in advance the technical expertise of the workers who will use it, the equipment that they will use, and the load that will be placed on the system. A tech specs document is appropriate and useful in this situation. But many interactivity projects have nowhere near as much certainty surrounding them. How many hits per day will your website get? Will the user have a fast machine? How much RAM will the user's system have? What conventions will the user understand coming into the program?

The killer problem lies not in these technical details; it arises from the very youth of interactivity design. A good programmer can look at an algorithm and quickly estimate how much RAM it will take and how fast it will run. That's not because good programmers are geniuses; they simply have lots of experience to fall back upon. As an interactivity designer, you don't have that rich background of experience on which to count—nobody does! We are all collectively making this up as we go along. You can't look at a single interaction component and estimate how smoothly it will function, how easily users will understand it, or how quickly they can operate it. Someday, years from now, there will be thousands of experienced professionals and library shelves full of books about the details of interactivity design. When that day comes, we'll surely have developed all sorts of rules of thumb comprising "standard industry practice," and then we can create detailed blueprints for our work. For now, our ignorance forces us to respect the need for flexibility.

Here's an example: In my Erasmatron project, I created a powerful scripting editor packed with features; only after it was fully operational did I realize that the time it needed to draw the screen was too long, breaking the natural flow of the interaction. I had to expend considerable effort to correct the problem, and I very much doubt that I could have anticipated it. If the project had involved several programmers and relied on a tech specs document, making the changes necessary to fix the problem would have required endless arguments about changing the tech specs; in the end, I would have settled for the slow screen, and users would have been cheated.

There are two primary considerations in deciding how large a role tech specs document should play in your project. The first is the degree of novelty in the project. If you're banging out a standard-issue 3D shooter game, most of your design is already done for you, and you'll have no problems using a strong tech specs document. Likewise for a straightforward information page on the web or yet another word processor. On the other hand, if you're off in the weeds designing something that's truly new and different, a tech specs document will make it more difficult to improvise; your programmers will hold it like a gun to your head.

The second factor determining the overall utility of a tech specs document is the size of the team working on the project. If this is a multi-million dollar project with a passel of programmers and an army of artists, you damn well better have a lot of documentation specifying just how all those efforts fit together. If this is a small-group effort, just you and a couple of others, you have more freedom to improvise and less need for tech specs.

Of course, if you're willing to treat a specifications document as an information document rather than a contract, it will have value in just about any project. Just make sure that everybody understands your freedom to change the specs without their approval.

Polish

Related to this notion of empirical design is the concept of a polishing phase for any interactivity design. All too often, the interval between "It works!" and "Ship it!" is a few days. There should be an interstitial phase here, which I call the polishing phase. During polishing, you're not trying to find bugs; you simply play with the software to find the little inconveniences and rough spots where the interactivity flow is broken. This is the stuff of subtle judgment; no one but the lead designer can make the final judgment as to the adequacy of the polish. Simply put, it must "feel right." This is perhaps the most subjective decision in the entire project, and you must schedule the time to make this decision with adequate research. Give yourself at least a week of polishing trials with the software before you freeze the design; I'd recommend a month as an ideal polishing period. You'll be under tremendous pressure to ship the product, but you must stick to your guns; polish is the only differentiator between a good product and a great product. Polish, polish, polish!

Convergent Testing

Software testing has traditionally focussed on finding bugs and thus has always been considered a technical task. While I certainly concede the necessity of such testing, I also insist that bug testing is not enough. There must also be user testing, which seeks to learn just how and where users get confused. I suggest that you use a convergent system. First, release test versions of the software to technically adept users who can overlook the minor glitches that we all expect. These testers will identify deeper-level problems with the design and suggest ideas you might not have thought of. The best testers at this stage are your professional peers. Just turn them loose on the software and see what they say.

Next comes the serious-user testing. You carry this out with the non-professional users who will nonetheless be using the software heavily. With these testers you need a more intrusive approach to the reporting of problems. These testers will often misconstrue the nature of the problem, reporting something that doesn't go to the heart of the issue. You can accept written test reports from them, but you must follow these up with a telephone call and some direct interaction. Ask some probing questions; find out what's really bothering the tester. Often, you can address the tester's complaint without necessarily implementing her suggested solution.

Last comes naïve-user testing. Select testers who don't know much about their computers, who don't dive into software, but who might still want to use your product. Do not send them the software and ask them to report back; they will not be able to articulate any problems they encounter. Sit down with them in their own environments, let them start the program, and watch them as they use it. Make them talk out loud about their mental processes and ask them especially to voice every single question that pops into their minds as they work. Take copious notes. Back at the lab, collate all the points of confusion from your various testers; if you see a common factor, redesign the offending feature.

Storyboards

One of the most important and subtle benefits of the Web has been its enticement of a great many talented nontechnical people into interactivity design. Those people have brought with them techniques and ways of thinking that have enriched a field that was narrowly technical in outlook. The largest group of immigrants has come from the field of visual arts, and they have brought with them one technique that I wish they'd left behind: storyboarding.

Many designers are deeply wedded to the storyboard, so I want to make my points with pinpoint accuracy, describing the aspects of storyboarding that are useful as well as those that are pernicious. The two positive benefits of storyboarding for interactivity design are sketching and team coordination. We all know how expensive graphics can be for any interactive product; with a graphic artist sketching rough diagrams of the various screens, we can preview the basic image before we spend all the money needed to implement it. That's good. The other benefit of storyboards is the way that they give every team member a clear visualization of the various screens of the design. That's good, too.

But now we come to the dark side of storyboarding. As soon as you assemble those sketches into a sequence—a storyboard—you have insinuated sequentiality into your design, and sequentiality is intrinsically non-interactive.

Recall Chapter 7 and its Crawford diagrams. The first diagram in the chapter was this:

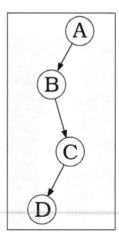

This is the storyline, the bad old linear design that we try to make as thick and bushy as possible when we want interactivity. Linearity, sequentiality—these are the antithesis of interactivity. A user marching down the primrose path that you have laid out for her has no choices, no options, no verbs. She can't speak because you have muzzled her. That's not interactivity. A storyboard is a device for linearizing images; by using it, you prejudice the design process against interactivity. I have nothing against sketches or passing them around; just don't assemble them into a deliberate sequence. Toss them together in a loose pile, not a strict sequence. Call it a storypile.

My second objection to storyboarding is that some people think that it constitutes a useful planning document for interactivity design, like an outline for a document or a blueprint for a building. Storyboards are excellent planning tools for video productions—but video is not interactivity! If you want to design video, by all means, please do so, but don't poison this field with an insidiously misleading tool, and don't try to pass yourself off as an interactivity designer when your true talent is as a video designer. A storyboard is not only misleading, but also inadequate—there's plenty of stuff to consider that can never be shown on a storyboard.

All interactivity projects should be led by a designer broadly educated in the arts and able to program. Teams should be organized functionally rather than by background. Don't overspecify the project in advance. Polish, polish, polish! Test convergently. Don't rely on storyboards.

13

ADVICE FOR SPECIFIC FIELDS

In this chapter, I apply the grand principles I have pontificated upon through this book to each of a number of specific fields of endeavor. Although you may not have a direct professional interest in any of these fields, the comments may prove interesting.

Game Design

Computer-based interactivity got its start in game design. While other fields were slowly groping their way toward interactivity, game design was reveling in it. Well-designed interactivity has always been central to the success of games; hence, game designers possess highly developed sensitivities for interactivity. Certainly designers from other fields would do well to examine game design closely. You can learn as much from the turkeys as from the winners; for each game, ask yourself, "What makes this game so good (or so bad)?" Your answer to that question will almost always be founded on some aspect of the interactivity in the game.

The central design issues in game design now concern the character of the interactivity: specifically, the nature of the thinking that the game demands of its user. The shelves team with games, but there are only three basic thinking elements in all current games: hand–eye coordination, puzzle solving, and resource management. All games combine these three elements in varying degrees.

Hand–Eye Coordination

Games that use hand–eye coordination move quickly and demand fast reflexes. Information races through the interactive loop at high speed. The user's brain activity is concentrated in the cerebellum, which handles the lower-brain functions associated with sensation and motor processing. The process of mastering a game requires the player to short-circuit normal sensorimotor processing. Information normally travels upward from the cerebellum into the cerebral cortex for what we might call conscious processing. If we see a bee, the cerebellum might handle the basic processing of recognizing it as a small, active, living thing, but the recognition of it as a bee requires higher-level processing, and the decision to take action will involve additional objective factors such as the presence of a window between the person and the bee. Thus, information spreads upward from the cerebellum into the cerebrum, wanders through there, integrating with other bits of information, and then passes back down into the cerebellum as instructions to swat the bee, close the window, or move away.

The beginning player of an action game goes through the same process, but as he learns the game, the amount of information flow through the cortex diminishes, reducing processing time and yielding faster reflexes. The player teaches lower levels of his brain to respond directly to the game's stimuli. A master player has cut out a great many of the cerebral middleman neurons, confining processing as closely as possible to the cerebellum. Such players report an altered state of consciousness while playing the game at their best; the highest levels of cortical processing are suppressed, and the player loses awareness of his surroundings. Another symptom is the experience of losing track of time: the player suddenly jerks himself out of the altered state of consciousness and realizes that it is three o'clock in the morning.

This brings us to one of the unhealthy effects of action games: their narcotic effects on consciousness. Common sense tells most people that the dull expression and trancelike behavior of action game players is unhealthy, but it has been difficult to nail down the gut-level feeling. If we think of this behavior in terms of altered states of consciousness, then we can recognize some of the appeal and danger of the activity. By shutting down consciousness, the player obtains relief from whatever demons haunt him. It is precisely the same behavior that alcoholics and drug addicts display, undertaken for the same reasons, and with essentially the same behavioral effects. Troubled persons can banish awareness of their pain by immersing themselves in long hours of action-game playing.

Another factor is, of course, the violence. Often the stimuli in a game are dastardly monsters in desperate moral need of extirpation, the player obliging with firepower of biblical proportions. Not all games are violent, of course. In some games, the violence is euphemized. There are also plenty of completely nonviolent, fast-action games.

The role of violence in computer games generates plenty of debate, especially after it was learned that the murderers in the Columbine High School massacre in Colorado were aficionados of violent computer games. All games must have conflict to drive the interaction, and violence is the simplest and most intense form of conflict—hence, the predilection for violence in so many computer games. But simplicity and intensity are not the sole measures of quality in any human experience. Candy boasts the simplicity and intensity of sugar, but it hasn't monopolized our diets. True, our less worldly wise gourmands (children) overpartake of this food, but we all outgrow the short, sweet satisfaction of candy and turn to more subtle tastes to entertain our palettes. In the same way that the intense pleasures of candy, cartoons, and comic books command the entertainment enserfdom seize the attention of our children, only to be eventually outgrown, so too does the craving for violence represent a phase in the maturation of some individuals. The real problem with violence, then, is not that it is unethical, but that it is ultimately boring. Once you've seen a million eviscerations, you've seen 'em all.

The challenge to computer game designers is to engage some other portion of the human psyche, probably something a little further up the brainstem. One such mental engagement is the solving of puzzles.

Puzzles

Puzzles, in their pure form, are completely noninteractive. They hide a solution, and the player must experiment to divine that solution. The puzzle makes no active effort to foil the player's efforts; its strength lies in its obscurity. The classic example of the use of obscurity was the adventure game that required the player to pass an obstacle by feeding a dead fish into a slot in a vending machine. The wonder of it is that so many players praised the game for its surpassing counterintuitivity!

While adventure games provide the purest example of puzzle games, game designers have been slowly fusing puzzles with other elements of the design to imbue them with some dynamism. For example, a jumping game can be seen as a puzzle with moving parts. The player must learn to run, jump, and duck in a precise sequence to achieve victory. A puzzle might even include some active elements to chase the player, in which case it certainly provides some interactivity. But where does puzzleness fade into interactivity? A player blasting sneaky monsters could just as well be said to be solving the puzzle of their algorithms—once he understands their style of fighting, he can massacre them at his leisure. The difference between puzzleness and interactivity lies in the perception of the user. So long as the user does not understand the algorithms driving their behavior, he perceives his opponents to be operating with free will, and therefore believes that he is interacting with them. Once the player understands the behavioral algorithms, the interaction collapses and becomes a puzzle.

Some confusion surrounds the integration of puzzles with other forms. For example, one popular design alternated puzzles with video sequences. Supposedly, the combination of "interactive" puzzles with noninteractive "movies" yielded "interactive movies." This supposition presumes that interleaving constitutes integration. If you shuffle together a deck of hearts and a deck of spades, you don't get a deck of sparts or heades—you get a deck of hearts and spades.

In general, puzzles have done little to advance interactivity design. While there have been a number of successful pure puzzle games, such games are weak in interactivity and do not represent enduring lines of development; they tend to come and go as fads. Designs that incorporate puzzles compromise their interactivity to obtain the challenge offered by the puzzles.

Resource Management

Resource management games, sometimes called strategy games, operate at a cerebral level; they present challenges requiring high-level processing. The most complex of such games demand integration of huge amounts of disparate data and detailed assessment of its consequences. There are many variations on this theme: military strategy games, explicit resource management games, and role-playing games. All of these games require the player to juggle limited resources to optimize performance in pursuit of some goal. In military strategy games, the military units constitute the resources that are used and expended in pursuit of victory. In role-playing games, the attributes of the player-character constitute the resources to be used in overcoming opposing players, thereby obtaining additional resources. In explicit resource management games, the player must marshal limited amounts of food, money, population, or other resources in pursuit of the goal.

Most of the variation in resource management games comes from integration of resource management with other styles of game play. For example, the classic conquer-the-world games combine straightforward military resource management with economic resource management: the player uses military units to capture cities that generate new military units. Another approach is to integrate a military strategy game with a hand–eye coordination game: position your military units and then fight the battle hand to hand. This approach goes back to the early 1980s. There have also been attempts to combine resource management with puzzle games. Some role-playing games do this by presenting the player with puzzles along the way.

Where to Go from Here?

Game designers have tried to pump life into these forms by two main strategies: technological advancement of old designs and odd new combinations of existing forms. The technological advancement approach took a great leap forward with the onset of 3D display technology, but this approach is nearing its technological ceiling: the improvements yet to be made can do little to boost the game experience. The utility of the combinatorial approach is also fading; almost all of the available combinations have already been experimented with.

It would appear that game design has exhausted its creative potential. However, I can offer a few suggestions for new veins of creativity to mine. The first of these is the exploration of alternative thinking styles. Each of the existing basic genres relies on a fundamental dimension of human thinking: hand–eye coordination, random creativity for puzzles, and careful calculation for resource management. Additionally, most of these games rely heavily on spatial reasoning. This suggests two other dimensions of human mentation that might prove worthwhile.

The first of these is verbal reasoning. I don't mean the use of words to present fundamentally mathematical problems; rather, I refer to the use of linguistic processing in the human mind. Such processing abilities far exceed our capacity for formal logic in their depth and richness, but designers are often at a loss to comprehend the potential of this approach, largely because our verbal reasoning is deceptively automatic, and most designers are so steeped in the tradition of spatial reasoning that it boxes in their imagination. Consider, however, that a riddle is a verbal puzzle, and a conversation is a purely verbal interaction. Consider the possibilities of any political interaction game (corporate politics, government political intrigue, geopolitics, and so on). Spatial reasoning is useless in such games; their interactions are manifested verbally. Consider also the classic mystery genre. This genre has done well in both cinema and literature, but the attempts that have been made in the games field have not been successful. I suspect that mystery games have failed because they do not effectively bring verbal reasoning to bear.

A second dimension of mentation is affective or social reasoning. Most male designers have little appreciation for this dimension, but it is one dimension of specialization for females. I find it ironic that game designers constantly worry about how they might go about designing "games for girls." The question is framed in such a way that the answer is to put a cute bow on the head of Pac-Man and call it Ms. Pac-Man (which is what Atari actually did). If the question is reformulated to "How can we utilize affective or social reasoning in our designs?" then we have a constructive challenge that can guide us to a solution. Unfortunately, this dimension of human thought differs so much from that employed in current designs that the solution will require a major effort. I have been working on the problem for ten years now, in the form of interactive storytelling, and have succeeded only in laying the foundations.

Some designers will protest that computer games generate plenty of emotion, citing the moments of elation or terror they have experienced in the better games. This logic confuses affective reaction with affective interaction. While the player may experience moments of reactive elation or fear, the interaction itself involves no emotional effort. Indeed, some games seem to have the reverse effect, deadening the player's senses of sympathy and empathy by mechanically inflicting suffering and death in amounts never approached in the bloodiest of movies.

Consider, for example, the aggregated body count generated by one computer game: Doom. Assume that 5 million people played this game. Next, assume that each player has played the game for an average of ten hours—long enough to figure out how to survive. Last, assume that the average Doomster kills one monster every ten seconds. While there are wimps who can't perform to that standard, many players do much better. Putting these numbers together, I calculate a body count of 18 billion. Compare this with the Holocaust, surely the most emotionally intense incident in human history, in which 6 million people were killed. One computer game has generated the virtual analog of 3,000 Holocausts without any concomitant emotional impact.

Large Verb Sets

Games have traditionally sported a small vocabulary of verbs, because the early games had to operate on joysticks with little expressive capability. Design styles have therefore concentrated on creating a small set of all-purpose verbs capable of executing a variety of tasks. The ideal game boasted an elegant, tightly knit set of verbs. This suggests an alternative design avenue to explore: the creation of large, loosely structured verb sets. Instead of hard-wiring the verbs directly into the program code, they would be stored in some sort of table defining their capabilities. Broadly defined verbs would be replaced with narrowly applied verbs. Such designs would face many new difficulties, such as how to communicate to the user which verbs are applicable in any given situation. Nevertheless, the strategy of large unstructured verb sets opens up new realms of game design.

Marketing Constraints

Sad to say, the greatest obstacle to creative development in the computer games industry lies on the marketing side, not the design side. Suppose, for example, that some genius were to design a game bursting with affective and social reasoning. Such a game would be completely new—and that would be its death sentence. What sane publisher would risk a million dollars on development costs for a game genre with absolutely no track record? In the good old days when games cost $50,000 to develop, risks like this were occasionally acceptable, but nowadays there is no point in spending that little—such a game would surely fail because of its necessarily low production standards. Publishers must either commit a ton of money or walk away from the design, and they will all choose the latter course, even though they know the game might be a major breakthrough. As one publisher told me back in 1984 about Balance of Power, "This is a great game and I really hope that somebody else publishes it, but I simply can't justify the risk." Besides, they figure that, if it turns out to be a success, they can have a competing clone on the market within 12 months.

But let's just suppose, for the sake of argument, that our genius designer finds a publisher foolhardy enough to risk a million dollars to develop the game. Having done so, the publisher must then find a distributor crazy enough to stock the game. If you think that publishers are hidebound, you should see distributors! These people have no sense of duty to the future whatsoever; they run their businesses purely by the numbers. They will not carry a game unless they have comparable sales data from previous, similar games to assure them of success. If our genius's design truly is creative, then there will exist no previous similar games—and the distributors are certain to reject it.

But let's again be irresponsibly optimistic and assume that some distributor somewhere feels lucky and opts to take a fling on this game. Now that distributor must convince the retail outlets to purchase it. Why should a retailer risk precious shelf space on a complete unknown, especially when there are so many proven performers to show? Standing on the sidelines, we might all urge her to "just give it a chance," but for those whose livelihood depends on getting the right mix of products that will move off the shelf, being charitable with shelf space only guarantees business extinction.

What the hell—in for a penny, in for a pound! Let's just suppose that we find a reasonable number of retailers in a charitable mood. They give our grandly creative new game a few inches of shelf space. Now everything depends on the store sales staff. Why should they bother to even look at the game? They know what sells, and that's what they'll recommend to the customers.

And here we come to the greatest obstacle of all: the customers. What kind of customers will visit the games shelves? Answer: customers who have purchased and enjoyed previous games—the old games whose traditions our game is breaking away from. The young fellow looking for the latest, most spectacular shoot-em-up is not going to be interested in some wimpy affective-reasoning game. Who wants to work things out with the bad guys? Just blow their friggin' heads off!

Of course, there are plenty of people who would be interested in our creative new game: grandmothers, little girls, guys undripping in testosterone. They'd surely be interested in our game and might even buy it. But these are exactly the people who don't browse the game shelves, because they already know that computer games are vaguely tawdry exercises in violence and geek-think.

Thus, the entire system is stacked against the creative new designs. It's a social system—a community—that has over the years learned, by dint of much pain and loss, what works and what doesn't work, and how little latitude there is for deviation from the norm. One brave company can buck the trend, but the distribution system is too big for that company's heroism to accomplish anything.

Ah, but what about an evolutionary approach? What if we slowly insinuated elements of affective or verbal reasoning into existing games, richening the mixture every year? That is unlikely to work because there's no bridge population of customers to carry us over the gap. There aren't many shoot-em-up-loving little boys who might occasionally want to make friends with the monsters. There aren't many doll-playing little girls who might fancy occasional recourse to a double-barreled shotgun. Unless the global environment changes dramatically, human beings will not evolve into turtles, because the jump is too great.

Educational Software Design

From the earliest days of personal computers, we have hoped for great contributions from them in the educational field. Results have been spotty; some impressive advances have been chalked up, but my overall reaction to the state of educational software is disappointment. Let's start by examining the two areas of greatest success: early learning and simulation.

Early Learning

The early-education field has generated lots of activity as well as great commercial success. We now enjoy an abundance of excellent software for the under-10 age group. Why have these designers succeeded where so many others have failed? The answer, I think, lies not in the design but in the problem. Young children lack dense reasoning skills; their learning process is less conscious and more immediately experiential. The greatest challenge in early education is presenting the content in a manner that attracts and retains the child's attention. In a roomful of boisterous kids, this demands consummate skill, but a computer program has the huge advantage of handling one child at a time. Moreover, it's easy to dress up the content in lots of animated eye candy. Teachers can't be talking dinosaurs that morph into the letters of the alphabet.

Another crucial feature of the computer for early education is its immediate responsiveness. In a roomful of kids, each one's behavior must be constrained in some fashion, and kids don't like such a passive stance. Their little minds are going a mile a minute, and they want to do things. The computer can keep them fully occupied, bending all that energy in the right direction.

Given these huge advantages, it's no wonder that early-education software has been so successful; the genre is one of the perfect applications of the computer. However, we should not draw too many conclusions from this success. Watching the Green Bay Packers make mincemeat of the Platte County High School football team doesn't teach you much about how to play football. We need to examine a tougher problem.

Educational Simulation

Educational simulation programs have shown little in the way of commercial success, but nevertheless remain very successful in design terms. In other words, there are plenty of great educational simulations out there, but they're not being sold commercially; most were created by teachers and are shared with the community. The strength of this software lies in the fact that it concentrates on processes rather than facts. As I've claimed elsewhere, facts are dead, uninteractive, but processes are the basis of interactivity. Simulations can't help but be interactive! The most impressive simulations are generally those in the physical sciences, especially physics, because the designers can zero in on an isolated process and simulate it easily. In other fields, the most important ideas are not so easily reducible to the mathematical terms required by the computer, and so simulation is more difficult to do well.

Guidelines for Educational Software

With these successes in mind, I can offer educational software designers three broad guidelines.

Eschew Exposition

As I explain in Chapter 19, the original educational technology is play, an intrinsically interactive process. The early attempts at formal education in most ancient societies took the form of a group of students gathered around a master, engaged in discussion; note how deeply interactive this process is.

Sometime around the founding of the medieval universities, formal education took a wrong turn. Perhaps it was the close association of learning with religion and the coincident concern with enforcing religious orthodoxy, but for some reason the medieval universities shifted their focus from discussion to lecture. Education shifted from an interactive process to a one-way broadcast of information. The mistake was exacerbated by the invention of the printing press: now learning was enshrined in books, and of course, there's no arguing with the authority of a book. Incidentally, my old friend Erasmus resisted this drift; his many writings on education excoriate mindless memorization of facts and extol an active role for students. He also recommended play as a healthy part of education.

But Erasmus was a voice in the wilderness; educational systems became obsessed with imparting facts rather than developing the process of thought. This is a natural result of the discomfort we feel with the abstract nature of thought, compared with comfortable, tangible fact. We can even see some of this today in the emphasis on test scores as a means of evaluating educational success. The brevity and legal rigor required of a test push it away from abstract process and toward concrete data. It's easy to ask a student when Columbus discovered America and then evaluate the correctness of the answer; but ask the question that makes history important—why did Columbus discover America?—and the answer becomes long winded and impossible to grade by clear, rigorous, legally defensible standards.

All the positive trends in education have, at the same time, made worse the problem of data intensity. The adoption of mass education required methods with economies of scale; interaction has no economies of scale and so was slowly pushed into the background. Every new educational technology or medium tended to work against interactivity. Cheaper textbooks encouraged teachers to simply assign readings; snazzy lecture halls with demonstration equipment reduced students to passive audiences; overhead projectors, slides, movies, mimeographs, and all the other paraphernalia took us ever further away from interactivity.

I remind you, though, that all of this—the entire style and approach of the last thousand years—is the newfangled technology, the untested fad. The tried-and-true educational strategy, bearing the stamp of approval of millions of years of natural selection, is play. You don't see kittens sitting quietly in nice neat rows of desks, watching attentively as some old fogey of a cat stands in front of a blackboard showing anatomical diagrams of a mouse with approach angles and attack vectors. Play isn't some namby-pamby educational strategy; as any cat can tell you, it's a jungle out there, and you need solid education if you are to survive.

Therefore, your first task as an educational software designer is to break loose from all the old expository prejudices that have entwined themselves around your neurons. You must stop thinking of education as a process by which a better-informed person transmits information to a less-informed person. Instead, you must think of it as an active process in which a student hones thinking processes by trying them out in a catholic panoply of experiences. Your role in this process is that of an assistant, not a commander.

In practical terms, this means that you must not include simple facts in your software. Dressing up a fact in multicolored animation with stereo sound does not give it life; it's still dead, Jim. You must examine your design minutely, looking for every fact that is not necessary for the student to make a decision, and then coldly expunge such facts.

The obvious objection to this rule is that some facts are essential to any discipline. The physics student must learn the value of the Heisenberg constant; the biology student can't avoid memorizing the basic taxonomy of life on earth. If facts aren't permitted in software, the student will be crippled. My answer to this objection is simple: use an appropriate medium, of which there are many. Put the facts in textbooks, or lecture, or videos, or slides, or handouts. Don't ask software to handle material that it's not well-suited for; you'll only produce lousy software.

Embrace Process

The rejection of facts does not leave the educational software designer bereft of content; there remains a huge, and much more interesting field of inquiry to handle: process. Biology isn't about the names of species; it's about how life works—the processes of life. Linguistics is not a compilation of foreign languages; it concerns how languages operate, how they change, how they are learned. If you focus your attention on this process-intensive thinking, you'll design better educational software.

The collision between process-intensive thinking and data-intensive thinking (see Chapter 17) is nowhere more poignantly demonstrated than in the sequence of "why's" asked of a parent by a young child, culminating in an exasperated "Because that's the way it is!" The process-intensive style of thinking is uncomfortable to most people; it will not come easily to you. Perhaps you will never feel at home with the abstraction of process-intensive thinking; if so, I fervently pray you to get out of the way and pursue some other grail.

All this translates to educational software design in a simple concept: the educational content of your design lies in the algorithms you create, not the data you store. Your students can't interact with a fact or an image; they can interact only with a process or an algorithm. Suppose, for example, that you are designing a program about the European discovery of the New World. A data-intensive approach would present this as little more than lists of discoverer's names, dates of discovery, and landfalls. Nina, Pinta, and Santa Maria; San Salvador and Cape of Good Hope; de Gama, Vespucci, and Drake. Whoop-de-doo.

One process-intensive approach might focus on the mechanics of geographical discovery. This would require a sailing simulation. How should the student allocate precious space in the hold for food and fresh water? How large a crew should be taken? Is it better to take one big ship or several smaller ships? How does one navigate in unknown seas with no means of determining longitude? How does dead reckoning work? A simulation of this nature could be made simple for younger students and more complex for older students. The younger students could skip the navigational problems, while older students could wrestle with the problems of securing royal patronage.

Another process-intensive approach might focus on the motivations for discovery. The simulation might place the student in charge of a European spice trading company, competing with other companies in garnering the fabulous wealth of spices. What is the fastest route to the Orient? How do the costs of overland transport compare with those of sea transport? Would a route through the Mediterranean, with transhipment at Suez, work better than the route around Africa? Is there a Northwest Passage to the Orient?

For philosophers, why not set up a Socratic dialogue? Take any of Plato's dialogues, put it into the computer in simple hypertext form, and then add lots of alternative responses and counter-responses to the existing material. Granted, this is hard-wired branching, but let's face it: mathematical equations for Socratic thinking are still a long ways off—you'll have to make do with simpler algorithms.

Political science has plenty of great opportunities for simulation; I wrote Balance of Power, a geopolitical simulation, in 1984, when computers were much less powerful than they are today. The challenge here is to reduce complex political thought to mathematical formulae. Most academics balk at such heresy; they rightly object that any such mathematical expression would grossly simplify the underlying idea. While this is true, the fact is that every freshman poli-sci lecture is an oversimplification. No teacher has the time to present a rigorously correct explanation of the subject matter. We all simplify whenever we teach, giving our students scaled-down versions of the truth. As they advance through the material, we refine the presentation of the material at each level. So the principle has long been established: we can simplify the presentation of the material. Mathematical approaches are merely another form of simplification. The only serious issue is whether the mathematical algorithm falls too far short of the educational level being presented.

Another objection is that many of the simpler equations make assumptions that constitute hidden biases in the simulation. This is a non-issue; an easy solution is ready to hand. When I designed Balance of the Planet, an ecological simulation, I needed formulae for the effects of a great many ecological and economic processes. I settled on simple linear equations with proportionality constants. For example, my equation for radioactive pollution emerging from nuclear power plants was simple:

```
radioactivity deaths = danger factor * number of nuclear plants
```

The danger factor was crucial to the simulation: if it were to be too small, the simulation would unfairly reward a nuclear-heavy strategy; if it were to be too high, it would bias the simulation in the other direction. My solution was to allow the student to tinker with the danger factor, to adjust it upward or downward. This, in turn, required the student to think carefully about the ideas behind that number. This approach transformed a difficulty into a higher level of education, for the student would naturally feel some obligation to research the basis of a number before changing it.

Understandably, these process-intensive approaches require a great deal of work. But our task is to develop human minds, not stuff data onto a floppy disk. Any idiot can spew information all over students—and a great many of them do. If you want to develop students' minds, you have to prepare materials that challenge and exercise what is most important about students' humanness: their ability to think. And the same thought applies to your own humanness: are you a teacher or a talking book?

Let Them Play!

All mammals are born with an instinct to learn by playing, and that instinct in young humans is powerful, more powerful than the sex instinct in adult humans. It is a testament to the towering failure of educational institutions that they have been more successful in suppressing playful human curiosity than all the repressive laws in the world have been in suppressing unseemly human sexuality. Perhaps we should recruit teachers for vice squads. The human youngster is blessed with a powerful drive to learn by playing. Damming that freshet of energy and diverting it to passive information absorption is a stupid waste. Let them play!

"But play teaches the wrong things: jumping and running, not reading" goes the objection. Only because the toys we give children teach the wrong things. The skills we want them to learn—reading, arithmetic, biology, algebra, economics—are all intrinsically interesting and fun. We should not treat them as foul-tasting medicines that must be coated in thick layers of sugar to be palatable. *Sesame Street* has proven beyond any doubt that something as mundane and dull as the alphabet can be enthusiastically embraced by children if it is presented in a playful fashion. The secret of *Sesame Street* is not in the cute puppets, but in the fact that the letters of the alphabet are *used* rather than merely presented. They are used in songs, in words, in jokes, and in skits. They are held up, handled, tossed about—played with. The audience engages in merely vicarious play, but play is so powerful an educational strategy that even indirect play works better than exposition. Imagine the effect if Big Bird & Company marched into your home every day and engaged your kids in their routines. There have been a number of attempts to accomplish just that with a computer, but so far the quality and intensity of the play has fallen short of the original. But it points us in the right direction.

The fundamental error of most educational software is the attempt to graft unrelated play onto the subject material. The worst of these (widely recognized as such) are the various arithmetic-teaching programs that reward correct answers with snippets of videogame play. The designer's task is to elicit the intrinsically playful elements of the material. This is why you must abandon the notion that your material consists of facts; there is nothing playful about a fact. Every attempt to make facts fun will surely fail.

For example, the method foisted on me to learn multiplication was the traditional memorization of multiplication tables. I burned those tables into my brain. I can still remember the special feeling that 7 x 8 = 56; perhaps my teacher praised me specially that day. Yet I didn't grasp the concept of multiplication until graduate school, and I daresay most adults don't ever grasp it. They can do the calculation but never understand why.

Yet multiplication is a simple concept. If I had been taught by more playful, process-intensive methods, such as playing with boxes and balls (this many boxes with this many balls in each gives how many balls?), I would have gotten the idea of multiplication at the direct experiential level necessary for understanding. Moreover, in a playful environment, I would have more quickly recognized the utility of arithmetic. I did not start to use arithmetic for anything other than school until my late teens, about 13 years after I had started learning it. Thirteen years is a long time for a kid to take something on an adult's word. I could have been given colored tiles and rectangular surfaces to cover with them; the applications of multiplication would have become obvious. With a computer, all sorts of wild geometric shapes are possible, and so all sorts of arithmetic combinations become available.

Many years ago, Warren Robinett demonstrated the utility of play-based educational software with a magnificent program called LogiGators. It taught Boolean algebra to young children by allowing them to play with logical gates.

The one serious obstacle to a play-based approach is the difficulty of process-intensive thinking. Most educators find the method so alien that they are at a complete loss at designing playful, interactive teaching materials. I ask only that the brighter educational software designers master the technique and make it part of their intellectual culture. Its superiority guarantees its eventual success; social osmosis will accomplish what this book cannot.

Application Software Design

Application software covers a lot of ground: spreadsheets, word processors, database managers, email programs, photo-retouching programs, CAD programs, painting programs, web browsing programs—all those programs that we use to get some work done.

The traditional manner by which we design such programs is a multi-step process. First, some genius defines a need and comes up with a way to meet that need with a computer. This leads to version 1.0 of Candidate Killer App. Most of the time, it turns out to be a Wimp App, but sometimes we get a Fierce App, and rarely we get an honest-to-gum Killer App. Then everybody else jumps on the bandwagon and begins the process of design by feature accretion. Eventually we end up with such a humongous heap of features that somebody comes out with a Lite version that distills the discombobulated heap of features down to a reasonably compact pile. Then the Lite version starts putting on weight, and the process starts all over.

What Does the User Do? What Does the Computer Do?

My first suggestion is that the starting point for designing any application must be to ask two questions: "What does the user do?" and "What does the computer do?" The most general answers to these two questions are: "The user does something deemed useful," and "The computer does something computable." Your first task as a designer is to flesh out these questions, making each increasingly specific until they match. Remember: you are acting as an ambassador here, a mediator between two parties who think in completely different terms. Your task is to get them onto common ground, even if they don't know it. Here is the sequence of answers to those questions for a word processor:

User does:	Computer does:
Something useful	Something computable
Writes a letter	Converts letters into numbers
Enters text	Organizes letters on the page
Evaluates resultant text	Presents resultant text

A great many programs answer the second level of the first question with "The user makes something," usually a document of some kind: letter, report, spreadsheet, presentation, photographic image, painted image, drawn image, web page, and so on. Other programs, including a few of these same ones, answer the question in another way: the user plucks useful tidbits of information from a huge pile of data. Database programs do this, as do web browsers.

The third generic answer to the question of what does the user do is that the user communicates something; this is the function of email programs. The fourth answer, rarer than the previous three, is provided by programs that control electrical devices, such as home-control programs that turn on and off lights, heaters, and other household equipment: the user controls something.

The second-level answer for the second question is always the same: the computer processes information. It calculates numbers and moves them around.

Thus, all application programs permit the user to do one or more of these four actions: make, find, communicate, or control. If you can't clearly phrase your design using one of these four verbs, then either you don't have a clear idea of what you're trying to accomplish, or you have a truly revolutionary idea. All application programs accomplish their user service by calculating numbers and moving them around.

The next step in the design process is to move to the third level of the questions. Can you describe in more detail what the user is making, finding, communicating, or controlling? Can you describe in general terms what kind of numbers the computer will calculate and move around and roughly how it might do so?

Suppose, for example, that a client comes to you wanting a program to help her schedule her employees at a small factory in a developing country. The employees are adherents to a religion that requires each one to perform devotions at specific times of specific days, and each individual has different times and days. Moreover, each individual has different skills with the different pieces of machinery in the factory, so they're not directly interchangeable. Last, the client's mix of orders is constantly changing. One week she wants to glue 10,000 hairpieces onto little furry toys; the next week it's assembling 25,000 model airplane boxes.

You interrogate the client, trying to determine the problem that most bedevils her. What does the user *do* that is most tedious and time consuming? Her answer is immediate and emphatic: with the constant mixing around of employees and machinery, the poor factory manager is going crazy. So you have your second-level user goal: the user wants to schedule her employees. The computer will be calculating blocks of time, mixing and matching employees with machinery and products. We'll call this combination EMP.

User does:	Computer does:
Something useful	Something computable
Schedules employees	Calculates EMP characteristics of blocks of time
Enters EMP data	Combines time blocks into a working schedule
Evaluates resultant schedule	Presents resultant schedule

This little list doesn't solve any of your problems for you, but it gives you a clearer idea of what the problems are. It specifies what the user does and what the computer does. That's a better start than most projects get.

Note that the fourth and final entries in the two lists fit together. The software does something, and the user evaluates the result. We start at the most general level for each of the two parties and bring them to convergence.

Convergent Iteration

Interactive solutions to many problems tend to be convergent iterations as opposed to the one-shot approaches of yesteryear. Before interactivity, your scope for altering your work was limited; most alterations required hours of tedium. Before spreadsheets, for example, most budgets were hand calculated and horribly tedious to amend. This distorted the budgeting process. It was crucial to get your budget estimates right on the first try—submitting changes afterward always angered the boss. Since changes were so difficult to make, everybody overestimated budgetary needs; if the extra money turned out to be unnecessary, it would be spent on departmental goodies. With interactive spreadsheets, the budgeting process has become more incremental; alterations can be integrated into the budget more smoothly. People still abuse the budgeting process (that's politics), but they now have one less excuse for doing so.

Consider word processing in this light. What, precisely, is the value of this software? I consider that its value springs from its acceleration of the naturally iterative process of writing, which seldom comes out right on the first try. We write down our sentence and then reread it to evaluate its fidelity to our intentions. It's never good enough, so we scratch out unsatisfactory words and rewrite them. Sadly, the combination of hand, paper, and pencil is slow, and the process of editing makes a confusing mess of the page. Word processing software accelerates and neatens this process. We delete, rewrite, cut, and paste at speeds that would astound our quill-using ancestors.

Thus, the computer's contribution in word processing is quite trifling in nature: it merely organizes the letters on the page for us. Two factors make this trifling contribution so valuable: first, we put so many characters on the page that keeping them all straight is a tedious task. Second, the linear nature of language imbues the words at the beginning of the document with great consequence: change "that jerk" to "our good friend" early on, and the position of every letter afterward could well be changed. Recalculating all those positions would be a huge and boring task for a human brain, but the computer eats this kind of problem for breakfast.

Thus, in productivity applications the computer acts as a partner with the human brain, tackling a narrow group of problems that the brain handles slowly. The brain-amplifying effects of this are serendipitous benefits. For example, the first spreadsheet, VisiCalc, was offered to Apple Computer to publish, but the marketing experts at Apple rejected it. Its calculational abilities were obvious but easily duplicated with a cheap calculator; why, then, would anybody pay serious money for it? What the experts failed to foresee was the way that instantaneous recalculation made financial calculations an interactive process. Before spreadsheets, financial calculations of any size were too laborious to permit much fiddling around; once the budget was hammered out, the cost of recalculation forbade tinkering. With spreadsheets, managers could experiment with a variety of financial options before committing to one. This experimentation—play—was unknown prior to 1981, but it is now universally applied. Here, the benefit was the interactivity made possible by rapid calculation.

The information loop in most application programs is based on hypothesis testing. The user sets up (at high initial cost) a computer model of the intended document, budget, mailing list, or whatever. Then the user plays with the model: Will this read better if I move this clause up front? Can I balance the budget if I cut down on massages for the employees? If I sort for female customers in Wisconsin, can I detect a pattern in their purchase decisions? The user tries out many variations and closes in on the final result. It's a convergent process in which two agents, user and computer, alternately listen, think, and speak. Each agent contributes the kind of thinking that it does best. The computer adds, subtracts, multiplies, divides, ORs, ANDs, and EORs; the human exercises judgment and applies human values in evaluating interim results.

Ergo, whatever task you contemplate, ask not how to computerize it; ask how subtasks currently requiring great care can be replaced with iterative guesswork that converges to the final solution. A diamond cutter gets just one stroke, and it had better be right; wouldn't it be better if he could use a computer to chip away at that rough diamond, removing tiny bits until it was perfect? That's not likely in the foreseeable future, but the principle of iterative solution can be applied to a great many tasks. Indeed, your software need not actually solve the user's problem. It can still be useful if it merely provides a way of organizing the elements of the problem so that the user can incrementally approach the solution.

The iterative process breaks down into four components, two each for human and computer; together, they form a more narrowly defined version of the interactive loop:

1. The computer offers the user a carefully defined set of editing options that permit all user-conceivable changes.

2. The user chooses from among the available set of editing verbs.

3. The computer applies the chosen edits and recalculates the state of the document or product.

4. The user evaluates the result and determines how it falls short of the desired ideal.

Let's use the foreign factory manager to show how this might work. Until now, the client has juggled schedules in her head. But with success came growth and more employees; with so many employees, juggling schedules in her head no longer works. It would be nice if the software could do the entire job for the client, but there are too many intangible factors to put into algorithmic form. She can't have these two employees working on the same machine at the same time; they're both sloppy, and together they're bound to screw up something. She would prefer to have this employee at work when she's around, because he gives her good reports on how things are going on the shop floor. No computer could ever handle such intangibles—but we don't need the software to get all the way to the solution. We need it only to get close enough that these intangible factors are the only ones that the client needs to worry about.

The software should allow the client to specify the basic factors—constraints on each employee's schedule, ability of each employee to use each machine, machinery and time requirements for each product manufactured, and so forth—and then view the resulting schedule. Presumably, the client will look over the schedule for a moment and then mutter "that won't do; those three employees all need a lot of supervision, so I can't have all three here at the same time." So the client rearranges the schedule slightly and then observes the result. The computer handles the busywork of laying out the schedule, while the user handles the high-level decisions and the special cases, iterating the process until convergence yields the ideal schedule.

We normally think of computer software as tackling problems with mathematically definable results, but in fact the most interesting applications are those that permit maximum expression of human creativity. A spreadsheet, for example, may indeed be seen from the computer's point of view as nothing more than a vast collection of straightforward calculations, but from the user's point of view, a great many delicate judgments are built into a spreadsheet. A word processor does nothing more than arrange letters on a page, but the user sweats the composition. A painting or drawing program provides the user with the means to draw neat, clean lines, circles, and other image components, but the human creativity at work is far the more important.

Thus, there remain two broad strategies for advancing applications software. The first is the creation of editing verbs that more closely approximate the user's creative impulses. Painting programs, for example, could offer us a higher-level set of drawing primitives, such as human faces and bodies. The user in such a case might be able to edit the face by specifying changes that make the face longer, the hair bushier, or the skin older, for example. Word processing programs might be able to make a sentence more assertive, tighter, or more diplomatic. Photo-manipulation programs might be able to identify image components and accentuate, enhance, or diminish them. "Soften the pig, shrink him, and move him further back in the background" would be a perfectly reasonable command in such futuristic programs.

The other broad strategy for advancing application design is the tackling of problems that are at present beyond the reach of simple editing and recalculation. Imagine, for example, a comics drawing program that included in its verb set drawing primitives more closely attuned to the various styles of comics art. The user might then specify his desire for a pretty girl sidekick and then adjust her appearance with commands such as "prettier but less sexy," "spunkier," or "more lithe." A great range of human creative activities demand much tedious effort to realize small creative goals; if the tedium can be separated from the creative effort, therein lies a potential for application software.

And that's all there is to application software design <riotous laughter>.

Website Design

Let's start by assessing the effectiveness of the Web as an interactive medium. Specifically, how well can it listen, think, and speak?

The Web's ears are adequate but unimpressive. Its primary mode of listening is through hotspots and, to a lesser extent, through typing and a few supporting gadgets such as pop-up menus. Hotspots are certainly the best simple, general-purpose input scheme. You can crowd thousands of 'em into a single web page, or you can have just one. Moreover, the size of a page's hotspot vocabulary is (or should be) instantly obvious, which helps the user feel confident about his choices. But hotspots are weak with sequential or compound commands. If our user wants to see the blue portrait of an old woman painted by Picasso sometime during 1933, he will have to navigate through a maze of single-query pages to get what he wants. That's slow and clumsy. Fortunately, textual input gives us some relief; a perfect example is provided by any of the various search engines.

The Web's fatal weakness lies in thinking. HTML is a completely inadequate language for any kind of thinking. Fortunately, Java provides us with a good processing language, given the constraints of platform independence and security. So far, however, use of Java on the Web seems to have fallen far short of its potential, possibly because many Java interpreters remain unreliable.

Last, we turn to the area in which the Web shines brightest: speaking. My oh my, how the Web can speak! It's got graphics, it's got animation, it's got sound, music, video—even voice telephony! The only comment I can make about the speaking skills of the Web is: enough, already! The stuff we already have is great, fabulous, wonderful, but there remain enormous problems in other areas, especially thinking. All of our efforts should be directed at equipping the Web with bigger brains and bigger ears. The efforts we put into giving it a bigger mouth are almost pointless now. It's like putting an even more powerful engine into a rocket-propelled car with six-inch wheels.

One aspect of web speaking, though, remains unsatisfactory: bandwidth. It's difficult to splatter wonderful images and sounds all over a user who sits at the far end of a slow and narrow pipe.

Strategies for Improving the Web

The main improvement that we all hope for is a dramatic increase in bandwidth. There's no question that users operating at 1 Mbps experience a completely different web than those of us who struggle with 56K modems that actually deliver an average of 20 Kbps. While higher bandwidths are steadily penetrating the consumer market, the sad fact is that the slow-modem users will remain, at the very least, a significant minority for years to come. (By the way, you should be careful interpreting the available data. While most regular users of the web are coming in at speeds in excess of 256 Kbps, that sample is biased by usage; most of the slower users don't spend much time on the Web because it's so damn slow. The actual market may be pretty fast, but the potential market is much slower.) Accordingly, website designers will not be able to assume high bandwidths; websites must still be designed to operate adequately at low bandwidths.

But there's another strategy for improving the value of a website: make it smarter. The Web's biggest problem just now is that it is viewed more like a library than a playground. Most users are on the Web to gather information, but our notions of gathering information are still dominated by the concept of the encyclopedia or the sales catalog. And by golly, if we think of the Web that way, that's what it will become: a musty old digitized library. Yuck!

It's surprising how deeply this attitude insinuates all thinking about the web. Most of the central features of most websites (hyperlinks, search facilities, and so on) are designed to help the user find things faster. This all fits neatly with the current grain of the Web: it talks volubly, listens weakly, and thinks like a worm. With this combination of features, people design websites that talk, talk, talk, listen a little, and never think. This is not interactivity! If we want to take advantage of the potential, it is imperative to bolster the Web's weakest link: its thinking.

Consider, for example, how much more effective the web would be if I could find exactly what I want on my first attempt at searching. I usually must examine 20 different pages before I zero in on what I want; at 20 seconds per page, that's six minutes to do one search! If I could always get exactly what I want on the first attempt, then I would experience an effective throughput 20 times greater than what I now have—roughly equivalent to 400 Kbps over a standard phone line! To get exactly what I want takes more intelligence from the web, not more bandwidth.

To demonstrate this problem, I went searching on the Web for trial records from colonial America. When I entered the words "trial records from colonial America" (not grouped into a single search string), I got 6,700 hits, 14,400 hits, and 34 million hits using three different search engines. The best hits on these three engines had the following text:

"Salem witch **trial records, colonial America**"
"**Colonial America** Lecture Hall and Chatroom. Western Canon"
"Salem Witch **Trial** Hysteria; Settlements, ships . . . New England Pilgrim Criminal **Records**. Religion in **America**. Beginnings to . . . US History—**Colonial** Cycle First . . ."

Now, suppose that the engines had been as smart as a human being, but didn't know anything specific about trial records from colonial America. It would then search using a variety of appositives: {trial, court, criminal} {records, documents, transcripts} from {colonial America, American colonies, early America}. That human would also know to group adjectives with the nouns they modify (for example, "trial" with "records" and "colonial" with "America"). These concepts are simple enough to be computable, so why haven't they been implemented yet? (Perhaps they have; if I had a faster connection, perhaps I might have found such an engine.)

Here's another way to look at it: right now, Google boasts that it spans 2,073,418,204 pages of webspace. That's a lot of pages, but suppose that you saw a game on a store shelf boasting that it offered 2 billion moves. Would you be impressed? What if you saw an ad for a word processor hyping the 2 billion different documents that it could produce? Or a spreadsheet that could handle 2 billion different budgets? I certainly wouldn't be impressed by any of these products; I would expect to be able to get uncounted zillions of game moves, documents, or budgets out of my software. The count of web pages looks impressive only when the pages are hand-built. But wouldn't you prefer a web that permitted you to get a page custom designed to give you precisely what you want, rather than merely sample a great many pages that might come close?

This next major transformation due for the Web will be the transition from fixed pages to custom-built pages. This transformation is already underway; whenever you use a search engine, the results are presented in a custom-built page. Why aren't *all* pages on the Web custom built? Rather than crawl through a pile of pages, why can't the user simply say what she wants and get it?

The reason, of course, is that you can't do any processing in HTML; it's a page description language, not a processing language. If you want to do any processing, you have to use something else—Java is the most likely candidate, although several other methods have been developed. The problem is, too few people design websites to use Java, largely because Java is too daunting for most website designers to tackle. And so the Web marches onward to a dead expository future.

The first question to ask yourself in designing a website is *not* "What information do I want to provide to my user?" It is instead "What do I want my user to be able to *do*?" There are plenty of situations where the user wants to get something, most likely information, and for these you have a large palette of well-developed tools. However, most of those tools involve little in the way of processing. I believe that search systems on the web must and will evolve toward greater process intensity.

One of the leading innovators in this direction is Amazon.com. Starting with a simple listing of books, Amazon has added new searching dimensions. Having found a book, the user can view other books by the same author, other books purchased by purchasers of this book, "Top 10" lists of similar books, and so on. The end result is the best single source of information about books on any topic.

But you should also consider whether the user can make anything or control anything using your website. There are plenty of precursors to this goal on the web. Online games are certainly not about getting information; they enable their users to control something (a game). There are also a few sites that permit a user to assemble some pretty email out of standardized components and send it to a friend. These, I think, offer us the best inklings as to the future of the Web.

For example, some websites already permit the user to assemble a computer using a base platform and custom options. There are plenty of products that come with gobs of confusing options, and the retail clerks in the stores can never provide a clear idea of exactly how all those options interact. A well-designed website could permit you to explore all the variations and choose the best combination for your needs and budget, knowing exactly what you are getting and exactly why.

A related possibility is the creation, not merely the assembly, of custom products. If you want a customized mouse pad with your photograph on it, wouldn't it be nice to simply provide the image as part of your order on the website? How about supplying your body measurements to a clothier, specifying which dress or shirt design you'd like made? Almost any product can be usefully customized. Why not provide the customer's name and driver's license number on any small, expensive item susceptible to theft? Put it on a hologram that cannot be modified, only noticeably removed. Microscopically etch the same information on any piece of jewelry. Replace those damn designer labels on most clothing with the customer's name on a snazzy label; at the very least this would eliminate laundry problems.

Why not give consumers access to expensive equipment through the Web? This is already done in many industries: circuit board designers can submit their designs to a board maker who runs them off and ships them. Why not extend the concept to the consumer level? Wouldn't home handymen be overjoyed to find a website that custom manufactures little metal widgets necessary to fix old fixtures? If the step from web-delivered specifications to machine requires no human intervention, it would be cheap enough to work. A great many hobbies, such as woodworking, frustrate their aficionados with those crucial components that simply can't be made with home tools. What if a website offered hobbyists the chance to get that part with the 0.001-inch tolerance, so that the hobbyist could concentrate on the rest of the work? How about a coffee retailer who invites you to specify any mix of any beans? A chair manufacturer who uses your body measurements to make an ideal computer chair? A game whose monsters can be tailored to look like your boss or brother-in-law? A toy that looks just like a child's relative or includes the names of the family members in its spoken vocabulary?

These are examples of the user making something on a website. They often require extensive specifications; the website itself should include the software that the user designs her product with. This requires a lot more processing—but that's the whole point: if you add more processing, you get better interactivity and greater opportunities.

Now let's turn to the possibility of letting the user control something on the Web. As I mentioned earlier, online games do this already. But there are plenty of other processes that a user could operate via the Web. Some sites let a user create an imaginary portfolio of stocks and then manage it online, watching how the portfolio appreciates or depreciates. This would certainly help people understand the market and prepare themselves for real investments and thereby make them more willing to invest real money—a worthwhile feature for any online stock brokering operation.

Simulations are the most common form of "running something." It seems a shame that the Web has so much educational information and so little educational simulation; it's rather like making an educational video of a book, turning the page every few moments. Some of the material on the web is unquestionably static information: prices for Beanie Babies, temperatures in Cleveland, and so forth. But much of the educational material could benefit from heavier reliance on simulation.

Browsing

Last, we come to the most common function on the Web: browsing. I am pleased to see how rapidly we have developed design standards for hyperlinks on the web. Despite the impressive progress, we still have a long way to go with hyperlink design at websites; we all have great horror stories of websites with an Alice-in-Wonderland feel to them.

The nature of a website changes as it grows. Almost all websites grow by accretion: a svelte little ten-page site gets more and more pages pasted onto it until it's a sumo-site. This is dangerous, because the hyperlinking mechanics of a site shift as it grows. Typically, websites grow by adding more leaves and establishing a more elaborate tree structure.

For example, suppose that your user wants to learn about Thomas Jefferson. The user goes to a history website and there finds a page on American history, with the following hyperlinks:

Colonial | Revolutionary | Presidents | Civil War | Westward Expansion | Robber Barons

Thomas Jefferson would belong in either the Revolutionary or the Presidents link, and conceivably, even the Westward Expansion link. Which to choose? The correct answer should be: any of these three, because he fits them all. Unfortunately, most websites are designed as trees, with Jefferson pigeon-holed into whichever box the designer prefers. This ensures that some of the users will go down the wrong path, search fruitlessly in its environs, and then retrace their steps to the higher-level link before chancing upon the correct link—an unnecessarily long and frustrating path.

There is absolutely no reason why information at a website must be organized in a tree structure. There's nothing about the nature of computers, the technology of the Web, or the limitations of HTML that imposes a tree structure upon designers. That tree structure is a figment that we impose upon our designs. "Branching thinking" is to website design what "linear thinking" is to creativity.

Branching design relies on a single type of hyperlink: the vertical link. Another common link is the express uplink, which jumps directly to one of the top-level branchpoints on the website:

Home | Site Map | Customer Service | Contact Us | Catalog

What we need more of is the crosslink, which jumps horizontally across the tree, fuzzying the branching structure so that it looks more netlike. In other words, the history website just described would have links to Thomas Jefferson from both its Revolutionary and its Presidents pages. Thus, an important rule to remember:

As a website grows, the percentage of crosslinks must increase.

Alan Cooper in *About Face* makes an important point: the designer must not impose the implementation model onto the user model. In other words, don't let the way you think about designing it affect the way that it's presented to the user. Most websites are designed backwards: organized by available information rather than anticipated user questions. I'm sure that it makes one proud to organize all sorts of information into a tidy little tree, but users seek answers, not trees. Start with the user questions that you want to answer and design forward from there.

The big idea here is that the information you present on the website, be it commercial, academic, or personal, is not merely the content of the individual pages. Information exists in a structure, and the way you structure the information on the website is just as important a component of the message of the site as the manifest content of the pages. In other words, the hyperlinks you create are just as much a part of the delivered content of your site as the images and text. The universe is not a tree with zillions of independent leaves of fact—it's a unified whole. As Galileo observed, we can see the entire universe in a glass of wine. The light reflecting off the glass, refracting and sparkling inside the wine, the thermal convection patterns in the liquid, the mechanical sloshing of the wine, the chemical interactions with the air—it's all right there for us to see. Your website must capture the unity of its content or it's nothing more than a useless pile of pages.

Sadly, this grander style of thinking still escapes many designers. They seem to think of themselves as "page designers" rather than "website designers." There are zillions of beautiful pages out there in gallimaufried sites. Would that site design attracted as much attention as page design!

Last Thoughts

You can't interact with information; it's dead. Information can't listen, and it can't think; all it can do is speak. Therefore, if you set out to provide information, then you have guaranteed that your website will be dead and noninteractive. You are not providing information; you are answering questions. The distinction is crucial; if information were the object of the user's search, then she would simply download your entire website. The more info the better—right? But that's not what happens. Users don't want to have gigabytes of spurious information sprayed all over them. Each one wants a small amount of specific information. Expository media provide information, which is one-size-fits-all in character—and normally too much to be useful. The web allows us to give answers, not merely information, but an answer must be tailored to the user. You're a tailor, not a cloth maker. You are not providing information; you are rendering a service. The distinction between providing information and answering questions is the difference between a book and an answer. You possess an ocean of information, but your user seeks only a sip.

Thus, you should think of your site as "Mr. Know-It-All helps you find the answer to your question!" rather than "It's all here for you to find—somewhere." A website is not a dead stack of paper; it is an interacting agent that can serve the user. You are not designing a tree structure; you are designing an expert who listens and thinks. The next big step in web evolution will be the integration of greater processing into websites. Java is the most likely means by which this will happen. Website designers who can't work in Java (or whatever replaces it) are doomed to become page designers.

The Web is the most dynamic design enterprise in human history. No other medium can match its mass of experimentation, its speed of communication, or its ease of modification. The umpty-zillion pages out there provide us with a gene pool of staggering size, loaded with all sorts of truly odd ideas. All of those odd ideas are like genetic mutations; even though most of them are junk, occasionally a good idea comes along, and when that happens, other designers can discover and spread word of that idea in a matter of days, and they can copy it in a matter of weeks. And so the cycle of design accelerates. Perhaps the web has reached a critical mass that allows us to dispense with deliberate design; perhaps we need merely permit random mimetic mutations coupled with our own selection to advance its evolution. Wouldn't it be ironic if this pinnacle of human design advanced beyond deliberated human design?

> *Game designers should explore other dimensions of thinking, in particular verbal reasoning and social reasoning. Educational software designers should concentrate on process, simulation, and play. Application designers should seek a convergent process by which the user makes, finds, communicates, or controls something. Website designers should get more processing into their sites by applying Java.*

14

DEDICATED DEVICES

One of the fascinating aspects of technological development is the way in which steady incremental improvements in a technology can occasionally alter the technology so much as to yield sudden leaps. Civilization itself arose from such a leap; people had been practicing small-scale agriculture for thousands of years, but at a certain point the efficiencies of the technology became great enough to permit the high population densities necessary for urbanization. From there, it was only a hop, skip, and a jump to standing-room-only subways.

Computer technology is just now taking this kind of leap, albeit a much less significant one. The price of raw computing power—CPUs and RAM—has fallen far enough that we can now discard the old notion of a single, mighty CPU surrounded by a host of peripherals performing a host of tasks. Instead, we can now build a host of smaller machines, each one dedicated to a particular task. Cell phones are one such example—lurking somewhere in the innards of your phone, there lies a microprocessor with as much horsepower as graced personal computers not so long ago.

There will likely be two broad, overlapping classes of dedicated devices: secondary devices, meant to augment conventional PCs, and independent devices, meant to perform some standard function requiring little interaction with a PC. We already have plenty of products in both classes. Digital cameras and portable PIMs (for example, the Palm Pilot) are used in conjunction with a PC. We also have plenty of independent dedicated devices, such as calculators, thermostats, and appliance control processors. Dedicated device technology has been around for a long time. Indeed, the kick-start for the whole revolution was the Intel 4004 processor chip, designed as a processor to be embedded in an appliance. It grew into the 8008, a general-purpose CPU. So dedicated device processing actually predates personal computing. What's new is the likely efflorescence of this technology in the next decade, brought about by smarter and cheaper processing.

The two broad classes of dedicated devices will likely have correspondingly different user bases. The secondary devices will cater to PC users and so will likely sport a more complex interaction. The independent devices, on the other hand, will perform some of the functions of the PC for less technically astute users, and for these purposes, replacing the PC. More important, they will probably create entirely new functions.

General Comments on Dedicated Device Design

We can all agree that VCRs, irrigation timers, thermostats, car stereos, and myriad other devices are often idiotically designed these days, and much improvement is required. Part of the problem is the way in which complexity snuck up on us. In the old days, a thermostat was a simple device: you set the dial to the temperature you wanted, and that was that. Nowadays, thermostats are much more complex: they often have a daytime temperature and a nighttime temperature, with different schedules for weekdays and weekends. But the interaction with the user has not kept pace with the capabilities of the hardware. The same can be said for most other dedicated devices. Hence, the first requirement is that designers of such devices recognize the need for increased attention to the difficulty of using the damn things.

Some designers object that cost considerations force them to rely on such primitive user interfaces. But allow me to present you with an interesting way of viewing the cost trade-off. Suppose that you are the chief designer for Dandy Doodads, Inc., and you are finally souping up your flagship product, the Dandy Doodad, with a built-in computer chip. This chip has plenty of horsepower, so you design in all the clever features you've always wanted to put in. You're feeling quite proud of yourself until you realize that one of your cleverest new features, the Doodad demagnetizing feature, for some odd reason simply cannot be addressed through your user interface. In other words, you can demagnetize like crazy, but it's impossible to provide the user with a means of ordering the Doodad to demagnetize. Sadly, you disengage the feature, kicking yourself for the extra $2 you spent on the hardware to enable this feature. But what the hell, you might as well leave it inside the Doodad—it would seriously delay the project to design it out. The user, of course, has no way of activating the feature or even knowing of its existence. The value of the demagnetizing feature to your customer is precisely zero.

Now suppose that you have come up with a means to permit your user to activate the demagnetizer, but it's quite complicated. The user must carry out a whole series of actions in precise order and with perfect timing. It's all explained in the manual, but, truth be told, few people can execute the command properly. The value of the demagnetizing feature to your customer has risen above zero, but is still low.

Now suppose that you've cleaned up the user interface so that a normal person can use the feature, but there's still a lengthy manual to read before he can understand the process. The value of the demagnetizing feature to your customer has increased slightly.

Last, suppose that you've come up with the ideal solution: there is one magic button on your Doodad that says "Demagnetize," and pushing that button takes care of everything. Now the value of the demagnetizing feature to your customer has finally reached its full potential.

In other words, a feature that is not understood is less useful than a feature that is fully understood. Spending money on features is worthwhile only if the user can readily access those features. It would have been smarter to spend some of the money allocated to the demagnetizing hardware for user interface hardware. Money you spend on interface hardware is justifiable because it makes all the expensive internal stuff more readily available to the user. If, from the user's point of view, that feature is not accessible, then as far as he is concerned, the feature doesn't exist.

RTFM

The software industry has slowly come around to the realization that Read The Manual—RTFM—is no excuse for bad user interface design. Yet designers of dedicated devices seem to be far behind the software people in this regard. This is doubly pernicious; user manuals for software are usually stored within arm's reach of the computer, but user manuals for hardware are quickly lost or, if saved, squirreled away in some cranny far from the user at her moment of need. As a close-to-home example, I challenge you to locate the user manual for your watch.

Indeed, getting users to read the manual in the first place is asking a lot. If people really were that conscientious, we wouldn't need seat belts, air bags, banisters, tempered glass, smoke alarms, and safety goggles. But people aren't conscientious; they are impatient, cocky, and lazy. They are also your livelihood. So are you going to engage in wishful thinking, or are you going to design a product for the actual, paying human beings who will not read your manual?

A simple measure of the quality of any design is the size of the user manual. The perfect design requires no user manual whatsoever; its function is so obvious that the user need not study anything. If you have to explain how to use it, then you haven't done a good enough job.

So now let's consider each of the three steps in interactivity as they pertain to dedicated devices.

Speaking

Dedicated devices don't boast a megapixel display with 32 bits of color; in most cases, the best you can design with is a liquid-crystal display (LCD). Most dedicated devices have too little display capability. It is insane to save a dollar of manufacturing cost by imposing egregious contractions and undecipherable labels on the user. One of these days, we'll have a juicy lawsuit wherein some user interpreted DGR, meaning "danger," as "degrease," thereby igniting a fire that burned down the house and put him in the hospital, etc. And when we do, the blame will fall squarely on the idiot who tried to save a few cents on the LCD. Do you want to be that idiot?

The machine age has cursed us with a cacophony of contractions; while each one individually might make sense, the overall effect is stupefying. Remember that human language has redundancy built into it. That's because people can misread anything. I have misread the "SinkMaster" label for a garbage disposal as "StinkMaster"; I read a billboard for an air show, "Wings Over Moffett," as "Winos Over Moffet." Imagine what I could do with contractions!

So don't push the contractions too hard. In general, you should contract only a few of your labels; if more than 25 percent are contracted, you're pushing too hard. Follow the standard conventions for contractions; don't get creative. If you use the displayed label anywhere else in the product materials (manual, attached short instructions), use both the full term and its contraction in quotation marks. If possible, augment the contraction with additional information to help the user guess its meaning. Perhaps an icon might prove useful—but be careful, because icons can easily mislead if you use them too heavily. Use an icon only if there's an obvious and natural candidate.

Now for some specifics on the LCD to use. First, you're better off spending more money on a bigger black-and-white LCD than on a color LCD panel; at small pixel counts, the eye is more adept at spatial resolution than color resolution. Second, stuff in the biggest LCD you can afford; the bigger the LCD, the more you can say to your user. Most dedicated devices are penny-wise and pound foolish with regard to LCD use; they go to great lengths to minimize LCD cost and then pay extra costs to make the device usable with such a tiny LCD. The primary cost of an LCD display is the pixel addressing circuitry; doubling the size of the array adds one address line. Overall size can be an important consideration in some applications. The pixels themselves cost next to nothing; if you're going to have a display, why not make it as big as possible?

For example, my cell phone sports an LCD with 2,048 pixels. This may seem like a great many, but in fact it's minuscule—a single icon on my computer screen takes up 1,024 pixels, and it's in 24-bit color, while LCDs are single-bit black and white. The manual for this cell phone is over 100 pages long and probably cost several dollars to print. By doubling the size of the LCD, the user interface could have been simplified, reducing the size of the manual and its associated printing costs. While the money saved on the manual would not cover the increased cost of the larger LCD, the reduction in customer service costs very likely would.

My cell phone boasts so many features that it requires nearly 60 different screens. No customer can reasonably be expected to memorize all those features. The designers have succeeded admirably in reducing the size of the cell phone; unfortunately, one must lug around a large and heavy manual if one wishes to actually use the cell phone.

Take full advantage of the periphery of the LCD. You can hard-print labels on the surrounding plastic that the LCD can point to with just a few pixels; the higher contrast of the plastic allows you to use smaller print. I have mixed feelings about the use of fixed internal LCD labels. These are regions of the LCD that are permanently set to display a particular pattern or message; thus, a single bit of information (such as "battery low") takes up a lot of screen space. Better to move such messages to the periphery and point to them with a blinking arrow.

Animation should be used only for annunciators, never for conveying meaning. While animation is powerful and expressive, it is already used and understood worldwide as an annunciator; do not overburden animation with additional uses. Blinking should be reserved for telling the user that something is wrong or for highlighting a selected item.

Sound output can be provided with simple piezoelectric buzzers. Single-tone buzzers have outlived their usefulness; only the simplest of applications can benefit from a single-tone buzzer. Moreover, the inclusion of small CPUs inside dedicated devices makes it easy to use more complex waveforms.

Sound can be used for three functions: acknowledgment, immediate feedback, and annunciation. Too few dedicated devices provide acknowledgment of user input; given the fact that many buttons and switches on dedicated devices are often recessed to prevent inadvertent actuation, it is all the more important to acknowledge deliberate button presses. I believe that every device with such protected switches should provide a short, muted beep to acknowledge every user input.

Given the low cost of LEDs and LCDs, I have difficulty imagining situations in which a designer would want to use sound for immediate feedback. Talking to a user with custom beeps and boops seems foolish—but I have seen some devices that attempt exactly that. About the only such beep that seems to work here is the two-tone "uh-oh" beep that indicates a problem.

The primary use of sound output is for annunciation: grabbing the user's attention when she might be attending to something else. The problem these days is that we live in an over-annunciated world; the classic example of this is the tizzy of activity set off by a single cell phone ringing in a crowded restaurant. Because your dedicated device must coexist with a thousand others, you must work harder to make your annunciations clear and distinct. You should certainly set the volume, pitch, and repetition rate of your annunciation sound to match the urgency of the situation you wish to communicate. Only the must urgent situations should be announced with high volume, high pitch, and rapidly repeating sounds; scale these down for less pressing matters.

The past few years have seen the increasing use of iconic sounds. We signal our car to identify itself; it responds with a distinctive whoop-whoop sound that we have all come to recognize. Cell phones chirp, cars tinkle their warning of lights left on—and on and on it goes. I have mixed feelings about such iconic sounds. The human ear's talent for recognizing a wide array of sounds gives us a huge palette for iconic sounds; however, there's plenty of potential for a digital

Tower of Babel. Designers should differentiate between public annunciations, which might be presented in an auditory environment containing similar annunciations, and private annunciations, which are safely emitted in a confined auditory environment. Public annunciation must be in some way customized to the user; this eliminates the cell-phone-in-the-restaurant problem. An easy way to customize an iconic sound is to append a second sound to it. Private annunciations are less problematic, but the designer should still strive for a distinctive iconic sound.

A better solution is voice output, which comes in two styles: prerecorded and synthesized. The former is best used with devices requiring limited amounts of annunciation. Certainly automobile internal computers could benefit from prerecorded voice output to handle the many warnings currently presented by a confusing variety of bongs, beeps, and buzzes. As the need to announce events and situations increases, these iconic sounds will lose meaning from their overabundance, and designers will have no choice but to use voice output.

If the device must announce a great variety of messages, voice synthesis is required. Voice synthesis has high initial overhead, but once you've set up the ROM with the phoneme data, you can control it with short strings of phoneme tokens.

Thinking

Thinking is just as important a component of interaction as speaking; even simple devices can benefit from a modicum of intelligence. Most dedicated devices offer as their primary function something that is not intrinsically a computing task, so the algorithms you use will not be the primary delivered value of your device. Instead, you will use thinking to head off or straighten out points of confusion with your user. A thermostat, for example, could benefit from intelligence by knowing that certain patterns of use are absurd. You don't put a cooling cycle immediately after a heating cycle; you don't have heating cycles less than ten minutes long. Indeed, there are lots of patterns of use that are unlikely. Most designers take a black-and-white approach to user control: some things are utterly impossible, and everything else is possible. But with some intelligence on the part of the device, you can provide more discrimination here. You can judge various patterns of use as either impossible, unlikely, or reasonable. Thus, the user who wants to turn up the heat at 3:00 A.M. can still do so, but the thermostat might balk and require him to assert himself first.

Listening

As with conventional PCs, listening is the most difficult design challenge with dedicated devices. The number of buttons on our devices has steadily expanded until now we are faced with absurd equipment. The remote control for my TV/VCR has 46 buttons; 8 of those buttons get 99 percent of my use, and 18 I have never used. This is why I feel that LCDs are a better approach for now. Most of those unused buttons could be grouped in a series of LCD screens that would present the information in a more organized fashion. However, arranging layered screens demands much care; the worst offenders here are cell phones and GPS devices. Befuddled users often randomly browse through displays until they find what they are seeking.

You could also have buttons around the periphery of the LCD that take on different meanings (defined by the LCD label) in different contexts. Remember, at any given moment, a user's needs are narrow; presenting her with unusable buttons is bad form. However, your organization must be crystal clear to the user; otherwise she'll get mad trying to figure out how to get the damn thing to give her access to a needed command.

Touch-screen LCDs are excellent devices; only their expense prevents me from recommending them wholeheartedly. Nevertheless, if you have a complicated input structure, you might find the touch-sensitive display worth the expense.

Mechanical buttons must provide feedback to the user. Tactile feedback (you can feel the button move as you press it) is always best. However, some devices require membrane switches that are flat and sealed against dust and water. Rugged they are; usable they aren't. Without any feedback, the user never knows how hard to press. I once had a thermostat whose switches required several pounds of force to actuate; I hated that thermostat. Always include a beep response to presses on such buttons.

Many dedicated devices use paged menus to provide complex input options. The user does not see the entire menu at once; the menu must be entered, and the user must scroll through the menu options, one item per page. While this scheme is serviceable, it is also clumsy and likely to confuse the user. If the user does not think of his goal in the same terms used by the designer, searching through all the menus becomes a cumbersome task. This provides another argument for larger LCDs; if you can fit the entire menu on a single screen, the full benefits of menuing become available.

Using larger LCDs requires the use of cursors, and here arises a tricky problem: should the cursor float, hop, or jump? Computer mice float; the cursor can move smoothly from any position to any other position. Unfortunately, this requires something like a mouse to implement well; most dedicated devices can't have mice. A hopping cursor moves in small, regular steps under the control of four cursor keys. It can go anywhere on the screen. A jumping cursor moves in big steps from one active item to another. This ensures that the cursor is always on a valid input. However, a jumping cursor requires you to space all accessible items in regular order on a rectangular grid. If the active elements of the display do not line up in neat rectangular arrays, the user can never be sure which way to jump to get from one active element to another.

Dedicated devices are tough to design because of tight cost requirements for additional hardware. Such expenses are justified because easy accessibility to features is just important as the features themselves. Touch-sensitive screens are best, but conventional black-and-white LCD screens are adequate if surrounded by mechanical buttons that can be relabeled.

15

WHY LEARN PROGRAMMING?

In Chapter 12, I specified programming ability as one of the qualifications for an interactivity designer. I realize that this specification generates resistance and resentment among many readers. In this chapter, I intend to provide a more complete rationale for this specification.

It is a bitter irony that the people best suited to design interactive products are the least inclined to learn the programming necessary to do so. I have tried—Lord knows I've tried—to prod, shame, encourage, and teach people to learn programming, but I'm up against deep-seated fears and prejudices that no amount of sweet reason or fire and brimstone can overcome. Part of the problem arises from Two Cultures prejudice (see Chapter 27); some comes from fear that is mongered by programmers; throw in a little natural human laziness, and you have an unbeatable combination. In this chapter, I intend to do battle with that windmill.

Piece o' Cake

Programming itself is not as difficult as people have been led to believe. Programmers have an economic interest in promulgating the myth of programming as rocket science, and they push that myth for all it's worth. You need only consider the lessons of Chapter 10, "Bloopers," to realize just how easy it is for programmers to make something simple seem impossibly complex. True, programming demands some effort to learn, but it is not of the same order of skill as, say, brain surgery or jet piloting. It's closer to accounting, writing, or cooking. Granted, each of these skills has its brilliant artiste practitioners who work at rarefied levels of excellence. But the majority of practitioners in these fields are normal people, not flaming geniuses, and you wouldn't feel presumptuous to try your hand at any of them. Programming is no different. You should not permit yourself to be intimidated by all that self-serving programmer hokum.

Don't Take No Shit

Our culture has learned the importance of accountability in guaranteeing good behavior, and through much of the past century we have erected forests of accountability rules for all walks of life. Everything we do has a paper trail: receipts, time cards, signatures, notifications—gad, what a snowstorm of paper! Yet we do it because we know that accountability is the best defense against human perfidy. Yet programmers operate with almost zero accountability. In the 14 programming projects I have completed over the past 19 years, I have never had a single line of my program code vetted by another programmer.

There's a good reason for this: anybody talented enough to evaluate my code has more profitable things to do than play quality-control inspector. The field has expanded too quickly; the demand for programmers has always exceeded the supply, so there are no surplus programmers to provide quality-control services. And you can be certain that programmers, being human, take full advantage of the lack of accountability. Knowing that there's nobody to look over their shoulders, they indulge in behaviors ranging from petty insubordination to bald-faced lying.

There's no escaping the requirement of programming for interactivity projects. Sure, you can hire programmers to do that work, but the less you know about programming, the more easily you can be victimized. A knowledge of programming will not render you immune to programmers' shenanigans—I myself have been deceived by programmers working for me. But the more you know, the less money and time you'll lose on this problem, and the fewer design compromises you'll be forced to make for the sake of the programmers. You'll always have to take shit from your programmers, but a knowledge of programming lowers your merdivorousity.

You Can't Drive from the Back Seat

Programming is where the rubber hits the road in interactivity design. I don't like that fact; it violates my design aesthetic, which calls for greatest weight to be assigned to the highest levels of design. Design should not have to dance to the tune called by programming, but that's the way things are. If you can't program, then you can't call the tune. If you can program, then the tough trade-offs between design goals and technical constraints will be made inside your own head, rather than over a meeting table with an obstinate programmer.

Nor can you lead a team from a position of ignorance. My wife is a manufacturing executive, but she makes a point of getting out on the assembly line and twisting a screwdriver shoulder-to-shoulder with the workers. Her ability to command willing obedience is derived from their knowledge that she understands their tasks. One of the basic principles of strong leadership is: never ask a subordinate to do something that you could not do yourself. Business is full of brash young executives who don't understand this principle, who rail impotently at the recalcitrance of their subordinates, earning only their insolent derision. If you refuse to learn to program, this is the position you'll find yourself in.

Understanding

Programming is more than the means of actualizing interactivity design; it is intimately associated with the concepts of interactivity. You can't dismiss it as a minor factor best delegated to junior employees. The ideas of programming closely parallel the ideas of interactivity. Divorcing interactivity design from programming is an unnatural act.

Moreover, you stand to gain so much by learning to program. No other area of human intellectual endeavor is so purely and sparely logical. (Mathematics is pure but not spare.) It is certainly an alien way of thinking, but your mind is capable of playing that role. As they say, travel broadens, and the journey into the weird, cold world of programming will broaden your mind—but you have to learn the language!

Interactivity Designer as Go-Between

Here's a gross but illuminating generalization: the human brain is a pattern-recognizing system, while the computer is a sequential-processing system. The fact that the computer's thinking is so orthogonal to human thinking constitutes a challenge to the designer, but it is also the source of the computer's utility. After all, if computers were just scaled-down versions of our own brains, what good would they be? Who would ever turn to an ignorant, dummied-down brain for help? When was the last time you asked a two-year-old for career advice?

The essence of every software designer's task is to create a harmonious and productive relationship between these two orthogonal styles of thinking. To do this well, the designer must understand both styles of thinking deeply enough to bring them together in a productive fashion. Herein lies the fundamental reason why computers suck: programmers don't understand human thinking, and designers don't understand computer thinking.

The problem is similar to that encountered by European explorers when they discovered new societies. How did the two parties communicate? The Europeans often had along with them a translator who spoke the language common a few hundred miles away, but who could barely make out the language of these new people. The natives might have a local on hand who knew some other languages, and between them the two intermediaries could just barely understand each other. Imagine yourself, then, as Meriwether Lewis talking to his interpreter, who talks to a Mandan interpreter, who talks to the Mandan chief. Imagine the frustrations and misunderstandings inherent in such a situation. Don't those frustrations and misunderstandings remind you of your relationship with your computer? It's the same story: you're talking to the computer through the intermediaries of a software designer and a programmer, neither of whom can bridge the gap between you and the computer. What a mess!

The only way to tackle this problem is to find a genuine translator who understands both languages, a single person to act as go-between rather than the two middlemen we now use: designer and programmer. That single translator has to be you, the interactivity designer. Ergo, you cannot call yourself an interactivity designer until you truly understand how the computer thinks—which means that you must be able to write software. You need not execute the programming task on every project, but until you understand the computer well enough to take over the programming task if necessary, you simply aren't equipped to design interactive applications.

Most people will take umbrage with this conclusion, and many will seek to refute it; some, possessed of blunter emotional acuity, will try to dismiss this entire book, and those few with the bluntest emotional acuity will want to discredit its author. It is a painful truth to acknowledge, I admit. It implies that decades will pass before we develop a community of truly expert interactivity designers. Worse, it implies that most people today are excluded from that community, relegated to second-class status. Yet I would caution those whose feelings have been hurt with the observation that any truly worthy endeavor cannot be, and should not be, assimilable in a quick gulp. Every reader of this book can surely boast of vast expertise in at least one field of endeavor, expertise built on a long heritage of previous effort and acquired at the cost of years of training and practice. Were interactivity design to violate this principle and admit to the ranks of its experts persons with a smattering of experience, then what point would there be in writing or reading a book such as this? What challenge could so lightweight a field offer to a truly talented or creative person?

Learn to program.

16

SOFT MATH

Simulation requires the use of soft math, which is a simplified and approximated variation on academic math. A variety of rules of thumb are offered.

Every interactivity design uses a mental model or simulation. *Simulation* is a dangerous term; it connotes a mathematical exactness that is appropriate only in physical systems. The interactivity designer roams a wider world, one in which mathematical exactness is often out of the question. Yet the language of the computer is mathematical in style and content. This disjunction cleaves the interactivity design community into two groups: those who insist on confining their efforts to mathematically definable problems, and those who refuse to contemplate the use of mathematics in their work. The first group imprisons itself; the second group enfeebles itself.

Soft Numbers

There is a path out of this trap, which I shall call "soft math." This is the unrepentantly sloppy application of simple mathematics to solve problems that could never be solved rigorously with honest, god-fearing mathematics.

Consider: how many days are there in a year? You say 365, right? Not quite; 365 is only an approximation. The true value is actually 365? days; that's why we have leap years. But, strictly speaking, 365? days is also an approximation; we drop the leap year on centuries not divisible by 400. That means that the true value of the year is actually 365.2475 days. But even this answer is wrong, because the true value of the year, as measured by astronomers, is 365.24220 days. Er, actually, even that number is off by a little, because the earth's rotation rate wobbles a little; every December 31 at midnight, the people in charge of maintaining our time standards make tiny adjustments in the official time—normally a few thousandths of a second. So here are some values for the length of a year:

365 days

365¼ days

365.2475 days

365.24220 days

365.24220 days plus an annual fudge

Which of these numbers is "correct"? We could bury ourselves in endless philosophical debate over this problem; indeed, it could be argued that there exists *no* correct value for the length of a year, because it's always changing by minuscule amounts. But there is a workable solution: let's not try to be dogmatic and simply use the best number for the task at hand. In other words, a number isn't just something that you polish bright and shiny and mount on your fireplace lintel; it's something that you use in some sort of calculation. If I want to buy a year's supply of pills and I take one pill every day, then I want 365 pills, not 365.24220 pills. If it's vitamin pills I'm buying, and they're so cheap that it doesn't matter, I'll be happy to buy a bottle of 500 pills. On the other hand, if I'm 48 years old and want to know how many days I've lived, I'll use the 365? days value to get 17,532 days.

The point of all these silly calculations is that a number is not just a dead hunk of data; it's something that you use, and the use to which you put it determines exactly how "much" number you need. Refer to Chapter 17 and its deeper discussion of this operational definition of reality.

This concept is so important that I'll kill a few extra trees with another example, this one concerned with distance. I can tell you that the distance from my home to town is 5 miles, but that estimate is accurate to only about half a mile. The distance from my barn to my house is 450 feet, give or take 5 feet. My barn is 32 feet long, with an error of maybe a couple of inches. When I cut a 2 by 4, I normally aim to get the cut good to within a 1/4 inch or so. When I'm making a knife, I try to get the parts shaped right to within about 1/100 of an inch. Here I have five numbers, each of which is measured to a different degree of precision. That's because I'm putting each of the numbers to a different use. I use the distance to town to estimate travel time and gasoline consumption; half a mile of error won't make much difference. I use the distance to my barn to calculate the length of a fence; 5 feet of error is acceptable in purchasing fence materials. I'll be nailing that 2 by 4 against a corner fencepost; it has to line up properly, but it'll bend a quarter of an inch if need be. The knife parts have to fit together neatly without obvious seams; most people can see and feel edges bigger than 1/50 of an inch, so if I keep everything to 1/100 of an inch, my knife will look and feel nice.

Soft Formulas

Now I want to apply this concept in another way, a surprising way: this concept applies to formulas just as well as it applies to numbers. After all, what is a formula but a way to obtain a number? Suppose my hardware store sells fencing by the meter; I have to convert that 450 feet (plus or minus 5 feet) into meters. The formula for converting feet into meters is

```
meters = feet * 0.304800
```

so I need 137.16 meters of fencing. But what's the point of worrying about that last 0.16 meter when the original measurement is good to only 5 feet (a meter and a half)? What's the point of sweating the formula when the numbers are sloppy to start with? It'd be better for me to use 140 meters and stash away the few feet of extra fencing for a chicken coop or something.

Let's extend the concept a little further. I'm building a bridge over the creek; I need to buy some struts to place diagonally in support of my kingpost. How long should they be? The correct formula is

```
length of diagonal = length of kingpost / sine (support angle)
```

Now the kingpost is 8 feet high, and the support angle is 45 degrees. But jeez, the sine of 45 degrees is $1/2^{\sqrt{2}}$, and that square root is 1.414 something. What the hell; just assume 1.5 and buy a 12-foot timber. I can cut it down to size on site.

Next I'll take it a smidge further. I'm planning a garden for my wife; to keep the deer out, I'll need a 10-foot high fence completely enclosing it. I plan it as a square 100 feet on a side, so I'll be needing 400 feet of fencing. But when I get to the hardware store, I find that they'll sell me a 500-foot standard roll of fencing for only a few dollars more than the custom-cut 400 feet. I want to decide if the extra money for the 500-foot roll is worth it, so I ask myself, how much more area would that add to the garden? The extra 100 feet would make it 25 feet larger, or 125 feet on a side. For any square, this formula is true:

```
area = length²
```

But jeez, I can't multiply 125 by 125 in my head. Besides, I don't want the total area; I want the increase in area provided by the extra fencing. If you care to dredge up tedious memories from your freshman year in high school, you'll recall the quadratic equation:

```
(a + b)² = a² + 2ab + b²
```

So I can set it up as

```
(100 + 25)² = 100² + 2 * 100 * 25 + 25²
```

I still can't figure out 25^2 in my head, but I do know that the 100^2 is the previously planned area of my garden, and I can see at a glance that 2 * 100 * 25 is a lot bigger than 25^2. So let's just fudge the equation by ignoring the 25^2 part. Hence, the difference in area is just 2 * 100 * 25, which is 50 *100, which is 5,000. In other words, the extra hundred feet of fencing will give me an extra 5,000 square feet of garden.

Note that I shamelessly changed the formula: I threw away the b^2 part. But for my purposes, getting to 5,000 square feet was close enough, so I skipped the extra work—and the correct answer, 5,625 additional square feet, isn't that far from my quick guess.

This basic concept of approximation can be applied to *any* mathematical calculation of *any* size or degree of complexity. You have to keep in mind just how much accuracy you need to get the job done, but you don't have to waste mountains of time on getting it perfect.

Suppose now that I'm working on an interactive storytelling program, and I need to figure out how angry one of my characters would be if he were insulted by another character. That depends on how ugly the insult is, and how much of a temper my character has. So here's my formula:

```
Anger = Temper * Ugliness
```

This is not a mathematically or psychologically correct formula expressing the intricacies of human emotional reaction and brain organization. It leaves out lots of other factors that, in truth, would affect the angry character. But it works, and for my purposes it's good enough. So I use it without fear that some Math Zeus will strike me with a thunderbolt.

This is what I mean by soft math. This is not a test, and you will not be marked wrong if your answer is off by 0.04. This is the grubby world of interactivity design, and you have a job to do. Just get close enough; you can always go back and refine your formulas later if they turn out to be insufficiently accurate.

Blasphemy!

Some people from the arts and humanities are discomfited by this concept. It seems somehow blasphemous to reduce the richness and subtlety of human existence to mere numbers. How can we reduce the complexity of an insult to a single number? When one of Shakespeare's characters calls another "Thou slander of thy heavy mother's womb," how can a simple dumb number like 29 truly capture the richness of the jab?

The answer lies in the fact that we are not attempting to capture the richness of the insult, but only one small aspect of that insult: its ugliness. True, ugliness is not objectively measurable as would be something like word count or number of syllables. But what's wrong with applying a little subjectivity here? Is subjectivity not intrinsic to the arts and humanities? The issue here is not *what* we deal with, but *how* we express ourselves. What's the difference between rating an insult as toothless, weak, minor, moderate, sharp, or vicious, and rating it as 20, 30, 40, 50, 60, or 70? Quantitivity does not exclude subjectivity.

If you want blasphemy, try this out for size:

```
Beauty = Lies + Murder + Suffering
```

You can certainly blaspheme using mathematical methods, but the blasphemy lies in the content of the message, not its form.

Applicability

Some people disdain this easy-going approach to mathematics; they argue that it's fine for mere games, but their designs, be they productivity applications, educational software, or websites, demand precision. This is true only to the extent that you design pedestrian programs. If you're designing a word processing program and you want to show the user a page count, it's pretty hard to mess up that calculation, and you certainly don't have to worry about getting 3.14159265358979323 pages. But what if you're going beyond the word processing designs of 1980? Suppose, for example, that you're designing a word processing program that will give your user advice on the writing style of a document. You would, of course, use one or more of the many formulas for clarity of writing, and that would help; but why not include other assessments? For example, you might want to provide an assessment of the amount of bureaucratic language in a document. You should be able to devise an approximate algorithm for determining the bureau-speak content of a document—but it sure won't be precise. It's easy to look for words like "actualize" or "implement," to count all the misapplied suffixes (-ize, -tion, -ate, -ify, and so on), and to count acronyms, but are there other factors in writing that are characteristic of the bureaucratic style? This is where your judgment and experience come into play— use them!

Or how about a "speaking style" detector? This is one of my weaknesses in writing: I write like I talk. It's not good; the written word breathes differently than the spoken word. I'm certain that some harried editor out there could come up with some simple rules for assessing the "spokenness" of a document. Such rules wouldn't be mathematically rigorous, but they would nevertheless be useful.

Here's an example for educational software designers: you want to design a program that interacts with your students. You don't want to merely spray information all over their faces; you want to respond to each one individually. There are already some primitive algorithms for this; they count how many times a student gets an answer wrong, and once the error count climbs too high, the program suggests (or transfers to) a simpler level of material. But this can easily be bettered.

Consider those tedious question-and-answer programs. The computer poses a question or problem, and the student enters or selects an answer, which the computer determines to be correct or incorrect. Surely such programs could be upgraded to, say, the 1950s by adding algorithms that detect particular common errors and divert the student to special material devoted to those errors. Of course, if you don't already know those common errors, you're not qualified to teach the subject. When I taught physics, there were plenty of mistakes so common that I resorted to acronyms in grading them. One such mistake was getting the units of measurement confused. Students would calculate energy in kg-m/s or force in kg/s. To think of all the times I had to walk a student through those remedial lessons! This kind of tedium is what a computer is good for.

You website designers need soft math even more than the educators. Why are web designers so stuck on designing dead sites? The user's interests are assessed solely by the page visited. If you're visiting our fruit page, you'll probably want to see the apple, banana, orange, and peach pages, so we put links to them on the fruit page. But why should a site's response be so static? There's more information about the user's interests in the pattern of pages visited. Even the simplest pattern data can reveal much. A user who returns to the home page frequently during a single visit is clearly engaged in exploration and therefore is something of a beginner to the site; once the site recognizes this, it can use alternate, beginner-level pages that highlight the best pages for beginners to visit and downplay the more advanced pages. But what formula should you use to identify a beginner? How many returns to the home page finger the user as a beginner?

You could define a half-dozen attributes that might be estimated for each page and then assign a value to each one. In other words, you might estimate, for each page, its pinkness, quantity of animation, use of ads, quantity of static imagery, amount of textual information, and jazziness of design. You could then keep track of the pages a user visits, accumulating the net value of each of the attributes. After you've accumulated enough information, you have a profile of your user; why not use that profile to steer her? Websites are growing so large that they have their own internal search engines and other navigational aids; how about a little intelligent assistance as well?

All of this requires you to use more math. Fortunately, you've already learned all the math you need. You can do wonderful things with high school freshman algebra, and if you use your sophomore geometry, you can design algorithms at the cutting edge of interactivity design—that's how primitive the state of the art is. The four basic arithmetic operations (addition, subtraction, multiplication, and division) can accomplish almost everything you would want. It's mostly a matter of learning how to use these tools effectively. For example, I recently learned how to use a crowbar. It's such a simple tool, I had always underestimated its utility. But once I learned the difference between the curved end and the straight end and how to use them properly, I suddenly realized just how much power I wielded with that simple tool. I started looking around for things to split, separate, or dismantle.

An Example

Here's a problem from interactive storytelling:

The human player is about to do something to Computer Character Fredegund. Perhaps it's something nasty, perhaps it's something nice—we don't know in advance because the human player has free will and must be permitted to make his own choice. Meanwhile, Computer Character Mary is observing the human player's actions. What will Mary's reaction be? Let us assume, for purposes of simplicity, that the only variables here are:

1. Whether the human player's action was nice. (Nice)

2. Whether Mary likes or dislikes Fredegund. (Likes)

3. Whether Mary is pleased by the human player's action. (Pleased)

This third variable is the one we want to calculate.

Here's an obvious and common approach to solving the problem, expressed in simple pseudocode:

```
IF Nice AND Likes THEN Pleased
IF NOT Nice AND Likes THEN Displeased
IF Nice AND NOT Likes THEN Displeased
IF NOT Nice AND NOT Likes THEN Pleased
```

This approach is weak because it is instantial in style. It is a case-by-case, nit-picky approach. There is no generality to it, no principle at work. It is, in my own terminology, data intensive. It is clumsy and inflexible. It is also simplistic.

Here's a slightly better approach:

```
Pleased = NOT (Nice EOR Likes)
```

This Boolean equation says exactly the same thing that the earlier set of four equations says, but it is superior, for two reasons. First, it is more efficient; it consumes less program space and executes faster. Second, it is a clearer statement of the actual principle at work. It gets right to the point. In a single sentence, it defines the principle at work, whereas the first approach requires four sentences to make its point. Thus, this second approach represents a deeper understanding of the principle at work than the first approach. A thousand years ago, swordsmiths knew the steps required to make carbon steel, but it wasn't until this century that we understood why those steps worked. This understanding permitted many improvements on the process. In the same fashion, the second approach points the way to the third and best approach:

```
Reaction = Niceness * Affection
```

In this approach, I have replaced the Boolean variables Pleased, Nice, and Likes with the arithmetic variables Reaction, Niceness, and Affection. For example, the variable Affection can range from, say, –100 to +100. Niceness spans a similar range. This equation thus says everything that the earlier approaches say, and much more. To appreciate the power of this formula, you should try out a variety of numbers between –100 and +100 in the formula to see what answer you get for Reaction. For example, if Mary's Affection for Fredegund is zero, then it doesn't matter how nice or nasty the human player's action is; whatever the value of Niceness, it will be multiplied by zero, which will always yield a result of zero for the reaction. In other words, if Mary has neither affection or disaffection for Fredegund, then Mary doesn't care what I do. The equation also allows a graduated appraisal of Mary's reaction. She isn't just a robot who is either pleased or displeased; she can have shades of reaction. In other words, the generality of the solution has increased. The first solution addresses exactly four cases. The third solution addresses myriad different cases.

Notice that, as we moved from the first approach to the third approach, the solutions became more difficult to understand. That third equation takes more mental effort to grasp than the first set of IF-THEN statements. This is the reason why so few designers use such methods—they are more difficult to understand.

Rules of Soft Math

1. *Quantify it.* Whatever your design problem is, ask yourself what kind of number or measurement you could use to tackle it. Remember to think operationally—you're not looking for the "correct" number; you're looking for the number that you can use to the benefit of the user. Don't hesitate to quantify seemingly nonnumeric factors. You can think of your user's impulsiveness by counting how many times she erases something entered or backsteps. Sure, that's not really impulsiveness, but it's a usable approximation, something you can apply to make your design more responsive. Don't waste time on philosophical arguments about what a label really means. You're using the word *Impulsiveness* in your design, not the real world, and like Humpty-Dumpty, you can use it to mean whatever you want it to mean, no more and no less. You could call it *Zargonosis* if you wanted, but *Impulsiveness* might help you keep your intent in mind.

Lord Berkeley said "To measure is to know," It's just a game, of course—talking about a user's Impulsiveness, Error-Proneness, Spelling-Correctness, and so forth may seem rather silly—but once you've dreamed up the variables, you can start to apply them in useful ways. You'll probably get some of them wrong, but if you refuse to dream them up in the first place, you'll never get off the ground. Crawford's Corollary to Berkeley's dictum is ". . . and to calculate is to understand."

2. *Either* means addition. Once you have some variables, you need to figure out how to put them together to calculate useful numbers. What's the right formula to use? Just talk about it in plain English. Suppose you want to decide how liberally you should issue cautionary warnings to your user. What kind of user would benefit from such warnings? *Either* an error-prone user *or* an impulsive user. Ergo:

```
Warning Frequency = Impulsiveness + Error-Proneness
```

Subtraction is really the same thing as addition, only in the opposite direction.

3. *Both* means multiplication. If I say that a character's reaction to an event depends on *both* the Niceness of the action and the character's Affection for the object of the action, then I express this as a multiplication:

```
Reaction = Niceness * Affection
```

4. The difference between addition and subtraction, or between multiplication and division, is often a matter of how you define your factors. In the previous example, I could have used a variable Hatred instead of Affection, and then my equation would have read:

```
Reaction = Niceness / Hatred
```

Subtraction is similar. If I want to calculate how much money I have left after tax day, I'd be tempted to do it as a subtraction:

```
Money Today = Money Yesterday - Taxes Paid
```

But there's a more optimistic way of thinking about it:

```
Money Today = Money Yesterday + Tax Refund
```

Of course, both formulas yield the same result, because if I paid taxes, then Tax Refund is negative, and if I get a refund, then Taxes Paid is negative.

5. If you're confused with subtractions and divisions, redefine your factors. If you don't like the subtraction equation, then use Tax Refund and flip to addition. Use whichever form is easiest.

6. Sometimes you need fudge factors. These are numbers you grab out of thin air to make a formula work better. For example, consider the earlier formula for giving warnings to an errant user:

```
Warning Frequency = Impulsiveness + Error-Proneness
```

Suppose that you measured Impulsiveness by the number of times the user backtracked; that would give you a regular number like 4 or 9. But suppose that you measured Error-Proneness by the fraction percentage of times that the user made an error; that would be a number between zero and one. If, in one case, Impulsiveness were 4 and Error-Proneness were 0.3, then your Warning Frequency would be 4.3. That's not fair to Error-Proneness! So let's just scale it up to level the playing field:

```
Warning Frequency = Impulsiveness + (10 * Error-Proneness)
```

That 10 that I inserted is a fudge factor that I just made up. It might be too big; I'll just have to use the program a while to get a sense for how well-tuned my fudge factors are, and perhaps I'll come back and adjust it during the final tuning stages of the design process.

7. Watch out for division by zero. If you use division, you always have to be on the lookout for a formula that divides a number by another number that just happens to be zero. For example, suppose that I cooked up this formula:

```
Gorgonzolaness = Typing Speed / Frequency of Error
```

Suppose now that my program encounters some inhuman typist who simply doesn't make mistakse. When this formula is computed, the program will look up the value of Frequency of Error and find that it is zero. When it puts that zero into the formula and divides Typing Speed by zero—kaboom! the program crashes. There is no computer in the world that can gracefully deal with a division by zero, because division by zero is mathematical gibberish.

This may surprise you; after all, computers are omnipotent, right? Well, division by zero is rather like what Captain Kirk used to do to befuddle rampant computers.

Suppose that you are carefully following along as Mister Master Chef on television shows you how to bake garlic oysters, and halfway through he says, "Now this is a very important step . . ."—and the TV dies! What could you do? The dog gets oysters tonight. The same thing happens when a computer program encounters division by zero. It crashes. Modern operating systems are smart enough to throw up firewalls and confine the damage to your program, but there's nothing that can save your program once it hits that division by zero.

Fortunately, division by zero is easy to fix. You can tell the programmer to check for zero and abort the calculation if it appears. Or you can just add something to the denominator, like so:

```
Gorgonzolaness = Typing Speed / (Frequency of Error + 1)
```

Now you're safe—most of the time. If Frequency of Error were ever –1, then you'd end up dividing by zero again. So this technique works only with variables that can't go negative.

8. It *will* happen to you! Don't ever, ever tell yourself that any factor can't ever take on some dangerous value unless you have absolute mathematical proof that it won't happen. Don't tell yourself "None of my users will ever be that fast"— someday, somebody will be.

9. Keep it short and simple. A formula with two factors is easy to figure out, a formula with three factors takes some effort, and a formula with four factors is well-nigh impossible for most people to understand, unless it's simply arranged. For example, what does this formula do?

```
Gorgonzolaness = Typing Speed / (Errors - (Tax Refund / (Money Today + 1)))
```

I can't make sense of it either.

Simulation is the art of playing games with numbers and formulas to emphasize what is important and ignore what is not. In the real world, much mathematical sloppiness is necessary. You can do great things with math as simple as high school algebra. To measure is to know, and to calculate is to understand.

PART THREE
THEORY

17

PROCESS INTENSITY

Underlying interactivity design is the notion of process-intensive thinking.

One of the deepest and most fundamental polarities in the universe is that of entities versus operations: facts versus principles, knowledge versus ideas. This polarity is so profound that it shows up over and over in many fields, each time in a different guise, but the basics are always the same.

In philosophy, one pole might be called the *operational definition of reality*: reality is as reality does. We think about the universe as an intricate webwork of processes, which as a whole generate reality. The other pole is reality is a set of objects: the universe considered in terms of things. The objects, of course, interact with each other, but the essential truth is the set of objects. Are you a glob of organic chemicals and water? Or are you perception plus digestion plus locomotion plus thinking plus . . . ?

In linguistics, this polarity presents itself as the distinction between noun and verb. These are the two absolutely necessary fundamental atoms of language. The other atoms (adjectives, prepositions, adverbs, and so on) are fundamental (not composed of the first two) but not absolutely necessary. You can build a language with nouns and verbs and leave out all the other grammatical types. But you can't construct a language without nouns or verbs.

In computer science, the polarity concerns the two most fundamental units of computation: bits and machine cycles or, in other terms, data and processing. Again, these are fundamental requisites of computing. You can still compute without printers, color monitors, mice, or keyboards, but you absolutely must have some memory for the data and a CPU for the processing.

Physicists talk about waves and particles, and these correspond to the preceding examples. Clearly, particles correspond to objects. I think it acceptable to think of waves as processes because a wave is a dynamic process in which something (often energy) sloshes from one form to another repetitively. Unless physics has greatly changed since I was in graduate school, you can be confident that any solvable physics problem can be solved with either wave mechanics or particle mechanics.

How about economics? Here we encounter goods versus services. Goods are objects, while services are processes. These are the two fundamental forms of economic output. You can't have an economy without both of these.

We can even extend the principle into the arts: in storytelling, we can distinguish between the character-based story (object) and the plot-driven story (process). And despite Hollywood's intense efforts, it remains impossible to create a decent story without *some* plot and *some* character, although I am told that the movie *Godzilla* made an impressive attempt in this direction.

Now I'm going to present some grand generalizations about this deep polarity. In each case, I'll try to exemplify the point with reference to the disciplines I've mentioned.

Duality

Duality is the notion that one can successfully (if clumsily) address any problem by hewing to one of the forms (object or process) or by using any mix of the two. Indeed, we recognize that any given situation will be most easily handled with some particular mix of the two forms. Thus, philosophers could, if they wanted to, achieve an all-inclusive definition of reality using some fluid mix of the operational approach and the object approach. Linguists will tell you that a word can readily switch from verb to noun and back again. I could call myself a person (object), but I could also refer to myself in verb terms as a human *being*: a human-type act of existence. Indeed, in English we have a formal mechanism for converting a verb to a noun: just add the suffix *-ing* to the verb root and presto! you have a gerund. We have no formal way to nounify a verb, but we extemporize; sometimes we simply pressgang the noun into a verb.

Duality is clearest and simplest in computer science. It is widely recognized that any computable problem can be solved with a range of algorithms combining data and processing in any mixture. We can use a table-driven approach that consumes lots of bits and few cycles, or we can try a formula-driven approach that uses lots of cycles and few bits—as well as almost any combination of the two. It's a matter of how many bits and how many cycles we have to play with, and how clever we are.

One of the big discoveries of twentieth-century physics is the wave-particle duality. You can talk about any physical phenomenon as either a wave or a particle, even though the mathematics used to describe these two are fundamentally different. In some cases, the particle equations are the most useful, and in other cases, the wave equations yield the greatest utility—but there remain plenty of phenomena that require us to use both particle physics and wave physics.

Economics offers no challenges to the principle; we can intermix goods and services willy-nilly. As somebody pointed out recently, it's impossible to unambiguously determine whether McDonald's sells goods (burgers) or provides services (food preparation). Is McDonald's a service providing customers with fast, hot meals, or is it a distribution system for all-beef patties, lettuce, onions, pickles, and sesame-seed buns? In writing this book, have I provided a service (intellectual edification) or a good (a hunk of paper)?

On to storytelling: writers, being naturally opinionated, tend to divide into tribal units, one supporting the character-based approach and the other touting the plot-driven approach. Yet each side grudgingly acknowledges the necessity of the other. They are arguing primacy, not necessity. And (just as some things are pretty clearly goods, particles, bits, or nouns, while others are more obviously services, waves, cycles, or verbs), so too in drama do we have some stories that are pretty clearly character based, and others that are pretty clearly plot-driven.

Nounism

Despite the apparent symmetry between the two extremes of the polarity, we humans seem to have a strong bias towards the object pole. I'm not sure why; perhaps it arises from our sensory system, which handles objects so much better than processes. Perhaps it's the temporal permanence of objects versus the temporally diffuse and narrow existence of processes. Perhaps it's merely our language; most languages seem so much more facile with noun phrases than verb phrases. Indeed, 60 percent of the first gurgling vocalizations of infants will eventually develop into nouns; only 20 percent will become verbs. There are a few exceptions, of course, including one Native American language that seems to verbify almost everything—but such exceptions are notable because they are so weird.

Certainly a contributing factor to our prejudice in favor of objects over processes lies in the inherent abstraction of processes as opposed to the concreteness of objects. This abstraction, however, lies at the heart of the power of process. Thus, the very factor that makes process so difficult to deeply comprehend is what gives it its power.

An easier way to recognize the prejudice of nounism is to note the historical trends in some of the above-mentioned fields. In computer science, for example, we have seen an explosion of creative activity in the last decade arising from the wide availability of PCs and the Internet. But has anybody noticed that the preponderance of this creativity has expressed itself in—and been measured by—the huge number of bits that have been made available? Between CDs and the Web, we now have humonga-bytes of images, sounds, text, numbers, and all manner of other data. But consider this: we have also built enough computers (and made them so fast) that every day, civilization expends humonga-cycles of processing time. And what are all those cycles doing? I'd guess that almost *all* of those cycles are wasted in wait loops, as the computer sits for eternities (in its own time scale) waiting for the rare keypress or mouse click. And even the cycles that aren't wasted are used almost entirely for shuffling bits around: moving an image from a CD to the screen, a sound from memory to a speaker, and so on. An infinitesimal fraction of the cycles we generate every day are used to actually process anything. We push numbers around a lot, but we seldom crunch them. It seems a great shame to use this wondrous processing machine to shuffle bits around; is it not unlike using a human being endowed with character and feelings and soul to bail water from a canal to a field? It would seem that, in terms of truly utilizing the power of the computer, we still have a long way to go.

The history of physics shows our noun prejudice even more clearly. Isaac Newton gave us a pretty good system of mechanics for particles back in the seventeenth century, but we didn't get decent wave mechanics until the nineteenth century. We solved the easy part (to us) two centuries before we tackled the hard part.

To see noun prejudice in economics, observe how long economics devoted itself solely to goods. The realization that services are just as important came towards the middle of this century. But the trend is ontogenetic as well: economies themselves grow from goods orientation to service orientation.

Process Intensity and Data Intensity

To express this polarity in terms most appropriate to interactivity design, I use the concept of *process intensity* versus *data intensity*. Process intensity is the degree to which a program emphasizes processes instead of data. All programs use a mix of process and data. Process is reflected in algorithms, equations, and (to a lesser degree) branches. Data is reflected in data tables, images, sounds, and text. A process-intensive program spends most of its time crunching numbers; a data-intensive program spends most of its time moving bits around.

The difference between process and data is profound. Process is abstract, whereas data is tangible. Data is direct, whereas process is indirect. The difference between data and process is the difference between numbers and equations, between facts and principles, between events and forces, between knowledge and ideas. It's easy to memorize a number, a fact, an event, or knowledge, but consider how much more difficult it is to appreciate an equation, a principle, a force, or an idea.

Processing data is the very essence of what a computer does. There are many technologies that can store data: magnetic media, punched cards, punched tape, paper and ink, microfilm, microfiche, and optical discs, to name just a few. But there is only one technology that can process data: the computer. This is its primary source of superiority over the other technologies. Using the computer in a data-intensive mode ignores its true nature and its greatest strength.

The Crunch-per-Bit Ratio

Because process intensity is so close to the essence of "computerness," it provides us with a useful criterion for evaluating the value of any software design. That criterion is the ratio of operations per datum, which I call the *crunch-per-bit ratio*. An operation is any process applied to a datum, such as an addition, subtraction, or logical operation or a simple Boolean inclusion or exclusion operation. A datum in this scheme can be a bit, a byte, a character, a number, a pixel, or a sonel: it is a small piece of information.

To demonstrate its utility, I shall apply this criterion to word processing software. Suppose that you are going to write a book with your word processor. Suppose further that you are omniscient in the subject matter of the book, impeccably organized, and a perfect typist. You simply sit down at the keyboard and start typing as you compose, making not a single mistake. After many days of work, you have your book, but what was the point of using a word processor? You could have done the same thing on a typewriter. In short, as far as you're concerned, the word processor has no advantage over the typewriter. Now let's estimate the crunch-per-bit ratio: it was zero, because not a single word or character was actually crunched by the program. The words moved directly from your keyboard to the printer with no significant intervening processing. Hence, zero crunch per bit makes a word processor no more useful than a typewriter.

Now suppose that you discover that your omniscience was less omni than you thought, and there are a few little mistakes that you need to clean up. You go back to the word processor, make a few minor changes, and print the new manuscript. Now you can say that the word processor delivered some advantage compared to the typewriter, but not a stupendous advantage—you could probably have managed with a little cutting and pasting and perhaps retyping a few pages. Again, let's estimate the crunch-per-bit ratio: it has gone up from zero to a small value because you have manipulated some (but not most) of the data in the file. Hence, a small crunch-per-bit ratio yields a small benefit.

Now suppose that you are older and wiser, and you realize that your manuscript is riddled with errors. You need to change the spellings of many words, you must completely reorganize the book and most of its chapters, and you really should change its layout, too, while you're at it. You can thank your lucky stars that you have a word processor. You'll be doing intensive reprocessing of the data as you move things around, execute massive search and replacement operations, and in general crunch the hell out of your manuscript. Obviously, the crunch-per-bit ratio is high, and this is the situation in which the word processor shines its brightest. Your word processor is most useful when you use it to do lots of crunching. Hence my conclusion that crunch-per-bit ratios indicate the overall utility of a design.

The same analysis works with other applications. Spreadsheets show their greatest value when you recalculate the same data many times with many different variations. If all you do is enter the numbers and print the result, you're not getting much value from your spreadsheet. Database managers earn their price only when you have them sort, search, report on, and otherwise munch the data in many different ways. Photo-retouching programs are worthwhile only if you do a lot of touching.

The same is true with games: the higher the crunch-per-bit ratio, the more "computery" the game is and the more likely the game will be entertaining. Indeed, games in general boast the highest crunch-per-bit ratios in the computing world. Consider how little data a player enters into a flight simulator and how extensive are the computations that this data triggers.

This applies just as well to the web. A data-intensive web page simply downloads its text, images, and sounds to your computer; a process-intensive web page does lots of calculations to personalize the page to meet your precise needs. Aren't those snazzy personalized pages that come out of search engines and buyer recommendation sites more useful than those bland pages that say exactly the same thing to every user?

The crunch-per-bit criterion also works well in the negative sense as an exposer of bad software ideas. For example, the early days of the personal computing era were darkened by a stupid idea called a checkbook balancing program. This piece of software was universally cited whenever anybody was boorish enough to question the value of personal computers. A checkbook balancing program would take all your checkbook data and figure out the true balance. You simply typed in all your checks, and it figured your balance. It wasn't vaporware, either; there were lots of these checkbook balancing programs floating around. The thing was, nobody ever seemed to use them. Why not? Nobody seemed to be able to say just why, but they just weren't practical. Let's apply the notion of process intensity to checkbook balancing programs. Every number entered from the keyboard is either added to or subtracted from the checkbook balance, but the addition or subtraction happens just once for each check or deposit. That's one operation per datum—a low crunch-per-bit ratio, demonstrating the inutility of checkbook balancing programs.

Nowadays, we have personal finance programs such as Quicken; they increase the crunch-per-bit ratio by using the financial numbers in additional ways: sorting by expense categories, grouping by dates, organizing reports that permit detailed examination of some special aspect of the financial data. By increasing the crunch-per-bit ratio, these programs crossed the threshold of utility and became worthwhile. If they had not made these changes, we wouldn't be using them.

We can even apply the process-intensity principle to bad games. Does anybody remember that smash hit arcade game of 1983, Dragon's Lair? This was the first videodisc game, and its glorious cartoon graphics created an instant sensation. The press rushed to write stories about this latest grand breakthrough; consumers threw bushelsful of quarters at the machines; and Atari frantically initiated half a dozen videodisc game projects. Amid all the hubbub, I alone stood unimpressed in my ivory tower, nose held high in contemptuous dismissal, disappointing reporters with wet-blanket comments that this was merely a fad. And sure enough, within a few years these videodisc games had disappeared from the scene. How was I able to correctly perceive that the videodisc game was doomed to failure once its fad value was exhausted? Simple: its crunch-per-bit ratio stank. All that data came roaring in off the disc and went straight onto the screen with barely a whisper of processing from the computer. The player's actions did little more than select animation sequences from the disc. Not much processing there.

An Objection

Here's an argument sometimes raised against my claim:

But both process and data are necessary to good computing. An algorithm without data to crunch is useless; hence, a good design establishes a balance between process and data.

While this argument is fundamentally sound, it does not suggest anything about *where* the proper balance lies. It merely establishes that some amount of data is necessary. It may well be that the proper balance between process and data is 90 percent process and 10 percent data; this objection does not suggest or imply any particular balance. It certainly does not suggest that data deserves emphasis equal to that accorded to process. And it certainly does not disagree with my assertion that the crunch-per-bit ratio should be large. Indeed, my criterion agrees that zero data is a Bad Thing; if there is zero data, then the crunch per bit ratio is mathematically undefined. We need to think harder about where lies the proper balance between process and data.

Personal Thinking Styles

Unfortunately, our attempt to find the ideal balance between process and data is hampered by our own prejudices. Most people are saturated with noun prejudice, and their thinking is consequently slanted. The embracing of process intensity in our thinking involves some degree of rejection of data, more as an act of discipline than necessity. All too often we grab for the simple fact that answers our immediate question, rather than grappling with the underlying principle. This is a natural and forgivable act of laziness—but do we expect to accomplish anything worthwhile through laziness?

Some people might bewail this ugly prejudice that colors our approach to reality, but I am not one of them. I see this as opportunity, not injustice. If everybody else wants to limit their thinking in some fashion, then I can leverage my poor mental abilities by concentrating on what other, smarter people don't think about. For many years, I have worked hard to grok the operational approach, to bring it close to the innards of my thinking. It is, I confess, quite alien in style; my brain resisted stubbornly. Yet my experience proves that it can be done.

Remember the first and most important question every interactivity designer should keep in mind: "What are the verbs? What does the user *do*?" That question is about verbs, not nouns. Interactivity lies on the process side of the spectrum. It's not inter-object-ivity—it's inter-*act*-ivity.

We all know that precise logical thinking requires discipline and effort; it is an artificiality that we impose upon our nonsequential brain cells. At heart, when we think logically, we're faking it. But fake or no, the results are indisputable: that kind of thinking is what allowed us to trod the moon. So the best of us grit our teeth and endure the unnatural act of logical thinking. Process-intensive thinking is even stranger, even more unnatural; it demands even greater discipline and greater effort. But if sequential thinking took us to the moon, where might process-intensive thinking take us?

If you would be an interactivity designer, learn to think operationally.

18

LINKMESHES

Trees generate a geometric explosion in the number of nodes required. You will recall from Chapter 7 that the branching tree structure creates a huge problem: the number of nodes increases dramatically as you add more branchpoints. Before you can create many viable options, the tree becomes too large to be buildable. The general solution to this problem is a *linkmesh*, a tree with loopback links and state variables. The set of state variables you choose is critical to good interactivity design.

In Chapter 7, I introduced you to the Crawford diagram and the basic architectures of interactive design. In this chapter, I shall explore these architectures at a deeper level.

Recall that the simplest architecture is linear, and that this structure is noninteractive.

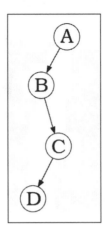

To go interactive, we use a tree, which can suffer from the problem of the geometric explosion of nodes:

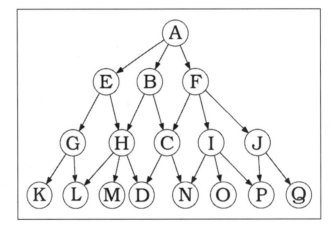

I presented some ameliorating strategies in Chapter 7, but in this chapter I shall present a more fundamental solution: the linkmesh. As with the Crawford diagram, a similar structure is used in computer science, known as a *directed graph*, but again, some subtle differences are just enough to make use of this term inaccurate in our setting—and we wouldn't want all the computer science people getting mad when we use *their* term in *our* way, would we?

A linkmesh is a tree with two crucial additions: reverse flow and state variables. Perhaps you noticed that in both linear and tree structures, the user always moves downward. Why shouldn't the user be able to reverse direction and move upward? Suppose that we made one small change in the tree:

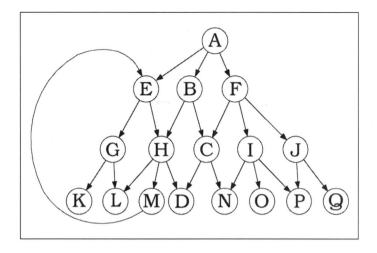

This one change has profound effects upon users' experiences, for now they can move from node M back up to node E and from there to nodes H and D or some other pair. They could even repeatedly move E-H-M-E-H-M and follow that loop forever. Such behavior might seem boring, but look how easily it changes with the addition of another reverse flow arrow:

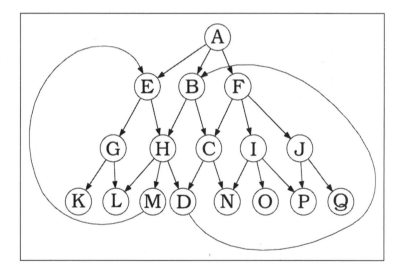

Now the user can move E-H-M-E as before, but then take another path from E through H, then D, and back up to B. With a few more reverse flow arrows, we can offer the user hundreds of paths through the linkmesh. Consider just how many paths there are through this mathematically idealized linkmesh:

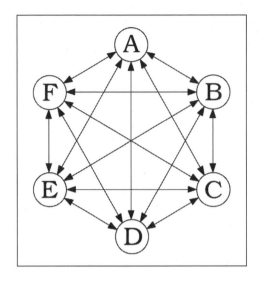

Theoretically, there are an infinite number of distinct paths through this linkmesh, but if you wish to limit the length of a path to, say, six steps, then there are 46,656 distinct paths. And that's with only six nodes! Note also that this design completely eliminates the notion of directionality that characterizes the tree. The tree has a top and a bottom, but this design can be approached from any direction. Clearly, this theoretical ideal would never be attained in practice; every program must have a beginning, a middle, and an end—hence, the necessary imposition of some directionality on the otherwise symmetric design of the linkmesh.

With just a few more nodes, the number of pathways explodes geometrically. For example, a 10-node mathematically ideal linkmesh would permit one million distinct paths with only six steps. Thus, with linkmeshes, we invert the problem we had with trees, transforming it into a benefit. A tree requires a geometrically exploding set of nodes to provide a small increase in the number of paths. A linkmesh creates a geometrically exploding set of paths for a small increase in the number of nodes.

This concept, by the way, is not especially new; it is a variation of the concept of looping in programming. As every programmer knows, a program without a loop just isn't worth writing. In the same way, an interactive application without a linkmesh just isn't worth designing. That's because a linkmesh is actually just a loop seen through a different dimension.

State Variables

There may be 46,000 different paths through the hexagonal linkmesh shown in the preceding section, but they'd be pretty boring; after about the tenth visit to node C, you'd probably be bored out of your skull. But there's one other trick that makes this architecture worthwhile: state variables. These are numbers that change during your passage through the various nodes. An easy example comes from the old videogame Pac-Man. The player moves through a simple maze with 34 nodes. If that were all there was to the game, it would have been better known as Boring-Man. But there are also pills to eat and ghosts to evade. These additions constitute state variables; as the player moves through the maze, those state variables change. Thus, when the player comes to node #27 the first time, she might find Pinky and Blinky above and to the left of her, so she would rather move down or to the right. Later, however, the player might find herself right back at node #27, only this time Pinky and Blinky are both below her, so she will choose to move up. The maze (linkmesh) has not changed, but the state variables have, and this change gives new significance to each node.

The concept of state variables applies equally well to more serious applications than games. For example, imagine a polygon like the hexagon shown earlier, only this polygon has 101 nodes, one for each key on a keyboard, and they are completely interconnected. This is the linkmesh for a word processor; the state variable is the user's previous path through the maze. Thus, if the user has just begun typing the word *circle* and has typed the letter *c*, then the next choice in the linkmesh would be *i*, but a little later the user would find himself right back at the same old letter *c*. This second time, however, the succeeding choice would not be *i*; it would be *l*. Now, this may all seem like a convoluted way to describe the familiar task of word processing, but sometimes a fresh way of conceptualizing something affords new insights into improving it. For example, if we visualize the linkmesh for that word processor, we will note that it is not a perfectly symmetrical 101-sided polygon; some of the links are highly probable, and some are less probable.

There's nothing obviating the use of state variables in trees. But the full utility of state variables is best realized by linkmeshes. That's because a tree already contains some of the user's state variables implicitly in the user's location (for example, "you couldn't have gotten here unless you previously found the silver key"). A linkmesh cleanly separates history from location. In an ideal tree, you can determine the user's history from his current location in the tree. In an ideal linkmesh, this is impossible: a user could have arrived at any node by any path.

Designing State Variables

The tree structure is simple to design but tedious to implement: all you must do is specify all the nodes and their connections. The linkmesh structure is more complex; you must also design the state variables and how they change during the user's traversal through the linkmesh; fortunately, this greatly reduces the amount of busywork that you would face with a tree design. Thus, a linkmesh substitutes cleverness for tedium. Here are some techniques for designing state variables:

Simplest is a Boolean variable representing the user's arrival at a node. At the outset of the interaction, the user has not yet visited the node, and the state variable has a value of FALSE. Later, however, the user enters the node, and we set the state variable to TRUE. This crude trick is the basis for most adventure games. If you enter the Secret Closet, you'll see the Golden Key, which can itself be treated as a node. By entering that node (picking up the Golden Key), you set the Boolean variable "Does the player possess the Golden Key?" to TRUE. Much later in the adventure, you encounter the Castle Gate node, which is the only entryway to the Treasure Room node. At the Castle Gate node, the program consults the Boolean variable "Does the player possess the Golden Key?" If the value of the state variable is TRUE, the program permits the player to open the Castle Gate and enter the Treasure Room.

For a more serious example, consider this: You've just opened your word processor and are looking at a blank page. In a stroke of perversity, you decide to save the blank document, but lo and behold, your word processor won't allow it. That's because the Boolean variable "Has the user entered any text yet?" is still FALSE; it won't be set to TRUE until you enter at least one node (type one key).

An even more pertinent example is provided by the now-universal practice of Preferences dialog boxes. Whenever you set a preference (for example, "Don't warn me before doing . . ." or "Auto-save my document every 10 minutes"), you are setting the value of a state variable. State variables make it possible to customize the program to the user's tastes.

The next step up is the counting state variable. This variable starts at zero and counts the number of times you do something. For example, a password-protection scheme might have a challenge gateway ("Please enter your password now"). You type your password incorrectly and enter it; the program rejects the password and tells you to try again. If it's smart, it might also add one to the count of the number of attempts you have made. After, say, three or four attempts, it might reasonably conclude that you don't know the password and you're just guessing, at which point it could gently advise you to go look up your password, or perhaps terminate the program, or perhaps call 911 to report an attempted break-in.

From here we graduate to fully arithmetic state variables: numbers that are calculated by special formulas for various reasons. For example, a personal finance program will have state variables for how much money you have, how much you spent on groceries, and so forth. These state variables will be added to or subtracted from each other depending on whether they're income or expense. The nodes you encounter, though, are always the same. There's a node for entering a check's amount, another for declaring whether it's income or expense, another for specifying the other party, and so on. Once you've learned the basic nodes of the budget-calculating program, you use those nodes over and over, entering lots of checks, credit card debits, and so on, and steadily changing the state variables.

Here's another example: In my interactive storytelling technology, each node represents one action taken by one character. Of course, one character might repeat the same action a number of times, or we might see different characters using that node at different times. Suppose that the node is "Character A punches Character B in the nose." We might well have a state variable for how much each character likes every other character. Then, whenever a character enters this node (that is, punches somebody else in the node), we reduce the amount of affection that the punchee holds for the puncher. The same node can be re-used many times, but the state variables change. After the fifth time he gets punched in the nose by Big Bully, perhaps Nerdy Wimp will pull out his handgun (he's American) and blow that bastard's head off.

Choosing State Variables

The set of state variables you choose is critical to the usefulness, colorfulness, or flexibility of your linkmesh. If your state variables are too few and too simple, then your linkmesh will be thin and repetitive. On the other hand, if you make your state variables too numerous and too complicated, you'll lose intellectual control of your linkmesh. As I discuss in Chapter 26, the nature of control in interactivity design is more indirect, more abstruse than the control we are familiar with in conventional design. Remember how many paths there can be through even a small linkmesh. You cannot possibly trace each of those paths explicitly; you must instead think in more abstract terms about likely behaviors. All too often, we fail to anticipate a particular combination of path and state variables, and our linkmesh screws up.

Here's an example of loss of control from a distantly related field: lawmaking. After all, lawmaking is an indirect process. Police don't stand over every citizen, evaluating each person's behavior and making snap judgments as to what is right or wrong. Instead, we have abstract laws that attempt to define precisely what kinds of actions are unlawful, and then police and courts apply those abstract laws to particular instances of human behavior. Sometimes the lawmakers fail to anticipate one of the paths through the legal linkmesh. So it was in the 1970s, according to a possibly apocryphal story I have been told. A furniture maker decided to build a furniture factory in a poverty-stricken parish in Louisiana. He'd get cheap laborers, and the region would get desperately needed jobs.

But wait! Congress had passed a new law designed to prevent the increase of air pollution, and it was quite clever. Recognizing that some of the pollution emanating from factories is impossible to prevent, the law did not require new factories to achieve zero emissions. Instead, itthey required the owners of new factories to approach other factories in the area and purchase for them equipment that would reduce their emissions by the same amount that the new factory would add. This would yield the most cost-effective way to keep emissions stable, because there would always be some filth-belching factory that could, for a small cost, be made a bit cleaner. Everybody was quite proud of this new law; it seemed to strike the best balance between environmental protection and economic development.

Unfortunately, this particular area of Louisiana was so poor that there were *no* factories in it at all—this furniture factory was to be the first. Ergo, it was impossible for the furniture factory to obey the law; there were no emissions to reduce in the first place.

Everybody scratched their heads about this problem for a while. The Environmental Protection Agency, charged by Congress with enforcing the law, was loathe to make an exception; with the amount of money at stake nation-wide, a single exception could trigger a host of lawsuits demanding special exemptions for everybody else. Particularly frustrating was the fact that the factory's emissions would be a small amount of shellac and other heavy organic compounds: not pristine stuff, but nowhere near as insidious as many of the chemicals used by modern technology. In fact, many deciduous trees emit tiny quantities of the same stuff from their leaves as part of the photosynthetic process. This generates a bluish haze that can be quite thick in areas blessed with huge deciduous forests, such as the Great Smokey Mountains (the tree-haze is the reason for their name).

Somebody put two and two together and hit upon the solution. Everybody agreed that this would in fact satisfy the requirements of the law. And so it was that the owner of the factory bought several hundred acres of forest and cut down every last tree—thereby eliminating a source of pollution approximately equal to the pollution the factory would add.

This is an example of lawmakers' losing control of their linkmesh. And if you don't watch out, you will surely do something just as stupid someday.

Lawmakers don't have any control over the complexity of the situations they face; you do. If you equip your design with so many state variables of such complexity that you don't understand it, you will lose control—guaranteed. Therefore, the best strategy is to use only a few simple Boolean variables in your first designs, and then expand the size and complexity of your state variables as you develop experience.

Historybooks

As I mentioned earlier, an ideal linkmesh gives no clue to the user's history; this means that, if you wish to use the user's history, you must store that history in a data structure that I call a historybook. A well-designed historybook permits the implementation of the limitless undo capability I describe in Chapter 19. There's lots of useful information buried in a historybook, if you're willing to look at it statistically and make some soft-math calculations. For example, a historybook makes possible a reasonable "intrusive macro facility." Given a moment of user inactivity, a program could scan the historybook, looking for patterns of behavior. Well-defined patterns of input could be noted, as well as the differentiating factor in each case. At this point, the software could interrupt the user and offer to carry out the repetitive task, with the user supplying only the distinguishing data. The degree of intrusiveness of this agent could be made adjustable by the user.

Some designers object that a historybook would require prohibitively large amounts of RAM. I disagree. A historybook is a record of user activity; how many bytes of data can a user enter in a single session? You need store only 10 bytes of data to record every user action: the location of the mouse cursor at the moment of the event, the content of the event (mousedown, mouseup, keypress, and so on), and the time of the event. If you want to get snazzy, you could make the record extensible with another 4 bytes. Even a busy-beaver user typing and mouse clicking at the rate of two events per second, working without a break for an eight-hour work session, would require only about half a megabyte of RAM to store all that work.

As I mentioned earlier, ideal trees have their historybooks built directly into their structures. Ideal linkmeshes carry no history whatsoever in their structures. Ergo, a linkmesh with a historybook, provides everything that a tree can provide, and it's easier to build. And when you add state variables, you have an immensely more powerful structure with which to design.

In interactivity design, you should think in terms of linkmeshes, not trees. A linkmesh is unique in three ways. First, it has linkages that loop back to earlier nodes, thereby weakening the absolute directionality of trees. Second, it requires state variables to differentiate repeated passes through the same node. Third, it requires a historybook to function best.

19

PLAY

Play is fundamental to interactivity. It is the original educational technology, dating back millions of years. Despite our protestations of deadly seriousness, play pervades much of our culture. The most important rule emerging from an understanding of play is the requirement of safety. Play has two major ingredients: *agon* (competitiveness) and *paidaia* (frolic). We must keep them separate.

A Naughty Metaphor

To understand interactivity, we must look deeper into the human soul and comprehend the fundamental human drive that renders interactivity so powerful. That drive is the instinct for play. Interactivity is only the outward expression of play, the mechanism by which play is executed. To use a racy metaphor, interactivity relates to play as copulation relates to love. The interactivity designer who lacks a strong sense of playfulness is like the man who has mastered pelvic gymnastics but cannot love. I don't have anything to contribute to the lore of love, but I can cast some light on play.

Understanding play is important to all interactivity designers, not just game designers, because play is fundamental to our culture and our mental makeup. From our brain's point of view, interactivity and play are the same thing. Play *is* what happens in a serious application. Yes, there's a lot of work involved, but especially in the crucial early phases, when a user is learning your program (and deciding whether to commit to it), much of what happens is intrinsically playful. It's not child's play; it's mature play. The difference between child behavior and adult behavior is not so great as to require an entirely new term; the difference is a matter of degree. Kiddie food (candy) is blatantly pleasurable to eat, whereas adult food has greater variety and depth, but it's still a kind of food. Kiddie reading (comic books) has bright, intense colors with strong lines, simple characters, and polarized plots; adult reading covers a wider range of topics, has more subtlety and less direct stimulation, and takes a great deal more effort to appreciate, but it's still reading. Kiddie video (cartoons) starts off with a bang; it delivers the laughs within seconds of its opening. Adult video, on the other hand, may take 30 minutes to set up its dramatic context. Whereas kiddie video has simple, direct conflicts with clean outcomes, adult video twists many strands together and delves more widely and deeply into human behavior.

Computer games are of a kind with candy, comic books, and cartoons, but this reflects the failure of computer game design, not any intrinsic limitations of the medium. Adult play is surely deeper and more subtle, takes more effort, and covers a wider variety of topics than child play. Consider these examples:

- The owner of a small business putting nice creative touches on her company newsletter

- The corporate drone dedicating long hours to the creation of a multimedia extravaganza for a meeting presentation

- The market researcher fiddling about with the customer database to find odd combinations of customer types

- The news reporter carrying out background research on the web, getting carried away following fascinating but marginally relevant threads

These are all play behaviors. Yet they are also work behaviors. The two are inextricably interwoven. And they are certainly no waste of time. All of these workers are expanding their skills by trying out new ideas, exploring new areas. Has anybody noticed how easily and smoothly American business picked up all the skills necessary to use personal computers? Typing, file management, back-ups, email, spreadsheets, word processors—millions of people picked up these skills in a matter of a few years, and most of them trained themselves without going back to school. Adult play made this economic miracle possible.

Historical Roots of Play

Play is often thought of as a modern creation, an indulgence of the leisure class made possible only by the modern ability to provide food, clothing, and shelter with less than full-time labor. On the contrary, play's historical roots go back much further than Thorstein Veblen; they predate even the evolution of humankind.

Let's jump way back in evolutionary time, all the way back to the origin of felines. What, precisely, are kittens up to when they play? We all acknowledge that they're having fun, but they are actually engaging in serious educational pursuits. Their antics are focused on three activities: stalking, pouncing, and wrestling.

Stalking, the delicate task of closing in on prey without alerting it to the hunter's presence, demands more than soundless movement; the hunter must keep the prey under constant, intense observation so as to notice prey suspicion behavior and freeze accordingly. Yet the cat must also plot a noiseless path through twigs, dry leaves, and grass; how can she allocate her limited optical resources between the two tasks? With practice, she learns to recognize prey behaviors likely to prolong prey inattention for long enough to divert the eyes to path scanning. Of course, this requires practice.

The pounce is the crucial act of the hunt; a well-executed pounce ensures success just as surely as a poorly executed pounce guarantees failure. At such close ranges, the probability of detection grows perilously high; hence, every centimeter of additional pounce range is precious. But the transition from stalking posture (loose, extended, delicately balanced) to pouncing posture (tight, compact, square) involves major body movement and diminishment of the view of the prey. Ideally, the pounce itself should be executed silently even though it necessitates a violent exercise of musculature. A higher arc is preferable, as it provides some scanning time to precisely locate the prey and position the paws perfectly, and it keeps the cat out of the prey's horizontal visual field longer. Again, the many fine judgments involved cannot be conveyed through the genes; they must be learned through experience.

Last comes the actual kill. Here the cat faces the most dangerous problem. While a mouse's claws are tiny, what with all the thrashing about they can easily damage the delicate structures of the eye. How can the cat bring her killing weapons (her teeth) to bear on the prey when the most vulnerable part of her anatomy (her eyes) are just two centimeters away from her teeth? Again, there is only one answer: experience.

Any cat who would acquire this vast compendium of experience through actual mouse hunting would surely starve before mastering the lessons. Hence, play. Kittens stalk, pounce upon, and fight with each other, thereby learning the skills of survival.

Evolution and Play

Thus, play arose during mammalian evolution as the natural method of education. Play is the behavioral analogue of genetic mutation. Just as mutations generate random changes in the DNA that are then tested against the objective realities of the creature's ecosystem, play generates random behaviors that are tested against the objective realities of the playmate's responses. The kitten quickly learns that an attempt to bite her playmate's face is easily countered with the forepaws; an attempt to bite the belly founders against the powerful kicks of the hind legs. If, for some random reason, the kitten attempts to bite the back of the playmate's neck, she encounters no effectual resistance. This, then, is the ideal way to dispatch prey, but it is always learned by play experience. By shifting adaptation from genes, which can generate at best one trial per generation, to behavior, which can generate several trials per minute, mammals are able to adapt thousands of times more rapidly.

Most mammals play, although the nature and extent of play behavior varies. Herbivore play is confined to mobility play (running, jumping, and the like) and hierarchy play (butting heads). Carnivore play tends to be more extensive, because carnivore food is a lot more interactive than grass. Primate play is even richer, and hominid play is the most complex of all. There are many answers to the question, "What differentiates us from other animals?" but one correct answer is surely, "We play more."

The most basic form of play is the gambol: jumping, running, and otherwise exercising the coordination of whole-body musculature. We see this form of play executed by almost all mammals and birds; it is a necessary means of learning how to coordinate the musculature. The phylogenetically earlier orders (fish, amphibians, and reptiles) are born fully coordinated; they are motor competent from the moment they hatch. But mammalian babies stagger about dizzily upon birth; they have no idea how to get all those muscles working in unison. It takes weeks or months of play to get everything working together. Human infants add vocalization to the standard gamboling play behavior. With its more prolonged childhood, human gambol play covers a wider range of activities, from simple running and jumping to more complex sports and games involving balls, fields with lines, and specialized rules. We even extend the gambol play into adulthood in the form of dance.

The point here is that play is not a historical accident or a frivolous diversion; it is a fundamental behavioral trait that serves vital needs. It is wired into our brains.

Play and Culture

Play is so fundamental to human existence that we seldom notice its pervasiveness. Johan Huizinga pointed out the ubiquity of play in *Homo Ludens: A Study of the Play Element of Culture*–an important book that I strongly urge you to read. He defines play as a voluntary activity, confined in both spatial and temporal dimensions, with formal rules. Huizinga proceeds to examine the play concept in a wide variety of human activities. I was astounded by his revelations about the universality of play. It shows up everywhere; Huizinga has chapters on play in law, war, art, philosophy, and poetry. Consider, for example, the law. It takes place within fixed limits of time and place: a trial in a courtroom. It is controlled by an extensive set of rules that are freely accepted (albeit by the people as a society, not as individuals) and absolutely binding. And there is certainly a feeling that a court of law is not ordinary life. The law takes place in its own little world, isolated from the rest of the world, and with a strong system of rules. Does that not sound rather like a game, or at least play? And why is it that the law has so many rituals? In Britain, barristers and judges alike still wear wigs. Why? They are playing, not in the sense of childishness or exuberance, but rather in the sense of isolating themselves from the real world to create a little self-contained world of justice. Nevertheless, a court of law shares much with a basketball court or a tennis court.

Moreover, the play concept permeates many aspects of our culture that we do not think of as intrinsically playful. When you're at a special place, during a special time, then special rules apply to your behavior. In a football stadium during a game, you are permitted to wear funny hats and to vent your aggressive instincts with greater freedom than would be permitted in normal life. At the theater, the reverse is the case: you play at elegance and overwrought civility; the theater frowns on an ill-timed cough even as the stadium applauds a megaphonic burp.

A revealing manifestation of play behavior is the establishment of costumes for a wide variety of roles. Bicyclists have their skin-tight attire, motorcyclists their leathers, and skiers their bright colors. You wear one kind of costume to play basketball, another for baseball, and a third for football. To what extent are these costumes truly functional, and to what extent do they serve to justify abnormal behavior by identifying the player with a role in which such behavior is expected? When I exchange my slouch hat for a tuxedo, my vocabulary jumps several grade levels. Do clothes make the man or do they make the role he plays?

Even some of our deepest religious and ethical ideas are founded in play. Why should we believe in the devil? Here is a personification of evil, a playful way of taking a complex subject (evil) and giving it human form (devil). Even I, an atheist, find it useful to talk about complicated issues of good in terms of god and the devil. To what extent are such references a matter of play or a matter of mentation?

Why is it that humor pervades all human interaction? Even the most serious of our activities is not immune to humor. In the midst of delicate arms control negotiations in Moscow, Henry Kissinger relates that a pause was reached when photocopies of working documents became necessary. He suggested that they simply hold the documents up to the chandelier. Everybody laughed. His Soviet hosts demurred. "Those cameras are too old; they were installed during Stalin's day. Why don't we use the cameras in the wooden paneling?" More laughter.

Oral arguments before the Supreme Court have been punctuated with jokes. In my oral examination for my master's degree, I replied to a tricky question by cracking an obscure academic joke; my answer was accepted. Alan Shepard hit a golf ball on the moon. A desperately wounded German soldier in

Italy in 1943 asked a nearby American to give him assistance in relieving himself. As the American helped out, the German smiled weakly and asked, "Do you realize that you're giving aid and comfort to the enemy?"

Play and Language

The word *play* has been applied with such catholicity that it is now verbal mishmash. My *Webster's Unabridged Dictionary* requires 21 column inches to define all the variations of the word *play*. The elementary verbs *go*, *eat*, and *do* require only 18, 5, and 8 column inches, respectively. For some reason, the word *play* is guilty of some kind of semantic imperialism, arrogating to itself vast tracts of semantic territory.

Huizinga addressed this issue with greater depth in his chapter titled "The Play Concept as Expressed in Language." He analyzed the way in which various concepts of play are expressed in a variety of languages. The lesson that emerges from this is that the concept of play extends over a huge range of activities. There is, of course, the conventional sense of play, but there is also the play of ideas, swordplay, play as the freedom of motion of a machine part, playing a musical instrument, a stage play, and the various erotic connotations of play (in German, a child born out of wedlock is called a Spielkind, literally, "play child"). The English word *lechery* is the only surviving remnant in English of the Old Germanic root *leik, leikan*, to play. Also striking is the fact that the Latin word for play, *ludere,* survives in English in *lewd*.

But there is another aspect of play that emerges from this linguistic analysis, and that is play as simulation. In Japanese, the most polite or formal means of expression is called *asobase kotoba*, literally "play language," and it communicates the notion that those we speak about are so refined that they only play at life. Thus, the polite way to say "I hear that your father died" is "I hear that your father has played dying." Even more striking are such words as *allude*, *collude*, and *illusion*, all of which are derivatives of the Latin *ludere*, and all of which refer to a sham, shadow, or simulated reality.

Consider the deep playfulness of language. What is a metaphor but a play on words? Why do we say "slower than molasses in winter" when we could just as easily say "very slow"? Why would we refer to the unreelected holder of the most powerful political office on the planet as a "lame-duck president"?

Play and Mentation

Two deep concepts emerge for me on contemplation of Huizinga's work. The first is the notion of play as modeling; the second concerns the subjunctive nature of play. When we play, we create our own little world that follows our rules. Unlike the real world, our play world makes sense. In the real world, good men die while evil men prosper, things break for no apparent reason. crops fail, the weather jiggles about arbitrarily. We feel at the mercy of arbitrary forces in the real world. But in our play world, we control the rules, and our rules make sense. There's a satisfying predictability in the play world. It's a world you can believe in.

The other aspect of play is its subjunctivity. We play "if-only" in our games. Once we have erected our imaginary world, we then explore it with experimental behaviors too risky to try in the real world. I shall have more to say on subjunctivity in Chapter 29.

These two concepts of play—modeling and subjunctivity—strike me as enormously important. They are the basis of something important about mentation. Modeling boils the world down to a clean subset, and subjunctivity explores the characteristics of that subset. This, it seems to me, is the foundation of creativity. The world is a complicated and messy place; we don't know what it will do next. By modeling the world in some fashion, we create a mentally manipulable version of the world. There are zillions of ways to model the world; we are always creating new models. A playful person is particularly good at making models.

When a little boy holds a stick in his hand and makes appropriately wet noise with his mouth, spraying saliva all over himself, and then swoops the stick down to a leaf on the ground and makes a loud explosive sound, he is modeling a jet bomber. You and I see a little boy spraying saliva on a stick and a leaf, but he has created a mental model of jet bombers.

By manipulating our model subjunctively, by asking what-if about its performance, we develop new insights into the world. Early developments in metallurgy were derived from the realization that molten metal is "just like water." I very much doubt that anybody ever successfully tested that hypothesis by direct sensory evaluation. But by thinking of molten metal as if it were water, early humans created the thought that it might be manipulated like water, by pouring it from cups. This realization catapulted us out of the Stone Age.

I am therefore tempted to ask, is there any aspect of human mentation that cannot be described in terms of model making plus subjunctivity? If not, what does that suggest about the place of play in the human mind? What I find so exciting about this line of thought is that it suggests that play behavior is deeply connected with human thought. Play behavior is not an aberration, nor a sideshow, nor idle recreation; somehow it is closely tied to the way that we think about the world.

Example: One of the most sensational intellectual developments of the last 100 years was Einstein's theory of relativity. There were actually two theories: special relativity and general relativity. What is most intriguing here is the trigger point for both theories. In both cases, Einstein could put his finger on the mental step that triggered each theory. In the case of special relativity, Einstein asked himself, "What would it be like to ride on a beam of light?" Think about the fundamental playfulness of this image. This is not hard, cold science; this is not abstract equations and formulae; this is a playful concept, a what-if game. And it was the trigger point for the theory of special relativity. Once Einstein started to answer these questions, his theory came tumbling out of the intellectual woodwork almost naturally. The same thing happened with general relativity. Einstein asked himself, "What would it be like to stand inside a closed elevator in space? How would you know if you were in a gravitational field or being accelerated?" This playful question led to the Principle of Equivalence, which in turn led to all sorts of conclusions about the nature of space and time.

Play Requires Safety

The foremost requirement for play is some provision for safety. The slightest inkling of danger will halt kitten play instantly. Many people, when first attempting some new skill, will do so only in privacy; it is socially dangerous to be seen as a bumbling incompetent. Indeed, this is one of the secrets behind the success of the personal computer: people can sit down with one and play with it behind closed doors, learning how to use it without the embarrassment of a teaching session. The original Olympic Games in Greece imposed a truce on all warring factions during the period of the games; any perceived danger would ruin the atmosphere of athletic competition.

Safety extends further than the avoidance of mortal threat. The safety must be complete: physical, social, financial. Many people avoid game playing because they fear the social consequences of failure. Men and women always have difficulty playing together because men seek play dominance, which women find socially risky.

Even gambling falls under our conclusions about play. There are two groups of gamblers: playful gamblers and serious gamblers. Playful gamblers set aside some money to lose, treating it as an entertainment cost. Hence, they are not engaging in financial risk; they have already written off the money before they begin. Serious gamblers are taking financial risk, and they certainly are not playing.

Prejudice against Play

While play is universally conceded to children, many cultures place restrictions on overt adult play, driving much play behavior underground. Some playful adult activities are acceptable, while others are considered childish. Such strictures are enforced through standard socializing methods, which are powerful influences on our behavior. These are some of the common expressions we use to pressure others to refrain from play:

- "Grow up!"
- "Enough of fun and games"
- "When I was a child, I acted as a child. . . ."
- "Act your age!"
- "This is not a toy"
- "That's a Mickey Mouse course"
- "Are we having fun yet?"
- "That's not professional behavior."

The last few decades have seen a loosening of the strictures against play in this culture, but we remain uncomfortable with the notion of adults at play. This made some sense in the harsher economic conditions of yesteryear, which forced a child to accept a productive role early in life. In our times, however, economic productivity is primarily the result of education, and, as I explained at the outset of this chapter, play is the original technology of education. Thus, the tables have been turned on us; our well-developed mores against play are now in direct opposition to economic realities. I suspect that the USA, the quick-change, plastic-fantastic culture of the planet, will figure this out and embrace, develop, and refine productive adult play. And guess who'll be at the forefront of that social tidal wave?

Applying Play to Interactivity Design

So far I have only mouthed some of the vague universal truths about play; I now seek to explain how these truths can be applied in the real world of interactivity design.

When I was an undergraduate student at the University of California at Davis, the aggie school of the UC system, I learned a fascinating truth: cattle will more readily walk through curved fenced ways than through straight ones with corners; it seemed to have something to do with bovine curiosity. If you've ever tried to coax a half-ton cow into its proper enclosure, you can appreciate the value of this truth. In much the same way, you as interactivity designer must coax your user into discovering how to use your software effectively. You can put your shoulder behind his butt and give a mighty shove with a four-hundred-page user manual, but that seldom moves him more than a few inches, and there's always the possibility of a fecal reaction.

The trick, then, to motivating your users in the most productive direction is to engage their playfulness. Your highest priority is to encourage a sense of play-ful experimentation. From the uninitiated user's point of view, your software is an unknown tangle of opportunities and dangers. Your familiarity with the design blinds you to the imagined dangers the users fear; you have always walked across the room in daylight and cannot understand your users' darkness paralysis. Unlike you, the users can never truly know what lies inside the room, for they have never seen the design from the inside out as you have. Your users are attempting to move around inside a darkened room you have created; if you litter the floor with obstacles, the users will quickly learn to creep slowly along the floor, clinging to the few trusty landmarks they know. Instead, you want to keep the floor absolutely clear and the room laid out with such order and clean-liness that the user can dance from one corner to the other, confident despite the darkness.

This may sound like mere fanciful metaphor, harmless, cute, and without practical application, but I argue here an unorthodox position very much at odds with conventional practice. If you should doubt the significance and con-troversiality of my admonitions, I refer you to a commonly heard assertion:

"The Macintosh is just a toy."

I have no wish to partake in the platform wars pitting Apple Apostles against Microsoft Maniacs; that war is over. Microsoft won, and there's no point in refighting that nasty little conflict. In raising this issue, I am unconcerned with the advantages or disadvantages of either platform; my point is focused narrowly on the attitude behind the preceding assertion and its implications for interactivity design. Whether the Macintosh is or is not a toy is irrelevant; what's important is the fact that plenty of people are willing to characterize it as a toy in order to dismiss it as a computer. They readily acknowledge its playful character and hold this playfulness against it. The unstated assumption is the old Puritanical notion that playfulness is unproductive. This attitude remains just as strong now as at the height of the platform wars; just four weeks before writing these words, I received an email from a software designer noting that I use a Macintosh, and asking when I was going to purchase a "real computer."

It is imperative that such thinking be utterly banished from the minds of software designers if we are to advance interactivity design. I am not arguing that good designers use Macs; what's important is not the machine but the design philosophy. Playfulness is not a liability, it is an asset, and we should acknowledge the fact that the Macintosh design is more deeply playful than that of Windows.

A playful design philosophy will certainly indulge in occasional cuteness, although cuteness is neither a necessary nor a sufficient condition for playfulness. If an alert sound can be cutely pertinent (perhaps "Ah-ooga!" for an automotive program), such an indulgence can't hurt unless the sound becomes grating upon repetition. Use of color, delightful imagery, and other cosmetic factors can also be of some value. However, it is more difficult to actively encourage playfulness than to take care not to discourage it. You can lead the user to the playground, but you can't make her play; and it's depressingly easy to discourage the user from playing. Hence, the most useful advice I can give you is negative in format:

Don't Chastise Your User

Remember that play takes place only when users feel safe. They surely prefer to learn your software in privacy; do not intrude on that privacy by injecting judgmental elements into your design. If an error condition arises and you must notify the user of that error condition, your wording must clearly assert that the problem lies with the program's limitations, not the user's mistakes. In interactivity design, "The customer is always right" translates to "The user can never make a mistake." Don't hit her with the error message "You entered too many variables!"; don't even say "You are not allowed to enter that many variables." The *only* way to phrase this kind of error message is "I'm sorry, but I'm too stupid to handle that many variables. Could you please redo your input so it doesn't use so many variables?" The acknowledgment button to dismiss the error message should not be worded with an unapologetic "OK"; it should reinforce the message that the user didn't do anything wrong, that the problem lies with the software. My favorite label for such messages is "Shoot the programmer!"

Of course, recourse to error messages is an admission of failure to design well; a well-designed program has no error messages because the designer has already made error conditions impossible. Any software that can detect an error condition after the fact can anticipate the error condition before the fact. Don't ever fall for the programmer's line "That can't be done." It's a lazy programmer's lie, pure and simple. There are some situations, primarily involving keyboard input, in which the input of the user cannot readily be anticipated or acted upon in advance, in which case obviating the error would present the user with too many constraints. However, the problem here is in the realm of design, not programming.

The best approach is to render error conditions conceptually impossible rather than merely technically impossible. Here's a simple example: You decide to permit your user to assign up to eight names to some item in your design. The worst implementation, as I have already noted, is to chastise the user upon input of the ninth name. Slightly better is to dim the control that adds another name when eight have already been entered—but this leaves the user wondering why the control is dimmed. Better still is to put the names into a display box that can hold only eight names, along with a provision to enter a new name by clicking in the empty space. Gee, if there's no empty space left, there must not be any possibility of entering more names.

This admonition is a well-known rule of good user-interface design. My contribution lies not in repeating old saws, but rather in formulating a higher level of explaining them; this permits us to develop and expand the admonition. The important and easily learned negative rule here is: don't ever, *ever* do anything that might inhibit your user's playfulness.

Positive admonitions are harder to come by and are highly context dependent. However, I can cite one general rule derivative from the need for safety. This rule is encapsulated in the following heading.

Everything Must Be Completely Undo-able

Your users can't feel safe unless they are confident that anything they do is reversible. Imagine yourself in an unfamiliar situation, trying to decide what to do next, but you know one thing for a certainty: anything you do will be irrevocable. Once you take that plunge, you're unconditionally committed. How many times have you balked at such an irrevocable decision? I know men who just can't make a decision to get married, only because the decision requires commitment—irreversibilty. Yet marriage is a lot more reversible than many software operations.

Here, then, is the first design rule: every single verb you provide your user must be undo-able. Some programmers will, of course, complain that this is technically impossible. Not so! As a programmer, I know that the majority of software verbs are easily reversible. Some require more labor, the creation of more complex undo buffers. And a few, I agree, are difficult to undo. But undo-ability is never theoretically impossible. It's primarily a matter of how much work the programmer is willing to do. A secondary consideration is sometimes the expenditure of memory required for the undo. However, now that it is common for a program to demand megabytes of RAM, we can afford larger buffers for the Undo command. Recall, moreover, my earlier calculation that the amount of RAM commonly available now greatly exceeds the amount of information that a user can enter. We now have a large enough supply of breadcrumbs to retrace any path.

I therefore claim that we should provide undo-ability for the user's entire session with a program. In other words, the user should be able to go back to any point in the work session. There are two ways to accomplish this, and I think we should use both simultaneously. Both require us to keep track of every action taken by the user. The first allows the user to step backward action by action. In effect, the user says, "play back for me every step I have taken, but play them backward, until I say stop." The other approach is to work forward from some established starting point. The most obvious starting point is the most recently saved version of the work, but the user should also be able to specify other starting points by the time of their occurrence. In other words, our user would be able to tell the computer, "Go back to where I was five minutes ago. Then start playing my actions back to me in forward order. Stop when I click the mouse button."

I can see only two situations in which this would be technically impossible: first, those in which the computer obtains information from external sources, such as from a now-ejected floppy disk, a network, or environmental sensors. If the external source has changed in the interim, then undo-ability might not be possible. But this is only a possibility; undo-ability is certainly worth a try in such circumstances.

The second irreversible situation arises when the user input is not discrete, such as in a painting program when a user draws a wiggling line by holding down the mouse button and dragging, and the positions of the mouse at every point along the line are significant. The buffer to handle such an event would require several kilobytes of RAM; a great many such events would add up to a prohibitive amount of RAM. Even in this situation, infinite undo could still be implemented by saving the work file whenever the undo buffer grows full.

One way to limit the size of the undo buffer is to discard old actions. If the user has been editing a document for the last three hours, the need to return to the state of the document two hours and 45 minutes ago is microscopic. This is true, but the importance of undo-ability is not the actual execution but the sense of safety it imparts. If you're walking a tightrope, you want to know that there's a safety net underneath you. If you discover that the safety net has holes in it, even holes that you'll almost never encounter, your sense of safety still will be shattered. The purpose of infinite undo-ability is to banish fear, and fear is never a rational creature; it can be dispelled only with ironclad guarantees of safety.

A particularly irritating failure is the refusal of many text editing and word processing programs to implement the undo feature for global search-and-replace operations. The objections to such an action are based on assumptions that the undo buffer must be kept small. A willingness to allocate, say, a megabyte of RAM to the undo buffer would easily permit undo-ability for global search and replace.

A secondary benefit of infinite undo-ability is the elimination of all those damnable "are you sure" dialog boxes. If everything is undo-able, there's no need to double-check for accidental entries; they can always be reversed.

Infinite undo-ability does impose a new requirement on the program: it must be able to display the stack of undo-able commands. A user wishing to return to a point 10 steps back should not have to recall each step and its effects; a list showing those steps in their proper order can clarify the situation.

Again, I stress that none of this is technically impossible or even difficult; I have implemented all of these features in my Erasmatron program, which has some two dozen active data-entry windows and half a dozen completely different types of data entry. It took me less than a month; a good programmer should be able to do better.

All Experiments Must Yield Clear Results

Recall my description of play as a series of experiments. The user playing with your design will try a variety of experiments, and this is desirable. A few of the experiments will succeed, but most won't. I have already explained that you should not chastise the user for a failed experiment; now I take the concept even further: every experiment the user attempts must generate some kind of response. The user needs to know whether the experimental behavior accomplished anything, so you must acknowledge the experiment.

This feature is simple to implement; when you process the user's input, you attempt to recognize every input as meaningful. If you come across an input that makes no sense, issue a simple response. I prefer an inquisitive grunt for this response. The important thing is to make sure that the user knows that you saw what he did.

Some Interesting Design Experiments I Have Tried

I once faced a situation in which the user might want to rapidly step through a long sequence of simple operations, evaluating each by a simple criterion that reduced to a binary result: yes, this is something worth looking at; or no, nothing interesting happened. To ease the tedium, I added an audio indicator. I could have used a beep or a boop or some other colorless noise, but I decided to liven up the tedium with a bit of cuteness: the affirmative response was a high-pitched "Meow," and the negative response was a low "Woof." Both sounds were kept short in duration, so as not to irritate the user.

Another trick is the use of faces to communicate some emotion in dialog boxes. Back in the bad old days, we had to use copy protection on our games; this often involved a challenge dialog box demanding that the user enter the fifth word from the fourth line on page 27 of the manual, or some such nonsense. I was always embarrassed by these fascist techniques, but I acquiesced to their necessity. My favorite version of the challenge dialog box showed a Nazi, complete with monocle and scarred cheek, demanding to know "Are your papers in order?" In the Erasmatron, I embellished every cautionary dialog box with a scanned image of Desiderius Erasmus. Adding a face to a dialog box humanizes the interaction and encourages playfulness. Note also that facial expression is a powerful means of communication. Again, you don't want to use intimidating or judgmental facial expressions. Here are some examples of what I mean:

Are you sure you want to format the hard disk?

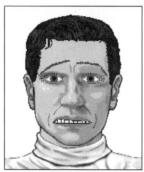

I don't have enough information to carry out your request.

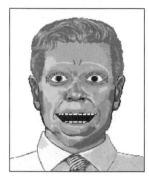

You've got mail!

The Dark Side of Play

In *Homo Ludens*, Johan Huizinga notes that the Greeks differentiated play into two forms: agon and paidaia. The first term refers to play as a competitive activity, a deadly serious pursuit within constraining rules; the second emphasizes play as a joyful activity. Thus, *agon* is the term we use to describe the activity of a runner at the Olympic Games, while we apply *paidaia* to a child throwing a ball.

These two aspects of play have nothing in common; how can they be joined in play? The catalyst that welds these two strangers together is interactivity. All play requires interaction of some sort. In the simpler kinds of play, the interaction need not be complex: the child throws the ball and it bounces back—from the child's point of view, this is surprising, interesting, and willful behavior on the part of the ball. But as we grow, bouncing balls lose their fascination, and we seek out interactive partners capable of richer behavior. Some of us, mostly adolescent males, get sidetracked and fixate on computers as interactive partners. Computers are such colorful and interestingly bouncy balls, and they are risk free; they never hurt our feelings. But most of us seek out other people as interactive partners, for the equality of interaction of social intercourse provides the most challenging and complete form of play.

Interaction can take place only where there is a perceived discrepancy of volition. The child throws the ball, in effect declaring, "You go away!" The ball bounces back; in the child's view, the ball answers, "No, I'm coming back!" The various angles, energies, and spins with which the ball bounces back are perceived by the child as manifestations of its volition. After much experimentation, the child figures out the laws of physics that determine the ball's behavior. This triggers a fundamental shift in the child's perception of the ball. It is no longer an agent with free will, capable of interacting with the child, but instead an inanimate object reacting according to natural laws. The now-volitionless ball is left lying on the floor as the child seeks out new agents with which to interact.

Let us now leap ahead to the mature adult interacting with another mature adult; this interaction represents the culmination of the long process that started with the ball. Let us imagine their discrepancies of volition in simplistic geometric terms. Where they are in perfect agreement, their volitions are parallel; where they disagree most intensely, their volitions collide head-on; and there are many intermediate cases where their volitions are at angles with each other. Where their volitions are parallel, there is no surprise, nothing to learn. They nod their heads in boring agreement. There is no information content in a field of gray. Sameness yields nothing.

Only where we have some perceived discrepancy of volition do we have a basis for interaction. How many times does a heated argument end with the realization that it was all a misunderstanding, that the perceived discrepancy of volition was not real—and now there is no longer anything to say, no basis for interaction? How many times does a child initiate interaction with a parent by fabricating a sham discrepancy of volition (being naughty to get attention)?

This explains the old and continuing failure to design successful cooperative games. Play thrives on the noncooperative elements, and withers where there is no discrepancy of volition. The child retains interest in the ball only so long as it appears to manifest discrepancies of volition—to go where it "wants" to go. As soon as the ball appears to obey laws of physics, the child loses interest.

This "blood and iron" philosophy of play may strike some as cynical, but I see no pessimism about human nature in it. The ugliness arises from two derivative phenomena. The first is the unwarranted extrapolation of the basic principle to absurd extremes. If discrepancy of volition is necessary to interaction, then greater discrepancy of volition yields greater interaction—right?

Well, it's illogical, and it leads us to the dark, intensely violent, ugly game designs in which the interaction takes its starkest form: kill or be killed. The error lies in confusing a one-sided Boolean relationship with the converse proportionality. This truth:

The absence of discrepancy of volition destroys interaction.

does not logically lead to this conclusion:

Greater discrepancy of volition yields greater interaction.

I will go so far as to concede that greater discrepancy of volition yields more *intensity* in the interaction. But intensity is not the same thing as richness or even quality. Greater amplitude does not make music sound better; more sugar does not make food more tasty; brighter colors do not make a painting prettier.

Agon in Paidaia's Clothing

But my main point here concerns a much more subtle error, one that pervades our civilization. It is the justification of agon (competitive play) through paidaia (joyful play).

I shall refer to the justice system in the USA to demonstrate this poisonous phenomenon. Do not think that the problem is confined to the justice system—it pervades our political system, our business culture, and our educational system. But I shall not waste your time with a tedious catalog of proofs; the example of the justice system should suffice to show the principle.

One of the trends in the history of civilization is the substitution of play—in its agonistic form—for conflict. For example, consider the evolution of systems of justice. Early justice systems were nothing more than socially tolerated vendettas. A clan would respond to a transgression against one of its members with an attack against the offending clan. Each individual looked to his own clan for justice. A gigantic step forward came with the substitution of state authority for the execution of justice. Thus was born the trial. But the earliest forms of trial took the character of blood-thirsty games. There was trial by ordeal or trial by combat. From our twentieth-century perspective, trial by combat is indistinguishable from simple vendetta, but in fact it represents a great leap forward, for vendetta is open ended, while trial by combat provides closure to the conflict. The rule of the game is that the outcome of the combat determines the outcome of the conflict. Two knights thundering down the lists with lances leveled toward each other represent the subtle shift of blood conflict into agon, and agon into paidaia. The points of the lances are the blood conflict; the rules of the joust are the agon; the pennants and cheering crowd are the paidaia.

After an English king was killed in such a joust, Western civilization shifted the balance even further away from blood conflict, but the element of agon remained unchanged. Within a century of that royal death, lawyers had so completely taken over the field of combat that Shakespeare was to write, "First, we kill all the lawyers!" The key observation here is that the legal system remained adversarial at its core. Instead of two knights charging down the lists in front of the king, we had two lawyers verbally jousting in front of a judge. The confrontation had been moved from the tourney field to the courtroom, and the blood had been cleansed from it, but the agonistic nature of the interaction remained unchanged.

There is no intrinsic reason why any system of justice need be adversarial in nature. Our system is adversarial only because it evolved from earlier adversarial systems, which in turn evolved from blood feuds. The modern lawyer can trace a direct line of descent from the tribal warrior.

And here is where we encounter the dark side of play. Somehow, agon gets mixed up with paidaia. Lawyers think that they are playing. They're not in it for the richness of the interaction; they're in it for the joy of victory. No lawyer has ever told me about a fascinating case that he lost. This agonistic element of their work is socially corrosive, yet lawyers sweep it under the rug of paidaia and rationalize it as a necessary element of a healthy justice system.

By acquiescing to an egregiously adversarial mentality on the part of our lawyers, we do for justice what the game Doom does for play. The richness—and therefore the educational or revelatory value—of the interaction is lost in the intensity of the confrontation. Yet the lawyer flashes his boyish grin and confesses, "Aw, shucks, I just like to win," and we indulge him his paidaia—and what we get is agon.

The term *play* is a Trojan horse of paidaia concealing a deadly cargo of agon. The rapist advises his victim, "You might as well just play along."

20

ABSTRACTION

As systems grow larger and more complex, they develop higher levels of abstraction to cope with the increasing complexity. Interactivity designers should apply this lesson to their work.

In this chapter, I'll be taking a long and roundabout approach to one of the deep ideas behind interactivity design. You'll likely find yourself growing impatient with the digressive nature of the material, but hang in there: the point I make is abstruse, and the preparatory material is necessary. In the next chapter, I'll show how this theory is applied.

Financial Abstraction

I begin with an examination of the development of financial structures. The earliest economic activity between sovereign groups took the form of direct exchange: "I'll give you this chunk of flint if you'll give me that cow." Because such transactions are as explicit and direct as possible, they are easy to evaluate and police. One party examines the cow, the other party examines the flint, they each see what they're getting, and once the exchange has been made, there is no further cause for interaction. Thus, the earliest forms of financial transaction were direct, explicit, utterly without abstraction.

The first level of abstraction was the introduction of money as a medium of exchange. Metals—not just precious metals such as gold and silver, but even base metals such as copper, lead, and tin—enjoyed a special position in the economy because (1) demand always exceeded supply, and (2) they were imperishable. The profound significance of this lay in the fact that a bar of metal could always be traded for something else, and, the nub of the matter, that everybody knew that it could always be traded for something else. Thus, if you offer me a bar of copper for my cow, I may not myself be interested in the bar of copper, but I know that I can always trade it to somebody else for something that I do want. Thus, I am willing to make the exchange.

An important point for later: This scenario presumes some population density and trade. If I don't run into many people willing to make trades with me, then I can't be so certain of finding a buyer for my bar of copper. The more people there are, the more confident I can be of finding a buyer.

There were only two drawbacks to the use of metal as a medium of exchange: First, there was the problem of knowing exactly how much metal you were getting. This problem was quickly solved by the introduction of simple scales for measuring weights, but it did impose a certain amount of hassle on the economy. The second problem was much tougher. People quickly learned the trick of alloying metals, mixing baser metals with precious metals and then passing off the result as pure precious metal. Just about every combination was used in ancient times, and it made trade more difficult. A variety of counter-measures were used, such as the touchstone, which, when rubbed against gold, showed a distinctive mark that roughly but unambiguously indicated the purity of the gold. Still, something better was needed.

That something better was the introduction of money. The new idea here was to have the government manufacture chunks of precious metal of guaranteed weight and purity. The government put its imprint on these chunks as a declaration of their honest value. Counterfeiting these chunks proved to be an expensive and difficult process; the cost of setting up the blast furnaces and striking molds was so high that you could recoup your cost only by making lots of counterfeit coins, and in the impecunious economies of those days, any operation moving large amounts of gold and silver would surely attract lots of attention and official curiosity. Thus, coinage provided a ready solution to the problem.

Of course, it also cost the local government to set up the mints, but if the city was big enough, the costs could be spread over many consumers and made worthwhile. Again, it was ever-bigger economies that both demanded coinage and made it worth the expense.

But note how coinage moved the economy to a higher level of abstraction. Now all fiscal accounts were kept in the otherwise arbitrary units of coinage. A rich man might be worth 10,000 tetradrachms—what does that mean? In a simpler economy, a man's wealth might be measured by the number of cattle he owns. That makes sense. But this—well, it's more abstract, isn't it?

The next big advance in financial abstraction was the concept of debt. It's only a small step from "I'll give you one drachma for your cow" to "If you give me your cow today, I'll give you one drachma tomorrow." And then it's an even smaller step to extend "tomorrow" to, say, "next year." Of course, as soon as we talk about long-term debt, we get into problems of recording the debt. After all, I might conveniently "forget" my debt to you, or die before the debt is due. The obvious solution is to write down the debt and give the lender the piece of paper: an IOU.

In those days, travel was hard, slow, and dangerous. Wealthy people, the kind of people who wrote and received IOUs, were constantly on the move. Collecting on an IOU often proved a difficult matter. This led to a new level of abstraction: third-party collection. Here I am in Venice, with an IOU from you for 1,000 ducats. Unfortunately, you're in Bruges, hundreds of miles away.

I run down to the local banco, an operation set up by one of the wealthier citizens of the community, and hand him the IOU. He recognizes the signature, knows and trusts the debtor, and figures he'll have no problem collecting when the debtor gets back in town. So he pays me the value of the IOU—less a small handling fee, you understand.

This was an immensely important leap in abstraction, because for the first time, the concept of "value" was divorced from a tangible object. Instead of transferring wealth through tangible intermediaries such as precious metals, wealth could now be transferred through a piece of paper.

This worked only because the legal systems backing up that piece of paper were robust enough to command everybody's confidence. If the debtor tried to welsh on his IOU, the banker could haul him before the local magistrate and make him pay.

Once we had established that a piece of paper could carry value, all sorts of new abstractions were possible. One, paper currency, made it possible for governments to print standardized contracts (bills) that promised to pay the bearer some fixed amount of coin. Because everybody knew they could trust the government (!), the paper money was every bit as valuable as the metal coinage, and a lot easier to handle to boot.

Unfortunately, some governments have trouble balancing their budgets, and whenever a government gets into financial trouble, there is always the option of printing more money, an option that was exercised so often in the past that people lost confidence in paper money. It took a long time before governments realized that they had to have the discipline to refrain from printing excess money or they would poison their own economies.

If governments could print money, why couldn't individuals? I'm not talking about counterfeiting; I'm talking about personal checks. These might be thought of as standardized IOUs made more reliable by the inclusion of the third party, a bank. Of course, a scoundrel could still write a bad check, but such an act could now be recognized as a crime, whereas enforcement of an IOU required tedious civil litigation. The check represented an amount of money held in a bank account, which in turn is an imaginary object containing imaginary coins.

Then came credit cards. These set up accounts (imaginary containers) that themselves contain no money; instead, they contain the promise that the user will pay enough money into the credit card account to keep it solvent. This adds the abstraction of futurity to the system.

New levels of abstraction don't replace old levels; they are often layered on top of the older levels. Look in your pockets. You have some coins (precious metals representing value) and some dollar bills (pieces of paper representing coins), a checkbook (pieces of paper representing money deposited in a bank account), and credit cards (pieces of plastic representing an account that you promise to pay into).

Time to summarize: as economic systems have grown and matured, we have developed ever more advanced structures to control them, and the central motif of financial evolution has been increasing layers of abstraction. Greater size both requires and enables greater abstraction. Systems grow by adding layers of abstraction.

Political Abstraction

The same process has been going on with politics. Early political organizations tended to be direct, straightforward, and simple. But as social organizations expanded, they required additional complexity. Of course, the laboratory of history has had many experiments and variations, so the simplistic generalizations I'm about to make should not be taken too seriously. But the overall trend has been toward greater abstraction.

The earliest hunter-gatherer groupings needed little structure, so they have been called egalitarian, but anarchistic would be a better term; at low population densities, anarchy and freedom are indistinguishable. It was only with the adoption of agriculture that societies became large enough to require some artificial social coordination. This was first achieved through the headman, a powerful and respected leader who ruled by direct fiat. Later, as social units grew larger, the headman was replaced by a king. We democrats may see little difference, but in fact a major new concept was introduced with kingship: the concept of legitimacy of rule. A headman achieved his status by asserting it over all challengers; a king gained his only by adhering to some formula for succession. In many cultures, the law of succession was simple primogeniture. Whatever formula was used, any person violating the formula would certainly have to fight off an army of challengers to establish himself. The transition from headman to king was neither sudden nor smooth. Early kings still faced violent opposition upon accession to the throne; only much later did the rules of succession become so well-established that they commanded wide respect.

Constraints on the king's rule were applied only to succession; once in place on the throne, a king could pretty much get away with murder—which kings often did. However, as societies became larger, outrageous behavior in kings was less tolerated, and the notion that a bad king could be corrected by regicide took hold. Meanwhile a new level of abstraction was developing. It was at first merely a reaction to the excesses of kings, an attempt to bring them under some sort of rein. The Greeks tried direct democracy, but Greek democracy was an extended aristocracy—not that many people were given the franchise. The Roman experiment was, in my opinion, closer to the overall evolution of political systems. They created a temporary king called a consul and split the office in half to ensure that no single person could ruin everything. These two new elements (temporary and split) provided a major leap in abstraction: now the concept of rule was separated from the person of the ruler and invested in a new concept, that of political office. The ruler was not this or that Roman; the ruler was the pair of consuls, whomever that happened to be this year.

Along with this came another abstraction: civil and criminal law. Kings were also judges; if you had a dispute with somebody, you took it to the king, made your complaint, and accepted his judgment. But societies were getting too big; kings couldn't spend all day resolving petty arguments over missing sheep. Hence came the notion of a new office, the magistrate (enforcer of laws), and, of course, the laws that he operated under. The king made the laws and the magistrates applied them. It took only a minor adjustment to invest lawmaking power in the hands of a consul.

Parallel with this came another increment in abstraction: the congress, senate, or council. This was a body of wise or important men, small enough to debate issues but large enough to be vaguely representative of the population as a whole. Initially such groups operated in an advisory role to the king or consul, but later they were given more and more control over lawmaking.

Unfortunately, Roman society was not flexible enough to handle all those new abstractions well; with Julius Caesar, Roman society reverted to the kingly system, retaining a few of the democratic elements. And because kingship isn't as efficient with large populations, the Roman system soon stopped expanding, coasted for a while on its enormous momentum, and then slowly disintegrated. Things remained in a funk until the Renaissance, when rising populations again made direct royal rule too cumbersome. Societies were just too big and complicated to be run by one person.

The European kings saw the handwriting on the wall and adjusted their rule, some with more alacrity than others. The English were the least laggardly, steadily eroding the power of the king until today the monarch is superfluous. The French monarchy was a little slower to respond and paid for it in 1792; the Russian monarchy was even slower and paid an even higher price in 1917.

The big idea that replaced monarchy was constitutionalism—an even higher level of abstraction. A constitution is a law specifying how laws are to be made. Everything is defined by the constitution in terms of the office, not the individual. A constitution, after all, is just like a computer program, only its variables are political offices and the values they take are individuals. It specifies how the variables are changed (election or appointment) and how the variables interact (powers of each office).

Our political systems continue to grow in size and complexity. The next level of abstraction—federalism—was first tried in the U.S. constitution and is now being gingerly approached by the European Union. Federalism creates an aggregation of distinct constitutions organized cooperatively. Each state in the federation retains internal sovereignty, delegating external affairs to the federal government. Thus, federalism is the next level of political abstraction after constitutionalism. Federalism's downward manifestation, devolution, is also being experimented with in a number of countries. I suspect that federalism will be the guiding theme of political history in the twenty-first century.

Again, the basic message is clear: as we've gotten bigger and better at politics, we have added higher and higher levels of abstraction to our political systems.

Computational Abstraction

Now let's talk about the process of computation. Its simplest form is counting. In the earliest days, counting was as direct a process as could be imagined: you made one mark for each item you counted. We still use this process today, making four hash marks before closing the group of five with a diagonal mark, but the basic scheme of counting with rows of marks has been with us for a long time. Archaeologists have found bones a hundred thousand years old with rows of scratch marks incised on them, obviously some sort of counting mechanism. What were our ancestors counting? Antelopes? Phases of the moon? IRS returns?

Later our counting systems took on a higher level of abstraction with the introduction of symbols for larger numbers. Every culture had its own system, but the Roman numbering system is typical. For small numbers, the simple slash mark was retained as an I. V stood for five slash marks, X stood for 10, L meant 50, C meant 100, and M meant a thousand. You still counted by making a long sequence of marks, but at least this system saved some space. The system worked for counting large numbers of things, as suited the needs of a more complex civilization, but it was hell to perform arithmetic with.

The next big step in abstraction was the Hindu concept of numerals. There were three big ideas here: first, the creation of a separate numeral for each of the 10 digits in a decimal counting system; second, the introduction of a numeral for zero (how do you show zero slashes?); third—and most abstract—the concept of decimal places: that a number consisted of a set of numerals, each numeral multiplied by an implicit power of 10. We learned it in second grade, but this was rocket science for the ancients. And before you dismiss their obvious stupidity, I challenge you to define the way the system works in purely theoretical terms. You may know how to use it, but on a theoretical level it is quite abstract.

The Hindu system traveled through the Islamic world and made its way to Europe, where it was called the Arabic system.

The next level of abstraction used this layer as its foundation. The newfangled Hindu numerals made arithmetic easier. Of course, the Hindu system required some fairly complicated procedures, but like any complex tool, once you learned the system, it was faster.

This didn't happen in a vacuum. The needs of European business drove the development of arithmetic. Financial transactions were themselves growing more abstract, and this growing financial abstraction demanded concomitant computational abstraction to figure out who got how much money.

Next came the substitution of a variable for some imagined number. Again, finance led the way. In earlier, more primitive days, loan terms were specified by actual monetary values. My loan contract with you might stipulate that I will give you 50 ducats, and you will pay me 55 ducats next June. But as the economy heated up, and transactions became more common, merchants began engaging in what-if games. What if I borrow enough money to buy the whole shipload? How much would I make? In these circumstances, people began to think in more abstract terms about such concepts as principal and interest rate. Some banker got tired of telling Marcello that his 40-ducat loan would cost 10 ducats a year, Antonio that his 120-ducat loan would cost 30 ducats, and Francisco that his 240-ducat loan would cost 60 ducats. Instead, he need merely post a sign that said "Today's interest rate: 25% per annum."

Note that this number was more complicated than the earlier numbers: it presumed some computation. By itself, the number 25% meant nothing at all to Marcello, but he need merely multiply 25% by his desired 40-ducat loan to obtain the actual interest: 10 ducats. Marcello started thinking at a higher level of abstraction.

Once we had jumped to this level of abstraction, algebra was the next level of abstraction (a Persian mathematician had invented the discipline long before; Europe didn't catch up with the idea until there was money to made in it.) Marcello could think in terms of an equation:

```
annual interest = interest rate * amount borrowed
```

Now we were putting variables together in equations; this allowed us to think in higher and more powerful terms.

From there, mathematics took off in its own direction, introducing even more abstract concepts such as operators and groups, but I won't follow that trail. Suffice it to say that the advance of mathematics has generated increasingly higher levels of abstraction that reach beyond the ken of most people.

Biological Abstraction

Biological systems have also evolved in the direction of increasing abstraction. What I mean by this is that the more complex organisms devote greater biological effort to more abstract traits. The simplest one-celled organisms concentrate on the basics: getting food and reproducing. As we move up to larger creatures, we see the addition of locomotion, which in and of itself is not of direct value to the basic goal of reproduction. But locomotion grants access to a larger food supply and a wider range of possible mates, so it indirectly supports the two basic goals of the organism. In the same way, sensory mechanisms provide only abstract support for nourishment and reproduction. Much the same thing can be said about immune systems, which have evolved an ever-more abstract approach to dealing with the ever-more abstract assaults of invaders. Particularly striking is the success of the AIDS virus, which pulls its trick by moving up one level of abstraction, attacking the immune system rather than the organism.

But the most spectacular example of biological abstraction is the development of the nervous system. In its earliest forms, it was a simple detection and control system, providing direct connection from stimulus (pain) to response (retraction of affected body part). Later, nervous systems expanded to provide additional computational power, giving organisms greater ability to react to their environments with sensitivity and discrimination. And, of course, the human brain represents a profoundly abstract piece of biological machinery, much of which is unallocated at birth. Here's a big blob of biologically expensive tissue whose job is not precisely defined by the genes—it learns what it needs during early years of life. How's that for abstraction!

Thus, biological systems have grown larger and more complex primarily by adding new layers of abstraction. Those layers are patent in ontogeny—the development of an organism from conception to birth. A fertilized human egg is initially the same as a paramecium, but as it grows it passes through many stages vaguely similar to the phylogenetically earlier orders of life. And the most distinctively human trait of the fetus—the brain—is the last thing to develop. Indeed, by the standards of other mammals, human babies are born prematurely; they require three more years just to complete the basic development of the brain.

Abstraction and Interactivity Design

At last the time has come to bring home my point. The general lesson from all these examples is that, as systems grow bigger and more complex, they evolve more abstract structures to cope with the increasing complexity. This is precisely what we are doing with computers: moving our endeavors to higher levels of complexity. Consider how much more complex the common conception of a document has become since the introduction of word processing. Back in the 70s, I was aware of such factors as tabs, margins, and line spacing, but now I regularly include such factors as font, font size, style, indentations, justification, tabulation, headers, and footers in my document preparation. Note, too, that all of these factors are abstractions of the printed page. Moreover, I prepare more documents these days than ever before. Word processing has advanced simultaneously in volume, abstraction, and complexity.

Or take spreadsheets. The first spreadsheet, VisiCalc, was a rudimentary tool for handling financial calculations, but the current monsters have huge libraries of statistical and trigonometric functions and are used for purposes ranging far beyond budgetary calculations. As part of this process, though, spreadsheets have grown in both complexity and abstraction.

Image manipulation programs (drawing, painting, and photo retouching) have similarly evolved from obvious and tangible beginnings to astounding levels of abstraction and complexity. Gradient fills, palette adjustments, and mathematically advanced filtering algorithms have been added to the simple drawing, rectangular selection, and other schemes of yesteryear. These additions are not merely more complex: they are more abstract as well, and they are used with more and bigger images because they're so useful.

Last, I direct your attention to the growth in abstraction on the web. As more and more pages popped up, we needed a higher level of abstraction for handling the web; hence arose the search engine. As more material flooded onto the web, we started seeing specialized search engines, and now we have pages that offer lists of search engines—an abstraction of an abstraction. At the same time, we have seen the languages of the Web increase in abstractive power. HTML has grown through the addition of more abstract constructs, such as frames and tables. Java has made possible a gigantic leap in abstraction in our designs, and the Web will grow even more because of it.

Transforming Observation into Design Practice

These observations provide us with a useful way of thinking about the design process for interactivity. It seems that a great many designers attempt to improve an existing design by adding greater complexity; all too often this yields what I call *humongous heap* design, in which features are simply shoveled onto an ever-larger pile, until the pile grows so large that even the designers themselves cannot grasp its operation, at which time design growth peters out from intellectual exhaustion.

A more productive alternative would be to concentrate on the level of abstraction of the design rather than the amount of complexity. Greater complexity emerges automatically from higher abstraction; therefore, abstraction should drive the design process, not complexity. For example, if I were to attempt to design a better word processor, I would not look for new features to add; I would begin by asking myself, "What is the deeper essence of a document?" I would seek some more abstract way of conceiving a document. Perhaps I would think of it as a communication rather than a document. Perhaps instead of visualizing words on a page, I might think in terms of organization of ideas—this would yield a word processor based on an outliner. Or perhaps I would think not in terms of the final result, but in terms of the interactive process by which a writer creates a document. What goes on in the writer's mind does not look like a printed page; perhaps an abstraction of that process would lead us to a better word processor. This might entail some specialization in target audiences: a word processor for novelists whose starting points are characterization and plot. Or perhaps a word processor for bureaucrats whose abstractions are a set of nothingburger sentences customizable with appropriate obfuscatory passive verbs, verbified nouns, and acronyms. Indeed, any formulaic style of writing can be addressed with a specialized word processor that incorporates the central abstracting formula.

Abstraction and Website Design

Website designers can enhance the utility of their sites by thinking of their work in more abstract terms. It's not just a collection of pages grouped into a tree structure, with some crosslinks added for fast navigation; it's an information structure. The basic tree structure is quite practical with small websites of a few score pages, but imagine how badly it breaks down with a website with 100,000 unique pages. As our websites grow in size and complexity, we need a higher level of abstraction to stay on top of the problem. Search engines help, but they abdicate any responsibility for organizing the website more efficiently. We must learn to think more in terms of information organization than information presentation. This new abstraction will require more intelligence of its users and more thinking/processing power of its providers; higher levels of abstraction in other systems have always demanded more of all concerned. Later, we'll need to move website design to higher levels of process intensity. This will require the use of languages permitting higher levels of abstraction than HTML.

Abstraction and Educational Software

I for one have grown bored and frustrated with all those tedious products that dish out facts like Twinkies off a production line—and the addition of sound-track, illustrations, and video only adds icing and colored sprinkles to the Twinkies. Much educational software operates at the lowest level of educational abstraction: the presentation of fact. Higher levels of abstraction will be necessary to tap the power of the computer in educational applications.

The educational simulation is the first level of abstraction, and much has been learned about the use of educational simulations. My hunch is that the next level of abstraction will be variable simulations. We present younger students with tiny simulations, each making a small point. Older students encounter a wider array of ideas presented at a higher level of abstraction. The youngest student learns about Columbus discovering America; an older student plays with the spice trade; an even older student experiments with economic simulations of the period.

Another direction in which to explore abstraction is in the educational process itself. What goes on in a student's mind when first encountering, say, algebra? How are those ideas successfully integrated into the webwork of previous knowledge? It might be possible to open up new areas of educational software by abstracting the process by which the student learns, rather than the material that we wish to teach.

Abstraction is the key to strategic development of interactive designs.

21

INDIRECTION

Abstraction is an intellectual concept; indirection is one means of translating this concept into practice—but not the only means. Abstraction replaces tangible realities with grander intangible concepts; indirection is not quite so esoteric. It replaces tangible realities with tangible substitutes, representations, or pointers. These indirectors are smaller, handier, or more manipulable than their referents; if they aren't in some way more useful, we wouldn't bother with them. Think of abstraction as physics and indirection as engineering.

I'll use financial abstraction as my example; here's how the abstraction of the financial system in the previous chapter is manifested through indirection. The rock-bottom foundation of finance is the "goody"—some product or service that we desire. Coins, the first level of finance, are not themselves goodies; they are held to be equal in value to goodies. Thus, I can exchange some of my coins for some of your goodies. The only reason I bother with coins is because they are small and light; I can carry them around in my pocket a lot more easily than I could carry a cow. The next level of abstraction is paper money, which is even easier to carry around, because one bill of a standard size can be worth $1 or $1,000, whereas coins would have to be larger for larger denominations, and we'd be stuck with either pin-sized pennies or pizza-sized $1,000 coins. But remember that the paper money refers back to coins; indeed, for many years, paper currency had to be backed up by gold. The U.S. government would store enough gold in Fort Knox to guarantee that owners of dollars could always cash them in for gold. The dollars stood for the gold. (Later, we dumped the gold standard. Dollars are no longer guaranteed to be redeemable for gold—but that's a technicality.)

The next level of abstraction is the check, which is even more convenient because we don't have to put together a combination of bills and coins to obtain a particular amount of money; a check is like a customizable-value dollar bill. Again, however, the check is not the same thing as a dollar bill: it's a representation of a dollar bill—not quite as tangible as the dollar bill, but handier to use. It points to a bank account that has the dollars in it.

The next level of abstraction, the credit card, is realized with an even greater level of indirection. The credit card is just a pointer to a financial account that acts as an anticipated repository of money. The credit card points to the account with its credit card number. The credit card account is a grandly abstract construct. It has no physical existence; in the deepest bowels of some monster credit card institution, you will not find a little box of coins with your name on it.

To summarize: Abstraction is manifested through indirection. Indirection substitutes a convenient indirector for the real thing. That indirector can represent the referent, substitute for it, or point to it.

Constructs

The crucial component of any indirection scheme is the *construct*, a scheme for getting to the referent from the indirector. The construct for dollar bills used to be quite simple: I could walk into any bank and demand that they replace my dollars with gold or silver. Checks have a slightly more difficult construct: the bearer of my endorsed check can't go to any bank to convert it to dollars; the check must be taken to my particular bank. The credit card construct is even more complicated: the creditor's computer calls up the credit card company's computer and collects the dollars electronically, using special green electrons.

Thus, the construct is the procedure you must follow to get from the indirector to the referent. Constructs are everywhere; they are so fundamental to our existence that we never notice them. Words are indirectors: the word itself is just a sound that we associate with something in the real world. When I say "cat," you mentally substitute your concept of the animal for the word.

Two factors determine the utility of a construct: the compression factor and the effort of translation to its referent. I use the term *compression* metaphorically; it does not refer to a reduction in size, but rather a reduction in clumsiness. Thus, a coin has a high compression factor for a cow, but a low compression factor for a jewel, which is why you find jewels and not cows inside treasure boxes. The word *cat* is a short, handy compression of "that little furry animal that purrs, eats mice, and has two erect ears on the top of its head." In general, language provides high compression factors for the ideas it represents (except in the hands of bureaucrats and politicians):

*"He can compress the most words into the
smallest ideas of any man I ever met."*
—Abraham Lincoln on another politician

Suppose I buy $10.56 worth of gasoline. Wouldn't the $10 bill and some change be easier to use than the credit card? This brings us to the other utility factor in constructs: the effort of translation to the referent. The credit card's 12-digit number goes straight into the computer, and the processing from there is lightning fast, perfectly accurate, and absolutely, positively reliable (we think). Not much effort there. But if I hand the attendant a $10 bill and some change, think about how much effort is involved for both of us: I have to carry around enough cash to cover my anticipated spending, the gas station attendant might have to make change, might make a mistake in the process, might try to cheat either me or the owner, might get robbed, and has to dispose of the cash safely at intervals. All of these problems impose extra effort. Thus, while a $10 bill might be itself "more compressed" than a 12-digit number, this is more than compensated for by the additional effort required to handle the $10 bill. The real point of constructs is to reduce the total workload, which in turn depends on how easy the construct is to "carry," how "far" you have to carry it, and how much work you have to do to "translate" it back to its referent.

By the way, this takes us back to Chapter 17 and the concept of *process versus data*. The data is the compressed item; the process is the translation back to its referent. As I pointed out there, you can always put together any mixture of process and data. In some cases, data is easier to work with; in others, process is easier, so you find a balance that minimizes your total effort. Processing a credit card purchase takes a lot more computer cycles than making change for a dollar bill, but computer cycles are faster and cheaper than human brain cycles.

Carrying Indirectors across Gaps

A construct "carries" an indirector across some "distance" to a destination, where the referent is somehow reconstructed. In the case of interactivity design, there are six gaps to bridge in the interactivity loop:

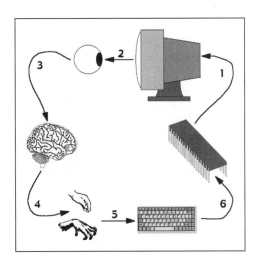

In moving information around this loop, the information must be converted at each step into some different form and transmitted across a gap. Let's take the simplest example: the path from keyboard and mouse to the computer. We'll concentrate all of our attention on the keyboard. The keyboard has a wire that goes into the computer. By the way, you may not have known that most keyboards have a pretty complicated chip inside that could fairly be considered a computer in its own right. Now, from the keyboard's point of view, a keypress is a connection between two wires in a matrix. When you press the Q key, the keyboard doesn't sense *Q;* it senses a connection between, say, vertical wire 4 and horizontal wire 2. As far as the keyboard is concerned, that's the reality of the event. However, that's not what the keyboard sends down the wire to the main computer; its computer chip looks up a kind of Morse code for that combination and sends that code down the wire. Your one keypress triggers a bunch of electronic pulses traveling down the wire to the CPU.

That might sound like a complicated process, but there's a good reason for it: that wire that runs from the keyboard to the computer is out there in the world, exposed to slings and arrows, chewing puppies, yanking users, EM-radiating transformers, and all the other dangers that the wires inside the computer are protected from. It's easy for the signal to get messed up by all that noise. Remember, the construct is supposed to carry the stuff across the distance—this presumes that the stuff actually gets there! To guarantee noise-free delivery of the signal, the keyboard codes it up in a Morse-code-type construct that is almost impossible to screw up. It sends the Morse-code down the wire to a circuit inside the computer, which reconstitutes it as the computer code for *Q* and presents it to the computer for processing.

Thus, your own indirector for *Q* is a key on the keyboard; pressing that key causes the keyboard to convert that indirector into another indirector that is well-suited to moving down the wire to the computer. When that indirector arrives at the computer, it is converted into another indirector, the computer code for *Q.*

Consider how complicated all this is, yet the connection between keyboard and computer is the cleanest, simplest, most reliable connection in the entire loop. I hope this instills in you a respect for the difficulties you will face in designing constructs to cross the other, more difficult gaps.

So let's trace each step in the process and discuss some of the constructs available. At each step, we'll be dealing with a pair of entities, each possessed of its own special strengths and weaknesses in receiving and transmitting information. We'll need a construct for each pair, one that takes advantage of each part's strengths while skirting each part's weaknesses.

Step 1: CPU to Monitor

I have good news for you: the CPU-to-monitor step is well understood and well supported at every level. At the hardware level, all computers have display boards that reduce the amount of computer effort required to keep a video display running. At the operating system level, every computer has a great many built-in programs meant to simplify the task of moving information from the computer to the display. As a programmer, I need merely order the computer to draw something (a line, some text, or an image), and the operating system does all the work. Finally, at the highest level (programming), we are blessed with a huge force of eager programmers who just love to create snazzy graphics on computers. Thus, you should have no problem dealing with this step.

Step 2: Monitor to Eyeball

Our accumulated wisdom about the monitor-to-eyeball gap is maintained by the community of graphics artists. I will not presume to offer a lesson in that field; let me merely note that there are a great many powerful constructs for communicating information to the eye. The retina is capable of deciphering color, texture, motion, and edges. That's one reason why text characters are always composed of lines, curved or straight: the retina quickly recognizes the edges to decipher the character.

Step 3: Eyeball to Brain

The eyeball-to-brain may sound like a superfluous step already covered by the graphic designers, but the problems they are best at solving aren't quite the same as the problems we face as interactivity designers. They have much useful advice to offer us, but I think it graces us to consider the problem from another point of view as well.

Fortunately, the brain is able to bring vast amounts of mental resource to bear on the interpretation of constructs. This permits a great many highly compressed constructs to be used. Perhaps the most impressive of these constructs is written language: in reading we take in a tiny amount of information and translate it into some pretty complicated and abstract ideas. My favorite example is the (only distantly correct) statement, "Ontogeny recapitulates phylogeny." (This is the notion mentioned earlier, that an organism developing from conception to birth retraces its evolutionary past.) With just 33 bytes of data, we can communicate an idea so complicated that entire books have been written on the subject.

Another powerful brain capability here is the facial recognition processor. Our brains have special circuitry for analyzing human facial expression. This is not merely a culturally learned capability; much research has demonstrated that infants can recognize and differentiate faces and facial expressions. Anthropologists have shown that the basic facial expressions are universal and independent of cultural differences. Both of these observations point to a wired-in capability. Even more interesting is the research into micro-expressions. These are quick expressions that flash across the face in a fraction of a second. They happen so fast that neither the expressioner nor the audience is consciously aware of their existence, yet careful experiments have demonstrated that the audience definitely, if subconsciously, perceives and recognizes the micro-expression. For example, when a person lies to you, he has difficulty maintaining eye contact; his eyes will flash away briefly. We all know this and thus arises the demand, "Look me in the eye when you say that!"

Consider what this implies about the processing capabilities of the human brain in handling facial expressions. There's a great deal of processing involved in feature recognition: transforming the texture and shading information into cheeks, eyebrows, lips, and so forth. Next, that feature information must be translated into emotional expression (this expression is angry, that expression is happy). Yet, all this processing is carried out in a fraction of a second. Clearly, a great many neurons are dedicated to this processing.

The movies take advantage of our natural brainpower in processing human facial expression. The sequence that best exemplifies this for me is from the very first Star Wars movie. Luke Skywalker et al. have escaped from the Death Star in the Millennium Falcon and are making their getaway, pursued by enemy fighters. There follows an intense action-packed sequence in which Luke and Han Solo shoot down the enemy fighters. What is most striking about this action sequence is its reliance on faces to communicate action and emotion. You would expect such a sequence to be all zooming spaceships, roaring turbolasers, and billowing explosions, but in fact such imagery occupies only half of the display time of the sequence. The other half is taken up by character faces: frightened, concentrating, worried, triumphant. George Lucas knew that special effects get you only halfway there. You need facial expression to cinch the communication.

Facial expression is not the communicated reality, but rather an indirect representation of the communicated reality. The important idea being communicated by facial expression is emotion, but the facial expression is not the same thing as the emotion; it is a representation of the emotion. In other words, facial expression doesn't depict emotion—it represents emotion. It is an indirect indicator of emotion, but the indirection of the expression is compensated for by the speed with which the brain can translate that indirect representation into an interpretation of emotion. Thus, although a tremendous amount of processing is involved in deciphering the construct, this processing is already hardwired into the brain, so it costs very little in terms of effort.

Step 4: Brain to Hands

Whatever the brain decides, it must express to the computer through the hands. The construct used here is simple: one nerve extends from the brain to each muscle; the brain sends a signal down that nerve, and the muscle contracts. The complicated part, figuring out the timing and sequencing of all those muscle contractions, is carried out inside the brain, so the information travelling to the muscles requires little compression in a construct; it just needs to get there fast.

Step 5: Hands to Keyboard and Mouse

Here we have the most tangible of the six steps. The hands communicate information by pressing buttons and moving a mouse. Unfortunately, pressing a button sends exactly one bit of information—not much to work with. If we have a hundred keys on a keyboard, then we can send 7 bits with one button press, and prefix keys such as Shift, Alt, Control, and Command add another 4 bits—still not much data. Hence, all those button presses have to be assembled in long, complicated sequences to communicate anything. We type lots of words per minute, and we click, drag, and double-click madly and give ourselves repetitive stress injuries. The construct used here is whatever you, the designer, can cook up to reduce the number of keystrokes and mouse clicks for the user. This is why interactivity design is important.

Step 6: Keyboard and Mouse to CPU

This last step lies outside our reach as designers; the wiring from keyboard and mouse to CPU is fixed. On the sixth step, the Designer rested.

An Example of Constructs at Work

To see constructs at work, let's use the brilliant example Scott McCloud used in his wonderful book, Understanding Comics. Here is my own rendition of Scott's much better artwork:

We start with a photograph of a face on the left. This is reality, plain and messy. To its left is an abstract face. Next comes the even more indirect representation: the word *FACE*. Last comes a verbal description of a face.

Consider now the constructs required to interpret the various representations of a face. The leftmost representation, of course, requires no construct because it is *not* a representation—it is a direct depiction. There is no abstraction, no indirection; therefore, no construct is required. As we move to the left, we encounter increasing abstraction and must apply increasingly abstract mental constructs. We must interpret the word *face* to understand the first textual representation. The second representation requires us to interpret the words and assemble them geometrically to envision a face.

Indirection in Programming

Computer programming uses indirection in an especially simple and clear manner. Allow me to walk you through some of the lessons that programmers have learned about indirection. Let's start by talking about numbers. You can refer to numbers in a program in many ways. The simplest and most straightforward is to explicitly provide the number. For example, suppose we wish to determine whether if a value has grown too large. So we have an IF -statement, like so:

```
IF MyVariable > 25 THEN...
```

But programmers know that this way of expressing a value is often undesirable. Suppose that I have three or four places in my program where I repeat the same test on MyVariable. This is trouble waiting to happen, because the odds are high that if I later need to change the 25 to, say, 26, then I have to hunt down every case of IF MyVariable > 25 THEN... All I need is to miss just one case, and I've got myself a messy, ugly bug.

Of course, every beginning programmer knows the solution to this problem: at the beginning of the program, you define a constant called, say, TestConstant, and you set it equal to 25. Then your code should read:

```
TestConstant = 25
(many lines of intervening code)
IF MyVariable > TestConstant THEN...
```

The big advantage of this approach is that, if I choose to change TestConstant from 25 to, say, 26, then I change it at a single place in the program. This greatly cuts down on stupid bugs. Of course, I also have to write one extra line of code.

This is all pedestrian programming, but there's an enormously important point here: the solution involves recourse to a higher level of indirection in the representation of the number. The old, dumb way used the direct value, but the solution used a representation of the value (TestConstant) instead of the value itself. In other words, the line

```
IF MyVariable > TestConstant THEN...
```

tells the computer to go back and look at whatever value was assigned to TestConstant. It doesn't present the value itself, it instead represents the number with a name.

But this is only the first level of indirection. The clever programmer might wish to change the value of TestConstant during execution. At first, its value is 25, but later on, she wants it to be 26. To do this, she turns TestConstant into a variable with the name TestVariable. This is a more powerful approach; you can do all sorts of snazzy tricks with it. You can einsure that the IF -statement is will triggered under different conditions. If you want TestVariable to be 25 in one situation but 26 in another situation, you just change its value at the right time. But there's a bit more work involved in making the variable work. You have to declare the variable, specifying what kind of variable it is. Then you have to initialize it. Thus, there are now two extra lines of code to write:

```
Short    TestVariable;
(many lines of intervening code)
TestVariable = 25;
(many lines of intervening code)
IF MyVariable > TestVariable THEN...
```

Moreover, the program is now a bit harder to understand. When you were using a constant, you could always check its value by simply looking up its definition in the program listing. But a variable is much trickier to check up on.

You have to halt the program in mid-flight and examine its value with a debugger. Granted, this is easy work, but it's still more work than simply looking up the constant declaration.

Note the drift: in moving from constant to variable, we increased our programming power and gave ourselves interesting new capabilities. But at the same time, we added one more line of code for each level of indirection, made the program harder to understand, and increased our workload.

But it doesn't stop there. We can take our problem another level of indirection higher by replacing the variable with an table of variables referred to by a pointer. This pointer an index into the table of variables. Now, why would we want to do this, you might wonder. The advantage is that the pointer or the index can be easily and simply altered to point to completely different values. Thus, an index of 1 might point to a value of 25, while an index of 2 might point to a value of 57, and an index of 3 might point to a value of 19. The big difference here is that now we are contemplating changing the value of TestVariable, doing so frequently, and using a large variety of numbers that bounce all over the map. We are now thinking in broader terms about TestVariable. It could be almost anything, and it will be many different things at different times. And this approach will require quite a few extra lines of code to initialize all the values in the table.

Searching and sorting huge amounts of data can be made much faster by using pointers. Entire books have been written on this technique. My point is that the central idea behind these powerful methods is the use of the indirection of a pointer. Indeed, some of the most powerful methods involve double indirection: that is, pointers to pointers (or *handles,* as they are called). Such methods can be truly mind-boggling, requiring a great mental exertion to decipher. Once you figure them out, though, they are truly powerful and elegant.

Indirection also costs computer time. When you use a constant, the computer goes straight into the object code and runs fast. When you use a variable, the computer has to load the value from RAM, a slower process. When you use a pointer, the computer must first fetch the pointer and then dereference it to obtain the value, an even slower process. And when you use a handle with double indirection, the computer must go through two dereferencing processes before it can finally fetch the desired value. Obviously, indirection slows down the computer in much the same way that it boggles the mind.

Note this also: our mental image of TestVariable has shifted. When we were low on the scale of indirection, it was easy to think about what TestValue represented: it was a single number, 25. Now a single value like 25 is something you can wrap your fingers around, something clear and almost tangible. But as we have moved up the scale of indirection, our mental image of the value has grown fuzzier. First it was a number, 25. Then it was a name (TestConstant) representing a number, 25. Then it was another name, TestVariable, representing a variable whose value was initially 25, but might change later. Later, it became a pointer or an index to a value in a list of values. Are you starting to become befuddled? Is all this indirection making you think too hard to keep up with what is intended? If so, then you are experiencing the other half of the representation/depiction tradeoff. As I have already shown, higher levels of indirection permit more power and expressive range, but they also require greater amounts of interpretive labor, and they presume larger programs. You don't need double indirection for a checkbook balancing program; you do for a big spreadsheet.

Here's another example: Imagine that you've got a huge website with several hundred pages up and running, and you have your standard high-level navigational links placed on each page. But now the client wants you to add another high-level navigational link. Under older versions of HTML, you had to laboriously go through each of the pages, inserting the new HTML code that includes the additional link. What a tedious job! Under later versions of HTML, though, you can design each page with a frame, which is defined just once. You change the frame, and all the web pages containing the frame are automatically updated. Aren't frames wonderful? Note, however, that each one of those pages with the frame actually contains an indirector—a pointer—to the frame. Frames are nothing more than a new form of indirection introduced into HTML.

Applying Indirection to Output

So far, I have spoken about indirection solely in terms of communication. It is also possible to use indirection in another manner entirely: to calculate output directly. There are three broad classes of output indirection: zero indirection (that is, utterly direct), combinatorial or indexed indirection, and calculated indirection.

The utterly direct approach is the most commonly used method these days, largely because it is the easiest to understand and produce. You simply prepare whatever it is you wish to present to the user, store it somewhere, and then dump it onto the user at the appropriate moment. I'll offer you two examples of this process: one using a human face, and the other using some text.

Here's an example of utterly direct text:

"Hector had a long, sharp, heavy sword hanging at his side. Drawing it, he swooped like a high-flying eagle that drops to earth through the black clouds upon a tender lamb or a fleeing hare. Thus he charged at Achilles."

And here is an example of an utterly direct face:

The second type of indirection, indexed or combinatorial, is most easily understood with a headline generation algorithm for the *National Enquirer* involving random combinations of Princess Diana, reincarnation, abduction by flying saucers, abnormal births, and revolutionary diet plans ("Two-headed baby abducted by space aliens; returns with secret message of peace from Princess Diana"). We could, for example, prepare a suitable headline with the following simple algorithm:

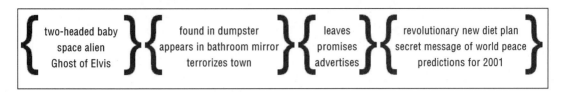

You randomly select one of the three items in each bunch and then string them together to get your combinatorial headline.

But you can take this idea much further. Here is an example of what I call Tinkertoy Text from my program, the Erasmatron:

<SubjectNom> {appears|looks} {quite|very|most} {distraught|upset}. "The {barbarians|Saxons}!" <SubjectNom> blurts. "They've {stolen|robbed me of|made off with} <NumberObject1Value> of my cattle!"

This little jewel can turn out hundreds of variations on the basic sentence, such as:

Percival looks most upset. "The barbarians!" he blurts. "They've made off with 87 of my cattle!"

or

Isolde appears quite distraught. "The Saxons!" she blurts. "They've stolen 45 of my cattle!"

or many other combinations.

Combinatorialism can also be used graphically; here is an example:

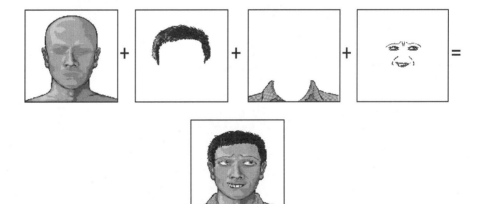

What makes the combinatorial approach so useful is that you can use a great many basic components in many different combinations:

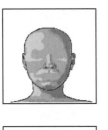 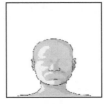 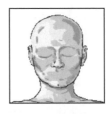 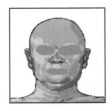

As you might imagine, with this approach you could easily generate zillions of faces.

The third type of indirection is the most powerful: calculated indirection. This method uses equations to figure out how to generate the output. My Tinkertoy Text scheme has a whiff of calculation in it; the term <NumberObject1Value> is replaced by a numerical value. It can figure out the name of a character and insert that where required; it can even substitute pronouns for proper names. However, it can't calculate tense endings, plurals, case endings, or most other aspects of natural language; such calculations are too difficult.

My face display system uses some calculations. The lips, for example, are calculated with consideration for mouth width and lip thickness. However, a much better approach is the use of fully synthetic facial displays, which calculate a face from basic knowledge of human facial anatomy. These are now in use in Hollywood and will soon become available at the less stratospheric levels at which we now work.

Communicative Power of Indirection

Directness is powerful. If you and I are having a heated disagreement, and I were to bare my teeth and snarl, the directness of my expression would have greater impact upon you than if I passed you a note saying, "I am angry." Indirect expression is never as immediate or punchy as direct expression, because indirect expression must travel through several layers of computation inside the brain before it makes its point. This is why movies are generally more popular than novels, and television is more popular than radio.

But directness is a two-edged sword; it has advantages and disadvantages. Most designers are acutely aware of the advantages of directness, but ignorant of its disadvantages or of the corresponding advantages of indirectness.

Consider this example of the detrimental effects of over-specified depiction: Suppose that you wish to communicate a simple idea about home safety—that you shouldn't leave electrical wires lying about on the floor. Now, you could communicate this with representational text like so: "It is unsafe to place electrical cords across walkways; people might trip on them." That's pretty good. But golly gee, wouldn't it be more impressive to make a video depicting the problem? Here's old grandpa shuffling down the dimly lit hallway. His eyes aren't so good. The camera at floor level shows his foot catching on the electrical cord. Next, a slow-motion shot of his face as he loses his balance, and then a full shot of his body crashing into the floor. Then we follow up with normal-speed sounds of voices crying out, "It's grandpa! He's hurt! Call an ambulance!"

This is certainly dramatic video. But consider its message. Does it say that electrical cords are dangerous to everybody, or only to old people? Perhaps a viewer might tell himself, "Since there are no old people in my home, I don't need to worry about this problem." Or perhaps the viewer will draw the conclusion that the problem lay in the poor lighting in the hallway. The video doesn't address your situation or my situation; it addresses a single case. We are expected to generalize from that single case to a variety of cases, but that process of generalization is fraught with confusion. It is entirely too easy to generalize incorrectly. Is the tale of grandpa's fall a warning about the frailty of old people, or the dangers of poor lighting, or the hazards of electrical cords left in the open? The video leaves these questions unanswered.

Note that the indirect textual representation has no such problems. It clearly specifies the scope and nature of the point being made. It is a more precise communication; it has clearer focus; it gets its point across more accurately than the video does.

There's another advantage to indirectness: it is not only more precise;, it also offers more expressive possibilities. Consider the lines from this Bob Dylan song: "And take me disappearing through the smoke rings of my mind, down the foggy ruins of time, far past the frozen leaves, the haunted, frightened trees, far past the twisted reach of crazy sorrow." Consider the expressive richness of these words. Their power springs from their indirectness, from the power of the combinations that the words permit. Consider, too, the futility of trying to communicate these phrases with direct depiction. Just what would "the foggy ruins of time" look like? I suppose that you could come up with an image that does the job, but could any actual depiction have the suggestive majesty of the representational phrase? And then there's "the smoke rings of my mind"—even further beyond the reach of direct depiction. The indirectness of representation makes possible an expressive range that completely outstrips direct depiction. What indirectness lacks in immediacy, it can gain in reach.

Here's an objection: User interfaces have evolved from indirect, representational schemes such as DOS to more direct, depictional schemes such as GUIs. Does this evolution not suggest that more power is obtained through direct approaches? This argument would have merit if DOS had actually made use of all that indirection. Remember that out of the zillions of things you could say in DOS, only a few actually accomplished anything. All the advantages of indirection were thrown away. Thus, there was no trade-off in moving from DOS to GUIs, and so the GUI advantage in limiting conceivable states was the dominant consideration. If the old command-line interfaces really had used all of the possibilities of textual input (that is, if they could understand and respond to a command such as "load my last word processing document"), then GUIs would never have stood a chance.

Putting Indirection to Work

Your task as interactivity designer is to concoct useful forms of indirection for your customers. What abstraction can you perceive that covers a great many tedious tasks, and what kind of user-manipulable indirector would make this abstraction available? A good place to start is to search for some task that has grown in size so that the old, more direct means of implementation are becoming tedious. Consider fonts in a word processor, for example. In the good old days, we had maybe a dozen fonts, and they were all available on a single menu. But nowadays, there are thousands of fonts to choose from. It would be nice to have them all available, but I don't like cluttering up my Fonts menu, so I leave many out. Here's a perfect place for a higher level of indirection. An obvious means of addressing my goal would be to characterize fonts by their most common function: body text, title text, and decorative text, for example. This would permit us to have three shorter font menus instead of one big one, but that's not what I'm driving at. Let's imagine a day in the not-too-distant future when our user is perpetually online and has fast access to thousands of fonts. It would then behoove us to organize our fonts by their characteristics: body text, header text, decorative text; wide or narrow characters, rounded or angular characters, and so forth. The indirectors are the described characteristics; each indirector points to a group of fonts. Users get easier access to tons of fonts.

Thus, using indirection is a matter of finding the ideal abstraction and set of indirectors for the task. Most people find the abstraction task more difficult to handle than the task of creating indirectors; they should pursue the design problem by sniffing about to find a good indirector. The more cerebral designers should try their hands at designing a good abstraction, from which an indirector can be deduced. But there's no hard rule here—some problems are most quickly solved by the more theoretical approach, and some are most quickly solved by the direct approach.

Scripting Languages

Many products extend their functionality by means of custom programming languages. An example is the query language on many websites that you use to specify what you're searching for. Such languages go by different names:; some designers call them scripting languages; others call theirs macro languages. Such languages are seldom learned by most users; they're just too much trouble for everybody but the hardcore enthusiasts.

My own cross is *grep*, a little language used in advanced text editors to specify all kinds of text patterns. For example, with grep, I can tell the text editor to search for all occurrences of any text string with the characters CASE# followed by two digits, and when it finds such a text string, to insert a zero in front of the first digit. This will sweep through all my text, replacing CASE#27 with

CASE#027, and so forth for any combination of numerals. And that's not all; with grep, I can tackle much more complicated situations. The problem is, grep is hard to learn. To this day, I still keep a three-page summary of grep programming rules next to my computer, and I consult it whenever I need to use grep.

These scripting languages commonly suffer from three design errors, all arising from a programmer-centric view of reality. First, their design goals are poorly thought out; their underlying motivation appears to be "let's add a small programming language to it!" Since programmers live and breathe programming languages, most have their own ideas about what makes a good language and can't resist the urge to design one. There's only one good reason to add a scripting language to a product: to improve the expressiveness available to the user by adding a capacity for indirection.

The second design error is making this capacity too large. Indirection is confusing; it must be administered in small doses. Programmers, though, are hardened addicts with such high tolerance for indirection that they can't help themselves—their designs are invariably too abstract for normal people. Programmers want power; they bitterly resent any constraint on their power. This was one of their objections to the Macintosh; it wouldn't let the user into its innards to perform unnatural acts. But DOS systems permitted any outrage— which in programmer eyes was a desirable trait.

Third, these scripting languages are expressed in unnecessarily programmerly terms. For example, the term *loop* is inappropriate for civilian use. Normal people don't think of such operations in sequential terms; they say, "Do this for each of these" to describe a repetitive operation. Or they give a single instance and then say, "Do the same thing for all the others." Yet all loop constructs in scripting languages require their users to specify the range over which the loop is to operate. The notion that a dataset could be defined as a closed set that is operated upon as a group seems alien to programmers. Another programmer arcanity: the use of a loop index as the primary component of the loop. Normal people don't think in terms of loop indices; they think in terms of corresponding actions for corresponding parts. Designers would do well to dispense entirely with loop indices and think in terms of sets of manipulable objects, with correspondence established in some simple fashion.

Let's use grep as an example. Its power and flexibility are impressive, but a dumber version would be more accessible to real human beings. Here's an example of a search facility containing the most important features of grep without all the arcanity:

Find/Change

Find text that:

Begins with:	Contains:	Ends with:
CASE#(0-9)(0-9)		

Change it to text that:

Begins with:	Contains:	Ends with:
CASE#0(0-9)(0-9)		

0-9	A-Z	⌐→	▶	•	☐ Whole Word
Any numeral	Any letter	End of Line	Tab	Anything	☐ Case Sensitive

[Change All]   [Change]   [Change, Find]   (Find Next)

In this example, the notion of looping is intrinsic to the "Change All" button, but there's nothing complicated about it.

There's a simple two-step formula for making looping implicit: include a means for the user to define a set, and add commands ending with -est, such as best, biggest, heaviest, and so forth. All of these words imply a looping search through a dataset. You could also use several other terms implying looping: average, standard deviation, total. There is also, of course, the ability to apply a verb to all members of the set.

Some scripting languages include a "watch me" facility for writing the script. The user doesn't have to learn the scripting language itself; instead, she tells the software to "watch me while I perform this task." The program records the sequence of commands and turns it into a macro. The difficulty with these schemes is how to loopify them. Selecting the set of manipulable objects on which the macro will execute is fairly easy: all of the files selected in a dialog box, all of the image frames in the selected portion of the movie, all of the records in the selected dataset. The trickier part is specifying the roles of each component in the macro. For example, suppose that I want to copy a small rectangle from the lower right corner of each frame of my movie and paste it into the center of the preceeding frame. How can I tell the computer that the frame parts of the macro are variable, but the rectangle selection and copying and pasting operations are fixed? There are two solutions to this problem.

The first and simplest is to have the user execute the desired procedure three times. On the first execution, the computer simply records the procedure. On the second execution, the computer notes the differences between the first and second executions, generalizing those differences to apply to the entire set. On the third execution, the computer compares its expectations with the user's entry to confirm that it understands the procedure; a discrepancy here triggers a request for additional examples. In our movie example, the computer would see that the rectangle selection, copying, and pasting operations are constant, but that the two chosen frames bear a constant relationship to each other: the recipient always preceedes the donor. This method is great for simple tasks but becomes overly tedious with more complex tasks.

A second method is to break down the parallelism of the interface and rely instead on a strictly sequential interface. In the preceding example, we would constrain the program to display only a single frame at a time. That way, the user must explicitly include the "go to preceeding frame" command in his procedure. The drawback of this system is that it forces the human to operate more like a computer, with a narrow focus of effort and lots of small, tedious steps.

Indirection is the means of implementing abstraction. Constructs are formulas used to translate indirectors back to their referents.

22

LINGUISTICS

To listen well, the interactivity designer must create a language of interaction between the computer mind and the human mind. Since you'll be getting into the language-design business, it might help to know a little about linguistics. Natural language won't save your neck. Two possibilities are considered here: inverse parsers and creoles.

My fundamental definition of interactivity declares that each of the actors "speaks" to the other. In normal conversation, the medium is natural language, which can't yet be used in computer-based interactivity. It is time to consider this matter of language in more detail.

Most discussions of user interface are bottom-up discussions of the language of human-computer interaction. They explain the various buttons, icons, and other doodads, laying out rules for when and how to apply them. They remind me of the old-style grammar books, laying down strict rules about what is proper user interface, without considering the dynamic nature of language. The user interfaces we will use in 10 years today will be much different than those we use today. Perhaps the user interface grammarians can benefit from this process, issuing new, up-to-date editions of the iron rules even as those rules plastically mutate. I will here attempt to take a top-down approach, describing the underlying principles of language design as they apply to the interaction between user and computer. Because these fundamental rules will still apply many years from now, there will be no need for you to purchase a second edition of this book. There go all those extra royalties for me. Ah well.

Although I have often spoken of "the language of interaction" as if it were unique to each application, there exists a larger language of interaction that is common to the entire computing community. It is the set of conventional devices—buttons, check boxes, scrollbars, and the like—that are common to all programs. Thus, there are two languages of interaction to consider: the local dialect that you design for your application, and the general language that we as a community use. This chapter will consider both languages, but the emphasis will be on the community language.

Why Not Use Natural Language?

Before I begin, let me lay to rest an obvious objection: why not use natural language? Sad to say, natural language comprehension lies beyond our grasp, nor is a complete solution likely in the immediate future. This is because so much language comprehension relies on a knowledge of the world in which we live. Computer science researchers like to offer "Time flies like an arrow" as an example. Normal people understand it instantly, yet the computer cannot because it can read it three different ways. The word "time" can be a verb, an adjective, or a noun. As a verb, the sentence becomes a command to measure flies as if they were arrows. As an adjective, the sentence becomes a declaration that a particular subclass of flies—time flies—prefer an arrow, presumably to eat. As a noun, the sentence suggests that the dimension of time moves quickly and linearly. Of course, most people have no problem disambiguating this sentence, for we all know that there's no such fly as a time fly, and nobody in his right mind would ever want to measure fly times in the manner of an arrow. But this disambiguation is dependent upon a detailed knowledge of the world. If you don't know about the many types of flies (houseflies, tsetse flies, botflies, horseflies), and you don't know about the process of timing and how an arrow might or might not be used in such a process, then you can't understand the sentence. And so far, we have not equipped any computer with that much knowledge of the world.

In claiming that the computer will not soon understand natural language, I prefer to use sentences that require detailed knowledge of the intricacies of human behavior: "The guy who was looking at my wife the wrong way just laughed when I called him on it, because he's built like Sylvester Stallone; but then my brother showed up, and my brother is built like Arnold Schwarzenegger." Anybody can understand that sentence immediately, but not so the computer. To make sense of this sentence, the computer would have to understand the details of human sexual relationships (bachelors to women, husbands to wives, husbands to bachelors, brothers to brothers) as well as the characteristics of two Hollywood actors and likely male behaviors during sexual conflict. And how is the computer to understand the frequent use of metaphor in language: "When he saw my brother, he took off with his tail between his legs."

Could we not at least use some reasonable subset of natural language? Tempting as this solution might seem, it is riddled with problems, the most important of which is blindness paralysis. Any reasonable subset of natural language will exclude some other reasonable subset of natural language. Although you as designer can easily convince yourself that the dividing line between the two sets is obvious and natural, your user will never see it this way. This puts you in direct violation of the rule that you should maximize the ratio of accessible states to conceivable states. Your user will always conceive natural language expressions that you cannot handle.

It gets worse. You won't be using natural language in isolation: everybody else will be using it, too. Of course, another designer's implementation will likely include a rather different "reasonable subset of natural language." What's the poor user to think when Program A recognizes a reasonable natural language expression while Program B does not? A user working with a dozen different programs will need to master a dozen different dialects of her natural language.

But wait—it gets even worse! This dialectation extends temporally as well. With each passing year, each new version of each application will improve its reasonable subset of natural language, meaning that the dialects are never stable.

This problem cannot be dismissed with the observation that users must already learn multiple user interfaces that regularly change. In the first place, user interfaces today are primarily visual, with a laudable closure that clearly communicates what cannot be done as well as what can be done—most of the time. A natural language interface does not declare its limitations so obviously. In the second place, current user interfaces don't conflict with an already well-developed and heavily used human standard.

History of Language Design

Your task as an interactivity designer is to create a language of interaction ideally suited for your task. Fortunately, you have a long history of earlier attempts at language design from which to draw inspiration; unfortunately, few designers seem to be aware of this history. Ergo I present:

A Short History of Language Design

Our times burst with so much communication that we have lost the polish and refinement that our media-deprived forebears prized. Not having the technology to worry about RAM, backups, closeups, or sidebars, they devoted their energies to linguistic technology such as synecdoche, metonymy, and catachresis. The first formal artificial language was musical notation, originally a simple scheme for denoting nothing more than basic note sequences. With the development of better musical instruments and a demand for more music in the Renaissance, the notational system grew more expressive through a series of incremental innovations.

At about the same time, Italian businessmen were learning that their increasingly complex business transactions required better notation for keeping track of things and calculating payments; they adopted the combination of Arabic numerals and the arithmetic procedures these numerals facilitated. Your calculator and spreadsheet have probably blinded you to the revolutionary significance of this little innovation:

$$
\begin{array}{r}
57 \\
\times 38 \\
\hline
456 \\
171 \\
\hline
2166
\end{array}
$$

but this little combination of geometry and numerals blew open the doors on all sorts of financial problems. You can thank those Renaissance Italian bankers for this along with the comparable schemes for long division and double-entry bookkeeping.

This started the ball rolling on a variety of other notational advances that eventually grew (with considerable borrowing from Arabic sources) into the language of mathematics. Thus, by the seventeenth century, we had two well-developed artificial languages: musical notation and mathematical notation (algebra). Realizing the benefits these languages conferred upon their disciplines, some adventurous thinkers wondered if it might be possible to design languages for other disciplines. The first efforts were directed at "philosophical languages" that might liberate philosophers from the maddening vagaries of natural language. This goal wasn't really attained to any reasonable degree until the work of George Boole some two centuries later (ever heard of Boolean algebra?), but the light bulb had been turned on.

For the first few hundred years, things went slowly, but the next big kick in the pants came with the realization that many Eurasian languages were grouped into a large family now called Indo-European. This triggered a frenzy of activity in analyzing the relationships between languages, which in turn led to an understanding of a variety of basic principles of language development. And that led the brazen thinkers of the nineteenth century to believe that they could improve on nature. You probably know about the most successful of these, Esperanto, but it wasn't the first. There were plenty of others: Volapük (cleaned-up German with politically useful token words from other European languages), Latino Sine Flexione (cleaned-up Latin), and Romanal (another cleaned-up Latin) were just a few. All of these languages boasted rationalized spelling, declension, and conjugation. They all fell afoul of nationalistic vocabulary preferences.

In the twentieth century, several attempts were made to get around this political problem with "context-free" vocabularies. These used logical systems for eliminating the arbitrariness of word assignments. In effect, they were structurally organized vocabularies. Proceeding from an arbitrarily selected set of one-syllable roots expressing fundamental concepts of human existence, they created new words by compounding these fundamental single syllables. Thus, the meaning of any word was logically derivable from its spelling. It was all wonderfully logical and utterly unlearnable, but it made for great academic fun.

Another attempt, more appropriate to our needs as interactivity designers, was Basic English, devised in the 1920s by a couple of linguistics professors. Their goals were to ensure that the less-educated classes would have a workable form of English, and to facilitate international communication. Their creation, Basic English, boasted a stripped-down vocabulary of exactly 850 words: 100 Operations, 400 General Things, 200 Picturable Things, 100 General Qualities, and 50 Opposite Qualities:

OPERATIONS (100 words)
come, get, give, go, keep, let, make, put, seem, take, be, do, have, say, see, send, may, will about, across, after, against, among, at, before, between, by, down, from, in, off, on, over, through, to, under, up, with, as, for, of, till, than, a, the, all, any, every, no, other, some, such, that, this, I, he, you, who, and, because, but, or, if, though, while, how, when, where, why, again, ever, far, forward, here, near, now, out, still, then, there together, well almost, enough, even, little, much, not, only, quite, so, very, tomorrow, yesterday north, south, east, west, please, yes

THINGS (400 General words)
account, act, addition, adjustment, advertisement, agreement, air, amount, amusement, animal, answer, apparatus, approval, argument, art, attack, attempt, attention, attraction, authority, back, balance, base, behavior, belief, birth, bit, bite, blood, blow, body, brass, bread, breath, brother, building, burn, burst, business, butter, canvas, care, cause, chalk, chance, change, cloth, coal, color, comfort, committee, company, comparison, competition, condition, connection, control, cook, copper, copy, cork, cotton, cough, country, cover, crack, credit, crime, crush, cry, current, curve, damage, danger, daughter, day, death, debt, decision, degree, design, desire, destruction, detail, development, digestion, direction, discovery, discussion, disease, disgust, distance, distribution, division, doubt, drink, driving, dust, earth, edge, education, effect, end, error, event, example, exchange, existence, expansion, experience, expert, fact, fall, family, father, fear, feeling, fiction, field, fight, fire, flame, flight, flower, fold, food, force, form, friend, front, fruit, glass, gold, government, grain, grass, grip, group, growth, guide, harbor, harmony, hate, hearing, heat, help, history, hole, hope, hour, humor ice, idea, impulse, increase, industry, ink, insect, instrument, insurance, interest, invention, iron, jelly, join, journey, judge, jump, kick, kiss, knowledge, land, language, laugh, law, lead, learning, leather, letter, level, lift, light, limit, linen, liquid, list, look, loss, love, machine, man, manager, mark, market, mass, meal, measure, meat, meeting, memory, metal, middle, milk, mind, mine, minute, mist, money, month, morning ,mother, motion, mountain, move, music, name, nation, need, news, night, noise, note, number, observation, offer, oil, operation, opinion, order, organization, ornament, owner, page, pain, paint, paper, part, paste, payment, peace, person, place, plant, play, pleasure, point, poison, polish, porter, position, powder, power, price, print, process, produce, profit, property, prose, protest, pull, punishment, purpose, push, quality, question, rain, range, rate, ray, reaction, reading, reason, record, regret, relation, religion, representative, request, respect, rest, reward, rhythm, rice, river,

road, roll, room, rub, rule, run, salt, sand, scale, science, sea, seat, secretary, selection, self, sense, servant, sex, shade, shake, shame, shock, side, sign, silk, silver, sister, size, sky, sleep, slip, slope, smash, smell, smile, smoke, sneeze, snow, soap, society, son, song, sort, sound, soup, space, stage, start, statement, steam, steel, step, stitch, stone, stop, story, stretch, structure, substance, sugar, suggestion, summer, support, surprise, swim, system, talk, taste, tax, teaching, tendency, test, theory, thing, thought, thunder, time, tin, top, touch, trade, transport, trick, trouble, turn, twist, unit, use, value, verse, vessel, view, voice, walk, war, wash, waste, water, wave, wax, way, weather, week, weight, wind, wine, winter, woman, wood, wool, word, work, wound, writing, year

THINGS (200 Picturable words)

angle, ant, apple, arch, arm, army, baby, bag, ball, band, basin, basket, bath, bed, bee, bell, berry, bird, blade, board, boat, bone, book, boot, bottle, box, boy, brain, brake, branch, brick, bridge, brush, bucket, bulb, button, cake, camera, card, cart, carriage, cat, chain, cheese, chest, chin, church, circle, clock, cloud, coat, collar, comb, cord, cow, cup, curtain, cushion, dog, door, drain, drawer, dress, drop, ear, egg, engine, eye, face, farm, feather, finger, fish, flag, floor, fly, foot, fork, fowl, frame garden, girl, glove, goat, gun, hair, hammer, hand, hat, head, heart, hook, horn, horse, hospital, house, island, jewel, kettle, key, knee, knife, knot, leaf, leg, library, line, lip, lock, map, match, monkey, moon, mouth, muscle, nail, neck, needle, nerve, net, nose, nut, office, orange, oven, parcel, pen, pencil, picture, pig, pin, pipe, plane, plate, plough/plow, pocket, pot, potato, prison, pump, rail, rat, receipt, ring, rod, roof, root, sail, school, scissors, screw, seed, sheep, shelf, ship, shirt, shoe, skin, skirt, snake, sock, spade, sponge, spoon, spring, square, stamp, star, station, stem, stick, stocking, stomach, store, street, sun, table, tail, thread, throat, thumb, ticket, toe, tongue, tooth, town, train, tray, tree, trousers, umbrella, wall, watch, wheel, whip, whistle, window, wing, wire, worm

QUALITIES (100 General words)

able, acid, angry, automatic, beautiful, black, boiling, bright, broken, brown, cheap, chemical, chief, clean, clear, common, complex, conscious, cut, deep, dependent, early, elastic, electric, equal, fat, fertile, first, fixed, flat, free, frequent, full, general, good, great, grey/gray, hanging, happy, hard, healthy, high, hollow, important, kind, like, living, long, male, married, material, medical, military, natural, necessary, new, normal, open, parallel, past, physical, political, poor, possible, present, private, probable, quick, quiet, ready, red, regular, responsible, right, round, same, second, separate, serious, sharp, smooth, sticky, stiff, straight, strong, sudden, sweet, tall, thick, tight, tired, true, violent, waiting, warm, wet, wide, wise, yellow, young

QUALITIES (50 Opposite words)

awake, bad, bent, bitter, blue, certain, cold, complete, cruel, dark, dead, dear, delicate, different, dirty, dry, false, feeble, female, foolish, future, green, ill, last, late, left, loose, loud, low, mixed, narrow, old, opposite, public, rough, sad, safe, secret, short, shut, simple, slow, small, soft, solid, special, strange, thin, white, wrong

The entire vocabulary of Basic English fits on a single page. Particularly impressive is the handling of verbs. There are only 18 verbs in Basic English: Be, Come, Do, Get, Give, Go, Have, Keep, Let, Make, Put, Say, See, Seem, Send, and Take. What makes the system work is the extension of these verbs with prepositions. You can go for a walk, go to the store, go out of the house, go in the tent, go over his head, go by the shop, go with your friend, go to the boss, go on a hunch, and so on.

As you can see, their system required heavy use of prepositions to cover the semantic ground stripped bare by their vocabulary depredations. By using almost every verb-preposition combination possible, they also created some truly confusing substitutions, and they also had problems with existing ambiguous combinations such as "go for." They designed a clever translation circular slide rule, the Panopticon, a word wheel for constructing sentences in Basic English. This was a mechanically operated combinatorial algorithm with seven nested disks of cardboard. You could rotate the disks in any combination and obtain a valid Basic English sentence. This demonstrates the computable algorithm behind the operation of Basic English. Unfortunately, despite the support of such luminaries as Winston Churchill, Basic English never caught on. Everybody seemed to prefer English Pro Version 43.1.4.

Basic English, revised and updated with new vocabulary, could become the basis for a semi-natural language for human-computer interaction. With a goodly amount of effort, we could build a complete, consistent, and closed database comprising the full meanings of the vocabulary of Basic English. The starting point of this database would be a simple table cross-referencing every word with every other word, specifying whether that pairing is legal. For example, we could cross-reference "male" with "wine" and find that this pairing is not legal, but the table would show that it is legal to pair "male" with "servant." With this table as our starting point, we could add a variety of semantic rules that would yield a language that is fully computable, understandable by humans, and useful. As yet, no work has been done in this direction. You may learn more about Basic English at www.basiceng.com.

Lessons from Linguistics

The obvious conclusion to draw from this history is that all attempts to replace anarchic natural languages with rationally designed languages have been inglorious failures. One man's logical language is another man's confusing mess—and a language community contains a lot of men (and even more people who aren't men).

Another lesson, derivable from linguistics but obvious in our own experience, is that languages change with time. The specifics of linguistic change offer some less obvious warnings for interactivity designers. The most common form of linguistic change these days is vocabulary change. We don't use *hogshead* as a measure of volume, because we don't need it anymore. And *email* wasn't in the Oxford English Dictionary last time I looked. We can expect some of the words of our user interface languages to drift into disuse with time, and we can surely expect to see new words arise; the butcon and the pop-up menu were not part of the original Macintosh user interface.

But vocabulary changes in other ways. Words take on additional meanings or drift into different meanings. I think that, as the amount of data we sling around increases, the tried-and-true scrollbar will be found inadequate to the needs of traversing a truly huge dataset, in which case something new will emerge: a super-scrollbar, perhaps, or perhaps something completely new.

Another important lesson from linguistics is the natural contraction of frequently used words. The automobile was initially called a horseless carriage. That got shortened to car. Shortening the length of a word is analogous to making a verb more accessible. The butcon bar across the top of many windows is just such a contraction: a way of making some commands more accessible. Expect to see much more of this in the future; interface languages are growing, which always increases the pressure for contraction.

A third lesson is that isolated speech communities spawn dialects that eventually grow into mutually incomprehensible languages. This shows up in the computer community in a number of ways. During the 1980s, Microsoft suffered from some insularity due to its location in Seattle; this isolation expressed itself in a rather unique style of interactivity design that many outsiders considered, um, odd. By now, fortunately, Microsoft has assimilated so many others become so large that it can lay claim to a kind of universality. *L'État c'est moi.*

The Clipboard

We can apply linguistic principles to better understand certain problems in interactivity design. One case is provided by the clipboard. This is the hidden vessel that contains whatever it is you cut or copy. When you paste, the contents of the clipboard are dumped into your assigned slot. Three problems darken the reputation of the clipboard: (1) you can't see its contents, (2) it cannot contain all types of data, and (3) you have only one clipboard; when you need to perform multiple moves, you can't assign one clipboard for each item to be moved.

Fortunately, a new interface concept is slowly replacing the clipboard: direct dragging of data from one location to another. This completely solves the first two problems. The third and fourth problems, it turns out, exist only in the minds of power users who expect too much complexity.

If you think in linguistic terms, the relationship between the clipboard and direct dragging becomes clear. As parts of speech, both are pronouns; the clipboard functions exactly like the pronoun *it*. Direct dragging functions exactly like the pronoun *this*. Using the clipboard could be narrated as, "Computer, you see this data right here? Copy it. Now paste it over there." Directly dragging data would be narrated as, "Computer, copy this to there." The conciseness of the second sentence compared to the first is analogous to the efficiency of dragging compared to using the clipboard. When using the clipboard, you must explicitly declare the meaning of *it* before doing anything. Moreover, *it* is linguistically weaker than *this* because the referent of *it* is indirectly expressed, while the referent of *this* is immediately available. Reflect: *it* is the most widely applicable and least explicit pronoun in the English language.

We can now apply our linguistic thinking to gain better insight into the use of the clipboard. Accumulating multiple entries into a clipboard would be akin to declaring: "Computer, see this right here? And this too? And this too? Cut it and move it here." The problem with this wording is instantly obvious: the pronoun *it* is singular, but the command refers to more than one object. The solution, of course, is to add a new word that explicitly declares plurality: *them*. If you are willing to create that special new word in your interface language, making certain that it is distinct from "it," then you can proceed with your accumulating clipboard—but not otherwise. And remember, too, that an accumulating clipboard is harder to understand when the contents of a clipboard are displayed as per my recommendations further on.

The idea of multiple clipboards likewise looks silly when you approach it from a linguistic angle: "Computer, see this? Call it 'It1.' See this? Call it 'It2.' . . . " Yuckers! Imagine framing a sentence with multiple pronouns of the same type: "When we tried to plug it into it, it wouldn't fit into the hole in it." Huh?

There is nothing intrinsically wrong with using a clipboard; after all, pronouns are very handy parts of speech, and to ban pronouns from a design would be as stupid as banning pronouns from language. The primary problem with clipboards is the same as that with pronouns: sometimes you can get confused over the referent of the pronoun. You must therefore make the contents of your clipboard perfectly clear to your user. One way to do this is to post a tiny clipboard window showing the contents of the clipboard. This need not be huge; showing the first three or four words would be enough to refresh the user's memory.

Another useful lesson from linguistics is that the pronoun *it* can be applied to any noun in the language; your clipboard should be the same. A clipboard should be able to hold text, formatting styles, formulas, numbers, images, video sequences, colors—any data structure that your program permits the user to edit. This can create serious problems with data typing. What if a user tries to paste "the quality of mercy" into a color specification slot? The answer to this, once again, is to display the contents of the clipboard.

It is tempting to solve this problem by creating a multidimensional clipboard. The clipboard can simultaneously hold every different data type: text, colors, numbers, images, and so forth. When the user pastes into a slot, the clipboard automatically pastes whatever it holds of that particular data type. Thus, the user could accumulate text, colors, and images into the clipboard and then paste into a color slot and have the color pasted, paste into a text slot and have the text pasted, and so forth. Again, the linguistic model shows the flaw in the thinking. We maintain only three flavors of personal pronoun: he, she, and it. Imagine trying to keep track of a dozen different flavors.

Some Possible Approaches to Language Design

I can offer two possible grammars for use in language design: inverse parsers and creoles.

Inverse Parsers

Parsing is the process by which a computer program analyzes the structure of a sentence to figure out what it means. *Inverse parsing* inverts the process: the computer program uses the structure of a partially completed input sentence to compile a list of acceptable choices for the user to peruse. We all use first-order inverse parsing whenever we use a menu whose menu items might be dimmed and unselectable. For example, if we consult the Edit menu looking for the Copy command, we might find that it is dimmed because no item to copy has been selected. The sentence we would like to say to the computer is: "This text—copy it." But before we can say "copy it," we must first say "This text" by selecting some text. The computer therefore dims the Copy menu item until we have selected some text.

The big idea behind inverse parsing is to extend this concept with additional steps. For example, suppose that I had an advanced computer that could send text to anybody in the world. Thus, I wouldn't need to copy and paste it into an email letter and then send the email letter; instead, I would just select the text and then use a magic menu command that says "send it to." The sentence I have entered so far now reads, "This text—send it to —." Obviously, I need to enter a third parameter: the person to whom I wish to send it. The computer would therefore whip up a menu listing all of my likely email correspondents, and I could select one person so that the complete sentence reads, "This text—send it to—Uncle Fredegund." We could go as far as we need to go, ending up with sentences like, "This text—send it to—Uncle Fredegund—via my PigNet account."

Yes, this is modal input, and modal input is generally a bad thing. *Modal input* is any system of input in which the meaning of a command depends upon what happened immediately beforehand. For example, suppose that we were to reverse the standard sequence of selecting something in a document and then applying an editing verb to it. That is, instead of selecting a paragraph and then deleting it, suppose that we first choose the Delete verb and then select the text to delete. This is dangerous because we might forget what we said a moment ago and become confused. We select Delete, and the phone rings; we talk for half an hour, turn back to the computer, and click a memo we were working on yesterday. Poof—memo deleted! We therefore prefer modeless input, in which each command always means the same thing, regardless of what preceded it. Modeless input is harder to screw up than modal input.

But the problem lies not in modeness per se; it is the likelihood of confusing the user. If we can prevent that confusion, then the argument against using a modal input scheme vanishes. After all, natural language is highly modal; the meaning of any utterance depends completely upon the context in which it is used.

The most common way of handling modal input is with the simple line input scheme, in which we type our commands. Partway through, our text input might look like this:

```
SEND/SELECTION/UNCLE FREDEGUND/PIGNET/
```

This might remind you of the bad old days of DOS, and in fact that is precisely the input scheme behind DOS and all the other simple parser schemes. The parser approach suffers a fatal flaw: there is no way to know in advance what text is legal and what text isn't. The user must guess commands, hoping that an experimental command like DET means determine rather than detonate. In an inverse parser, this problem is solved by replacing the freeform text input with a pop-up menu input scheme.

Imagine a simple linear sequence of pop-up menus, like so:

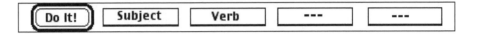

The user clicks Verb, and a pop-up menu offers a variety of verbs such as Open, Print, and Send:

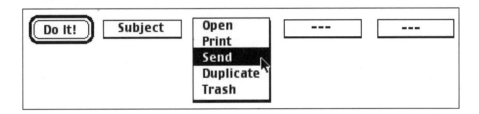

The user chooses, say, the verb Send, and the display now looks like this:

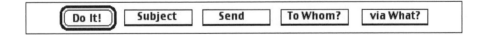

Clicking the Subject pop-up menu reveals a list of menu options for what exactly is to be sent: Selection, This File, A Disk File, and so on. The user chooses Selection, and then raises the To Whom? pop-up menu, filling in the recipient of the email. And so on until the sentence reads:

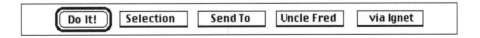

Satisfied with this input, the user clicks Do It. Poof!

This approach is subtly different from a conventional dialog box. This approach reads like a sentence; a dialog box is a spatial jumble of items. There wasn't a problem when dialog boxes were small, containing a handful of items.

But nowadays we see huge dialog boxes with—I do not exaggerate—dozens of items to be set. We even see dialog sub-boxes: dialog boxes inside other dialog boxes, raised with tab buttons or pushbuttons. We are stretching the concept of the dialog box beyond its natural range of applicability. For big jobs, we need a new approach, something that people can make sense of, and to find it, we must take advantage of people's most powerful built-in construct: language.

Let's take a common example: the clumsy and complicated schemes used to program VCRs to record television shows at different times. Here's how you would express such a set of commands in plain English:

"Mister VCR, I want you to record Channel 8 from 9:00 to 10:00 every Wednesday night. Also, please record Channel 4 from 6:30 to 7:00 every weekday night. Last, record Channel 37 from 8:00 to 10:00 this Thursday night."

Now let's just suppose that your computer was rigged to control the VCR. Then you would enter three commands, one for each clause in the sentence, and the first would look like this:

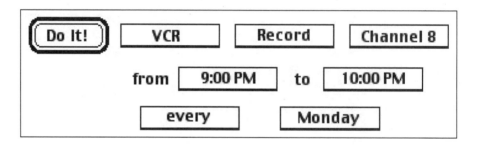

Note how the software inserted the prepositions *from* and *to* as soon as the verb *record* was chosen. It wouldn't be hard to improve this with self-shortening menus to close up the gaps and make the sentence even more readable:

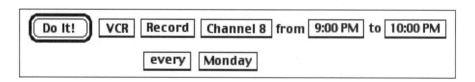

And here's what a dialog box to accomplish the same thing might look like:

Which of these approaches is easier to understand? There's no functional difference between these two methods; they say the same thing. But the verbal approach says its piece in a format that the human brain is more familiar with.

There is a difficulty in this approach: natural language teems with little cues that help us sort out what a sentence means and how to make sense of it. Sometimes they're just one or two characters tacked onto the ends of words: *-'s, -ed, -s, -ing*, and so on. Sometimes they are changes in the words themselves or use of auxiliary words: *have, had, will have*, or prepositions or adverbs. But the scheme I have shown would require that the verbs carry within themselves any such cues for inclusion, such as the two prepositions used in the example. This, in turn, would make possible some awkward situations if the user changes the verb in mid-sentence. When this arises in natural language, we just give up and start over with a new sentence; much the same would have to be done here.

There are numerous variations on the inverse-parser idea, but there are two core concepts: precalculation of grammatically acceptable options, and display of the sentence abuilding. They are, in a way, a hybrid of the old line-input user interface and the menu-driven user interface. I am certain that inverse parsers are better than conventional parsers, which place the user in the role of supplicant and the computer in the role of judge. The computer should never be the judge of the user; the computer must always be the user's servant. This is the fundamental reason why precalculated inverse parsers are superior to postcalculated parsers. However, I have reservations about applying inverse parsers to especially large or complicated problems; my hunch is that the scheme works best in the range of problems currently tackled by personal computers. By the time we master the scheme, people will be doing things on the computer too complicated to handle with inverse parsers.

Creole

Here's an approach that's closer to human verbal reasoning and less artificial, yet within the grasp of computability. *Creoles* are languages created spontaneously by the children of immigrants in a linguistically unstable community. They last for one generation and then fade from memory as the next generation learns the dominant language. Roughly speaking, creoles combine the vocabularies of two languages while falling back on a simple and standard grammar. Since creoles come out of the mouths of babes, they are believed to reflect the instinctive grammatical preferences of our species, whatever those might be. This belief is supported by the striking grammatical similarities between creoles created in different linguistic contexts.

I still don't grasp the fine points of creole grammar, but I can relate the basic points in a manner that reflects my simple-minded understanding of the subject. First, creoles rely on auxiliary words for conjugation. For example:

Hypothetical	English	Creolized English
Present tense singular	he walks	he walk
Past tense singular	he walked	he been walk
Future tense singular	he will walk	he gwanna walk

Second, creoles never coin new vocabulary; they borrow the vocabulary of the parent languages and impose their own grammar. This makes them easy to use; people don't have to memorize any new words. The grammar that they use is picked up with amazing speed, because it reflects our instinctive grammatical preferences.

Third, they are clumsier than modern languages, both in terms of utterance length and semantic resolution.

So here is a user-computer interaction in my hypothetical creolized English, with English commentary on the right:

"Foo, use the database that I been open when this morning. Tell me, how many records be in it?"

> *"Foo" is the nonsense word used to identify the computer. This ensures that it won't be confused with other text.*

"2867 records"

"Do sort the records by the field called Age. Tell me, what be the three highest numbers in the field called Age?"

> *"Do" indicates a command. "Tell me" indicates voice output. Labels are denoted with the prefix "called."*

"87, 74, and 74."

"Use these records. Do select the text in the field called Name in these records. Do recognize these texts as persons. Do start a letter to each of these persons, using for the address the text in the field called Address."

> *"Use" makes its object the topic of conversation.*

"But second record has no text in the field called Address."

> *An error message.*

"Do not use that one record."

> *Removes the bad record from the topic of conversation.*

"But tell me the text of the letter."

Unfinished business.

"The text of the letter be as follows: Dear Sir or Madam: Foo, paragraph, unfoo. We are having a special sale on wheelchairs this week. We have all kinds of wheelchairs: big ones, little ones, motorized ones. Come in and look them over soon. Foo, paragraph. Do apply the signature called Woody's Custom Wheels."

"Foo" and "unfoo" mark places where the user is popping out of the letter to give commands to the computer.

[The computer interrupts:] "But I can't find the signature called Woody's Custom Wheels."

Error message.

"Oops. Do apply the signature called Sedate Senior Mobility."

"But the text of the letter be not complete."

Unfinished business.

"That be the end of the text."

"Do confirm that be the end of the text of the letter."

The user should properly have called it "the text of the letter."

"Yes"

"Do confirm this letter." [The computer displays the letter on the monitor.]

"No. Do change all texts that be wheel cherry to be wheel chair."

Speech recognition error.

"Do confirm this letter."

"No. Do change all texts that be wheel chair to be w-h-e-e-l-c-h-a-i-r."

User gives up and spells the word.

"Do confirm this letter."

"Yes"

This exchange handles a complex interaction: database search, word processing, and mail merge. The creole is certainly up to the task, but the human would have to learn the narrow meanings of some of the terms. For example, the temptation would be to say "how many records are in it" when the correct usage is "how many records be in it." Collapsing all verbs down to their infinitives will not come easily to most people at first, but we can rely on an easy mental shift to "baby talk." We all instinctively know how to talk to infants, simplifying our natural language to make it comprehensible. We can do the same with computers, for lord knows they are certainly infantile in their linguistic talents.

I have not shown how the computer would handle unknown terminology, but the process of sorting out such misunderstandings, while tedious, would be straightforward and need only be invoked once for each special term.

Creoles piggyback directly onto voice recognition and synthesis technology. These two technologies are just now coming into their own, but integrating them into our designs requires grammar; creole could provide that grammar.

While the use of creoles may seem far-fetched, we must remember that the alternative of using genuine natural language is, strictly speaking, unattainable in our lifetimes. In practice, natural language processing systems will suffer from frequent breakdowns; users will eventually learn to speak baby talk to them. Since natural language systems will inevitably be much larger and slower than creole systems, and users will end up speaking baby talk anyway, and we don't *need* the expressive richness that creoles lack, what point is there in holding out for natural language? We could be using creole-based systems *right now*; all the technology we need is in place. All we need now is a major company to put its weight behind the idea; from there, its utility will cause it to spread quickly through the community.

Who Designs It?

With the passage of time, the community language of interaction will grow richer and more detailed and will impose itself more imperiously upon the individual designer, leaving less room for variability in the design of languages specific to the application. This makes the design of the community language of interaction all the more important to the community. An ugly political problem intrudes upon our intellectually pure considerations: who will define the community language of interaction? Three answers are available:

The first answer would be the company that is most successful in selling software. (Guess who that might be.) The winner of the market competition defines the language. This solution boasts a simple pragmatism: After all, the winner of the market competition pretty much defines the language anyway. Why not recognize the market realities and go with the market's flow? The problem we face is not so much getting it right as getting an "it" in the first place. We all know that multiple definitions of the language lead to confusion and anarchy. This problem is a matter of setting standards, and if one company has successfully set some standards, let's embrace that success as a benefit for everybody. Software designers will know what to design for. Consumers will know what to expect. Everybody wins.

But there are also flaws in this approach. The first is history: Look at Microsoft's track record in user interface design. Do you really want to surrender control of our human-computer interface to these people? Ack!

Second is the danger of granting a monopoly over what is essentially a public utility. Our experience with public utilities has shown that they are always slow and never efficient; finding ways to break them up has been one of the underlying sources of economic growth in the last few decades. We don't want to create a new monopoly.

Then there's the risk that a single company might use this monopoly power to benefit itself at the expense of consumers. Naah, Microsoft would never do that! Right?

A second approach is to grant the monopoly power to a disinterested group of wise old men, collectively known as a standards committee. The engineering industries have scores of these august bodies, dictating everything from the thickness of the insulation on a wire to the specifications for a computer language. Indeed, we also have experience with a standards committee for a natural language: the French have just such a committee that publishes the official dictionary for the French language. With all this operating experience, we will have no problem creating an effective standards committee for our user interface language. And its independence ensures that it won't show favoritism to any single company. Populated with representatives from industry and academia, it can command the respect required to make the standards stick.

On the other hand, there are some problems with a standards committee. First, standards committees are notoriously slow in getting anything done. The standards for the most heavily used computer language, C++, are perennially about five years behind industry practice. Every company that sells a version of C++ issues two flavors: a flavor that meets the ANSI standards, and a flavor with all the latest improvements; most programmers rely on the latter, falling back on the ANSI standard version in certain cases requiring broad compatibility with several dramatically different platforms and little in the way of modern features.

Furthermore, standards committees end up being horribly political. There will surely be at least one representative from Microsoft on any such committee, and perhaps a representative from Apple. These two will bicker endlessly, and in tense situations the Microsoft representative will likely threaten that Microsoft might not implement the proposed standard, thereby reducing it to irrelevance, if Microsoft doesn't get its way. This kind of thing has been known to happen on standards committees many times in the past.

Which leads us to the third problem with standards committees: in their efforts to find a politically viable solution, they sometimes end up concocting a ridiculous standard that nobody will ever use in its entirety, a bloated farce that crudely patches together completely incompatible ideas to get one overarching "standard." This way, everybody can go ahead with what they've already set their hearts on and still meet the "standard." In effect, the standard is defined to be anarchy. The standard for RS-232, a wiring and signal protocol for connecting computers, provides the perfect example: in practice, there really is no standard. Hooking up one RS-232 machine to another one frequently requires tricky measurements and occasionally an oscilloscope.

The third approach is to accept anarchy and call it democracy, although I'm not being as cynical as my clever turn of phrase suggests. The idea here is to decentralize the language-defining power, devolving it to all interactivity designers. This, of course, requires, to use the phrase used to promulgate democracy, an "informed citizenry"—interactivity designers must be knowledgeable about their business if they are to define the language used by the rest of us. But hey, you read this book; isn't that enough?

One argument for the democratic approach is that it is how natural languages keep up with changes in societies. As new concepts arise and old ones fade, the words for them are coined or forgotten. When was the last time you drank a firkin of coffee? Aren't you glad that you can refer to your means of transportation as a car rather than a horseless carriage? In the fast-moving world of computers, you can expect old interface concepts to die fast (joystick, parser, DOS, batch processing) and new ones to arise just as quickly.

The most compelling argument for democracy lies in its embarrassingly demonstrated superiority over the centrally planned approaches to user interface. The first coherent attempt to define a user interface standard was the research work undertaken at Xerox PARC in the 1970s. The revolutionary results of this work were embraced (or plagiarized, depending on your point of view) by Apple for the Macintosh. Apple went on to diligently enforce its user interface language, against a small amount of resistance from software developers, and the result was a pretty good language, but Apple's attempts to maintain the standard tended to stifle linguistic innovation. Apple tried to compensate by spending large amounts of money on research to expand the language, and it did a respectable job of upgrading the Macintosh language of interface. But several factors in the mid 1990s converged to degrade Apple's unique position as arbiter of user interface language. First, the introduction of Windows 95 created the first creatively viable alternative to the Macintosh language, and suddenly Apple found itself in a meaningful competition with Microsoft in the matter of designing a user interface language. Microsoft's user interface language was little more than a copy of Apple's, and so a bastard standard was born, whose illegitimacy encouraged individual developers to experiment. Suddenly, a plethora of linguistic innovations appeared, most of which were half-baked and useless. A few ideas, however, had merit. The software design community is just like any linguistic community: when people see a good idea (word), they used it themselves. New forms of expression appeared and were refined incrementally by the community.

A good example of this is the butcon, an icon that operates as a button. Now, there were many early versions of this concept; I myself used butcons in a published design as early as 1987. They were very close to the modern concept: 32-by-32 images with little images inside, all arranged in a geometric order. Clicking one inverted its color; click-and-release on one executed its associated command. It even had a pop-up text expression of its meaning, although it didn't operate in quite the same way that modern tooltips operate. Nevertheless, we can surely cite this as one of the many precursors of the butcon.

What converted the butcon from a vagabond concept to a linguistic standard was a series of embellishments, of which the use of color was probably the most important. Once designers could count on their users' having at least 8-bit color, they could create icons that actually meant something. The black-and-white icons of my design were, I admit, difficult to interpret. Color dramatically increased the expressiveness of the icons and pushed them over the brink of expressive utility.

Three other embellishments further improved their utility. Shadowing communicated that the icon was not merely a static image, but a button in three dimensions that could be "pressed." Placing the butcons in a horizontal bar at the top of the window allowed designers to grant special visual status to the most important commands, adding a new tier to the hierarchy of commands, above that of menus and below that of immediate cursor-cum-clicking commands on the imagery in the active window. Last, the tooltip phrase explaining the function of the butcon did much to overcome the visual ambiguity intrinsic to icons, and having this pop-up appear when the cursor merely hovered stationary over the icon was a big factor in making the device effective.

None of these innovations came from the labs of Microsoft and Apple; they arose spontaneously from the design community. I'm sure that plenty of designers will clamor to have their own work recognized as the ground-breaker, and I'm sure that somewhere in the archives of Microsoft and Apple there's software with some or even all of these elements. But what's important here is the undeniable fact that nobody can convincingly claim that he alone created the idea that everybody else adopted. It arose in bits and pieces, in numerous variations, until the community as a whole settled on the common factors that make the butcon work so well. And the process doesn't end here; people will continue to tinker with the butcon, and more embellishments will become part of the standard.

The butcon demonstrates the superiority of the democratic strategy over the centrally planned strategy. No individual designer, no matter how brilliant, can ever match the creative energy and mature judgment of an entire community of designers.

The democratic process exploded with the success of the web. Suddenly, there were thousands of designers putting up all sorts of crazy things on the web. We must admit that the great majority of those innovations were truly stupid: surely the "invisible hotspot" must rank high in any list of such inanities. But two factors more than compensated for opening the gates to the maniacs: the sheer volume of their contributions, and the vastly accelerated cycle of evaluation that the web offered. It's ridiculously simple for any nitwit to create a website, and most of them have risen to the challenge. Their complete ignorance of even the rudiments of interface design has enabled them to spawn a nightmare of demonic designs, hair-raising hyperlinks, and stomach-emptying structures. Yet, just as one genetic mutation in 10 thousand might yield a marginally more adaptive creature, the creative craziness of this group has occasionally, by towering dumb luck, generated a useful idea.

Add to this the hothouse atmosphere of the web, where word of mouth travels by email to designers who are online 16 hours a day, and you have a system that can detect rare innovations in a matter of hours, copy them in a matter of days, and improve on them in a matter of weeks. No consciously designed institution can match such performance.

Of course, anarchy has its drawbacks; millions of truly execrable web pages shout their confirmations of this truth. But this is the argument that elitists of all stripes have proffered for centuries. From Plato to the European aristocracy to the Communists, the belief that smart people could run the country better than the rabble has run deep. It took Thomas Jefferson and a couple of centuries of trial and error to demonstrate that the rabble could do the job better than the smart people. We are going through the same process in a couple of decades—it would have been faster if we had been blessed with a Thomas

Jefferson back in 1985. In the absence of that great genius, I will arrogate the mantle of the "20-20 hindsight Thomas Jefferson" and argue that we should at least understand and embrace the brilliant solution that we have already created and adopted. Whether it's a government, an economy, a natural language, or a language of human-computer interaction, so long as the community is large enough and intercommunicative enough, democracy works best.

The most powerful construct in the human mind is language. Designers who seek to communicate with that in mind would do well to study linguistics and to consider the linguistic implications of their decisions. We desperately need a standard language of interaction for the computing community as a whole.

23

METAPHOR

Metaphor is a common device in interactivity design, but its application is haphazard. Here I reduce metaphor to a series of simpler steps—but I do not address the higher creative issues it raises.

Metaphor is one of those irritatingly vague concepts—like consciousness—onto which thinkers have slathered tidal waves of words without ever accomplishing much. Sheer weight of verbiage has not served us well. Yet the concept requires our attention because it underlies so much of our work in interactivity. I request that the reader cut me some slack in this chapter; if we can revere Aristotle despite his failure to solve the problem of metaphor, then surely you can smile indulgently as I flounder around the topic.

Why should an interactivity designer worry about metaphor? Because at a deep level, every interactivity designer uses metaphor. The software jungle teems with metaphors. The trash bin on your desktop swarms not with flies, clangs not, and smells just fine, but you recognize it as a trash bin. Its relationship with a real trash bin is strictly metaphorical. A column of numbers on a spreadsheet is a metaphor. After all, the only reason we always place summed numbers in a column is because that's how we carry out the addition with pencil and paper. A page image in a word processor is *not* the same thing as the printed page: it is a metaphor for the printed page. The old sawcronym, WYSI-WYG (What You See Is What You Get) has a hidden gotcha: in between seeing and getting lies a certain amount of metaphorical transformation. The clumsy unreadable 9-point fonts on the screen leap into sharp focus on the printed page. And of course, every icon ever used is a metaphor.

First you must understand a little about the concept. By applying a small amount of neurophysiology, we can get a functional grip on the idea. Please inspect this image:

This is an easy image to recognize: a person holding a black ball. But now let's zero in on one small portion of the image:

Again, this is fairly easy to recognize as an eye, but now let's isolate even further:

Now, all by itself, just how easily can you recognize this as a pupil? When I use my photo-retouching software on this image, no transformation I can find will produce a circle for the pupil. Yet your visual system is capable of determining that it's a circular pupil. How? By a long and involved process called feature extraction. The first and simplest step in feature extraction is called edge detection; this processing is actually done by the retina and yields something like this:

Note how much cleaner this image is; much of the visual noise has been removed, and the edges have been sharpened. Another process is texture recognition, which allows us to guess the shape of three-dimensional objects (remember, the image we start with is only two-dimensional) by noting the way that the texture changes. For example, our mental software will readily note from the first image that the forehead curves away from the light as we move across it from left to right.

A third and quite powerful process is facial feature extraction. Our brains are wi ed up with lots of neural arrays for recognizing the subtle nuances of facial expression. Introspect as you inspect these "faces":

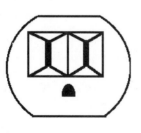

Automobile

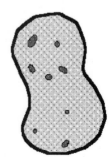

Your neural circuitry serves to superimpose facial features onto images. That's why you can see a circular pupil in the first image: it isn't circular, but your neural circuitry recognizes the overall pattern as that of a face and therefore (quite correctly) interprets the fuzzy image as a pupil, which it already knows to be circular. The trick lies in the recognition of the overall pattern. If we could eavesdrop on a brain sorting out that image, we might hear the following:

"Well, there's an oval shape; that suggests a face. Now look for eyes: hmmm, it's not so clear. I can make out one eye, but the other one is hard to see. Let's check out the next most important facial feature: the mouth. Again, there's a horizontal line at about the right place, but it doesn't extend all the way across. So far, we might have a face, but we'll need to verify some minor features. Is there a nose? Oh yes, that's a clear nose in exactly the right place. Hair? Yes, there's definitely hair along the top of the head. Ears? Yes, I think that's an ear on the face's right side. Correct facial curvature? Definitely along the forehead, and pretty clear on the cheek and chin. How about eyebrows, eyelid shape, and pupil? Well, again, they're quite clear on the right eye, but hard to see on the left. So let's decide this is a face. Now we'll go back and fill in the parts that we couldn't otherwise recognize. The left eye must be that little burble of pixels, and the mouth extends into the shadow, and...."

Here's the big idea that emerges from this discussion: to the brain, a face is defined as a collection of features: an oval shape with two eyes symmetrically placed about a third of the way down from the top, and a mouth about two-thirds of the way down, and lots of secondary features such as a nose, hair, ears, eyebrows, and so on. Put those features together, and you've got a face, as far as the brain is concerned. There isn't a person on the planet who would not recognize this as a face:

The brain is not an open-minded observer of reality: it insists on jamming everything it sees into one of its preconceived patterns, because pattern recognition is the fundamental technique by which neural circuitry works. This is important!!! We *never* see the world as it truly is; instead, we see it solely in terms of the patterns that we expect and are able to recognize. Every image we perceive is ruthlessly broken up into a set of features, and then those features are matched against previously established pattern templates until a match is found. The cardinal rule is simple: find a pattern match! No matter how confused or arbitrary an image might be, the brain will come up with the closest match it can. We look at the moon and see a man; we look at clouds and see dragons, flowers, or whatever strikes our visual fancy.

Herein lies the fundamental basis of metaphor. Any image that fits a predefined feature set is interpreted as the object defined by the feature set—even if we know that it isn't. We know perfectly well that an electrical outlet is not a face, yet our brains see a face in it. An outlet is "like" a face; it is an unintended metaphor for a face. A cane is not a leg, yet the sphinx threatened to kill Oedipus if he failed to recognize the metaphorical connection between canes and legs: they are both long straight things that support an animal as it walks.

Thus, your customer is a brain programmed, either from birth or from experience, with a bunch of "feature sets" that define things that the brain can recognize. If you communicate something to it, that brain will not recognize it for what it "truly" is, but will instead recognize it only when it fits into one of its preexisting pattern templates. That brain is not scientific about the recognition process; it will not withhold judgment until it has enough data to confirm the hypothesis. The brain will instead latch onto the best fit it can find, regardless of how weak the fit might be.

This is why we humans can be so destructively irrational. We Americans have read about Arab terrorists for so long that when we actually encounter an Arab face to face, we flinch, no matter how nice a person he actually is. My wife once pulled a bit of something out of her enchilada and it looked for all the world like some sort of multi-legged insect. Despite my careful examination of the object and confirmation that it was vegetable, not animal, my wife could not eat the rest of her meal, and the management, recognizing the realities of human vision, graciously refused to charge us for her meal, even though the cooks had made no mistake.

As always, there's lemonade hiding inside this neural lemon. It may yield lots of irrational results, but it also makes your job feasible. After all, if the human brain were obsessively literal and demanded absolute nonmetaphorical truth, how could you ever convince it that the pixels flickering on the monitor screen have anything to do with budgets, documents, or databases?

The trick, which artists have known for millennia and programmers still haven't figured out, is that we achieve more by stripping away detail than by adding it. The painter or cartoonist strives not to achieve photographic realism, but to strip away image detail to ensure that the brain zeros in on the precise pattern intended. Of these two images, the simpler one communicates "happiness" more quickly:

The simpler image communicates happiness better because all unnecessary detail has been eliminated. By giving the brain a bare minimum of information, we force it to recognize the pattern "happiness," even though there's not enough information to "truly" or "accurately" depict a human face. The only features presented are those necessary to trigger recognition of the mental template for "happiness."

In actual practice, metaphor is used more heavily in language than in image processing, and because language covers so much more mental territory than vision, metaphor is more powerful in language. The mechanism, though, is the same. Each word we use is a label for a feature set or template. Thus, when I use the word *leg*, I might have the following feature set in mind:

- Animate

- External

- Supports body weight

- Makes contact with ground

- Long and thin

- Moves when walking or running

- Stationary when standing

Now, the word *cane* matches five of the seven features in this feature set; since that's a mildly good fit, we are willing to metaphorically think of a cane as if it were a leg. A table leg is an even better fit because it matches six of the seven features. Thus, we are perfectly happy calling it a leg even though it isn't a leg (it does not satisfy the first feature requirement).

Metaphor Creation

Metaphor creation is a profoundly creative act, yet the basics can be reduced to five simple steps. These don't constitute a formula for the creation of the most profound metaphors, but they are serviceable for the problems of software design.

Step 1

List the features that constitute the feature set of the thing you wish to describe with a metaphor. You need not ensure that each feature is independent of all others; overlap is not a problem. For example, if I wanted to use leg as the receiving end of a new metaphor, I would use the feature set listed in the preceding section to complete Step 1.

Step 2

List all objects whose feature sets contain many features in common with your first list. Their feature sets need not match the feature set of the metaphoree; they need only share some features in common. This list could be huge, but the human brain is shockingly fast at sweeping through its knowledge base to find such things. Think how fast people can solve riddles.

For the leg example, here are some things I come up with: post, tree trunk, pillar, wheel.

Step 3

Compare each candidate's feature set with the metaphoree's feature set, noting features that match and features that don't match. Let's do it for *leg* and *wheel*:

Leg	Wheel
Animate	X
External limb	✓
Supports body weight	✓
Makes contact with ground	✓
Long and thin	X
Moves when walking or running	✓
Stationary when standing	✓
X	Round

Step 4

Isolate the mismatches: for the leg, they are *animate* and *long and thin*; for the wheel, there's only one: *round*.

Step 5

Metaphor requires you to use some of the matched features and ignore or negate each of the mismatches. For example, I would implement the wheel > leg metaphor by sweeping the issue of shape under the rug and focusing the reader's attention on matching features:

The jeep struggled desperately to find its footing on the steep slope, planting its wheels on the few solid rocks and lurching forward, only to slip backward on the loose gravel.

This metaphor emphasizes the action of foot and leg on difficult ground.

The truck dug its heels into the pavement.

Here we have an explicit substitution.

After he installed monster tires on his VW truck, Farley christened it "Shirley Temple Meets Arnold Schwarzenegger."

This metaphor negates the *animate* mismatch by setting up an internal comparison of animate objects. In other words, the relationship between Shirley Temple and Arnold Schwarzenegger is similar to the relationship between a VW truck and monster tires.

The motorcycle's circular legs drove him forward.

The adjective *circular* explicitly negates the *shape* mismatch.

In visual use, the metaphor has been successfully used in both directions. Cartoon characters running fast have their legs replaced with circular blur lines—but legs don't move in circles: wheels do. The metaphor is often enhanced with the addition of automobile or motorcycle engine sounds. In the reverse direction, I recall from many years ago a series of commercials by a tire company showing a car equipped with that company's tires streaking down the road by means of tiger feet instead of wheels. The tires were called Tiger Paws. How's that for metaphor?

Putting Theory to Work

At long last, I can apply these grand theories to interactivity design. You'll be attempting to communicate some abstruse concepts to your user, and you'll often need clean ways for the user to communicate with you. You can use metaphor to great effect here. You have two approaches: extending existing metaphors or creating new metaphors.

The main advantage of extending existing metaphors is that the user community is already familiar with them. Since the desktop metaphor is now universally familiar, an extension to this metaphor would be immediately understandable and quickly accepted. However, metaphor extensions suffer from two dangers of which you must be aware.

The first is the intrinsic limitation built into the concept of a metaphor. A metaphor is used when some features match and some features don't match. The creator of the metaphor must distort the expression to get around the mismatches. This works in narrow, constrained situations. But when you attempt to extend a metaphor, you are trying to widen its applicability. If the metaphor was competently designed in the first place, it may have little room for extension. Extending a metaphor often weakens its value.

A second danger arises from the temptation to extrapolate rather than extend a metaphor. A beautiful example of this problem is provided by the attempts to create three-dimensional desktops. The original desktop design is essentially two-dimensional in structure. We sometimes call it two-and-a-half dimensional because windows can overlap other windows. So every extrapolatory fool in the industry has jumped to the simple-minded conclusion that three dimensions are better than two and a half. They proffer "virtual offices" through which one may walk, accessing all manner of items. The most laughable expression of this concept is the virtual filing cabinet, which permits a $2,000 computer to lose information as quickly as a $50 filing cabinet can. Filing cabinets may be familiar, but they're also lousy ways of storing information—why do you think that we've all been moving our data from filing cabinets to computers in the first place? A virtual filing cabinet is as silly as one of the old horseless carriages that was designed to look and act just like a horse-driven carriage, except there were no horses. Computers allow us to organize information in so many useful ways; why would we ever want to revert to the old and clumsy spatial organization system?

All in all, I see little promise in extending existing metaphors. Perhaps in the early years, when a metaphor is young and unfamiliar, there is some value in extending it, but otherwise I believe that metaphor extensions are a waste of design time.

Instead, I prefer the creation of new metaphors. A tightly focused metaphor tailored to the precise problem at hand can frog-march your user straight to your meaning—so long as you don't try to squeeze too much out of it.

Metaphors are such an ubiquitous component of language that we have a huge statistical base from which to work. Look here: most of our language's words are essentially metaphorical; the roots on which they are built are sensory or motor in nature. Thus, the root word for *see* (Indo-European *ueid*, pronounced like *wide*) gave us *white*, *idea* (can you *see* why?), the suffix *-oid* (as in *trianguloid)*, meaning "looking like," all of the "video" words (*vision, visit, interview*), *witness, wit, wise*, and scores of others. Every one of these disparate words is a metaphor for seeing. Our words for mentation are all metaphorical:

"I don't grasp that."

"Ya follow?"

"He sure demolished that argument."

"You must be blind not to understand that."

"Despite my pleas, she would not hear me."

"I was too tired to carry the argument."

"This discussion is over; drop it."

"Run that by me one more time."

"What a dimwit!"

"Her reasoning left me cold."

"What a sharp tongue he has!"

Metaphor is so common, so everyday in application, that we quickly grasp customized metaphors: unconventional wordings that utilize novel metaphors. One study found that the average English speaker uses a thousand such one-shot metaphors every day. I used four metaphors in this single sentence:

A tightly focused metaphor tailored to the precise problem at hand can frog-march your user straight to your meaning—so long as you don't try to squeeze too much out of it.

One of the metaphors (*tailored*) is conventional; a second (*focused*) is familiar but not strictly conventional; a third (*squeeze*) is odd; and the fourth (*frog-march*) is downright peculiar—but they all work.

I therefore recommend the use of verbal metaphors in interactivity design. We already use quite a few of these: we run a program, crash the computer, browse the web, shoot an email to somebody, and so on. The computer field has been until recently dominated by science and engineering people (see Chapter 27), whose verbal skills typically fall short of their mathematical skills. This suggests that much opportunity remains for creation of other useful metaphors.

Time for an example. What if I try my hand at email programs? Consider attachments. Gad, what a clumsy term for including a file with a message! Some programs attempt to communicate this with a paper clip, but that metaphor strikes me as all wrong, because paper clips are used to join two or more sheets of paper. I think that the term *package* (or perhaps *parcel*) communicates the idea better. A package is a box with something inside. It usually includes a letter explaining the contents. That's more evocative of what we do when we send each other files. Moreover, it makes the interaction clearer. Create a box; put this file (and possibly more files) into the box; here's the letter to tuck inside; send the package.

Experienced users will object that this approach is no clearer than the conventional way to attach files. But there's a bias here: if you've already mastered the conventional way, then you are not a properly naive judge of the relative values of the two approaches. The real issue is, how do the two approaches work for raw beginners? Only field testing can decide the matter.

Here's another possible metaphor: a secretary instead of a mailbox. My email program allows me to sort old messages into mailboxes; I can define a mailbox by any criteria I want and then manually assign each incoming email to it. It can even automatically assign emails to mailboxes based on their authors. However, in real life, we often recall old messages by a variety of criteria: content is the most important factor, but author and date are also used. Moreover, in attempting to dig up an old email for reference, our recollection of its date and content (and sometimes even author) are often fuzzy. Imagine the busy executive poking her head out of the door and asking her secretary, "Tom, can you find that letter from What's-His-Name in Accounting about the travel invoices? I think it was last October." There is no mailbox system that can handle this task (as far as I know), yet it constitutes a fairly simple database search request. In other words, the problem is easily computable; our failure to solve it arises not from technical considerations but from our working metaphor: a mailbox. Whoever talked to a mailbox? Shift the metaphor to a secretary, and the feature becomes obvious.

Another area of email software needing a new metaphor is the address book. This is usually a list of names and addresses organized alphabetically. This concept worked fine when we had a few dozen correspondents, but nowadays we communicate with hundreds of different people. Address books are growing impossibly cumbersome. (This is yet another example of how, as problems grow in size, technology must shift gears to another approach.) We could try to extend the address book metaphor by setting up multiple address books—one for family, one for friends, one for colleagues at work, one for outside business contacts, and so on—but as I have pointed out, extending metaphors seldom works. In this case, it handles crossover cases poorly. ("Do I put Mary on the friends or contacts list? She's both.") Here again, the secretary metaphor would serve us better. Specifying "Gomer" as the recipient of the email clearly means the guy I've sent dozens of emails to in the last week, not Gomer Tziginopilis in Tahiti, and not Dr. Joseph Meningitis, the back specialist who treats me once a year. If I want to send a message to the doctor, I'd specify the recipient as "the back doctor." The secretary should be smart enough to scan previous messages for references to doctors and backs. When the secretary finds a match, it posts the true name and email address next to my entry—as any good secretary would. ("Tom, send this letter to the back doctor." "Ah, yes, Dr. Meningitis.") In other words, the secretary metaphor converts our problem from a list selection to a database search. Again, the crucial design act is not the technical act of creating a database engine; those are a dime a dozen. The key lies in finding a metaphor that suggests and supports the database search.

Another useful application of the secretary metaphor is the handling of junk email. There are already spam filters out there, but the filter metaphor is all wrong—too techie in style and not quite suggestive of its true function. An email secretary might scan each incoming email for a variety of factors: Does it come from a recognized correspondent? Does it include such words as *price, buy, opportunity, hot*, and so on? Does it include URLs? The secretary could note which emails are discarded rather than archived and use their content as models for other emails to discard.

Metaphor lies at the outer reaches of our understanding because it is so deeply embedded in our thinking. I much doubt that it will ever be reduced to "engineering practice," but interactivity designers are only half-breed engineers; they're also half-breed artists.

24

ANTICIPATION

The simplest forms of interaction involve little or no anticipation. However, as the interaction between two agents grows more involved, each agent begins to anticipate the other's behavior, which in turn shapes the overall interaction.

Hearken back to my original definition of interactivity: a sequential process in which two agents alternately listen, think, and speak. In particular, let's scrutinize that second step: thinking. There's an assumption hidden in there: that the thinking agent will, as part of the thinking process, anticipate the needs, capabilities, and goals of the listener in formulating her expression. In other words, when somebody says something to us, we don't just mouth off with the first thing that pops into our heads; we consider the speaker's situation in framing our response. This process of anticipation plays a large role in mediating the interaction. Indeed, a prime reason for interaction failure lies in erroneous anticipations. We all know this about conversations: "I didn't think you'd take my criticism of your proposal so personally!" It applies just as forcefully to other forms of interaction, and especially to human-computer interaction: "But when it asked me if I didn't want to save my work before quitting, I thought that Yes meant to save it!" So let's examine the role of anticipation more closely.

Know Thy Partner

My first observation is that anticipation requires some knowledge of the other agent. You can't anticipate the reactions of a completely alien interlocutor—which is why so many people have problems with software. Designers—who understand computers—fail to realize that their customers can't anticipate the computer's behavior as readily as they can. The problem is partly diminishing as more people become familiar with computer basics: concepts such as volatile RAM versus nonvolatile hard-drive memory, the irreversibility of many actions, and so forth. But computer systems are also growing more complex, creating new anticipation problems even as older ones slowly clear up.

This is why user interface standards are so important. Apple was way ahead of the industry when it established and enforced user interface standards way back in 1984. When Microsoft finally caught on and started copying those interface standards, legal considerations required it to alter the appearance and function of some of the standards, much to the confusion of the users. What Macintosh users called a scrollbar, Windows users called a slider. A Macintosh thumb became a Windows elevator. And so on. Fortunately, the two interfaces have slowly converged; we've even seen the Macintosh adopt a few elements that arose in the Windows world.

These standards create expectations—anticipations—for the user. For example, we all know that an icon bar always contains the most useful commands; a brief explanation of each command can be had by leaving the mouse stationary over the icon button for a few seconds. We know that certain key combinations will always accomplish the same thing: Command-Q on the Mac or Alt-Q in Windows will generally quit a program, Command-P will print a document, and so on.

There is more going on here than merely speeding up the interaction by replacing long commands with shortcut equivalents. There's more than reducing the amount of time that the user must devote to reading the manual. We are slowly coining a language of interaction between computer and user, a system that sustains a variety of anticipations on the part of the user. "If I do X, my hunch is that Y will result; let's give it a whirl."

Anticipation is a two-way street; if the interaction is enhanced by user anticipation of the computer, why can't it be equally enhanced by computer anticipation of the user? Our present attempts in this direction are encapsulated in the notion of "preferences." The user tells the software in advance what her preferences are with regard to the program's functions. However, most preference systems offer little more than customization or alteration of default settings. The best anticipation systems we have so far are the schemes that fill in text or forms based on recognition of heavily used strings of text. In other words, if you type "Aunt Mary Ellen" frequently, your software recognizes the phrase after you've typed "Aunt" and fills in the remainder for you. Such systems suffer from two problems: misfires and feedback for recognition.

Misfires occur when the software mistakenly fills in the text string where you don't want it. If, for example, I am writing a letter to my Aunt Nellie, and the computer fills in "Aunt Mary Ellen" for me, I shall be inconvenienced and possibly irritated. Designers have experimented with a variety of solutions to this problem. The safest—and least useful—requires the user to explicitly declare the phrases that are to be filled in automatically. This is a cover-your-ass solution, ensuring that the user can never feel irritated at you, even if it costs her more time. It is rather like an old-time secretary taking dictation who refuses to accept the boss's informal shorthand and insists that he declare every such contraction up front. I would expect such a secretary to be fired.

A better approach keeps track of the user's typing patterns, comparing them with dictionaries of common usages. It would then fill in text strings based on how oddly often they crop up in your typing. For example, if you are employed by a company named Quixerixicon, and your letters frequently contain references to the company, the software should recognize that name after just four letters and fill it in for you. This concept could be extended to regular vocabulary—if I type *vocab*, the only reasonable concluding phrase is *ulary* (yes, there's also the word *vocabulist*, but how often does that show up relative to *vocabulary*?). The concept could be extended even to the level of individual letters. If I type *q*, there's almost certainly a *u* following it (assuming I'm using English). Why not have the computer fill in that *u*?

The second problem is the real killer: such automatic filling in could readily interrupt the flow of touch-typing. The mental task of touch-typing allows us to move our spelled image of a word directly from our brains to our fingers. If we attempt to interpose a conscious subtractive process on this, typing *qick* when we mean *quick*, we'll end up typing more slowly. Moreover, the disjunction between seeing *quick* on the screen when we have just typed *qick* will surely break the flow of our composition. This applies just as well to long phrases. If I set out to type "Aunt Mary Ellen," but the software fills in the remainder of the phrase for me after I type *Aunt*, I will still experience a mental disjunction.

There is no solution to this problem, but the reason why there is no solution reveals a great deal about the nature of the problem. It's the speed of the typing interaction that kills us; a touch-typist's fingers move faster than his ability to process input from the computer. If the computer fills in a word for me, I don't realize it until my fingers have already typed four more characters, ruining the value of the computer's anticipation. The fill-in-the-phrase feature is thus a boon to hunt-and-peckers and a curse to touch-typists. Thus, software in such an application should monitor the speed of the user's typing and fill in for him only if he's a slow typist.

Few human-computer interactions take place as rapidly as typing. My fingers can tap out half a dozen keys in a second, each on a separate interaction. But all other tasks (clicking buttons, scrolling windows, selecting items from menus) take place at a much slower pace. Such tasks could more readily benefit from detailed anticipation.

Designer-Level Anticipation

There's another angle on anticipation in interactivity design: the anticipation that the designer brings to the process. There's precious little of this much-needed behavior in the design of software. When examining software, I often wonder, what were the designers thinking that the user would think? Were there any anticipations going on in their heads?

For example, I recently came across a blooper on eBay. I mistakenly entered a password that I use for another situation. The response presented to me was that either my username or my password was incorrect. Now what did the designers think this message would engender in my mind? They deliberately foisted an ambiguous situation on me; was it my username or my password that was wrong? Didn't they think it would confuse me? I ended up trying half a dozen combinations of username and password, trying to figure out the problem. Their defense, of course, is that when a user submits a username with a password, it's the pairing that is evaluated; the username cannot be separated from the password, and so a failure must include both parts. While they are technically correct, the designers should have given some weight to the confusion their message was certain to engender. It would have been more useful to evaluate the username first; if the username is valid for eBay, they should have responded with something like this:

The username chris_the_schmuck is a valid username, but the password you entered doesn't match that username. If chris_the_schmuck is your correct username, please reenter your password; otherwise, enter the correct username with the password.

If, on the other hand, the username didn't match any of the usernames on file, then eBay should have responded with:

We don't know who chris_the_shmuk is; perhaps you have mistyped your username. We suggest that you reenter the username with your password.

This approach clearly identifies the problem and immediately eliminates all possibility of confusion on the part of the user.

Another example of poor designer anticipation is the all-too-common practice of dumping overly technical explanations onto the user. For example, I have seen some programs that advise a user of a problem by notifying him that "the buffer is full." What could a designer possibly be thinking when including such a notification? What will a user think when confronted by such a blatant use of technical terminology?

Variations on Anticipation

General anticipation involves what the computer should know about everybody; personal anticipation uses what the computer knows about the individual user. General anticipation should be built right into the software and so should seldom be noticed—it's automatic, after all, and it makes perfect sense. We notice it only in its prominent absence. For example, it took the geniuses at Microsoft and Netscape several years to figure out that most people use web browsers to browse the web. If you're browsing the Web, you always use the URL prefix http:\\www. Yet they required millions of us to type those meaningless characters over and over again, because they just didn't anticipate that people would use their web browsers to browse the web. They finally realized what people were up to and dumped the required prefix characters. They've learned their lesson well; nowadays, browsers even recognize previously used URLs and provide auto-entry options.

Personal anticipation must be figured out from interaction with the user. As I wrote earlier, most designers require the user to take the initiative and declare her preferences up front. This suffers from the problem that the user often doesn't know what components of the software can be personalized. On the Macintosh, for example, many people still don't realize that they can substitute custom icons for their files and folders. The means of doing so is not at all obvious. Only the observation that other people do so has prompted them to inquire into the trick.

A truly idiotic solution to this problem is the "startup wizard" who quizzes the user when the program is first launched, asking for all sorts of detailed information that the software uses to custom tailor the software. The problem with this approach is that, all too often, personal preferences can't be developed until after you've had the opportunity to use the software. By that time, the startup wizard is gone, and there's no way to figure out how to get him back. If you use a startup wizard in your design, make sure that you tell the user how to bring him back without reinitializing the whole program.

The biggest hurdle we must overcome with anticipation is our pantywaist fear of relying on less-than-ironclad means of anticipating the user's desires. A great Macintosh example of this problem arises from the dialog box we must deal with every single time we issue a Print command. This dialog box allows the user to fill in all sorts of interesting variations on the central theme of printing the document: Do you want it sideways? Do you want to print all the document or some of it? How many copies would you like? The vast majority of Print commands issued by the vast majority of users require no such special decision making: we want one copy of our entire document printed right-side up. Yet think of the millions of users who, over the past 15 years, have had to wait the extra second or two to dismiss that useless dialog box to get their document. The time that they have lost dealing with an irrelevant dialog box certainly exceeds by a great margin the time that they would have gained by separately invoking the dialog box before printing. And the solution to this problem is so trivial that I still can't understand why something like this has not become universal: Command-P to print, Shift-Command-P to print with the dialog box showing up first.

Anticipation is almost always accompanied by uncertainty. We need to use probabilistic thinking in our designs. How likely is the most likely outcome of any choice offered the user? If an outcome is overwhelmingly likely, then it should happen without requesting confirmation from the user. Think of the computer as an assistant to a human. If you told your Man Friday, "File this contract," and all contracts have always been filed in the brown filing cabinet under the label "Contracts," would he ask you where to file it? What would you think of him if he did ask you? You'd call him a ninny—yet this is what software designers do all the time. So, are software designers ninnies?

There really isn't much work required to implement probabilistic anticipation. Your software provides the user with lots of choices. Examine each choice critically, asking how often you would expect it to result in a known outcome. Or how often a particular user would make the same choice in the same way. If you find that there is a clear preference for one of the choices, then you should consider making that choice for the user, automatically. In your preferences file, store a record for that choice indicating how many times the user has indeed taken Choice A, Choice B, Choice C, and so on. When one of those choices establishes a clear preponderance over the others, then make the choice automatically.

By doing so, you guarantee that most of the time your software will make the right choice and save the user some time. You also guarantee that your software will sometimes make the wrong choice and inconvenience your user. The ratio of the convenience benefit of a correct decision to the inconvenience incurred by an incorrect decision determines what you mean by *preponderance* in your decision to make a choice. If you are writing targeting software for nuclear warheads, the inconvenience of an incorrect decision is quite high, so that *preponderance* means *always*. But if you're considering a less ominous decision, you can lower the implied value of *preponderance*.

Your next step is to reduce the inconvenience imposed by a mistaken decision. The user needs to be made immediately aware of the decision and needs a quick way to countermand it. The latter task is trivial: implement the undo feature for the decision. Every automatically made probabilistic decision must be undoable! Making the user aware of the automatic decision is the tough task. If the decision entails a time-consuming task, then all you need do is post a window declaring that you are now executing some task and that the user can countermand the task by pressing a special key. If the decision immediately leads to other activity, then you have to be careful; you don't want the user to charge forward ignorant of the fact that you just made a decision for him, but you also don't want to force the user to explicitly approve of your decision—that ruins the whole point of the feature!

Once again, recourse to human experience provides an answer. Consider the protocols that have evolved for teams of people simultaneously carrying out complex tasks under the integrating control of a leader. Typically, each team member will call out her actions as she performs them, using a standard, concise phrasing. Team members are taught how to "leave the mike open" while still reporting vital information as it arrives. Such protocols are almost always carried out via the sound channel. because it can be shared by all and because it allows workers to keep their hands and their eyes on their primary tasks.

Our problem therefore calls for speech synthesis or pre-recorded voice. When the user chooses the Print option, the computer calls out "normal printing" and continues. The key to the solution lies in finding a quick back-channel way to represent the decision automatically made.

Levels of Anticipation

The zeroth level of anticipation is the null level: no anticipation at all. This was where we were back in the old DOS days. A computer was a machine, and your job was to push the right buttons. Nowadays, computers have moved up to the first level of anticipation: to some extent, they take the human condition into account as they function. Clearly, our immediate task is to expand the degree of such anticipation until computers operate with a reasonable understanding of the human context in which they work.

But there are further levels of anticipation: second, third, fourth, umpteenth levels of anticipation. It's easier to understand in human terms: Fredegund uses zeroth-level anticipation when he bluntly tells Gomer that he has been terminated; Fredegund isn't considering Gomer's likely reaction at all. Fredegund uses first-level anticipation when he gently couches the news in terms meant to salve Gomer's feelings. Fredegund uses second-level anticipation when he considers how he (Fredegund) might respond to his (Gomer's) answers to his (Fredegund's) questions. "After I tell him the bad news, he'll probably ask whether his performance had anything to do with the decision to let him go; if I answer yes, how will he respond?" (Side note: Psychologists use *intentionality* to describe what I am here calling anticipation.)

In second-level anticipation, we look ahead a step before we make our decision. If I do X, then the other guy will likely do Y, which will force me to do Z, so do I really want to do X in the first place?

Your biggest problem in using anticipation in software design is your exposure to blame. If your software insists on pig-headedly covering its ass at every turn, nobody can ever blame you for screwing up. When you anticipate the user's wishes, rather than requiring him to explicitly declare them, you perform a useful service at a small risk of being wrong. Good workers do this all the time, and when they do get it wrong, they apologize and recover. Shouldn't your software do the same?

Privacy

Anticipation requires knowledge of the other party; better anticipation requires more such knowledge. Thus, to really apply anticipation usefully, your software needs to know as much about its user as it can. Our current knowledge about our user is stored in a Preferences file; each application maintains one or more of these. The Preferences folder on my Macintosh contains 855 files amounting to 42 MB of hard disk space. Once again, we face the old problem of a good idea that has been outgrown. We need something better.

The seeds of a better solution are already in place. My Macintosh knows my name; when I install a new program that wants to know my name, it can find it automatically. Why stop with a name? Why not include address, telephone number, social security number, and shoe size in the standard user data file? Why not include our credit card numbers so that we don't have to run for our wallet every time we buy something online?

I don't stop there. Our software should compile every useful bit of information it can about us: our habits, our spelling oddities, and our email correspondents. The accumulation of this kind of data can dramatically enhance the performance of our personal computer software. The spam-killer software that I mentioned earlier would operate by noting which emails we trash without reading, looking for patterns in their content that are unique to such emails. Once it has reached an appropriate level of statistical certainty, it can start throwing out the worst examples automatically—leaving the questionable ones for us to examine. But this works only with an existing compendium of data on our past behavior. The smart address book that I mentioned in the same context would also require considerable background information on its user. To identify "the email from What's-His-Name in Accounting about the travel invoices that was sent last October" will require a vast amount of information—but it is all information that at some time has resided in the computer and could be put to productive use.

One might object that such information storage would gobble up too much disk space for its overall utility; and were we still using 1 GB hard drives, I would agree. But inasmuch as hard drives are now operating in the 20 GB range, I don't see a problem. Similarly, the digestion of all that data should not be onerous; most computers waste literally trillions of machine cycles every day. Why not put some of those cycles to use in background work?

This gets us into the swamp of issues surrounding privacy. We have all heard the terrifying stories about how easily our privacy can be breached by unscrupulous scoundrels on the Internet. We all agree that privacy is a good thing that should be protected. Nevertheless, I argue that there are good and valid reasons to compromise the privacy of the user. I do not argue for the reduction of privacy on the Internet; my goal is to point out the magnitude of the dilemma.

For most software designers, this matters little; the sensitive information is safely confined within the bounds of the computer, and the user need not fear its divulgence. But the Internet changes things. Website designers in particular face sensitive issues in doing their jobs well. Much of the information that other programs squirrel away on a user's hard drive must move over open telephone lines and be saved inside the host computer. There goes privacy.

I will use Amazon.com, one of the better-designed sites, as an example of how tricky privacy issues can be. The designers of this site have worked hard to make it intelligently helpful. With my permission, they have stored my basic purchase information (shipping address, credit card number, telephone number) in their computer; when I order a book, I need not endure the tedium of reentering this information, nor the risk of retransmitting it across the net. I have surrendered a considerable amount of privacy, but it seems a good trade-off to me.

But they don't stop there. They keep a record of my purchases and have built up a profile of my buying tastes in books. They use this profile to suggest new books for my consideration. It's a good idea, but what if my tastes ran to child pornography? How would I feel knowing that they have a file on me revealing my sick tastes? For the moment, my only fear is that someday some snoop will uncover my eccentric interest in Desiderius Erasmus—and what if someday my penchant for Erasmus becomes a crime?

Amazon.com could do a better job by logging my browsing as well. The searches I make, the books I look at, all provide even more information about my purchasing tastes, even if I don't proceed to make the purchase. This would require more intelligent algorithms, of course, but with the amount of data generated on the site every day, the designers would be professionally remiss not to utilize that data. This would give them an even more refined basis for recommending books.

But why stop there? Once they've mastered the on-site data, couldn't they do an even better job for me by considering data from other sources on the Web? They could estimate my disposable income by consulting publicly available information on my tax assessments; this might help them tailor the ideal price range for my purchases. They could swap data with other retailers to divine my other interests; since I've been buying electronics parts recently, perhaps I would be interested in a book or two about charge-coupled devices or universal asynchronous receiver-transmitters?

But a designer truly determined to do the best possible job for me would go even further: when I log on, the site would download software to my machine that would scan the contents of my hard drive to assess my interests. Here's an email talking about installing a hard drive; perhaps a book on upgrading computers would be nice. There's a spreadsheet with weather data; surely a book on weather measurement with computers would be interesting.

As far as I know, nobody has gone this far yet, and I doubt that anybody will soon develop software intelligent enough to analyze this data adequately. The important point, though, is that all of this conjectured activity is a perfectly reasonable application of a genuine desire to help the user. There's nothing malevolent in this breach of privacy. The effect of all of this intrusion is to create a private bookseller for the consumer:

"Good evening, Mr. Crawford. May I take your coat? How is your cat Khublai recovering from that abscess? I take it you're in a rather jubilant mood after receiving that royalty check? Perhaps you'd like to splurge on that 1532 edition of the *Colloquies* you've been eyeing. . . . Not yet? Very well, I've found an interesting work on language origins. It's a tad expensive but has some fascinating new theories. Something else? Did you know that Richard Dawkins has a new book out? Why yes, here's all the information on it. . . ."

Wouldn't that be nice? And who could be more discreet than a well-programmed computer? I'd be uncomfortable knowing that a human bookseller has such an intimate knowledge of my life, but a computer, being a machine, would make no judgments and tell no tales . . .

. . . unless something went wrong. Between greedy businesspeople and outright criminal hackers, there's plenty of reason for concern. All that personal information would not be truly secure—so some people have concluded that we should not allow it out of the barn in the first place. Perhaps this is the most prudent course for the moment. But the integration of information via networks is progressing with amazing speed. We have already placed most office workers permanently on a LAN, which is in turn connected to the Internet; the office worker who needs to look up a quick statistic can set aside the spreadsheet for a moment to grab the relevant page from the web. The personal finance program Quicken already permits users to log onto their site to obtain financial information for the program automatically. The benefits of integrating one's personal computer into the Internet are too great; more and more software will plug into the net to enhance its performance. As this trend grows, more and more interactivity designers will be caught between the desire to better serve the customer and the need to protect the customer's privacy. It is in the best interests of interactivity designers to support the development of strong privacy laws that protect users while permitting legitimate access to detailed personal information.

PART FOUR
SOCIAL AND ARTISTIC ISSUES

25

A HISTORY OF INTERACTIVITY

Presenting a cute tale sketching the difference between mass media and interactivity. No apologies are offered for the attempted humor.

It all started long, long ago, before DOS, before television, before cavemen. Mother Nature was screwing around with a new kind of critter, the mammal, and the basic design looked pretty versatile. On a whim, she tried giving some of the mammals bigger brains for more intelligence, and lo and behold, it worked! Critters with bigger brains seemed to do better.

But at a certain point the brains got so big that a problem emerged: what do you put in those brains? Mother Nature had gotten pretty handy at cooking up nervous systems that could detect, analyze, and respond to all manner of complicated environmental situations. Herbivore brains could combine sensory information from ears and eyes to detect approaching predators, analyze their motions, and plot the best routes of escape. Later, she concocted some snazzy evasion algorithms that permitted prey to zig and zag with just the right timing to throw off closely pursuing predators. But these were all hard-wired into the synapses; the critical information about how to do these things was encoded in the DNA, and the critter was born with the ability.

The bigger brains she was experimenting with were capable of all sorts of snazzy calculations. But bigger brains need more data, and that's what raised the problem. She was getting tired of hand coding the DNA with all those complicated neural algorithms. More important, she realized that she couldn't keep going this way forever; eventually she'd run out of DNA for all those algorithms, and the new 256-MB DRAM modules were a long way off. She fiddled around aimlessly for a few eons, trying various combinations, none of which seemed to work. Then she stumbled onto the solution with one of the minor orders, *felix*—that's the cats. The big idea was this: Don't bother programming the brain with all the behavioral techniques and algorithms. Instead, program the brain with the basics (eating, drinking, sleeping, walking—that kind of thing), and then add a special behavior whose function is to learn new behaviors. A behavior to learn behaviors—what a concept!

This raised a new problem: How could Mother Nature design such a behavior? How do you program critters to learn about their environment? A few million dead mammals quickly demonstrated that any explicit-learning system was just too vulnerable to minor problems. Every little programming bug crashed the species. She needed something that was robust, that would work in all kinds of different situations.

"Why not let them do it the same way I do it?" she mused. After all, she'd had a lot of fun playing with genes, trying out all sorts of combinations and variations, and every now and then she hit upon a recipe that worked. Sharks were one of her early successes. What an elegant design: clean, simple, and wonderfully efficient! She was proud of that one. On the other hand, she never could seem to get beetles right. She'd pulled out all the stops with them, trying all sorts of different schemes, but none of them quite rang the bell for her.

To get back to the story, she figured that she'd let her new "learning mammals" learn about their environment the same way that she learned about species: by playing. Of course, she played with genes, and they'd be playing with synapses, but that was only a matter of timing and generality. Her experiments took eons and affected millions of critters; these experiments—games—would take minutes and affect only the player.

So that was her plan: equip the learning mammal with a basic drive to try out all sorts of crazy behaviors (we now call it curiosity) and some sort of mechanism for noticing the results and remembering successful experiments. The remembering part was easy, and the random behavior generator was also pretty simple, but she soon realized that she needed to put a terminating gene in there; the damned silly adults were still playing games, getting themselves killed jumping out of trees, attempting to mate with predators, trying to swim across the ocean, that kind of thing. With that bug fixed, she had kittens that would play, but the evaluation algorithm was always a problem. It worked, but it was accident prone, and try as she may, she just couldn't get it working safely. Eventually she decided to call it a feature.

The cats worked out just great. When they were young, they were too small and weak to do anything worthwhile; they needed a few months to grow big enough to bring down a full-sized mouse. During that period of kittenhood, they would play with each other, trying out all kinds of stalking, pouncing, and fighting techniques.

These kittens were so successful, they even got around one of Mother Nature's biggest belly-flops: she had placed the most vulnerable part of the body, the eyes, right next to the primary killing weapon, the teeth. Before you can eat a mouse, you've got to kill it, and if you're going to kill it, you've got to bite it, and in the process, you're bringing your eyes within easy striking distance of a mouse's feet. All predators suffer from this problem. Mother Nature had tried to get around it in a variety of ways. She had moved the eyes all around the head, but some of those poor critters were walking into trees. She tried giving them big teeth, so they could kill in one quick bite, but then they had horrible dental problems. She tried making the predators so much bigger than the prey that they could get the whole prey inside the mouth in one gulp, but that required big predators nibbling like crazy.

But these clever little kittens solved the problem in a way she had never thought of. By practicing the whole stalk-pounce-bite-kill routine over and over again, they were able to polish it to perfection. They didn't change any of the techniques; they just reduced the error rate by endless practice, practice, practice. With that kind of quality control, they were able to take on prey not much smaller than themselves—quite a feast when it worked. And they didn't need to pack big-caliber teeth to do the job, either. These new smart mammals that could learn were quite a discovery, and she decided then and there to include this new learning-by-playing feature in many of her new models.

So Mother Nature played around with the formula. She tried a slightly different tack with the *canids* (dogs), emphasizing teamwork rather than quality control, and that worked pretty well. She tried all sorts of other experiments I won't go into now, but in one of her wilder moments, almost a fluke, she tried raising the ante by cooking up a critter with a big brain. It was ugly as sin: the skull had to bulge out like a gorged tick to hold all those brains, and the whole body was thrown out of balance by that monster head. When it ran, the poor thing's heavy head bounced around crazily, throwing the body this way and that, and all four legs would scrabble around trying to keep everything moving along. What a pathetic sight! She decided to tuck these losers into a small corner of the world while she went back to other, more promising experiments with dolphins and pigs.

But then there was an accident. A fairly sizable group of these pathetic ninnies managed to get themselves cut off from the main group when a tectonic plate shifted suddenly and dropped a strip of continent below sea level. All of a sudden, these monkeys were marooned on a big desolate island, surrounded by a shallow sea. Here's where that playfulness paid off: some of them went into the water to gather oysters and other shallow-water food. With their weight partially supported by the water, their ungainly bodies weren't such a handicap. They shifted from quadripedalism (four-legged walking) to bipedalism (two-legged walking).

I think you can see where this story is going. Rather than bore you with the details, I'll just wrap up this part with a quick "...and the rest is history."

One of the other themes that Mother Nature had been experimenting with was social behavior. The mammals were smart enough to permit some simple social behaviors, and she had found these to be quite useful in coping with a variety of problems. She kept refining her techniques, adding more and more social behaviors as she built bigger and bigger brains. She was having quite a bit of fun using the idea on primates, and of course the new hominids boasted lots of social behavior. But then she noticed that the hominids, equipped with scads of social-behavior genes, were starting to get themselves mixed up in messy and confusing interactions. It seems that Mother Nature had designed all the social behavior algorithms to handle what she called *radial* interactions. Each creature stood in the center of his own psychological universe, and all other creatures were scattered around it, some psychologically nearer and some further. Thus, each creature saw all social relationships in radial form: what do I care about this situation?

However, the new hominids were so intensely social that other kinds of relationships were taking on real significance to their behavior. Expanding on some ape behavior, they had developed gender-based specialization, with the females and children remaining in a relatively immobile central location, and the males looping outward on long hunts. This admirable food-gathering scheme ran afoul of their sexual algorithms: How was a male to have enough confidence in the paternity of his children to expend all the energy to feed them? He could never know what his mate might be doing in his absence.

At first Mother Nature treated this as a radial problem, trying to come up with ways to guarantee the paternity of every child, but every approach she tried proved to be buggy. But then she had a stroke of genius: what if she approached it as a three-party problem: male, female, and back-door male? This opened up all sorts of possibilities, because behaviors encompassing three parties can be extended to cover the entire clan. If these hominids could be made to understand the concept of a love triangle, could they not just as easily understand the concept of a "tri"-bunal: judge, plaintiff, and defendant? Or an alliance? This new concept bubbled over with possibilities. Recalling her earlier geometric notion of radial relationships, she dubbed these *circumferential* relationships: every individual remains at the center of his own psychological universe, but must now consider the relations between others, relationships around the circumference of the circle of his friends and family.

Humming happily to herself, Mother Nature set to work endowing her hominids with the algorithms necessary to evaluate circumferential relationships. After but a few minutes' work, she realized that this was harder to program than she had imagined. The radial relationships, involving only one outside party to consider, were fairly easy to define and address with simple emotions such as fear, affection, dominance, and so forth. But these circumferential relationships could combine in a dizzying number of ways; there were just too many to program an algorithm for each and every combination.

Mother Nature struggled with the problem late into the night, trying to solve the problem, but made no progress for hours. Just after midnight, she had a brilliant brainstorm. What if she simply reused all the existing radial algorithms, but applied them with variable subjects? In other words, all the algorithms that she had developed for, say, fear/dominance/intimidation in the radial form could be used circumferentially if she simply substituted another person in them. The original algorithms always assumed the thinker to be the subject (for example, "I am intimidated by his chest thumping"); she need merely plug in the ability to substitute another person in the subject position: "She is intimidated by his chest thumping."

This was a fantastic concept; her excitement grew despite her fatigue. If she could equip hominids with the ability to substitute another person in the subject position, the same trick could be used to substitute the original person in the direct object position: "She is intimidated by *my* chest thumping."

Mother Nature soon realized that there were two necessary extensions to the existing programming. First was the aforementioned ability to substitute another person in the algorithm, and second was the ability to recurse this thinking, to apply one layer of algorithm inside another layer. This allowed such thoughts as, "If I thump my chest, then she will be intimidated by my chest thumping, and she will attempt to mollify me, and she will give me her banana."

By this time, Mother Nature was bleary eyed and yawning, but there was one last detail to sort out: how to continue using the original algorithms for their original purpose, radial relationships? The answer seemed obvious: equip each hominid with an indirect means of referring to itself, the pronoun *I* for the preceding sentences. She set it all up with her hominids and then, exhausted, retired for the night.

The next morning, after tea, she returned to the lab to see how these new circumferentially adept hominids were doing. A single glance made her recoil in horror; the teacup fell from her hand and crashed on the floor. During the night, the hominids had developed consciousness! "Oh, shit!" she cried. "What hath I wrought?" Instantly she saw her mistake: that little pronoun *I*, that new variable that she had used to generalize her algorithms, had planted the seed. The hominid brains had developed that nascent ego and grown it into full-scale consciousness. It must have been the language feature that made it happen so fast. Once the seed of ego had been planted, the hominids plugged it into their primitive language systems, and then they started talking about themselves, accelerating the process!

She stared in wide-eyed horror at her mistake. Then she paced for hours, trying to figure out what to do. Despairing of a solution, she called an old friend.

"B.L., I've got a big problem." She explained the sequence of events.

B.L. couldn't resist a hearty laugh at her expense. "You really did it this time, didn't you?"

"C'mon, B.L., this is serious! I've got to do something! Help me out here!"

"You don't have a whole lot of options, M.N. You know what's going to happen next, don't you?"

"Of course: the little buggers are going to take over the world and wipe out everything else."

"Well, then, it seems to me that you have only one choice: reformat the whole thing."

"But B.L., I've got so much work in it. I can't just wipe it all out."

"Look, M.N., there's no stopping one of these infections once it gets started. You know that."

"But couldn't I just use an anticonsciousness checking program?"

"Sure, but those things seldom work; the little monsters just build boats."

Mother Nature sighed. "Okay, thanks for your help, B.L."

"What are you going to do?"

"I don't know. I'll think on it."

"Don't wait too long. Those buggers move pretty fast."

"I won't. Bye."

She couldn't bring herself to destroy the entire genome; there were too many good ideas in it, especially that learning-by-playing discovery. Perhaps, she mused, they'll never become too destructive. After all, it's the females who concentrate on the interpersonal relationships; they'll end up with the most highly developed consciousnesses, but the males are the ones who run the show. Perhaps the big lugs won't be bright enough to do much harm. I should at least give them a chance. I won't use the anticonsciousness program until they show unambiguous signs of developing civilization. She sat back to watch her little experiment take shape.

Meanwhile, Back on the Earth . . .

One fateful day, a Cro-Magnon named Gorkimedes found some red berries growing on the hillside. He ate them and then got sick. After throwing up the already paltry contents of his stomach, he headed down to the group's encampment for sympathy and some water to wash the taste of vomit out of his mouth. On his way down, he resolved to warn his compatriots not to eat the red berries. But as he walked into camp, he realized that almost everybody was there, and he'd have to thread his way through all 37 people, telling them one at a time about the red berries. Discouraged by the prospect, he slumped his shoulders and glanced away. His eye fell on a big flat-topped boulder. And that's when Gorkimedes invented mass media.

He climbed up on the boulder and began shouting to his friends and family, "Everybody gather round! Come listen to what I have to say!" Well, at first they all just stared at this maniac standing on a rock shouting, but pretty soon a few of the younger ones went over, and when the adults realized that Gorkimedes wasn't insane, they came, too. Standing up on that boulder, Gorkimedes could easily see all 37 members of the tribe, and they could all see him. "Listen up!" he announced. "Don't eat the red berries! They'll make you sick!"

"That's not true!" his uncle Gorkistotle shouted back. "I was eating some red berries down by the stream not 10 minutes ago, and I feel fine!"

"You mean those little hard orange-red berries that grow on the thornless bush?" Gorkimedes asked.

"Yep, they're the ones," came the reply.

"Well there you have it," Gorkimedes declared. "I'm talking about the big squooshy berries, deep red, that grow on the thorny bush on the hillside!"

And that's how mass media was invented. As he stepped down off the boulder, Gorkimedes exulted to his father, "Give me a place to stand, and I will tell the whole world!"

Everybody was terribly excited by Gorkimedes' discovery, because it dramatically increased the efficiency of language. With old, obsolete solid-ground technology, you could talk to only a handful of people at a time, but rock technology permitted a speaker to address 20, 50, maybe even 100 people at once. That was astoundingly efficient—and adding more people to the audience didn't cost a clam! This was itself revolutionary.

The first breakthrough in rock technology was the discovery of bigger rocks. From a bigger rock, a speaker could be seen and heard by even more people. Soon, speakers were addressing 100, 200, even 300 people from ever-bigger rocks.

The next step took tens of thousands of years, but it was a big one: the artificial rock. By piling bricks or cut stones on top of each other in big mounds, people were able to build platforms on which to stand, platforms high enough to permit one person to address hundreds easily. Mankind marched forward!

The Greeks came up with the next big improvement: the amphitheater. Basically, this is a rock turned inside out. The audience sits on the sides of a small valley, and the speaker stands in the middle of the valley, surrounded by people looking down on him. Because the slopes of the amphitheater are curved, more people can see and hear the speaker. Even more efficient! Progress progressed!

The Romans took the amphitheater to its ultimate form in the Coliseum. This was a huge artificial amphitheater, a bowl for people to sit in. They could pack thousands of people into the Coliseum, and one person standing in the center of the Coliseum could be heard by everybody, if they all kept absolutely quiet. Unfortunately, the Coliseum bumps up against the upper limit of capability of rock technology. That limit came not from the technology but from the human voice, which can get only so loud. It looked as if the March of Progress was pooped.

But there was already another solution ready to go: writing. It had been invented much earlier by Mesopotamian accountants to keep track of goods. I'm not kidding! The first written documents in human history were receipts for goats, sheep, and wheat. Later, the priests caught onto the secret, but writing didn't catch on until much later, when the Greeks managed to put all the pieces together. They swiped paper from the Egyptians and the alphabet from the Phoenicians and added one element all their own: the expectation that everybody should be able to read and write. Of course, "everybody" in those days didn't really mean everybody; after all, slaves, women, children, and foreigners didn't count. But if you were a man of substance, a participating member of the community, you were expected to be able to read and write.

What a difference that made! Suddenly, with a broad spectrum of people involved in reading and writing, the subjects of writing exploded out from the dull bills of lading, royal chest thumping, and temple hocus-pocus that dominated other people's writing. (Can you imagine reading that dreck for a living? Gad, it would be worse than programming financial databases for banks! Let's pause for a moment of silence to honor the archaeologists who patiently read through reams of this stuff trying to figure out what those people were up to.) But the Greeks started writing to each other about anything they felt like: family gossip, political diatribes, business advice, anything. And that in turn led to something altogether new: the realization that deliberately written things—books—could be passed from hand to hand, copied, and thereby spread to many people. At any given time, only one person could be reading a particular copy, but as the years rolled by, the audience for a book could get up into the thousands. Moreover, you didn't need to gather everybody together into a single location to get your information across to the multitudes. Copies of your book could travel all over the world, reaching people in distant lands without your ever even lacing your sandals. This was high tech! Once again, humanity lurched forward with the impetus of a new and more efficient way to disseminate information.

The pace of innovation was accelerating: a mere 2,000 years later, Gutenberg invented the printing press, and suddenly it was possible to make thousands of copies of a single book. It was so easy that printers could make money selling books for a pittance (at least, a pittance to your average upper-class oppressor of the people). More books were printed, which encouraged more people to learn to read, which made the customer base even larger—things just took off. The efficiency of communications took another giant step forward. Then came movies, radio, and television, which permitted a single person to communicate useful (and useless) ideas to millions of people at once. The efficiency of human communication now stands at dizzying levels of achievement. Let's all give ourselves a great big congratulatory hug.

But there's a catch. Along the way to greater and greater efficiency, we cut out all the interactivity. Language, in its original form, was highly interactive because it was mostly conversational—and remember, I used conversation as the defining metaphor for interactivity. Now recall Gorkimedes' warning about the red berries. His uncle Gorkistotle was able to interrupt him with an objection. There followed a public conversation between Gorkimedes and Gorkistotle, which was certainly interactive. But other parts of Gorkimedes' speech were not interactive. Hence, the total interactivity of Gorkimedes' warning was less than what people normally achieved in conversations.

It got worse as the rocks got bigger. Try to interrupt a speaker addressing a hundred people, and the speaker and the audience will likely show some irritation. With amphitheaters, the problem grew even worse, because there were even more people in the audience, and the social pressure to shut up was overwhelming. I very much doubt that any of the gala events staged at the Coliseum were even moderately interactive, except, of course, for the interactions between the Christians and the lions, but then they were the entertainment, not the audience.

With the printing press, we eliminated once and for all the theoretical possibility of interaction. At least at the Coliseum, a spectator in the farthest bleachers could feasibly shout, "Hey Caligula, when you gonna fix the potholes in the streets?" and although we can be reasonably certain that nothing of the kind ever actually happened, it was at least theoretically possible. But with the printing press, we dismissed even the possibility. Still, people tried to interact. Lots of people wrote letters to the authors of books (they still do today, but back then it was a bigger portion of the audience that wrote). There were "dueling pamphlets," ugly arguments carried out through the printing press. But the degree of interactivity was vastly reduced.

Look at the situation today. If the president of the United States comes on television to announce some important new decision, you don't stand a snowball's chance in hell of interacting with him. You could try writing him a letter, but you know it'll be read by some White House intern. Most people just give up and make raspberries at the TV screen.

Thus, as the efficiency of our communications has increased, the interactivity associated with those communications has been reduced to zero. And that's why, when you mention interactivity, traditional communications designers blink and say "Huh?"

26

CONTROL VERSUS INTERACTIVITY

In this chapter, I'll be talking about interactivity, plot, free will, determinism, quantum mechanics, and temporal irreversibility. Yes, believe it or not, these six things are all tied together. Moreover, they're tied together in a way that reveals some useful truths about designing interactive applications. Although the vehicle of discussion is interactive storytelling, the lessons of this chapter can be applied to any interactive design.

The starting point of the discussion is the conflict between plot and interactivity. There are theoretical reasons for this conflict, best seen from the point of view of the plot faction, most of whom are writers. Plot creation is, from their point of view, an enormously difficult task, demanding great talent and creative energy. The thought of allowing a user to mess up their carefully crafted plots raises their hackles. Knowing how difficult it is to get a plot to work well, they realize that any intrusion by the user into the process will only yield garbage. If interactivity requires the user to involve herself in the direction of the plot, then clearly interactivity and plot are incompatible.

Adding to this apparent incompatibility is the attitude of the other side. The protagonists of interactivity tend to take a dim view of plot. There is a possibly apocryphal story about id Software and the creation of Doom. There was, so the story goes, some dispute among the designers about the proper role of story in the game. One faction argued that there should be some story element to tie everything together. The other faction argued that Doom was to be an action game, pure and simple, and that "we don't need no steenking story." Eventually, the anti-story faction won out, the losers left the company, and nowadays story is referred to within the company as "the S-word." That's the industry gossip.

So what we have here is an apparent incompatibility between plot and interactivity. It would seem, from both theoretical considerations and direct experience, that plot and interactivity cannot be reconciled. This, in turn, implies that the dream of interactive storytelling is a chimera.

The central issue that we face here is not new. In slightly different terms, some of the brightest minds in human history have struggled with this problem. The results of their efforts might prove illuminating. Now, you might wonder how a problem in interactive design could have attracted the attentions of august thinkers in times past, but in fact they weren't concerned with computer applications. They were working with a bigger problem: the classic theological problem of free will versus determinism.

It goes like this: God is omniscient and omnipotent. The unfolding of history is predetermined; everything that happens in the universe happens according to His benevolent design. There are apparent evils in the universe, but these are all part of God's wise plan. This includes the actions of people as well as the actions of natural phenomena. Thus, a terrible disaster is an "act of God," but so is a murder. How, then, can human beings have any free will? They are pawns in the hands of an omnipotent God. If we did have free will, then God would be neither omnipotent nor omniscient, for then He would neither control nor know what we might do. But if He is neither omnipotent nor omniscient, how can He fit any definition of god? Thus, free will clashes with determinism.

The connection with interactive design should be obvious. Determinism in theology is analogous to plot in storytelling. Free will corresponds to interactivity, for how else can a user interact without the exercise of her free will? Indeed, we can make the analogy more explicit by viewing the creative person as the creator of a miniature universe. The storyteller, for example, creates an imaginary universe populated by the story's characters. Like some omnipotent god, the storyteller decides the characters' actions and predestines their fates. To reverse the analogy, the history of the universe is nothing more than a huge story written by God that we act out. As Erasmus wrote long ago, "What is this life but a kind of comedy, wherein men walk up and down in one another's disguises and act their respective parts."

Every interactive designer creates a tiny universe and exercises godlike control over that universe. A website is a tiny intellectual universe with its own laws and logic; it is a complete and consistent unit. Yet, the user of a website clearly exercises free will in perusing it. What difference is there between the artist as god of storytelling and the designer as god of the website?

Here's a counterargument: "Free will in the real world could be an illusion. After all, God would want us to think that we have free will, but in fact He has already determined our actions for us. We think that we are making our own choices, but in fact our choices are predestined. Even if we try to assert our free will by deliberately making apparently arbitrary decisions, that, too, can be explained as God's plan for us."

The debate took a new turn about 70 years ago with the Heisenberg Uncertainty Principle and the introduction of quantum mechanics. The Uncertainty Principle established that the behavior of the universe was fundamentally random. That is, the most basic processes that underlie the functioning of the universe are unpredictable. Even the simple act of measuring the position and velocity of any particle cannot be carried out without some unavoidable, unpredictable error. This blows determinism right out of the water. If you can't even be sure where an electron is or where it's going, then you certainly can't be sure what a complex system like a human being will do. And if the fundamental processes of the universe are at core random, then there's no way that they can follow a predestined course. Predestination just went down the tubes.

But this was not a triumph for free will. Quantum mechanics replaces determinism with randomness. We aren't predestined to go to hell; it's all a flip of the coin. That doesn't make you feel any better, does it?

Quantum mechanics also had another consequence: not only did it shatter determinism; it also shattered temporal reversibility. This is the notion that the laws of physics can work backwards in time just as well as they work forward. Before quantum mechanics, physicists were embarrassed to admit that they could not explain why time always moves forward. In the entire structure of physics, there wasn't a single fundamental reason for time to be unidirectional. The fact that time is unidirectional was a baffling reality for physics. But quantum mechanics changed all that. (Warning: At this point, I am expounding personal opinions rather than generally acknowledged truths.) For example, the final destruction of Maxwell's Demon (an imaginary creature who violated the Second Law of Thermodynamics, thereby challenging the unidirectionality of time) was not accomplished until Leon Brilloun used quantum-mechanical arguments to finish him off.

But it's easier to see the relationship between quantum mechanics and temporal irreversibility if you think in terms of the Uncertainty Principle. This principle establishes that information knowable about the universe is finite. Now combine this fact with the knowledge that information "draws interest"—that is to say, information gained about a physical system at one time can be combined with information obtained about that system at a later time to gain even greater knowledge of the system, in a manner that exceeds the simple sum of the measured information. The longer you wait between measurements, the more interest (additional information) you can earn from a second measurement. This, of course, would permit you to gain infinite amounts of information about the universe, thereby violating the Uncertainty Principle. Besides, the total amount of information in the universe is finite. The resolution to this apparent quandary lies in the fact that information degrades with time because of the Uncertainly Principle. If you gather information about a physical system and then gather more information at a later time, you won't be able to meaningfully combine the data from the two measurements because the system will have randomly changed in ways that render the combination useless.

Thus, the Uncertainty Principle establishes temporal irreversibility. Time has an unambiguous arrow defined by the necessary degradation of information arising from the Uncertainty Principle.

Reversibility through Undo

But computer applications permit temporal reversibility within their universe through the simple, ubiquitous, and life-saving mechanism of the Undo command. We all know how handy this command is. Whenever we make a mistake, just select that Undo command, and poof!—the mistake disappears. But consider the Undo command from the point of view of a storyteller. That command reverses time, allowing you to jump backwards to a point before you made your mistake. In effect, you go back in time and change your decision.

The use of undo proves your possession of free will. If you type "pig-headed ass," then one could argue that you were predestined to type that phrase, but if you go back and retype it as "suffering from a misunderstanding," then there can be no argument about predestination. Temporal reversibility allows us to prove free will—at least in the tiny universe of a computer program. By the way, this is why infinite undo capability is important—it permits greater exercise of free will.

We don't get temporal reversibility in the real world. Wouldn't it be great if we had an Undo button on a remote control that allowed us to back up and do something over again? Alas, the real world is not so forgiving as the artificial world of a word processor. And this means that we cannot use temporal reversibility in the real world to prove our free will. Falling back on the theological discussion, this suggests that temporal irreversibility is God's kluge to cover up His decision to deny us free will, but allow us the belief that we possess it. If we could go back in time and change our decisions, then we could prove that we have free will. The fact that we can't suggests that maybe we don't . . . right?

Thus, we see theology, physics, and interactivity design all brushing elbows on the issue of free will and determinism. Indeed, the intellectual possibilities here suggest that a merging of interactivity design with theology could yield an exciting new field of research: experimental theology. Think of the possibilities!

An Alternative

As it happens, however, there is another resolution to the problem of free will versus determinism, one that embraces physics and rationalizes faith. It says that God is omnipotent with respect to process, not data. That is, God controls the universe through His laws, but not through the details. God does not dictate the position and velocity of every electron and proton in the universe; instead, He merely declares, "Let there be physics" and then allows the clockwork of the universe to run according to His laws. God's control over the universe has not lessened; it has instead become more abstract, more indirect, and therefore harder to perceive.

This approach provides us with the resolution of our apparent conflict between free will and determinism. God determines the principles under which the universe operates, but grants us free will to choose as we wish within those rules. He even works a little randomness into the system to ensure that we aren't automatons responding robotlike to our environments. The important point is this: God is a process-intensive designer—He specifies not the data but the process!

The same resolution works with the apparent conflict between plot and interactivity. If you are a data-intensive designer, then you are necessarily a deterministic one. Like some Bible-thumping fundamentalist, you insist that every single word you write must be obeyed literally by the characters in the story. The fundamentalist focuses all his beliefs on the data of the Bible rather than the processes behind it.

But if you are a process-intensive designer, then the characters in your universe can have free will within the confines of your laws of physics. To accomplish this, however, you must abandon the self-indulgence of direct control and instead rely on indirect control. That is, instead of specifying the data of the plotline, you must specify the processes of the dramatic conflict. Instead of defining who does what to whom, you must define how people can do various things to each other.

Perhaps you object that this is too esoteric, too abstract to allow the richness of tone that a good story requires. If so, consider what a story communicates. A story is an instance that communicates a principle. *Moby Dick* is not about a whale; it is about obsession. Luke Skywalker is a lie, but the movie's truths about growing up and facing the challenges of manhood are its real message. Stories are literally false, but they embody higher truths. The instances they relate never happened, but the principles they embody are the truth that we appreciate. They are false in their data but true in their process.

Given this, consider the nature of the communication between storyteller and user. The storyteller seeks to communicate some truth, some principle of the human condition. Rather than communicate the truth itself, she creates a particular set of circumstances that instantiate the truth she seeks to communicate. This instantiation is what she communicates to her user. The user then interprets the story, inducing the higher principles from the story's details. Note, however, the indirection of this process. The storyteller seeks to communicate some truth of the human condition; the user seeks to learn the same. Instead of just telling the principle, the storyteller translates the principle into an instantiation and then communicates the instantiation; then the user translates the instantiation back into a principle. This is truly a roundabout way to get the job done.

Interactive storytelling differs from this process in two fundamental ways. First, the process of translating principle into instance is delegated to the computer. The storyteller retains full artistic control, but must now exercise that control at a more abstract and indirect level. The basic scheme of translating principle into instance is retained, but is now performed by the computer. This, of course, entails considerable effort in algorithm creation. The second fundamental difference is that, because the story is generated in real time in direct response to the user's actions, the resultant story is customized to the needs and interests of the user, which compensates for any loss in polish with its greater emotional involvement.

Shrink not from this task; it may sound inhumanly difficult, but it is done all the time, and by amateurs, no less. Here's Grandpa taking little Annie up to bed:

"Tell me a story, Grandpa!" she asks.

"Okay," he replies, "Once upon a time there was a pretty little girl who had a pony. . . . "

"Was it a white pony?" Annie interrupts.

"Oh, my, yes, it was as white as snow. It was so white that the sunlight reflecting off its coat dazzled the eye. And the little girl and the pony would go riding along the beach...."

"Did they go riding in the mountains too?"

"Why yes, as a matter of fact, they did. After riding along the beach, they would ride up the green canyons, jumping over the brush and ducking under tree branches, until they came to the top of the mountains. And there they would play at jumping over boulders. . . . "

"I don't like to jump."

"Well then, instead of jumping, she would let her pony graze in the rich deep grass on the mountain's summit while she sat in the sun...."

And so the story goes on. Note that Grandpa does not respond to Annie's interruptions with "Shuddup, brat, you're messing up my carefully prepared plot!" He wants those interruptions, his storytelling thrives on them. Grandpa does not enter the room with a carefully planned and polished plot, all set to dazzle Annie. He comes in with basic principles of storytelling, and then he makes up the story as he goes along—in response to Annie's needs and interests. The story that he creates is their special story, just for Annie and himself, and no other story will ever be the same. Because it is their special story, it means more and has more emotional power than any high-tech Hollywood extravaganza. Yes, it lacks the careful plotting, the intricate development, and the glorious special effects of the Hollywood product. But its roughness is more than compensated for by its customization. Sure, Annie likes *The Lion King*—but she treasures *Annie and the White Pony*.

Now, if some schmuck of an amateur storytelling grandpa can pull that off, why can't we big-shot professionals do the same?

Other Points of View

The absurdity of the faux dilemma of control versus interactivity leaps out at us when we contemplate the design of productivity applications such as word processors. Can you imagine the designer of a word processor imposing a "standard business letter" on the user, permitting him only a few menus to alter the addressee, the subject, the date, and so forth? The word processor designer has no problem with control; the division of responsibility is clearly drawn: all the data belongs to the user, and all the process belongs to the designer. That's why design of word processors is now considered a solved problem.

Much the same applies to the other productivity applications. Your spreadsheet doesn't come equipped with your budget data on the CD; you provide the data, and it provides the processing. The same thing goes for photo-retouching programs, database programs, drawing and painting programs—the pattern is clear and successful. Note further that these are some of the oldest program families in the world of personal computing. They've gone through so many years of evolution that they've settled down into their optimum configuration: process from the designer, data from the user.

The web offers some difficulties to this view; after all, a web page is basically a collection of data with very little processing. It would seem, then, that the Web violates the division of responsibility so clear with productivity applications. This suggests to me that the web is not far down its evolutionary path. It needs more processing. It is still a pile of answers rather than an answerer of questions.

Turning It Around

Now let's turn this whole approach inside out and look at it from the negative point of view. What, precisely, have we learned from the many failed attempts at interactive storytelling? What is the precise nature of these failures? I would argue that all past efforts in this direction have not been interactive storytelling, but rather "interactivized stories" or "storyized games." At a structural level, they are not storytelling; they are stories. The difference here is profound: it is the difference between the process of storytelling and the result of storytelling (a story). Storytelling is not the same thing as a story: storytelling is an activity, a process, while stories are collections of facts, data. You can't interact with data—you can interact only with processes. Our current efforts at interactivizing stories are as pathetically ignorant as the efforts of Dr. Frankenstein, who saw life as a collection of body parts rather than an interaction of biochemical systems. If only we can stitch together the body parts, he thought, then we can create life. But body parts are not life—they are but the reified manifestations of living processes. Dr. Frankenstein might have kept on, adding more and better body parts, using higher voltages, better stitching techniques, but he was doomed to failure, because his approach was too reified, too thing-oriented and not process-oriented. In the same way, we pursue interactive storytelling by adding more graphics, more animation, more puzzles—more things—to our efforts, but we are just as doomed to failure.

The solution is to shift our thinking from the things of stories to the processes of storytelling. Indeed, the life sciences people have shown the way. Frankenstein was fictitious, but in fact the life sciences people have been making steady progress toward his goal by concentrating their attentions on the processes of life rather than the things of life. Molecular biology, the study of the basic chemical processes of life, is making great strides toward the creation of artificial life. We now toy with living systems, not by stitching body parts together and zapping them with high voltage, but by manipulating the DNA that controls organisms. This is a more abstract but more powerful approach.

In much the same way, we must shift our thinking from the gross parts of stories to the deep abstractions of storytelling. The people who focus their attentions on such details as cinematic technique in interactive storytelling are Igors looking for fresher, stronger body parts.

This abstract approach gives us ready answers to several of the commonly cited objections to interactive storytelling. If you think of an interactive story as a collection of story parts, then the objection that the user must play along with the story parts is compelling. But if you think of interactive storytelling as a process of responding to the user's interests, then behavior that is viewed as perverse in the old model is now seen as informative. "You don't like Juliet? How about someone more like Cindy Crawford? Or Mother Theresa?" If the user is absolutely determined not to play along with anything, then we can't cram entertainment down his throat. What's the problem with this? It's what he wants!

In like fashion, the complaint that interactivity works against the immersive experience is an artifact of the faux-interactive approach we've been using. We whipsaw our users when we present them with an interactivized story, for the interactive aspect of our creation demands activist behavior, but the story aspect demands passive behavior. The basic conflict emerges because the artist insists on taking the user down a predetermined path (as is the case with conventional stories), while at the same time demanding the user's active involvement in the course of the experience. "Let's do it my way!" is a selfish attitude that nobody will pay good money for.

For those readers who are atheists and therefore found the earlier discussion of theology off-putting, here's a different angle: Consider the political power wielded by the president of the United States. It is certainly greater than the political power wielded by any dictator or tyrant in history, yet the president has no direct control over anybody's path. He can't tell you what to eat for dinner, what clothing to wear, what job to work. Yet his power to influence tax policy, foreign trade, and a hundred other areas of life gives him vast power to influence your life. In a more primitive society, the leadership exercised more direct control over a population that was too dumb to take care of itself, but our notions of politics presume a sophisticated population that makes decisions for itself under the indirect control of the government. We have long since discarded the old notions that the population is divided into competent aristocrats and incompetent plebeians.

Yet in the field of the arts, we still cling to such archaic notions. We presume a black-and-white distinction between artists and nonartists. This artificial distinction then vests total control in the hands of the artists, and none in the hands of the plebeians. I would ask, are the plebeians so stupid, so dense, so utterly lacking in artistic sensibility that we cannot afford them some measure of artistic control? The fact that some people are more artistically advanced than others does not argue for total control on their part, only control at a higher level of indirection.

Trust the people. Trade direct control over a small pie for indirect influence over a larger pie.

27

THE TWO-CULTURES PROBLEM

Interactivity design lies at the juncture between arts/humanities and science/engineering. The chasm between these two cultures explains the dismal state of interactivity design. This chasm must be bridged.

About 40 years ago, a British philosopher named C. P. Snow pointed out that Western intellectual culture had bifurcated into two mutually antagonistic subcultures: an arts/humanities subculture and a science/engineering subculture. Much hand wringing was expended over the fear that this "two-cultures problem" might worsen. Technology without soul is antisocial, and art without technology is feckless.

I don't know if the situation has improved or deteriorated since C. P. Snow's time, but I do know that right now, it's bad, and the problems reach like a carcinoma's tentacles through much of the body intellectual.

Techie Pinheads

I am most familiar with the technical people, and I have plenty of nasty things to say about them. They're so bloody narrow minded! Not the best of them, mind you: the best scientists have always enjoyed and respected the arts. It's the rank and file who rankle me by defiling science with their small mindedness. The most obvious manifestation of their narrowness is their stunted lack of appreciation of the arts. Their literature library consists of a few dozen science-fiction books; while many enjoy music, their tastes lack catholicity, concentrating obsessively on some tiny niche in the vast universe of music. In the visual arts, they predictably go for affectless stuff: computer-generated mathematical patterns or integrated circuit layout patterns. Of course, theater, architecture, sculpture, or any of the more "obscure" arts are beyond their ken.

Sadly, many of them try to organize their lives, relationships, and feelings along logical or engineering lines. An argument with a spouse is transformed into a debate over efficiency; vacations are organized for maximum areal coverage or minimum travel times. The most absurd expenses for technical toys are rationalized on trumped-up grounds of productivity. I don't offer these observations to establish personal depravity; we all have our foibles, and these behaviors are mere peccadilloes. My purpose in this paragraph is to illustrate a mindset that in other areas has poisonous consequences.

Those consequences arise from an imaginary and artificial segregation of the arts from the sciences. Indeed, "segregation" is too delicate a term; the attitude is just another form of bigotry. Most S&E people hold arts and humanities to be intellectually flaccid, lacking the demanding requirements of the sciences. They disdain the ambiguities and subtleties of A&H as self-indulgent subjectivity, inferior to the disciplined objectivity of the sciences. S&E people consider themselves indubitably superior to A&H people. (Again, I exclude the better and brighter members of the S&E community from this generalization.) A&H people were the ones who couldn't hack the tough courses in school and ended up in the arts classes—which were little more than glorified basket-weaving courses. How many times was our brilliant S&E guy solicited for help with simple algebra by those A&H pansies? And remember how seldom he reciprocated such a request—as if he had time to waste on those A&E classes in the first place! Of course, there were many cute A&H chicks needing help, and so few S&E chicks . . . .

Yes, sexism gets intermingled with the intellectually bigotry. We can't deny that a strong majority of S&E people are XYs, and that, to a lesser extent, the reverse is the case with A&H. Those S&E males view A&H males with some contempt, and A&H females as fuzzy-headed sweeties. By contrast, they view S&E females with some trepidation. Clearly, such females are worthy of respect, but they can also be dangerous: should they prove superior in technical expertise, they could humiliate the S&E guy in the canine hierarchy of male S&E communities.

Thus, S&E people build a wall—they think of it as a floor—between themselves and the A&H people. They don't mix, they don't share ideas, and they disdain the values of the A&H people.

Artsy Anger

But now I turn my baleful glance toward the A&H people who, being human, are afflicted with their own foibles. They, too, narrow their perspective, but in different ways and for different reasons. At some unconscious level, they acknowledge a germ of truth in S&E's superiority complex. They, too, remember their school days and those humiliating science and math courses. It pains them to recall how stupid and incompetent they were made to feel. Homework problems that reduced the A&H person to helpless babbling would evince a patronizing smile and a breezy solution from their S&E friends. Even the brightest, most successful, and most confident student of A&H felt like a kindergartener in introductory physics.

Combine the proven but meaningless incompetence of the A&H person with the obvious sense of superiority of the S&E person (emotional subtlety is unknown to S&E people), and you have the makings of a deeply imbued resentment. Add the creeping invasion of technology into our daily lives (gadzooks! computers in the art studio! is nothing sacred?), and the resentment smolders. To top it off, let's have society lionize and reward Bill Gates and his like, and the resentment bursts into flame. A&H people resent S&E with a frightening but well-concealed intensity. They can't admit that resentment to others or even to themselves; it's not "adult." But its symptoms are obvious—and destructive.

Consider the laggardness of A&H's embrace of the computer. This endlessly capable device should have penetrated every realm of human endeavor all but instantaneously. S&E pounced on it, business embraced it, but A&H accepted it hesitantly. As the computer revolution surges irresistibly forward, A&H brings up the rear. Search the Internet for software; you'll find terabytes of S&E stuff, gigabytes of business programs, and a smattering of A&H software.

There is no justification for the paucity of A&H software; the world of A&H can benefit just as much from computers as any other area. Nor can A&H people plead poverty; a huge amount of software is written by amateurs and made available for free. The reason for this deficiency lies in the fear and resentment that A&H people bear toward the S&E world. The computer is, after all, S&E to the core. Attempt to purchase a computer, and the salesperson tests your technical expertise: how many megabytes? Will that be with a DVD and an internal modem? Will you take a Pentium IV at 1800 MHz or a plain old Pentium III at 700 MHz? You're going to spend a thousand bucks on a computer and you don't even know what a CPU is?

Pull your new computer out of the box and smell that high-tech aroma of plastic and electronics. Fire it up, and you face more tests. The operating system wants to know what options you desire—options expressed in acronyms that you never heard of. What's a TCP/IP? What if it fell out of the computer during unpacking? I bought 256 MB—that was a big decision that I'm proud of—but now the operating system is offering me more megabytes if I want them—but what's the difference between a virtual megabyte and the normal kind? You poor, dumb, presumptuous A&H brat; how dare you enter the S&E domain!

But the worst comes when, in despair, you turn to technical assistance. If you call some company's technical support line, the customer service rep treats you like an idiot ("Did you remember to plug it in?") and cannot conceal his impatience with your mental slowness. (Have you ever noticed that tech support people are almost always male, while every other business on the planet employs mostly women for customer service work, knowing that they are often better at human relations?) Once again, just like old school days, the S&E people are making you feel stupid. Bah!

Why Don't Artists Program?

Suppose, however, that you claw your way through the confusing and often inappropriate instructions. You now have a functioning computer. More travails follow as you attempt to master some of the standard applications: word processing, email, and so on. If you are so thick-skinned that you can endure these slings and arrows and press further, an even more chilling prospect awaits you. Like some computer game, you master each level only to be presented with a more difficult level—and the final level always has the biggest, meanest, toughest monster of them all. In your case, that monster is programming.

Software is the only thing that makes computers useful; the potential utility of a computer to any person is only as great as the supply of software pertinent to that person's pursuits. Whence comes such software? Most people answer that question with "programmers"—but that is incorrect. Programmers have nothing more to do with software creation than printers have to do with book creation. Both functions are necessary for the completion of the process, but with books we recognize that the truly hard part is not done by the printer, but by the author. Why can't we do the same with programmers?

Yes, programming demands considerable technical skill, but so does printing. A more convincing explanation is that writing a book is less technically demanding than creating a program. But step back for a moment and consider the amount of expertise that must be brought to bear on the task of writing a book. We'll not concern ourselves with the content—only the technical requirements. First is the mastery of the language used. We take that for granted because we have already learned that language, and we use it daily, but that does not permit us to ignore the requirement. Consider, then, that the author of a book has years of experience with the language and plenty of expertise in spelling, vocabulary, and grammar. There is also, of course, the requirement that the author master a word processing program, but that task is small compared to the previous one.

Closed A&H Minds

I submit the admittedly controversial claim that programming isn't difficult. I consider it to be a glorified form of accounting. I further submit that any normal human being can learn to program.

Yet my own experience disproves my claims. I have on two occasions undertaken to teach an A&H person to program. In each case, we used an easy, entry-level language, not the clanking, hissing monstrosities that professional programmers use. Both of my students were bright—no, brilliant—people with a pressing need to learn the material. And yes, I confess: both were cute chicks.

Both attempts failed. Both students made every effort, but in the end, their understanding of programming was too superficial to permit them to actually do anything, however simple, with their knowledge. They just didn't get it.

Yet I refuse to accept this result. I blame the students for their failure, but I don't question their intelligence, their effort, or their sincerity. These women were obstructed by their emotional orientation. As A&H people, they simply could not embrace the linear, disciplined thinking of S&E. I refuse to accept the excuse that the human mind, once set in its mode of thinking, is incapable of adopting any other mode; I have seen too many cases of normal people switching modes (under the right conditions) to accept that switching modes is an unusual or difficult task. When I taught physics for nonscientists, some of the A&H students were able to embrace and revel in the strict linear thinking of that field, and some could never get it. Strikingly, the difference between the successes and the failures was not intelligence, but an emotional openness, a willingness to try on different hats just for fun. But I was seeing these students in their early college years, before they had learned the mores of the A&H culture. It wasn't their mode of thinking that hardened later, but their sense of identification with A&H and its concomitant (and unnecessary) rejection of all things S&E, including its mode of thinking. Have you noticed that the phrase "linear thinking" is the A&H disparaging euphemism for "S&E thinking"?

Tribalism

Hence, we have an impenetrable wall between A&H and S&E, enthusiastically erected by both sides. Their tribal identities are well established; the pom-pom girls for each side whip up the barbaric anti-otherness cheers. "Hooray for our side! Boo-hiss on theirs!"

The penalty we pay for this tribalistic nonsense has been light for the last few decades, but with the advent of interactivity design, the problem punches us in the solar plexus. Interactivity design requires both styles of thinking, an integration of A&H with S&E.

You need only look at the software we have created to appreciate the magnitude of this problem. Consider computer games, S&E's attempt to apply the computer to an A&H kind of use. They're terrible! True, they're fine for the underdeveloped minds of kids, but how many mature adults actually enjoy computer games? Perhaps I should rephrase that question: how many non-S&E adults actually enjoy computer games? We all know the answer: precious few.

The reason for this failure is immediately obvious to any A&H observer: computer games lack heart and soul. They come in two flavors: nihilistic, blood-drenched orgies of killing and violence requiring fast reflexes and tricky strategy; and puzzle games that are pointless exercises in obscure logic, random guesswork, and tedious trial and error. Those poor S&E people don't understand the most basic truths of A&E, so they grind out endless clones of these two flavors.

Software Sucks

Consider now the sorry situation of computer operating systems. Let's be honest: Windows is a cruel joke on the innocent user. Like some twisted adventure game, it bristles with trap doors, hidden compartments, lurking monsters, rolling boulders, and secret doors. I'm quite certain that, if I use Windows long enough, someday I shall certainly find the captive princess hidden inside it.

I myself am afraid to mess with my PC because Windows' complexities befuddle me; its propensity for damaging error terrifies me. But I'm not the only person befuddled by Windows. When I get in trouble with it, I call my old friend Dave. Dave's a whiz with this stuff; he has assembled, configured, and fixed hundreds of PCs. He's had a variety of software jobs, many of them at a higher level of technical responsibility than programming. Despite all this expertise, Dave still has problems getting Windows to work. He slices through the easy problems, the kind that clobber you and me, with alacrity. But every now and then, I come up with a problem that stumps him. He always solves it in the end, but it's scary just how hard it can be for an expert like him.

Why are computer operating systems so blasted hard to use? I believe that the primary deep cause is the shortage of A&H people in the computer community. In the first place, S&E people don't mind technical messiness; indeed, they enjoy having more buttons to push. Because the A&H people have entered the computer marketplace late and in dribbles, computer makers cater to their primary customers: S&E people who don't mind messy user interfaces. Moreover, the shortage of A&H people makes it difficult for computer makers to find and hire A&H people with computer expertise. So we end up with an operating system that, if it were a person, would be institutionalized and sedated.

The Gloomy Prospect

The two-cultures war is now older than most of its participants. The world of computer games is soulless and antisocial, exactly as C. P. Snow would have predicted. Most of the artists engaged in interactive design have reduced themselves to utter fecklessness because they refuse to confront the technology of the computer on its own terms. They insist on treating the computer as nothing more than a souped-up version of the technologies with which they are already familiar. To these people, the computer's attraction comes from the ease with which they can now assemble exactly the same kind of art that they've been assembling for decades. The computer is an audiovisual device, a digital VCR/slide projector/tape recorder—nothing more. It's the Same Old Shit, digitized and a thousand times faster. The possibility that something entirely new might be in the offing does not seem to loom large in their thinking.

After many attempts to help the two warring camps cooperate in the colonization of the interactivity universe, I have come to the unhappy conclusion that this union will not come about any time soon. The two sides are just too far apart and too set in their ways to accept the kind of major change in thinking required to pull it off. When it does come about, my hunch is that the artists will lead the way, not the techies. The artists are lean and hungry, whereas the techies are fat and happy. Computer games make enough money to confirm industry prejudices; little change will come from that direction. The artists, at least, are still struggling, and out of all this struggle, a few pioneers will emerge who will show everybody else the way.

Prescriptions

Here's what you should do if you're from the S&E tribe: first, read some literature. Don't confine yourself to science fiction. It's not that I have anything against science fiction; some of my best friends are science-fiction writers. It's just that you need more breadth. When was the last time you read Shakespeare? There are zillions of great books out there, and they didn't become classics by wasting people's time. Spend some time with other art forms, but pay attention when you do. Some of that stuff is immensely clever, but you can't appreciate it with a quick glance. You have to take the time to understand the subtleties. If you doubt this, just go back and reread one of those classics you hated so much in high school. It'll read a lot differently from the perspective of a mature adult.

As for you A&H people, I have three specific recommendations. First, make no apologies and feel no shame for your supposed lack of intelligence; difficulty understanding technical material in no manner bespeaks stupidity. It's just a different dimension of intelligence. Second, indulge the S&E people their emotional clumsiness. Just as you can't hack calculus, they don't understand the human condition. It's not their fault that they act like clods; it's just their thinking style. Third, learn to program; you can't evade that requirement for interactivity design.

Last, to everyone I make a plea: we must not tolerate two-cultures prejudice. We must promulgate a cherishing of the bridge-building task between the two cultures. We must applaud those hardy souls who dangle in the chasm between the two cultures, drawing thin strands of community between the two sides. We must disdain those pig-headed fools who dig their heels into their side of the chasm and snarl epithets at the opposite side. The magic of the interactive medium is not to be found on either side of the chasm; it pulsates somewhere in the airy space between them, the void populated by a nimble few who clamber like monkeys on the thin skein of ropes that now constitute the only bridge between the two cultures. This is the territory we must explore and colonize.

Don't look down—it's a long way to the bottom.

28

INTERACTIVE STORYTELLING

Interactive storytelling is a new field in interactivity design, explicitly combining the artistic with the technical. It is not at all like conventional storytelling, requiring a more abstract approach.

This unconventional topic deserves special treatment because I think that it promises to become a major new field of interactivity design.

What Interactive Storytelling Is Not

My first task is to disabuse you of the many wrong-headed notions about interactive storytelling currently bouncing around. First, interactive storytelling is not some kind of altered computer game. Computer games are a well-defined medium placing a premium on action, animation, spatial reasoning, resource management, and graphic spectacle. These desiderata confine computer gaming to a subset of the population, mostly young S&E males. Interactive storytelling is aimed at the general population; hence, its desiderata are profoundly different. The story comes first: plot and character command more design attention than cosmetic factors. Moreover, interactive storytelling will attract a completely different set of authors, publishers, distributors, and retailers than computer gaming utilizes.

Interactive storytelling is not interactive fiction. The latter field is the next-generation text adventure; its adherents prize parser quality, puzzle depth, and mapping cleverness. Plot and character rank only secondary status.

Interactive storytelling is not digital storytelling. This term applies to the use of the computer in conventional storytelling as a tool for producing components previously handled with other technologies.

Interactive storytelling is not the same thing as interactive stories. This latter term is a misnomer and a technical impossibility. A story, once created, is frozen in place by its plot; interaction is impossible. A story is information, which cannot be interacted with. Storytelling, on the other hand, is a process—which can be interacted with.

The Difference between an Interactive Story and a Conventional Story

Let's consider an "interactivized" *Romeo and Juliet*. The original is a single story about a single couple in a single context with a single outcome. By itself, the story is meaningless; who cares about a couple of Italian twits who died hundreds of years ago? What makes the story compelling is its generalizable relevance to our lives. I'm not Romeo, but I, too, have been torn between conflicting personal loyalties. Thus, I may not learn from his precise example, but I derive benefit from a generalization of the forces at work in the original play.

Thus, an interactive *Romeo and Juliet* would *not* be about Romeo and Juliet; it would be about the collision between love and social obligations. This distinction is crucial to understanding the advantages—and disadvantages—of interactive storytelling. If you insist that an interactive *Romeo and Juliet* must be about Romeo and Juliet, then you must also insist that it follow the plot of the original play. But if instead you shift your point of view and require that an interactive *Romeo and Juliet* be about the collision between love and social obligation, then a great many plot developments are possible that remain true to the work.

Consider the nature of the truth regarding the collision between love and social obligation. Such truth is complex and multidimensional; nobody could reduce it all to a single statement. Yet understanding it is vital to our existence as human beings. So how can our wise ones communicate such truths to our younger ones? Storytelling is one way to do so, but a single story offers only a single glimpse at a broader truth. *Romeo and Juliet* shows us just one facet of this multifaceted jewel of truth. If we wish to understand the matter, we must have other glimpses from different angles. If in one such glimpse, Romeo and Juliet live happily ever after because they have found one resolution to the conflict between love and social obligation, then what is wrong with that? It would be false to *Romeo and Juliet*, but it would be true to the point and purpose of the work. So what's our goal here? Is our goal to kill off Romeo and Juliet or to reveal something about love?

Consider an analogy. Suppose I asked a painter to create a portrait of me. This painter is an artist who seeks to capture the essence of my nature in this portrait. She labors long and hard and eventually brings forth a portrait showing me with mouth open and index finger raised in profound expostulation. A true and insightful portrait, some would say. But now suppose that, displeased with this portrait, I engage another painter, who produces a portrait of me as programmer/writer/worker drudge, slaving away at the keyboard while the wonders of nature parade by unnoticed? This, too, would be a true and insightful portrait, but how do we resolve the conflict between the two portraits? Which is the "correct" portrait?

The difference between an interactive *Romeo and Juliet* and the original *Romeo and Juliet* is the same difference as that between Chris Crawford and a portrait of Chris Crawford. Yes, the portrait contains a single truth, powerfully made. (Who knows? Perhaps Ms. Mona Lisa was really just a dull Italian housewife, nowhere near as intriguing as her portrait.) But ultimately, it presents a single truth, where interactivity provides many viewing angles to truth. Some of those viewing angles will not be as dramatic or as powerful as others. We should not dismiss interactivity as inferior because it fails to winnow out the less revealing angles. Interactivity shows all of the viewpoints on a truth, strong and weak. Its catholicity of viewpoint is it strength; its undiscriminating nature is its weakness. Let us not c ndemn it for its weakness without also recognizing its concomitant strength.

Every word processor contains within it gazillions of potential letters and memos; every spreadsheet carries the seeds of countless budgets and profit/loss statements. We need merely supply the details to let the final result spring to life. It would be absurd of me to expect my word processor to write this book for me; the same lesson applies to interactive storytelling.

Abstracting Storytelling

After thousands of years of stasis, we are ready to move storytelling to higher levels of abstraction. What exactly do we mean by greater abstraction when we talk about storytelling? I don't know for sure—how could a Venetian merchant of 1360 A.D. understand a credit card? Our approach must be to move away from the specifics of storytelling and think in terms of the grander principles. We need to invent higher-level constructs. What relates to storytelling as a credit card relates to coins?

Recall that the storyteller has a Big Idea. He translates the Big Idea into a story. The story is not the same as the Big Idea; it is only a single instance of the Big Idea at work. He then communicates the story to the audience, and the audience induces the Big Idea from the example.

What if that first translation, from Big Idea to story, were not done by the storyteller but by the computer in collaboration with the audience? In other words, we simply transfer the process of instantiation from storyteller to computer. The storyteller still defines and controls the Big Idea, but rather than expressing the Big Idea through a single instance, he expresses the Big Idea itself in more abstract terminology. He communicates the Big Idea to the audience in the form of a computer program. The audience runs the computer program, which interacts with the audience in such a way as to spawn a story expressing the Big Idea while matching the interests of the audience.

It's obviously impossible to achieve a perfect match between creator's control and audience's interests, but this impossibility has always existed with conventional stories and has never been a serious impediment. So long as we can get enough overlap between the interests of the audience and those of the creator, the problem will not be serious.

Another, more important issue concerns the mechanics of this process. Exactly how does the storyteller express the Big Idea itself in more abstract terminology? What is the abstract expression of a story?

A story is a statement of the mechanics of the human condition. Its simplest form is, "X did this, and Y resulted," from which the audience induces, "If I do X, then Y will result." The step from "X led to Y" to "if X, then Y" is the fundamental induction of storytelling. (Yes, it's a classic case of *post hoc, ergo propter hoc*, but stories aren't exercises in logic.) And herein lies a crucial difference between conventional storytelling and interactive storytelling. A conventional storyteller expresses "X led to Y." An interactive storyteller expresses "If X, then Y." The conventional storyteller, being in total control, spells out every detail of X and Y. The interactive storyteller has no such control and must instead recognize the audience's version of X and generate a version of Y that properly corresponds to the stipulated X.

There's an immensely important idea here: that of creative collaboration between the designer of a program and the user of the program. With interactivity, we blur the hard lines that separate the creator from the audience. Instead of dividing the world into creators and dullards, we share creativity in a measured way. The audience gets just enough creative freedom to meet its needs, and the heavy-duty creativity remains under the control of the high-powered creators. With other media, we have a simple choice between artistic tyranny and artistic anarchy; interactivity permits something like constitutional democracy. The audience can do anything it pleases within the constitutional guidelines established by the artist. Isn't it wonderful? How small-minded are those who resist this magnificent new opportunity!

You might object: but what if the audience abuses its responsibilities? Look here: ksdhia wo;hkjnd kjh sdfast sd. I just typed a bunch of garbage. My word processor permits failure! But I'm a big boy; I can accept responsibility for my actions. If I type garbage, I don't feel bad if I get garbage coming out of the printer. And the same thing applies to interactive storytelling. What's wrong if the audience playfully experiments with perverse behavior and discovers idiotic results? Isn't that part of the truth of the universe, too?

Getting back to storytelling, the solution is to divide each party's contribution along the lines of process and data. Let the designer specify the processes of the story world, the dramatic rules under which it operates. Let the audience provide the data operated upon by the artist's rules. The artist's process plus the audience's data yields a single story. The same processes with another set of data yields a different story. This is interactive storytelling. Although the implementation is difficult, the concept is clear and simple. All the other crap floating around about branching, multiple storylines, interleaving, and so on is either irrelevant or secondary.

Now for an unfortunate aspect of narrative abstraction: it requires more work and bigger structures. Consider how financial abstraction makes sense only with bigger economies. The use of money makes sense only if I believe that somebody else will take my money in return for goods. If I live in a tiny world with just one other person, money has no utility. A credit card is useful to consumers only if there are lots of retailers that accept it, and it's useful to retailers only if there are lots of consumers who use it. Suppose, in a moment of twisted humor, that God had equipped medieval Europeans with the technology for credit cards. They still couldn't have used them, because their economies were too small to make them worthwhile. Most people didn't have any money to spend anyway. What's a starving peasant supposed to do with a credit card—buy a cellular telephone? A television set? What use is a credit card in a world without credit agencies, in which credit card slips must be carried on horseback to a processing center?

Or consider how political abstraction requires magnitude. Let's start off with the assumption that the Constitution of the United States is a good thing. Fine; let's use it for the Chris Crawford Fan Club. Unfortunately, the CCFC has only six members: Chris Crawford, Khublai Khat, Penelope Pig, Galahad Goat, Binky Burro, and Darth Duck. So, I will be the president, and Khublai Khat will be vice president, and Penelope Pig will be speaker of the house, and...wait a minute, who's gonna be the senators? And where will we get a House of Representatives? It's impossible to apply the Constitution to a small polity. With a group as microscopic as the Chris Crawford Fan Club, a simple dictatorship might be the only thing that works. (Knowing my luck, I'd probably be ousted and replaced by Penelope Pig.)

Here's the problem: the logical links between abstraction and system size point both ways. As a system grows more complex, it requires additional abstraction, but additional abstraction makes sense only with more complex systems. Thus, if we are to take advantage of narrative abstraction, we must also expand the content of our storytelling.

The basic concept here is to think of the larger issues treated by the story. Recall my earlier claims that a story is a single instance of a principle at work. Narrative abstraction requires that we tell the whole principle, not just a single example of it. Consider, for example, the simple morality tale presented in the movie *Fatal Attraction*. In the movie, of course, we present a single tale with a single outcome. The "best" outcome was a matter of some dispute; only after the movie was tested with a number of audiences and alternative endings was the "best" outcome selected. But there was clearly some uncertainty as to the best outcome; why did they have to discard the alternatives? The subject of adultery is not a simple black-and-white moral issue; if it were that simple, why is it so common? This is a complex issue, one that faces millions of men and women every day. Surely its complexity cannot be adequately addressed in any single story.

There are so many variables to consider in debating adultery. What if the wife is frigid? What if the husband brings home a disease? What if the wife is the one having the affair? What if she does it in retaliation for his affair? How does a one-night drunken fling compare with an extended affair? No single story can hope to cover all these issues. It can emphatically make an isolated point, but it can never address the broad issue. It can powerfully describe a single tree, but never the forest.

This is where narrative abstraction enters our vision. The subject of *Fatal Attraction* was not adultery but rather a single case of adultery. The subject of an analogous interactive environment must necessarily be adultery, not any single case of adultery.

This is why all the attempts to "interactify" existing stories are doomed to failure. You can't climb up in abstraction by taking a single example and magnifying it. Finance did not evolve by mere magnification; huge financial transactions are not carried out with forklifts moving gold coins the size of manhole covers. So long as you think about finance in terms of coins, you'll never get the idea. So long as you think about politics in terms of who gets to be king, you'll never understand democracy. So long as you think about anatomy in terms of eating and reproduction, you'll never understand why the brain evolved. And so long as you think about interactive storytelling in terms of individual stories, you'll never get the idea.

This demands far more of the storyteller than any single story ever demands. The conventional storyteller can contrive the situation to focus attention on the key point. The interactive storyteller must think in larger terms, must be more open-minded about her point. Instead of proving that a single case of adultery can be disastrous, she must instead treat adultery in all its guises and variations. There are cases in which adultery is understandable; there are cases in which it does little harm; there are cases in which it is despicable.

Here's another objection: what becomes of emotional power in such circumstances? *Fatal Attraction* scared the bejabbers out of a generation of husbands; how could *A Simulation of the Ethical Implications of Extramarital Sexual Liaisons* ever have that kind of impact?

Remember, we're talking interactivity here; there is always a huge emotional boost whenever the audience gets to control the action, even if the results aren't as dramatically powerful as those produced by the professionals. When Uncle Fredegund and Aunt Martha go to San Francisco, they stop by the Golden Gate Bridge to take a picture. Sure, it's not the best photograph ever taken of the Golden Gate Bridge; Aunt Martha is struggling to keep her hat from blowing away, and there are two brats strangling a seagull in the background. It would have been easier and cheaper for them to buy a picture postcard with a photograph taken by a professional photographer in a helicopter on the one day of the year when the fog and the light were absolutely perfect. But a few years from now, that amateurish photograph will have much more emotional power for them than the professional's work. If you're a professional artist, and you want to reach your audience, you want them in the picture. If you could combine your professionalism with their active presence, would that not be grand?

There is one problem that profoundly troubles me, though. The implicit assumption in storytelling is that the storyteller is wiser than the audience. The storyteller has some wisdom to impart to the audience, and the audience is prepared to accept her claim to wisdom. But the interactive storyteller must do so much more; she must be that much wiser. Is there anybody wise enough to create an interactive storytelling world? I don't know.

My Own Work in Interactive Storytelling

A number of researchers have approached interactive storytelling as a problem of simulating characters. I used this approach in 1987 with Siboot and concluded that it led nowhere. Its problem is its failure to focus on the verbs. Nevertheless, several worthy efforts have been made by concentrating on character simulation, and although I myself do not think it the best strategy, I do not question the possibilities inherent in these efforts. Interestingly, this difference of opinion as to the importance of characters versus verbs mirrors the classic argument in storytelling between character-based writers and plot-based writers.

I have spent most of the 1990s building a technology for interactive storytelling. It has been a huge task, and I have made many mistakes along the way, but I am convinced that my fundamental approach is sound and, indeed, the best overall strategy for achieving interactive storytelling.

My approach centers on the verbs available to the characters—remember the first admonition of Chapter 8: start with the verbs. Organizing the design around the verbs completely changes the technology and the design process—for the better, I believe.

The heart of my technology is the storytelling engine. The engine's basic task is to execute verbs. Each verb can lead to another verb, and so on, generating a long sequence of events: a story. The verbs are created and specified by the author. Each verb can generate a number of options for other actors. Which options are available and the rules by which those actors choose among the options are again specified by the author. The human protagonist is given control of one actor and makes the choices for that actor.

The engine uses an extensible personality model with several dozen personality traits for each actor. It automatically handles the direct interactions of actors, as well as their indirect interactions through conversations and gossip. Actors can learn of past deeds and react to them after the fact. They can anticipate the consequences of their revelations and selectively reveal information to each other. They can tell lies about each other and trace the path of gossip backwards to find its source. They can recall past favors and transgressions; they can pursue revenge and abort plans if new information causes them to change their minds.

The user's options are calculated by the storytelling engine and sent to the interface, which then presents them to the user for choice in a menu-like fashion. Typically, the user has three to seven choices, such as "Oh, yeah? Take that! (punch)"; "I'm really sorry I did that; please forgive me"; or "Kiss me!"

All of this is handled by a second program, the Erasmatron. The engine actually executes the interactive storytelling; the Erasmatron is the development environment used by the author to specify and edit the data and rules fed into the engine. The Erasmatron includes editors, navigational aids, and rehearsal tools. The big idea behind the Erasmatron is to make interactive storytelling technology directly accessible to artists. What makes this radical step possible is a transfer of the programming task to the artist in a form that is comfortable and accessible. I have created a special programming/storytelling language that jettisons all the picky trivia that make programming such a tedious process.

For example, the storybuilder does not type words in this language; input is made by selecting pieces and assembling them into larger expressions. This obviates syntax errors; it is impossible to say something wrong because the Erasmatron won't let you choose inappropriate items. Another feature is the use of strong visual cues. Relationships are spelled out on the screen in meaningful terms such as Affection or Greed, rather than with cryptic acronyms. Colors and underlining provide additional reminders. Wherever possible, the Erasmatron double-checks the artist's work to catch simple mistakes.

The first task of the storybuilder is to create a cast of actors. Each actor must be given a name and numbers for such personality traits as Libido and Gullible. The stages on which the drama takes place must next be specified, with rules of access for different actors. The props that are used during the story must be defined, and ownership assigned.

The main task facing the storybuilder is the creation of a large set of verbs. The verbs are really the heart of the story world; I believe that a good story world requires at least a thousand verbs. Each verb must have a set of roles. A role is a dramatic slot into which an actor might fit. For example, if Puncher punches Punchee, then one role might be Punchee's Best Friend, who presumably would come to the Punchee's defense. Another role might be Punchee's Girlfriend, whom we would expect to scream, rush to console Punchee, and possibly hurl a few epithets at Puncher. There could also be Intervening Bystander, who might step if the fight goes too far. We could even have Timid Bartender, who might want to duck behind the bar or call the cops. Whenever a verb is executed, each of the witnessing actors consults each of the roles, asking whether they fit that role. If the actor does fit the role, then he executes it, deciding which of the role's responses to choose. These decisions are made according to the rules and actor traits specified by the storybuilder. They can take into account details such as the properties of the stage on which the action takes place, the props available to the actor, even the past history of the story.

A comprehensive set of screen-test and rehearsal tools in the Erasmatron help the storybuilder assess the overall performance of the story world, identify problem areas, and correct them.

My interactive storytelling technology has not attracted much attention. I believe that its complexity drives people away. Most people are still hopeful that interactive storytelling can be achieved by some reasonably simple technology; the gargantuan intricacy of the Erasmatron is more than they are willing to tackle. Most people sidle up to the problem, bash their heads into it for a while, and then give up, only to be replaced by a new generation of naïve hopefuls. I started bashing my head against the problem much earlier than others and am blessed with a harder head; I was therefore able to bash my way through to a solution. When the demand for interactive storytelling grows strong enough, and enough heads have been bashed, people will hitch up their belts, take a deep breath, and reluctantly return to my hairy technology. As I write these words, my patent still has another 12 years. I can wait. In the meantime, you can look up my stuff at www.erasmatazz.com.

29

SUBJUNCTIVITY

 Language is a vehicle of thinking. Natural language is clumsy with subjunctive thinking. Interactivity provides a language that supports subjunctive thinking.

Let's hearken back to Chapter 25 with its silly story of the history of interactivity. Let's try it again, only this time with a different emphasis and style.

Imagine that you are Mother Nature playing around with your first little animals. Since they have to move around, you need a control system to make certain that the legs all operate in the correct order. That's pretty simple: a string of neurons controlled from a central point, sending the appropriate messages at the appropriate times. This is simple motor output control.

Your next big step is the addition of sensory inputs to the control process. It's easy to see how this evolved from small beginnings. The simplest version would be pain reception, which is nothing more than the final high-frequency squawk of a fatally damaged neuron. You simply establish than any saturated response (lots of spikes coming down the axons at the maximum frequency) constitutes a pain input, and your critter will respond to this with some sort of cathartic behavior (run! jump! jerk away!) This is a reliable system; it ensures that almost anything that's too much to handle (too much light, too much heat, too much pressure, too strong an odor) will trigger the pain response and a quick reaction.

Later, you can improve this system with specialized sensory receptors. You could attach a single photoreceptor neuron to the top of the head, and when it signals a sudden decrease in light input (possibly caused by the appearance of a large predator), your critter will scuttle away quickly. Later again, you could add more photoreceptors, and then optical imaging systems—which, of course, require more neurons in the brain to process all those images—and then other sensory inputs (auditory, olfactory, temperature, and so on).

The basic structure of your nervous system design is still pretty simple: a bunch of sensory inputs feeding into a bunch of motor outputs. But as your design grows, you encounter a new problem arising from its greater complexity: how do you process the more complex sensory inputs? After all, a sensory input of an object moving in your critter's visual field could be a predator, or it could be prey. How do you distinguish different responses based on subtle differences in sensory input?

This is, at core, a problem in pattern recognition. One pattern of inputs indicates prey, another pattern of inputs represents predator, a third pattern of inputs suggests a potential mate. You need a system for recognizing subtly different patterns and responding to them appropriately. The solution to this problem is the neural net, a group of neurons with multiply connected dendrites, multiple inputs, differential thresholds, and so forth. Such a structure can easily handle pattern recognition problems—and that, in fact, is what evolved.

This basic design takes you up through the reptiles, and it is wondrously effective. It can even handle a modicum of learning, in a highly condensed form. The trick here is to take all experiences and categorize them into a small set of operationally meaningful groups. For example, if your dinosaur tugs on a tree limb and hears it crack and nothing happens, then there's no reason to store that data. But suppose that the dinosaur tugs on the tree limb, hears it crack, and then suffers a blow to the head from the broken limb. The cracking sound is associated with pain—that's operationally meaningful, so it stores the cracking sound into a category that should cause it to flinch or respond cautiously. Call this category *fear*. Perhaps I am overrating the dinosaur's mental capabilities by attributing such an emotion to him. If that bothers you, you can call it proto-fear, dinosaur fear, or sub-fear. There will be lots of other experiences that go into the same category with the limb cracking sound: the image of a big predator, a cliff as seen from the top, a poisonous animal. The dinosaur doesn't have to engage in complex reasoning: the sensory pattern triggers the fear response, which then triggers the appropriately cautious behavior. The same thing would apply to other proto-emotions, such as lust, hunger, anger, and so on.

In other words, emotion is a primitive system for learning. Instead of having to memorize all of its experiences, the critter simply extracts the few features that are important for its survival and throws away everything else. This highly boiled-down, digested memory of events is emotion.

This idea rings true for me because of my work with interactive storytelling. I have spent years struggling with the problem of how characters remember the events of the story. It is possible, of course, to take a brute-force approach and have the characters remember everything, but I have found this method clumsy and wasteful. I can build a huge database of all the events in the story, but it is rarely consulted by the characters; this bothers me. What I'd like is a system that saves only the significant events; this would be faster to process and less wasteful of memory. Over the years, I have developed a multilevel system in which one level is emotion, a highly digested form of memory. All experiences go through the emotion processor and contribute to its memories; particularly significant events are given more detailed treatment.

Note, however, that if I didn't have much RAM, I'd have to rely on the emotional system exclusively. In the same way, the dinosaurs didn't have enough neurons to waste on detailed memories, so they developed the more efficient system of emotion. It was a great idea, and in fact it worked superbly. If it hadn't been for that damn asteroid, they'd still be running the show. There is no indication that brain size increased during the age of dinosaurs. They had a system that worked, and there was no point in changing it.

At this point, the mammals, losers and wimps though they were, took center stage. Along with various special traits, the mammals brought one special new idea to life's party: bigger brains with a completely new conceptual approach to processing—sequential thinking.

It's difficult for me to articulate just how tricky and special sequential thinking is. We take it for granted and love to disparage it as "linear thinking," but in fact sequential thinking is intricate business. I first sensed this when I began playing with digital electronics some 25 years ago. It was trivially simple to set up circuits that could handle direct stimulus-response relationships; you just slapped some gates together in whatever complicated pattern you desired. Yes, it could get messy, but in design terms it was easy to understand. Then came the day I tried to design a circuit that would process a sequence of bits coming down a wire. All of a sudden, life became vastly more complicated, because the circuit loses its instantaneous stimulus-response nature. You have to define a starting point for the sequence. Then you have to collect the first bit of information. Then you have to store that information. Then you have to wait for the next bit of information. How long should you wait? How do you decide when you've waited too long? What if the second bit of information comes in fast, but the third comes in slowly, and the fourth comes in fast? How do you handle such complexities? Meanwhile, you have to store all the incoming information in a convenient place and then bring it back out when it has been assembled. From this point, things get simpler: once the information is all lined up properly, processing it is just a straightforward pattern recognition issue. But getting it lined up in the first place is the trick.

Fortunately, this system can be built on top of existing pattern recognition neural circuitry. In other words, you can start with a conventional reptilian pattern-recognizing brain and add just a little bit of sequentializing circuitry, and all that sequentializing circuitry has to do is line up a temporal sequence of information into a spatial pattern and then hand the pattern off to the regular pattern-recognizing circuitry. With just that incremental improvement on the reptilian brain, all sorts of new behaviors become possible. For example, suppose that I am a small, wimpy mammal, and a big, nasty predator lunges at me. If I had nothing but direct pattern-recognizing circuitry, I'd have a tough time escaping, but with just a little sequential-processing capability, I have a big advantage: I can process momentum. Suppose that the predator is on the left side of my visual field, and I note that he is moving fast toward the right side of my visual field. By comparing the information on his previous position (left side) with his current position (right side), I can infer that he has lots of momentum toward the right—so if I zag to the left, I can probably shake him. The reasoning process need not be so academic, but the trick hinges on my ability to compare past information with current information: sequential information processing.

Well, if a little is good, then more must be better, right? That's what natural selection seemed to tell the mammals, because they started growing larger cortexes with greater sequential-processing capabilities. Mammals can remember route information, taking circuitous paths around obstacles to reach their destinations; this is an example of more complex sequential thinking. Then the mammalian predators pushed the envelope even further, inventing the concept of the hunt as a complex sequence of steps culminating in dinner. If you have any doubts as to the ability of mammals to engage in sequential thinking, just watch a cat stalk and capture its prey sometime. There's some pretty complicated sequential thinking going on in that furry head. Even more fascinating is the complex interaction between mammalian predator and mammalian prey. From stalking and evasion to the chase, the process is loaded with complex mental twists and turns as each tries to anticipate the opponent's move and counter it. By contrast, the mammalian hunter's relationship with reptilian prey is much simpler: the prey's defense lies in venom, camouflage, inaccessibility, or speed. There's nothing like the death dance between coyote and jackrabbit. And reptiles themselves don't hunt in the formal sense; that's too sequential. They wander around looking for an opportunity, and when they come across one, they strike; that's all.

Then came the primates, and they apparently "decided" to invest a higher percentage of their biological capital into even bigger brains. This gave them the capacity for more complex social structures than any of the other mammals had, which, in turn, gave them a competitive advantage. With the hominids, we saw the first evidence of tool use. Pause for a moment to consider how utterly alien tool making is to pattern recognition. It's not as if you can look at a chunk of flint and see cleanly scraped animal hides incipient in it. You have to think in a long, long sequence about how you could chip the flint to make it sharp, then carry the flint to a freshly killed animal, and then use the flint to scrape the meat off the hide. Moreover, you must anticipate doing this many times, for the very essence of a tool is something whose capital cost to create exceeds the return from a single use. This is highly sequential thinking!

Well, the cortex that handles all this sequential thinking just kept growing and growing, allowing more and more complex sequential thinking. Indeed, the growth of the human cortex over the past 3 million years can best be described as an explosion. It happened so fast that we just didn't have time to adjust to it. Look how the female pelvis has been rearranged to get that big fat head out of the womb at birth—what a pain! Human females don't walk, they kind of galumph along. High-heeled shoes are sexy because they accentuate the natural ungainliness of the female gait, which in turn is the direct result of our big heads. If we had small heads, high-heeled shoes wouldn't be sexy. Therefore, if you're female and are abducted by aliens, and they have big heads (as aliens are wont to do), just put on some high-heeled shoes to drive them into a frenzy and—on second thought, maybe that wouldn't be such a good idea.

Sequential thinking had many other manifestations for human adaptability. One of these, probably the most important adaptive trait, lay in more complex social structures, which were able to take on a more complex temporal dimension. That is, animals that have simpler brains build their social structures on a here-and-now basis: mate selection turns on immediately observable traits; social cooperation has no deferred or delayed elements. But hominids were able to build social structures that were more adaptable because they could extend over a longer time period. For example, altruistic behavior can sometimes take the form of deferred reciprocity. I'll give you some of my food today in the expectation that someday, when you have food and I don't, you'll return the favor. Another example comes from leadership: in most ape societies, leadership is assigned on the basis of simple, immediate dominance, but as the hominids developed, they were able to recognize the value of granting leadership to older, more experienced, but physically weaker individuals. Again, this is a reflection of the adaptive utility of extended sequential thinking.

But far and away the most significant factor in the cortical explosion had to be the development of language. Language is the basis of culture and the medium for modulating complex social relationships; its development by humans is the most significant milestone in the advance of human cognition. But we must not think of language development as a single point in the evolution of human cognition, for in fact the creation of language triggered changes in human society and mind that have reverberated right up until the present day. We are still working out the consequences of language.

Okay, so now we've got humans talking to each other, regulating their social interactions, and developing culture that they transmit through the generations. The next step is the expansion of languages. Clearly, we didn't jump from "Ook ook gronk" to "The quality of mercy is not strained" in one step; language had to develop from the simple to the complex. Along the way, though, the brain had to expand its capabilities to support ever more complex linguistic structures. First there were problems of parsing complex sentence structures (for example, "That, sir, is an insult up with which I will not put"). There was also use of indirection via pronouns, as well as indirection through abstraction (for example, chair < furniture < object or cat < mammal < animal). We also had to cope with contextually parsed utterances (sentences that make no sense until we add other information, such as "My marriage ended when I came home with lipstick on my collar"). All these elements had the twin effect of extending the power of language while demanding ever more cortical resources. Skulls ballooned, women groaned, and humanity marched onward.

The next measure in this bolero was agriculture and urbanization. Poof, now we've got civilization. But urbanization required food collection and transport, and as anybody who's dealt with the postal service knows, things sometimes get lost in transit. When those things are valuable, they can disappear all the more easily. So here we have some early Mesopotamian city surrounded by its hinterland of farms. The farms feed the city under some set of social rules (for example, "Your barley or your life!"). How does this system ensure that what the farmer sends actually gets to the city rather than the stomachs of the intermediaries?

This was a dumb little problem, one of those bureaucratic stumbling blocks that irritate great minds and delight petty ones. The solution was appropriately small minded: the bill of lading. Along with the shipment, you send some device that declares the goods being shipped ("three goats, five bushels of barley, one ox"). Then you sign it with some difficult-to-reproduce mark. The recipient checks the consignment against the bill of lading—well, it's pretty obvious. Initially, that bill of lading might be just a set of pictures with hash marks. After you've done this a few hundred times, though, you start to get sloppy with your artwork. That ox you drew becomes simplified to an ox head and then to a triangle with projecting horns (that, in fact, is the genesis of our letter *A*—just turn it upside down, and you can see the ox head with horns).

I won't go into any more details; suffice it to say that writing emerged from this dumb problem. But there was one hitch: writing in those early days was morphemic (each symbol stood for a complete word). There were no alphabets— which meant that you had to memorize the symbol for every word in the written language (sort of like the command sets for much of our computer software). Initially, there were only a few dozen words, and the system worked fine. But people kept wanting to write down more of the words they spoke, and the new symbols bred like rabbits. Pretty soon, you had to memorize hundreds or even thousands of little icons in order to read. What a pain! Because this process was slow and clumsy, it devolved to an elite group of highly trained scribes (like today's programmers), and writing itself was confined to only the most necessary functions: social coordination at a distance, record keeping, and so forth.

Then some Semitic hacker in a garage invented the alphabet, and everything changed, because now anybody who could pronounce a word could spell it, and therefore write it. And you had to memorize only a few dozen letters! This was literary anarchism; the scribes sputtered indignantly, clung to their morphemic writing systems, and went the path of IBM, Burroughs, and CDC. Tough luck, guys.

Meanwhile, the scruffy alphabet users weren't exactly burning up the road. As I explained in Chapter 25, the Greeks were the first group to break writing out of its hacker-created rut. And that, in turn, led to something altogether new.

To understand that new something, you must first appreciate one of the fundamental weaknesses of the spoken word. The problem is not in the spoken language itself but rather in the neural circuitry we use to process it. We have all this of great dedicated brain matter that successfully parses complex sentences with astounding speed—but it seems to be optimized for processing one sentence at a time. It's as if the sentence is the basic chunk of linguistic thought. You can recognize this sentence instantly wrong. But if you link two good sentences together in a non sequitur, the recognition of that non sequitur is idiosyncratic.

Ahem.

We are all acutely aware of this weakness in our linguistic processing; sometimes we use it to our advantage. The colloquial expression for this stunt is "the primrose path." How many times have you entered into a discussion with a person who starts off with a seemingly reasonable proposition, but then leads you down a primrose path, with one seemingly reasonable intermediate conclusion following another, until you reach an endpoint that you find completely objectionable? You've been had! Used-car salesmen and politicians are particularly good at this.

Because we've had this done to us many times (and we've done it to others, too), we don't trust the spoken word very far. Sure, I'll trust a short, simple statement, but if you start walking me down a long primrose path, I'll get suspicious. Indeed, the longer the primrose path, the more suspicious I become. It is entirely possible to create verbal analogues of those delightful M.C. Escher drawings in which perspective is spread over such an extended visual area that it can be made to contradict itself in the whole, even while maintaining the logic of perspective in any small portion of the picture. In the same way, any long verbal exposition can microscopically appear perfectly logical, while still contradicting itself in the whole.

Our skepticism is healthy, but it robs us of intellectual depth. If you can trust me for only a sentence or two, then we can't explore ideas deeply, can we? Consider, for example, Darwinian evolution. If Charles Darwin had been confined to explaining his entire idea orally, nobody would have understood or believed it—it's just too long and deep an idea. You can't handle big, complicated ideas with the spoken language.

Now let's turn that around and look at it from the other direction. Imagine what happened when the Greeks started writing about things. The written word is subject to more rigorous analysis than the spoken word, for the simple reason that you can go back and cross-check sentences against each other. If someone leads you down the primrose path, you can go back and reread the exposition, examining it critically for the sloppy logic or the tricky wording that permits the deceptive shift in meaning.

Because of this, you can have more confidence in the reliability of the written word. You can trust it more because it's subject to accountability. And this greater level of confidence permits writers to make longer logical forays, to explore ideas more deeply, to journey further into the world of ideas.

This was the basis of the cultural and intellectual explosion that was classical Greece. Have you never wondered why the Greeks seem to have started everything? I believe that it's because they had the first long-range intellectual tool: writing. The Greeks did to ideas what Henry the Navigator did to oceans.

You can see it the Socratic dialogues. They all have the same pattern: here's Socrates and his straight man. Socrates starts off with a proposition that the straight man challenges. Socrates then leads him down the primrose path, asking the straight man to verify the correctness of each step in the process. The straight man's contribution to the process is never more than a sequence of affirmative responses to Socrates' requests for confirmation. When they reach the end of the primrose path, the straight man always slaps his forehead and exclaims, "Golly gee, Socrates, I would never have thought that, but you sure proved it! What a surprising result!"

What strikes me about these dialogues is the giddy sense of excitement at the intellectual discoveries being made. Plato gets full of himself sometimes, all but congratulating himself on his cleverness. Clearly, this was new territory to the Greeks, and they reveled in the discovery.

The other striking observation is the merely exploitative nature of subsequent work. The Romans added a bit to the Greek cultural heritage, but the Roman contribution looks like little more that tidying up, filling in some loose details. We were well past the Renaissance before we started to make fundamental additions to the Greek foundations.

Thus, writing changed the way we thought. Don't think of it as a means of recording ideas; think of it as an instrument for exploring and examining ideas. Civilization grew from the heady exploitation of this instrument of thinking. Indeed, the written page can be thought of as artificial cortex, a technological means of augmenting the expansion of the sequential-processing portions of the brain. We humans were so impatient to grow more cortex, we went ahead and concocted an artificial version: paper and ink.

Misogyny and Sequential Thinking

A sidebar on Western misogyny sheds additional light on the nature of the revolution. All of the civilizations of the Greco-Roman era placed women in a secondary role, but Western civilization added an edge to the relationship. Was it due to some special nastiness on the part of Greeks and Romans? I think not, for Western misogyny survived Greco-Roman culture. The Christian church in the first few centuries approached gender issues with something like benign neglect, but the later church showed sharper anti-female prejudices. Why?

I think that the answer lies in the Western exaltation of reason. Recall from earlier parts of this chapter my observation that there are two fundamentally different types of thinking, the pattern-recognizing style of the earlier brain, and the sequential style of the outer cortical regions of the brain. Remember that writing was an extension of this sequential-processing system. And sequential processing was the underlying cause of the explosion of Western civilization. It therefore makes perfect sense that the people behind that explosion would elevate sequential reasoning to the highest possible status. You can see it in their philosophical writings. I can quote most readily from Erasmus, but many of his comments echo the classical philosophers. Erasmus's writings bristle with demeaning comments about women, yet when called upon to address women specifically, he demonstrates sensitivity, sympathy, and a remarkably liberated attitude. I had long struggled to understand the contradiction between his clearly declared respect for women and his frequent disparaging potshots. But there is a pattern: Erasmus the woman hater always refers to women in terms of their anti-rational behavior. He writes that somebody is "no better than an unreasonable woman," "just a silly woman," "possessed of a more-than-female irrationality." It's not women that Erasmus is disparaging; it's anti-rational behavior. He just uses women as the personification of such behavior.

Female social roles have long emphasized the interpersonal universe, whereas male roles have tended more toward the physical universe. The vast complexity of social interaction is more aptly handled with the pattern-recognition style of thinking. But the physical universe is more readily understood with sequential logic. Thus, men in Western civilization tended to emphasize sequential thinking, whereas women were stronger in pattern-recognition thinking. But remember: the underlying cause of Western success is sequential reasoning. If we exalt such reasoning, we concomitantly demean women. By celebrating our greatest successes, we trashed women. Oops.

Yet the exaltation of sequential thinking was the crucial step in the development of Western civilization. Our forebears had a fight on their hands: the human inclination is to rely on an ill-defined combination of sequential and pattern-recognition thought. The mongers of superstition, emotionalism, and tribalism could not hold their own against this rigorous style of thinking, so they resisted the change at every turn. This in turn evoked a combative response from the proponents of sequential thinking, which was often applied with too broad a brush. The sequentialists eventually won: the central value of Western civilization is the belief in a disciplined adherence to sequential thinking. It took a lot of hard PR work, but the point was won.

So now our story has come to the Renaissance. The developments that I recognize as important are all extensions of the process of writing: the invention of the printing press, of course, but also the whole concept of scholarly collaboration through publication of ideas. Later came the creation of secondary forms of writing: arithmetic notation, the use of Arabic (actually, Hindu) numerals, and the creation of musical notation. All these innovations extended the intellectual power of the writing instrument. And ideas began piling up on each other.

Once books became cheap enough for everyone to own a personal library, our thinking processes altered again. It was no longer necessary for people to cram their heads full of all the details of their existence; they could keep the requisite books on their bookshelves and refer to them as needed. It's difficult for us to appreciate just how much this has changed our mental habits. A few centuries ago, a person's intellectual prowess was measured by the amount of learning stuffed into his head. Nowadays, the most everyday office worker daily works with a larger database of facts than the greatest intellectuals of the Renaissance. With phone books, dictionaries, computer manuals, maps, and the wide array of specialist reference works each of us uses, we sit atop a mountain of information. We don't bother learning most of it by heart—all we need know is where to look it up. The confidence that gives us permits each of us to operate over a wider intellectual range. The secretary can spell check the boss's letter, the engineer can prepare a visual presentation, the carpenter can whip up an invoice for work performed. Some of this benefit, of course, comes from computers, but the deeper cause is the ease with which each worker can access the information necessary to carry out the foreign task. Even today, writing continues to change the way we think.

Here We Go Again

We're about to start the whole process again, only this time the trigger is not writing, but the computer.

What is the real significance of the computer? Is it a monstrous number-crunching machine, cold and inhuman, ready to obliterate humanity for computational convenience, as we pictured it in the 1960s? Is it a source of cheap thrills as a videogame machine, as we saw it in the 1980s? Or perhaps an office machine, a glorified typewriter? Just what is this thing, anyway?

I'd like to turn the picture upside down and suggest that we're asking the wrong question here. Imagine yourself in 1469, examining one of the new-fangled printed books, trying to divine the real significance of the technology. You might be tempted to focus your attention on the thing itself, the physical entity of the printed page, but you would be wrong. The importance of printing was not in the printed page itself, but rather in the ideas unleashed by the printed page, in the way it changed our thinking. In the same way, when we wonder about the significance of the computer, we are misplacing our attention. The computer is just the paper onto which and with which we write; it is no more important than the paper onto which Gutenberg printed his first Bible. Necessary, yes—but not the essence of the revolution. What was important about printing was the gathering, dissemination, and group discussion of ideas.

Computers are also changing our culture, but in a profoundly different way. I'm not talking about email, the Internet, word processing, or any of the other wonders of the last few decades; the truly important change is the way our thinking is changing as a result of our use of the computer.

Just as writing started as the preserve of a small group of highly trained scribes, so, too, has computer programming been the preserve of a small group of highly trained programmers. Just as the alphabet opened up the world of writing to the community at large, I expect new forms of interactive communication to open up programming to all computer users. Of course, such programming will not be able to hold a candle to the real programming that Real Programmers do. They will sneer at the new stuff in much the same way that the scribes dismissed the alphabet. Where writing gave us vastly increased power with sequential thinking, programming will give us vastly increased power with subjunctive thinking: the consideration of a problem or issue in terms of many possibilities.

Subjunctive thinking is one layer of thought more abstract than sequential thinking. In the latter, you lay out a long thread of ideas in order, arriving at some result or conclusion. In subjunctive thinking, you lay out a great many threads, all of them converging on the issue at hand, but each taking a different path. One's conception of truth morphs in subjunctive thinking into a more complicated being. Truth is no longer a simple matter of truth or falsehood; it is more a set of related conditional statements.

Our natural talents for subjunctive thinking are limited; we can keep only so many threads in our head at one time. But our talent for sequential thinking was limited to the length of a sentence, and writing allowed us to extend our sequential thinking to many sentences. In the same way, computer programming allows us to handle more threads.

Let me present an example of subjunctive thinking at work. Suppose that you are the manufacturing manager for a high-tech factory, and the boss sends you a memo instructing you to reduce your budget by 20 percent. The old, sequential way of responding to that memo might look like this:

> *Dear Boss:*
> *Your request that I reduce my budget is not workable. If I lay off some of*
> *the line workers, our output will not keep up with demand. If I cut*
> *down on electricity, the machines that make the product won't work. . . .*

Suppose, however, that you simply sent her your budget spreadsheet with a note:

> *Please examine this spreadsheet for unnecessary expenses. If you*
> *experiment with a variety of budget-reducing scenarios, you'll quickly*
> *see how little fat there is in the budget.*

This is a much superior communication. Instead of butting assertions with your boss ("You can easily cut 20 percent of our of your budget." "Can not!" "Can so!"), you can put the issues directly in her lap and let her experience the problem directly. When you try to communicate the ideas in English, you get a long collection of statements beginning with "If . . . ," most of which won't interest your interlocutor.

People are already doing this, and it certainly changes the way they work, but the effects have not sunk in yet; we have yet to change our habits to exploit this new capability. Moreover, we can do this with only a limited number of problems: spreadsheets, documents, and so forth. But the concept can be extended much further. For example, there is a weakness in sending the budget to the boss: the spreadsheet doesn't address the efficiency of the operation. The boss could easily argue that cutting one manufacturing engineer out of the operation would not significantly affect the manufacturing process. You would demur, and there you go again, butting heads.

To solve this problem, you need a new kind of document, a subjunctive document for your manufacturing process. Think of it as a spreadsheet for how the product gets built. This document would show how everybody's work fits together, what the dependencies are, and so forth. If you could create such a document, and then you could hand it off to your boss and show her how the loss of the manufacturing engineer would affect the entire operation.

Such a technology would not eliminate arguments; every simulation, model, or construct is based on assumptions. Certainly, two workers arguing over a proposal could each prepare a simulation showing why his or her own position is superior. But this way, the argument would be shifted from idiosyncratic particulars to the assumptions underlying the simulation—higher, more abstract principles. And it's always more productive to debate principles than particulars.

So here we have in programming a new language, a new form of writing, that supports a new way of thinking. We should therefore expect it to enable a dramatic new view of the universe. But before we get carried away with wild notions of a new Western civilization, a latter-day Athens with digital Platos and interactive Aristotles, we need to recognize that we lack one of the crucial factors in the original Greek efflorescence: an alphabet. Remember: writing was invented long before the Greeks, but it was so difficult to learn that its use was restricted to an elite class of scribes who had nothing interesting to say. And we have exactly the same situation today. Programming is confined to an elite class of programmers. Just like the scribes, they are highly paid. Just like the scribes, they exercise great control over all the ancillary uses of their craft. Just like the scribes, they are the object of some disdain—after all, if programming were that noble, would you admit to being unable to program? And just like the scribes, they don't have a damn thing to say to the world—they want only to piddle around with their medium and make it do cute things.

My analogy runs deep. I have always been disturbed by the realization that the Egyptian scribes practiced their art for several thousand years without ever writing down anything interesting. Amid all the mountains of hieroglyphics we have retrieved from that era, with literally gigabytes of information about gods, goddesses, pharaohs, conquests, taxes, and so forth, there is almost nothing of personal interest from the scribes themselves. No gripes about the lousy pay, no office jokes, no mentions of family or loved ones—and few discussions of philosophy, mathematics, art, drama, or any of the other things that the Greeks blathered away about endlessly. Compare the hieroglyphics of the Egyptians with the writings of the Greeks, and the difference that leaps out at you is humanity.

You can see the same thing in the output of the current generation of programmers, especially in the field of computer games. It's lifeless. Sure, their stuff is technically good, but it's like the Egyptian statuary: technically impressive, but the faces stare blankly, whereas Greek statuary ripples with the power of life.

What we need is a means of democratizing programming, of taking it out of the soulless hands of the programmers and putting it into the hands of a wider range of talents. What we need is analogous to an alphabet. In other words, we need some means of making programming accessible to people without requiring years of training. This idea is not at all new; people have been designing programming languages for beginners for decades. BASIC, Logo, Pilot, and Smalltalk are just a few of many such efforts, none of which has ever amounted to much. So why am I dragging out this dead horse for further abuse?

I think that the failures of the past arise from an underestimation of the amount of computer resources required to support the nonprofessional user. Here we come to a fundamental difference between computer writing and paper writing: computer writing is executed on a computer, whereas paper writing mirrors speech. Because computer writing must be executed on a computer, it is constrained by the limitations of the computer, and it must also consume some portion of the computer's resources. In times past, computer resources have been so limited that we could not afford to allocate much to the programming language. This is why we used low-level languages such as assembly language and C. But computers have grown vastly more powerful in the past decade. My current computer is about 2,000 times more powerful than the computer I used just 15 years ago. Yet the programming language I use on it, C++, does not consume 2,000 times more computer resources; I'd guess that it eats up maybe 50 times more resources. It's as if we were ditch diggers who've been using shovels all our lives, and one day we receive a shiny new bulldozer with the horsepower to do the work of a thousand shovels—but the blade on the front of the bulldozer is only three feet long, and so we can do only as much work as 50 shovels. What a waste!

Alan Kay once observed that, with the 8-bit machines, 90 percent of the computer's power was used up doing the work, and only 10 percent was available for making the user interface more effective. He allowed as how computers wouldn't get useful until those percentages were reversed. Well, we should have reached that point by now. If our computers of today are a thousand times more powerful than the 8-bit machines, then we could have 10 times the raw computing power of those old machines and still have 99 percent of the computer's resources available for user interface. This, I think, is the biggest failure of the computer industry: the standards of user interface quality have gone up by a factor of 10 while the basic hardware has improved by a factor of 1,000. Windows is nice, but it doesn't go far enough. We're way behind the curve.

So if we are to design a programming language for normal people, using modern computers, we want something far more glorified than BASIC, Logo, or even Smalltalk. This new language should be more removed from the mathematical constructs of conventional programming and closer to the grammatical constructs that we understand from natural language.

So how will we concoct such a language? I see two possible strategies; I don't know if either one will work. The first strategy is to build a series of small, special-purpose languages for single applications. We don't try to tackle some high-falutin general-purpose language; instead, we just build a bunch of narrow-purpose languages for particular tasks. We already have some of this in macro or scripting languages. As the years go by, we allow Darwinian factors to select the better language traits. Within a decade or so, perhaps we will be in a position to talk about designing a general-purpose language.

The other possibility is to simply make programming a necessity. I think that Apple has taken a good baby step in this direction with its AppleScript language. This is a general-purpose programming language capable of handling many of the mundane tasks of computing. Nevertheless, even AppleScript seems too steep for most users. Perhaps something founded on the Basic English proposal I offered in Chapter 22 might provide a gentler beginning.

Before you dismiss my demanding attitude as out of touch with reality, consider this: we now require our children to undergo years of tedious training to learn to read and write. It truly is a huge investment, reading—wouldn't it be wonderful if we could skip the effort? Sad to say, that's just not possible: every citizen must learn this tool so fundamental to our civilization. It demands a great deal of effort to learn, but the rewards are well worth it. Someday soon, programming will be just as important.

30

FUTURES

My own prognostications on the interplay of interactivity, society, and technology.

The computer revolution is, without doubt, the most dramatic jump in human history. This is an extreme statement, but I make it with due regard for the vastness of human history. Perhaps I can justify my wild claim with some rough quantifications. Let's start with one of the seminal technological events in human history: Gutenberg's invention of the printing press. The significance of this technology was that it replaced hand-copied books with much cheaper printed books. The reduction in cost made books available to many more people and thereby triggered huge changes in society. Yet the actual reduction in cost was only about a factor of 10. True, the beautiful illuminated manuscripts of the early fifteenth century were hugely expensive, but it's not fair to compare an illuminated manuscript with a printed book. For similar standards of quality, the price ratio was about 10 to 1.

Another big technological revolution was the Bessemer process for mass-producing steel. This lowered the cost of structural steel by roughly a factor of 3; as a consequence, cities all over the world leapt skyward, breaking the old three-story limit imposed by stone. Within a few decades, skyscrapers were stretching hundreds of feet into the air.

In this century, the Green Revolution of the 1960s is certainly impressive. A combination of hybrid seeds, fertilizer, and pesticides dramatically increased crop yields. The overall improvement is tricky to estimate because of uncertain assumptions about capital intensity and sustainability, but overall I'd say this revolution roughly halved the price of food. Human population continued its geometric growth.

In raw magnitude of technological advance, the computer revolution dwarfs these monumental moments in human history. In two decades, I have progressed from a Commodore PET computer with 8K of RAM, an 8-bit processor running at 1 megahertz, a cassette drive for nonvolatile storage, and a tiny black-and-white display to a Macintosh 8500 with 256MB of RAM and a 64-bit processor running at 230 MHz, over a megapixel of 32-bit deep color display, a 2-gigabyte hard drive, etc., etc. My Mac's CPU is 2,000 times faster than the PET's, its RAM is 32,000 times bigger, its display can present about 40,000 times as much information, and its nonvolatile storage is about 20,000 times bigger and hundreds of times faster. Overall, I'd say that this Mac outperforms the old PET by a factor of about 4,000, at about the same price (in constant dollars). In only two decades, computers have improved by a factor of 4,000, and the improvement continues unabated.

Let's summarize these guesses in a table:

Invention	Improvement Factor	Results
Printing press	10	Mass literacy, Reformation, democracy
Bessemer process	3	Skyscrapers, higher urban densities
Green Revolution	2	Billions more people
Computers	42,000	Computer games

Okay; I admit that computers have, in fact, wrought gigantic changes in society, and their power has only begun to sink in. Here are some of the factors at work.

Technological Progress

This is the factor that everybody dotes on. Golly gee, computers just get more and more powerful every day! The concept is formalized in Moore's Law, which states that computer chips will double in power for the same price every 18 months. In general, laws that involve exponential growth (as this one does) tend to apply for only short periods of time, but Moore's Law has been right on the money for nigh unto 30 years now. There's little reason to doubt that computer technology will continue to improve, at least at an attenuated rate, into the foreseeable future. Surely before I die, I will own a computer a million times more powerful than that old PET.

If this were the only factor to consider, computers and society would have a rosy future. But there are some other factors to consider, such as:

The Perception of Adequacy

The application of technology does not slavishly follow its power curve; it is limited by the popular need for its benefits. Paper clips used to cost enough for people to notice; nowadays, they're so cheap that nobody pays attention to them. If I were to invent a process that dropped the price of paper clips to one-millionth of their current price, would you use any more paper clips than you now use?

Let's face it; many of the basic computer applications are already nearing the upper reaches of their appeal. My word processor is quite good, and I'm sure that it could be better, but if Two Jerks in a Garage, Inc. (floated on Wall Street with an initial valuation of $20 billion), were to release a new word processor that is undeniably ten times better than my current word processor, would I rush out to buy it? I doubt it; my current word processor is probably good enough.

Human Limitations on Use

When automobiles were first mass-produced, they couldn't go fast; 5 or 10 miles per hour was about the fastest any sane driver would go. By the 1920s, roads were smoother, tires were better, and the typical automobile could manage 30 or 40 mph. By the 1930s, the risk of a catastrophic tire blowout and consequent loss of control kept speeds to about 45 mph. By the 1950s, better tire designs and wider, smoother roads had gotten speeds up to about 60 mph. But in the past 40 years, we haven't seen much increase in typical highway speeds. Technology didn't stop improving: just about every component of the current technology makes its 1950s ancestor look ancient. But the increase in average highway speeds stopped because one component of the overall system remained constant: the driver. Human reaction times today are no better than they were 40 years ago, and above 70 mph, our reaction times exceed our likely warning times.

There are already a few components of computer systems that have reached the limits imposed by human frailties. Our hands can't handle bigger keyboards, nor will our typing speeds improve. The color depth of most monitors now exceeds the color resolution of the human retina. Many computer games could easily run at speeds fast enough to seem a blur to the most hard-core videogamer. In many other areas, of course, there's still plenty of room for improvement, but we must remember that the human partner in the interaction has his own limitations.

Design Expertise

The printing press reduced the price of books overnight, but it took 50 years to sink its teeth into society. The technology to print a book comes more easily than the talent to write one; an entire generation had to grow up with the printing press before a cadre of talented writers arose to put it through its paces. The first media superstar, my old friend Erasmus, was born several years after Gutenberg unleashed his creation. An Erasmus could not have appeared before Gutenberg, because there simply weren't enough books lying around for one person to read the entire corpus of classical literature.

Such is surely the case with computers. We have plenty of programmers, but our accumulated design expertise in interactivity is paltry. Consider how poorly most workers in the industry understand interactivity; ask your colleagues to define it, and you'll likely get a scattershot of vague and contradictory answers. All the computing power in the world is useless in the hands of a Neanderthal.

Audience Development

The computer does not exist independently of its audience of users; after all, they're the ones paying for this revolution, and they call the shots. The capabilities of the technology are constrained by the acquired skills of its users. Thus, when personal computers first hit the streets in force in the early 1980s, a major obstacle was their reliance on keyboards. Most of the yuppies who comprised the initial market couldn't type; moreover, typing was commonly associated with secretarial work, and status-conscious executives refused to be seen using secretarial equipment.

My wife provides a typical example. She first encountered computers as a business tool in the early 80s, and she shied away from them. She would attempt something only with me standing nearby, and then only the simplest of tasks. By the mid 80s, she was reluctantly using my cast-off computers, hunting and pecking her way through simple memos and letters. In the late 80s, she embraced the technology, mastering spreadsheets, budget control programs, and word processors. Nowadays, she is completely confident using a computer and types using a hybrid of two-finger and touch typing.

It takes years for masses of people to develop the skills necessary to utilize a new technology. Computers are particularly demanding; progress in the field will be dictated more by audience familiarity than by technology.

Opportunistic Adjustment of Lifestyle and Workstyle

The other side of the coin is that, as people grow comfortable with a technology, they alter their lifestyles to take advantage of it. The alteration in lifestyle modifies the definition of the technology's utility. For example, email had zero utility to most people before, say, 1980. To whom could you write? Its communication functions were handled by letters and telephone calls. Snazzy voicemail systems in the 1980s made telephone calls even more useful. But email solved problems that people had never noticed before. With email, you don't need to waste several minutes on personal banter before getting to the point in a business call. You can make an exact copy of another person's email and forward it to others as a way of documenting your comments. You can respond to an email point by point, referring to each item by quoting it. Since email doesn't constitute much of an intrusion, you can use it freely at any time for the most minor of communications. And you can send copies to lots of people with no extra effort.

Businesses have changed their social behaviors in response to this. The chance meeting at the coffee pot has been downgraded in importance; encounters with important people at the urinal no longer offer quite the same opportunities that they once did.

These kinds of changes are more important to the future of interactivity than the technological changes. The interactivity designer must be more attuned to them than to technical developments.

Complexity of Interrelationships

The success of email cannot be attributed to a single technology, such as email application programs. Several technologies contributed to the universal embracing of email: local area networks, cheaper and faster modems, optical fiber (just in time!), less noisy telephone lines, and the Internet. Had any of these technologies failed to blossom, email might not have taken off. After all, email commands our attention only when lots of people are using it, and to convince everybody to join the system, you have to get every individual piece working well, fast, and cheaply. I don't think that the success of email was credibly predictable until just before it actually happened; there were too many contingencies.

The same thing applies in guessing the future of the revolution. Exciting possibilities abound, but each one depends on a morass of supporting developments, any one of which could kill it before it gets started. Back in the late 70s, the smart money said that bubble memory would sweep away rotating magnetic media (hard disks and floppy disks), but it didn't turn out that way, and there are more attributable causes for that failure than there are for the fall of Rome.

Winner Takes All

Every information-based technology enjoys huge economies of scale; selling one additional copy of the information costs you almost nothing. This confers enormous economic efficiency on all information-based technologies. The downside of these economies of scale is the winner-takes-all marketplace that naturally ensues. The biggest kid on the block enjoys such huge economies of scale that he can put everybody else out of business even with inferior product. The almost-textbook example of this tendency is the triumph of Windows over the Macintosh. In my opinion, at each point in time until the late 1990s, the Macintosh technology was superior to the competing Microsoft product—yet the good guys (or at least the guys with the best product) lost. There are lots of secondary reasons for Apple's failure, but the primary reason is simple: the Microsoft installed base was bigger than the Mac's installed base at every point in time. Superior product was not enough to overcome the relentless economic logic.

This unfortunate trait of the revolution throws a wildcard into its future. Suppose that two competing technologies appear simultaneously. Suppose further that one of the technologies is moderately superior. If the inferior technology is better funded, it can establish a stronger initial position in the marketplace and use the ensuing economies of scale to crush its competitor. Thus, the future course of the revolution will be shaped at least partly by the vagaries of funding at the expense of objective and rational factors. When you combine this with the previous factor, you get a future whose specifics cannot be reliably predicted.

Putting the Pieces Together

In assessing where the revolution is headed, the technological extrapolation is likely the least useful approach. Each of the other listed factors is, I think, more consequential to the future. The most important factor is likely to be continuing adjustments in lifestyle and workstyle. This is a positive factor that will drive the revolution onward, but to understand it, we must concentrate on what tasks people are now handling that might be handled more easily (with some adjustment in style) by the computer. We should not think in terms of the computer taking over some existing function and performing it exactly as in the past, only better. Email is not the same thing as a telephone call, nor is it the same thing as a letter.

The Short-Term Future

I will not make a fool of myself by attempting to predict specific developments, but I will identify three developments that I think will have a great impact in the short term.

The first of these is voice synthesis. Already pretty good, I think it is now poised to cross the threshold of consumer utility. By making user interfaces easier and more natural, it will make the computer more accessible to nontechnical users.

Next comes voice recognition. It is not as far along as voice synthesis, but offers greater gains in computer accessibility.

Last, and most important, is overall ease of use. Computers suck! They are too difficult to use. This is the primary obstacle to their wider employment, and thus overcoming it will be the primary driver shaping the future of the revolution.

The Long Term: From Computing to Interactivity

All revolutions, be they political, economic, religious, or technological, are initiated by specialists and co-opted by commoners. The intensity, dedication, and dogmatism of the revolutionaries melts into the pragmatism, diversity, and laziness of the masses. The computer revolution was launched, and is still dominated, by technological revolutionaries. They are certainly intense; listen to them gush all that techie drivel with such enthusiasm. Dedicated they surely are:

look how much they have to learn to install and use all those conflicting programs. And dogmatism is never far below the surface. Complain about the malfunctioning of his program, and the programmer will snarl "RTFM" at you. Just for kicks, tell a techie that you prefer the Macintosh, America Online, or BASIC; watch how upset he gets!

But already the commoners are making some dents. It took 11 years, but they finally dragged the techies, kicking and screaming, out of DOS and into Windows. And the commoners are starting to realize their power: note the large and successful line of books titled *(Technical Topic X) for Dummies*. The industry makes the commoners feel like dummies—but the covers of these books all show a defiant protester's sign.

The vulgarization of computers will necessarily follow their popularization. Technical values will be replaced by consumer values. Somewhere along the way, we'll stop calling it "computing" and give it a name that connotes its social function rather than its technical foundation. We probably won't use the term *interactivity*; the word's six syllables clatter off the tongue like a rickety freight train. But the concept of interactivity will be the intended gist of our meaning. The deepest essence of this revolution is not bytes or spreadsheets but the discovery of a new sentient being. True, that sentience is merely a faint prerecorded echo of the designer's sentience, but its genealogy is as nothing compared to its potential. This new sentient species is, in truth, just a faint image of ourselves, a darkened window into another person's mind—not his knowledge, but his thinking. This strange and wonderful species is dressed in traits we already know: video, audio, keyboards. But the element that fascinates us, captivates us, is the one element that is truly new and unique about it: interactivity.

Seven Lessons to Remember

1. Your software engages your user in a conversation. Your design task is to maximize the utility of that conversation.
2. Think about that conversation in linguistic terms.
3. What are the verbs? What does the user **DO**?
4. Speak less, listen more.
5. Thinking is the delivered content of all software.
6. Your software should do whatever a reasonable person in its situation would do.
7. *Dactylodeiktous* means "all fingers pointing at."

INDEX

B

Erasmatron (program) *(continued)*
  implementing undo-ability, 237
  not allowing inappropriate item
    selection, 344
  problem when designing, 101
  slow screen draw problem, 154
  timing results, 98–99
  Tinkertoy Text from, 261
Eric's Ultimate Solitaire
    (software game), 67
error messages, 234–35
errors, design, 109, 304–5.
    See bloopers
escape button (Esc), 53
evolution and play, 228
executable file, 135
executives, role of, 150
expansion/contraction, 24
expectations, false, 106–7
experimentation, 95, 153–54
expression, interactivity as
    form of, 15–18
expressions, facial.
    See facial expressions
extending sequentiality, 68
eyeball-to-brain gap, 257–58

F

facial animation, 25
facial expressions
  human brain's processing
    of, 257–58
  meaning of, 46
  in messages, 248
facial feature extraction, 293–94
false expectations, 106–7
Fast button, 140
Fatal Attraction (film), 343–44
"featuritis," 106–7
federalism, 247

feedback
  force-feedback mouse, 60
  as necessity for interactivity, 9
  sound for, 187
  tactile, 189
feelings. *See* emotions
females. *See* women
fields, 39–40
files
  extensions for, 135
  icons for, 66, 135, 136, 307
films, 9
financial abstraction, 243–46
first and second person, 116
flight simulators, 52
foldback, 79
fonts
  and algorithms, 34–35
  error messages
    regarding, 111–12, 132
  menus for, 64–65, 266
  size of, 22–23
  in word processor
    programs, 88–89, 266
footers, 250
force-feedback mouse, 60
formulas, soft, 197–98
frame rate, 24–25, *29*
frames, HTML, 262
Frankston, Bob, 17
free will, 324, 326
frolic. *See* paidaia
FSFM (full-screen, full-motion)
    video, 24, 26
full-motion animation, 26
full-screen, full-motion (FSFM)
    video, 24, 26
future of interactivity, 361–67
  audience development, 364
  complexity of
    interrelationships, 365
  design expertise, 364
  human limitations on use, 363
  long-term, 366–67
  opportunistic adjustment
    of lifestyle and
    workstyle, 364–65

Huizinga, Johan, 228–29, 230, 238
human attributes, enabling
    computers with.
        See anthropomorphization
human factors design, 11
human limitations, future of, 363
human thinking, vs. machine
    thinking, 31–32
human-human interaction, vs.
    human-computer
    interaction, 74
humanities. See arts/humanities vs.
    science/engineering
humongous heap design, 251
hyperlinks, 71, 179–81
HyperText Markup Language.
    See HTML

I

iconic sounds, 187–88
icons, 136
    See also tooltips
    in AppleWorks, 123
    for cursors, 57–59
    example of problems
        with, 130, 131
    for files, 66, 135, 136, 307
    menus for, 65
    that operate as
        buttons, 55–56, 288–89
    unrecognizable, 121–22
ILS system, 52
images
    See also animation; icons
    cursors for passing over, 59
    download time for, 119
    pixels in, 20–22
    programs for manipulating, 250
    recognition of, 290–94
immune systems, 249
indentations, 250
independent devices, 184
indirection, 251–67
    applying to output, 262–64
    carrying across gaps, 255–59
    communicative power of, 264–65

constructs, 253–54, 259
    in programming, 259–62
    putting to work, 266
    scripting languages, 266–69
individuality, 82
inflection, in speech, 28
information contribution,
    symmetry of, 70
information flow, measuring, 73
information, providing, 181–82
input devices, 50–62
    input devices, 60–61
    joysticks, 51
    keyboards, 51–53
    light pens and other
        devices, 61–62
    mouse, 53–59
inputting. See listening
intensity in interaction, 239
interactive loop, 69–74, 124, 160,
    174, 255
    browsing by hyperlink, 71
    convergent iteration, 72
    database querying, 72
    gaps to bridge, 255–59
    human-human interaction vs.
        human-computer
        interaction, 74
    keyword search, 71
    measuring information flow, 73
interactive storytelling, 327, 329,
    339–46
    abstracting storytelling, 341–44
    author's work in, 345–46
    building a technology
        for, 345–46
    vs. conventional story, 340–41
    technology, 221
    what it is not, 339–40
interactivity, 3–18
    automated, 14
    competitive advantages of, 16–17
    definitions of, 5–6
    degrees of, 6–8
    future of, 361–67
        audience development, 364

metaphors, 36–39, 291–301
  application of, 298–301
  bureaucratic, 39
  business, 38
  creating, 297–98
  economic, 38
  emotional, 39
  extending existing, 298
  geometric, 37–38
  importance of, 291–92
  in language, 272
  metaphorical
    transformation, 291–92
  musical, 38
  physical, 38
  solutions, 36
  spatial, 37–38
  transformation, 291–92
  visual, 46–48
mice. *See* mouse
military strategy games, 162
minute setting, 142
misfires, 304–5
misogyny, 354–55
mistakes. *See* bloopers in
    interactivity design
Moby Dick (Melville), *327*
modal input, 280
monitors, computer.
      See screens, computer
monitor-to-eyeball gap, carrying
      indirectors across gaps, 257
Morse-code-type construct, 256
mouse, 53–59
  buttons on, 55, 124
  complex expressions of, 67–68
  as interaction, 53–54
  vocabulary size of, 54–55
movies, 9
multimedia, 12
multi-step processes, 72
music, 27
musical metaphor, 38
musical notation, 273–74

N

narrative abstraction, 341–44
natural languages, 46, 272–73
  attempts to replace with
    designed languages, 273–77
  clumsiness with subjunctive
    thinking, 347
negativity, rule of, 87
nervous system, 249, 348
nested menu, 64
neural circuitry, 291–92, 352
Newton (PDA), 68
Ninth Symphony (Beethoven), 36
NNW (north-northwest) arrow
    cursor, 57
nodes. *See* linkmeshes; storytrees
non-interactivity, 9–10
  vs. interactive, 8–9
  non-interactive
    expressions, 43–44
non-technical designers, 32, 156
NorthernLight.com
    (search engine), 72
north-northwest (NNW) arrow
    cursor, 57
nouns, 208, 209–10
numbers
  referring to in programs, 259–60
  soft, 195–96

O

objects. *See* nouns
obstructionist stories, 80
operating systems, 336
operations, in Basic English, 275
operations per datum, 210–12
options. *See* verbs
organizational charts, 150–51
OS (operating system), 336
output. *See* speaking
over-specified depiction,
    effects of, 264–65

P

Pac-Man (game), 219
Page Setup box, 127
paged menus, 189
paidaia (frolic), 225, 238, 240–41
painting programs, 171
palette, 65
Palm Pilot (PDA), 68
Panopticon (word wheel), 277
paper money illustration, 251–52
parsers, text, 86
parsing, 280–83
participation, difference from
    interaction, 9
pattern recognition, 32, 200,
    291–92, 348, 355
pens, light, 61
Performance Specifications
    document, 152
personal anticipation, 306–7
personal finance programs, 212
personal thinking styles, 213
"Phaedrus" (Plato), 8–9
"philosophical languages," 274
phones, cellular, 186–87
photo-retouching
    programs, 125, 171, 211, 294
physical metaphor, 38
picture element, 20
pictures, drawing. *See* architectures
piezoelectric buzzers, 187
pixels, 20, 21–22, 186
pixel-targeting cursor, 57
Plato, 8–9, 354
play, 225–41
    applying to educational
        software, 169–71
    applying to interactivity
        design, 233–37
    competitive, 240–41
    and culture, 228–30
    dark side of, 238–41
    design experiments, 237–38
    and evolution, 228
    historical roots of, 227
    human desire for, 169–70

and language, 230
and mentation, 230–31
overview, 225–26
prejudice against, 232–33
provision for safety, 232
playful experimentation, 95
plays, 10
plot, 323–24, 327
pointers, 261
polishing phase, 155
politeness, 116–17
political abstraction, 246–47
pop-up animation, 25–26
pop-up menus, 25, 65, 87, 281
portable PIMs, 184
preferences, 87–88
preponderance, 308
Preppies (computer game), 27
prerecorded voice output, 188
primary data windows, 108
Principle of Equivalence, 231
Print dialog box, 127
printed books, 8–9
priorities, setting, 103
privacy
    not intruding in user's, 234
    and user data, 309–12
probabilistic anticipation,
    implementing, 308
problems. *See* bloopers
process intensive thinking, 207–13
    argument against, 212–13
    crunch-per-bit ratio, 210–12
    vs. data intensity, 210
    duality, 208–9
    and educational software
        design, 168
    and indirect control, 327
    nounism, 209–10
    and personal thinking styles, 213
programming
    democratizing, 359
    indirection in, 259–62
    lack of accountability, 192
    languages for, making
        simpler, 359–60
    looping, 218
    why learn, 191–94

progress reports, 109
project manager, 150
project team, 150–52
pull-down menus, 64
pushbuttons, 124. *See also* buttons
puzzle games, 161

Q

qualifications for designing, 152
qualities, in Basic English, 274
quantum mechanics, 325
querying databases, 72
Quicken (personal finance
    program), 212

R

radio buttons, 67, 124
RAM, 100–101, 235–37
random processes, 36–37
randomness, 325
ratio of operations per datum, 210
Read The Manual (RTFM), 50, 185
reality
    distorting, 43
    operational definition of, 207
reasoning
    social, 163
    verbal, 162–63
rectangle-selection cursor, 57
relativity, theory of, 231
resolution
    color, 22–23
    screen, 21–22
resource fork, 135
resource management games, 162
responses, delayed, 123–24
reversibility through undo, 326
revolution, interactivity, 14
reworded menu items, 126
Robinett, Warren, 170
role-playing games, 162
Romeo and Juliet (Shakespeare),
    340–41
rotation, 25

RTFM (Read The Manual),
    50, 52, 185
rule of negativity, 87
rules, design. *See* design guidelines

S

safety for play, 232
ScanDisk (program), 120
science/engineering vs.
    arts/humanities, 331–37
    artsy people, 334–35
        feelings toward
            science/engineering,
            332–33
        future of, 336
        need for in software
            development, 335–36
        recommendations for, 337
        why don't program, 334–35
    technical people
        feelings toward
            arts/humanities, 331–32
        recommendations for, 337
screens, computer, 21–22
    gaps in interactive loop, 256–57
    resolutions of, 21–22
    size vs. pixel count, 21–22
    touch-sensitive
        screen, 61, 68, 189
    vertical monitor screen, 61
    windows, fitting into five
        categories, 108–11
scripting languages, 266–69
scroll boxes, 124
scrollbars, 67, 124
scrolling menus, 65
search engines, 71, 90, 177
searches, keyword, 71
secondary devices, 184
secondary keywords, 72
"secret" icons, 121–22
security issue, 309–12
Seneca, 9
sensory inputs, processing, 348

verisimilitude, 33–34
vertical link, 180
vertical monitor screen, 61
vibration, 25
videogames. *See* game design
VisiCalc (first spreadsheet), 17, 173, 250
visual metaphor, 46–48
vocabularies, "context-free," 274–75
voice output, 188
voice recognition
        software, 59–60, 366
voice tonality, 27–28
volition, discrepancy of, 239

W

Walker, Dave, 136
watch cursor, 57
watches, 141–42
wave-particle duality, 208
Web, the, 175–81
    and abstraction, 251
    bandwidth issues, 41, 176
    browsing, 179–81
    future of, 41, 181–82
    overloading web pages, 119
    and soft math, 200
    strategies for improving, 176–79
windows
    alternate, 25
    primary data windows, 108
    screen, 108–11
Windows 95 operating system,
        135–37, 144
women
    for customer support, 333
    game design for, 163
    and sequential thinking, 354–55

word processing, advancement
        of, 250
word processor design vs. game
        design, 83–90
    criterion for excellence, 84–85
    decreasing number of
        conceivable states, 85–87
    hand-wired branching, 81, 89–90
    increasing number of accessible
        states, 88
    increasing number
        variables, 88–89
    replacing boolean variables with
        arithmetic variables, 88–89
    use indirection, 90
WORDPRO.EXE. (program), 86
workstyle, adjustment of, 364–65
wristwatches, 140
writing, 352–68
    and computer programming,
        356–60
    development of, 352
    in Greco-Roman era, 353–54
    modern-day use, 355
    non-interactivity of, 8–9
    in Renaissance era, 355
    and sequential
        reasoning, 354–55
    and subjunctive thinking, 356–58

Z

zero, division by, 203–4

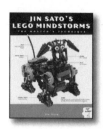

JIN SATO'S LEGO® MINDSTORMS™
The Master's Technique

by JIN SATO

Inspire the master builder in you! Jin Sato, the creator of MIBO, the Lego Hall of Fame robotic dog, teaches you how to think about and build unique robots with the LEGO MINDSTORMS kit.

2002, 364 PP., $24.95 ($37.95 CDN)
ISBN 1-886411-56-5

JOE NAGATA'S LEGO® MINDSTORMS™ IDEA BOOK

by JOE NAGATA

Over 250 step-by-step illustrations show how to build 10 cool robots using LEGO MINDSTORMS, with ideas for building many more.

2001, 194 PP., FOUR-COLOR INSERT, $21.95 ($32.95 CDN)
ISBN 1-886411-40-9

PROGRAMMING LINUX GAMES
Building Multimedia Applications with SDL, OpenAL™, and Other APIs

by LOKI SOFTWARE, INC. *with* JOHN R. HALL

This complete guide to developing Linux games discusses important multimedia toolkits (including Simple DirectMedia Layer) and teaches the basics of Linux game programming.

2001, 426 PP., $39.95 ($59.95 CDN)
ISBN 1-886411-49-2

STEAL THIS COMPUTER BOOK 2

What They Won't Tell You About the Internet

by WALLACE WANG

An offbeat, non-technical book that tells readers what hackers do, how they do it, and how to protect themselves. Includes coverage of viruses, cracking, and password theft, Trojan Horse programs, illegal copying of MP3 files, computer forensics, and encryption. The CD-ROM contains over 200 anti-hacker and security tools for Windows, Macintosh, and Linux.

2000, 462 PP., W/ CD-ROM, $24.95 ($38.95 CDN)
ISBN 1-886411-42-5

THE BOOK OF JAVASCRIPT

A Practical Guide to Interactive Web Pages

by THAU!

Rather than offer cut-and-paste solutions, this tutorial/reference focuses on understanding JavaScript, and shows web designers how to customize and implement JavaScript on their sites. The CD-ROM includes code for each example in the book, script libraries, and relevant software.

2000, 397 PP. W/CD-ROM, $29.95 ($46.50 CDN)
ISBN 1-886411-36-0

Phone:

1 (800) 420-7240 OR
(415) 863-9900
MONDAY THROUGH FRIDAY,
9 A.M. TO 5 P.M. (PST)

Fax:

(415) 863-9950
24 HOURS A DAY,
7 DAYS A WEEK

Email:

SALES@NOSTARCH.COM

Web:

HTTP://WWW.NOSTARCH.COM

Mail:

NO STARCH PRESS, INC.
555 DE HARO STREET, SUITE 250
SAN FRANCISCO, CA 94107
USA

Distributed in the U.S. by Publishers Group West

UPDATES

Visit **http://www.nostarch.com/interactive_updates.htm** for updates, errata, and other information.